LIVES ACROSS CULTURES

CROSS-CULTURAL
HUMAN DEVELOPMENT

Harry W. Gardiner
University of Wisconsin–La Crosse

Jay D. Mutter
Saint Mary's University of Minnesota

Corinne Kosmitzki
Southern Methodist University

Allyn and Bacon
Boston   London   Toronto   Sydney   Tokyo   Singapore

Vice President and Editor-in-Chief, Social Sciences: Sean W. Wakely
Senior Editor: Carolyn Merrill
Series Editorial Assistant: Amy Goldmacher
Vice President/Director of Field Marketing: Joyce Nilsen
Composition Buyer: Linda Cox
Manufacturing Buyer: Suzanne Lareau
Cover Administrator: Jenny Hart
Cover Designer: Suzanne Harbison
Photo Researcher: Sarah Evertson
Production Administrator: Rosalie Briand
Editorial-Production Service: Trinity Publishers Services
Text Design/Electronic Composition: Denise Hoffman

Copyright © 1998 by Allyn and Bacon
A Viacom Company
160 Gould Street
Needham Heights, Massachusetts 02194

Internet: www.abacon.com
America Online: keyword: College Online

Library of Congress Cataloging-in-Publication Data

Gardiner, Harry W.
    Lives across cultures : cross-cultural human development / Harry
  W. Gardiner, Jay D. Mutter, Corinne Kosmitzki
        p.   cm.
    Includes bibliographical references and indexes.
    ISBN 0-205-19182-7
    1. Ethnopsychology—Cross-cultural studies.   2. Life spans
  (Biology)—Cross-cultural studies.   3. Socialization—Cross-cultural
  studies.   4. Cognition and culture—Cross-cultural studies.
  5. Personality and culture—Cross-cultural studies.
  6. Developmental psychology—Cross-cultural studies.   I. Mutter,
  Jay D.   II. Kosmitzki, Corinne.   III. Title.
  GN502.G37   1997
  155.8—dc21   97-17766
                                                         CIP

Printed in the United States of America

10 9 8 7 6 5 4 3 2 1   02 01 00 99 98 97

CONTENTS

◇ CHAPTER THREE
CULTURAL ASPECTS OF PHYSICAL
GROWTH AND DEVELOPMENT 55

◇ CHAPTER FOUR
CULTURE AND COGNITION 79

◇ CHAPTER SEVEN
CULTURE AND SOCIAL BEHAVIOR   163

◇ CHAPTER EIGHT
THE FAMILY IN CULTURAL
CONTEXT   193

◇ CHAPTER NINE
CULTURE AND HEALTH   223

◇ CHAPTER TEN
LOOKING TO THE FUTURE   253

FOREWORD

This book is a substantial accomplishment. I have been aware of its development for several years, occasionally receiving reports on its progress. In fact, because I reviewed their initial book prospectus, I had a little influence on the nature and depth of the coverage that Harry and his coauthors, Jay Mutter and Corinne Kosmitzki, finally attained.

This book is a first. It covers the entire human life span, never losing sight of culture, which is at its center. It is current, theoretically and pedagogically sound, balanced, and above all it is authoritative without being stiff. It reflects Gardiner's personality and teaching style, both of which can be called engaging, energetic, anecdotal, and down to earth. I assume his coauthors have the same style in their respective teaching obligations. It certainly shows throughout the book.

A little historical background and some personal recollections will help explain the importance of this book and a few factors and events that contributed to its development.

In 1967, shortly after returning from two years in Germany, I accepted a one-year appointment in the Science Education Department at Oregon State University in Corvallis. This was my first academic appointment as a new Ph.D. from the University of Minnesota. I was hired mainly because I expressed a strong interest in orienting my career around cross-cultural psychology, which in the mid-1960s was still in diapers as a new and promising development in psychology.

This position involved, in part, holding periodic seminars with the Science Education faculty and a group of visiting science educators from several Asian countries. This meshed very well with my interests but not so well with my preparation.

During these seminars, a number of issues and topics were freely discussed, including when in a child's life certain science concepts should be introduced and how, the nature of children's thought processes, and the role played by peers and family. One of my main tasks was to discuss key factors in cognitive development, with special emphasis on Jean Piaget's theory. Although I was not, and am not, a developmental psychologist, at Minnesota I had received an introduction to the ideas of the late, famous Swiss developmentalist. Quite well known in Europe at the time, Piaget and his works were just being introduced to educators and researchers in the United States.

Hardly knowing where to look for the kind of information I needed, I had few guiding resources. I recall fumbling through several seminars, perhaps doing a job that might, if one was in a charitable mood, have been called adequate. I wasn't fully aware at the time—and few were—that Piagetian developmental psychology was to become instrumental in contributing to the tremendous growth spurt that cross-cultural psychology was about to experience. A glance at the international literature on cognitive development and related research on moral development will support the view that were it not for Piaget's interesting and seminal ideas, the pages of journals at the time would have been relatively barren of cross-cultural data and information.

If I had the book you are now holding with me back then, my job would have been not only joyful but I also could have impressed those foreign science educators perhaps to the point of their attributing magical powers to me.

During the same period in the mid- to late-1960s, other related developments—independent, coincidental, and convergent—were taking place. All of these activities coalesced and contributed to the acceleration of the establishment of cross-cultural psychology as a force to be reckoned with in the growth of psychology as an internationally viable enterprise rather than just a Western preoccupation.

One of these developments was a weeklong seminar held in 1966 at the East-West Center in Honolulu. The focus of that seminar was to discuss international developments in psychology. I didn't attend that seminar and didn't even know about it until later (at the time I was still trying to figure out Germany) but have since met most who did attend.

One of the attendees was Harry Gardiner, the senior author of this book. This shows that Harry has been at the business of trying to fathom the depths of culture for over thirty years, concentrating all the while on human development in teaching, research, and applications. This is an almost unmatchable track record and displays admirable consistency in career goals and orientation.

Back to the future. This book is going to make it easier for a lot of people around the English-speaking world to understand the numerous complex interactions between culture and the developing person. Thirty years ago I would have paid a king's ransom for it during the period when I thought I knew a little about psychology and culture but was soon to learn that what I knew was a drop in the bucket compared with what I have learned over the years about cross-cultural psychology. Fortunately, this book is going to teach me even more.

Students who are assigned this book as a text are in for a treat, for it is as good a guide to the literature and to the issues on culture and human development as one would want.

This book is a welcome addition to the extensive cross-cultural literature. The authors are to be congratulated for their efforts and for a job well done.

Walter J. Lonner
Professor of Psychology and Director
Center for Cross-Cultural Research
Western Washington University
Bellingham, Washington

Walter J. Lonner is an author, editor, and contributor to numerous books on cross-cultural psychology, including coeditorship of *Psychology and Culture* (1994) and *Counseling Across Cultures,* 4th ed. (1996). He was founding editor of the *Journal of Cross-Cultural Psychology* and currently serves as senior editor. Dr. Lonner is a charter member of the International Association for Cross-Cultural Psychology. He served as its president (1986–1988) and, in 1994, was made an honorary fellow of the association.

PREFACE

Our principal goal in writing this book is to bring a cross-cultural dimension to the study of human development across the lifespan. Our focus on major developmental topics provides a global and multicultural perspective by introducing the reader to contemporary as well as classical research. Basic principles and research findings are connected to practical everyday situations in order to foster an understanding of, and appreciation for, development as it takes place in diverse cultures throughout the world. Owing to its range of content, this book can be assigned as a core text in developmental courses or as a culturally sensitive supplement to monocultural texts used in psychology and related disciplines.

The three of us who wrote this book are teachers and cross-cultural researchers with extensive experience in small college and large university settings in this country and abroad. It is our shared belief that behavior is best understood when the characteristics of the individual and those of the environment, including social settings (family, school, culture) and the activities taking place within and between them (social interactions, personality development, cognitive change), are viewed as reciprocal and interdependent. This is the theme that weaves its way through the pages of this book.

✧ THE BOOK'S MAJOR THEMES

This volume differs from most books on cross-cultural psychology in a number of significant ways. Most notable is its effort to integrate a variety of important viewpoints and perspectives. First, there is a *cross-cultural perspective* designed to provide opportunities to expand awareness and sensitivity to global similarities and differences in human development and to reduce any ethnocentric thinking on the part of readers, whether conscious or unconscious. By helping readers to experience variations in behavior not normally found in their own societies, this perspective contributes to an understanding of human adaptation. Perhaps most important, this approach encourages readers to look more closely at the interconnections among culture, development, and behavior.

Second, a major emphasis is placed on *cultural-ecological and developmental contextual models* that recognize the bidirectional or reciprocal influence of individuals and their surrounding environments. Particular attention is given to understanding development within the framework of Urie Bronfenbrenner's *ecological systems approach* and Charles Super and Sara Harkness's concept of the *developmental niche*. Each of these approaches will be fully explained in Chapter 1.

Third, this text takes a *chronological-within-topics approach*. As the table of contents indicates, selected topics, for which a substantial literature of cross-cultural research exists, are discussed chronologically. This approach demonstrates how behavioral processes evolve and change as individuals in a variety of cultures pass from infancy and childhood through adolescence and into adulthood and old age.

These themes make this book a unique contribution to the field of cross-cultural human development. We hope you will agree and that you will enjoy reading and learning from it as much as we have enjoyed writing it.

◇ ORGANIZATION OF THE BOOK

In the introductory chapter, we define cross-cultural human development and provide a historical context for the increasing interest in cross-cultural research. In addition, the major themes of the book are presented and illustrated.

Chapter 2, "Culture and Socialization," focuses on ecological systems, the developmental niche, and cultural variations in the socialization of behavior. Following the chronological-within-topics approach used throughout the book, discussion centers on such behaviors as sleep, feeding, and crying during infancy; aggression and formal versus informal learning during childhood; adolescent rites of passage; and adult interpersonal relationships.

"Cultural Aspects of Physical Growth and Development" are examined in Chapter 3, with particular attention to the role of nutrition and prenatal care during the early period of development; cross-cultural studies of physical change in adolescence; and cultural reactions to physical changes associated with the transition to adulthood, including menopause and senescence.

In Chapter 4, "Culture and Cognition," attention is given to the theories of Piaget and Vygotsky and some of the variations in cognitive development across cultures.

Chapter 5, "Culture, Self, and Personality" looks at the development of self and personality, beginning with temperament in infancy and progressing to the emergence of the self-concept in childhood, identity in adolescence, and personality changes during adulthood and aging.

"Culture and Issues of Sex and Gender" are examined in Chapter 6, including a discussion of some universal gender differences and cultural influences on the socialization of females and males. Attention is given to cultural views of marriage and other long-term relationships as well as to gender roles and status in old age.

In Chapter 7, "Culture and Social Behavior," culture and social development are presented. The chapter opens with a focus on ecological contexts and early child-caretaker relationships; moves to influences of family and peer culture during the years of childhood and adolescence, work and leisure activities in middle adulthood; and concludes with a discussion of social support and well-being in the years of later adulthood.

Chapter 8, "The Family in Cultural Context," looks at the birth process and variations in the family life cycle across cultures, including differences in parental belief systems and cultural views of mate selection, parenthood, and grandparenthood.

Issues related to "Culture and Health" are examined in Chapter 9. Topics include cultural differences in children's health, adolescent eating disorders, depression, and cultural views on caring for the elderly, many of them victims of dementia and Alzheimer's disease.

Finally, in Chapter 10, "Looking to the Future," the major themes are briefly reviewed, with suggestions for applying some of the theoretical approaches considered more culturally useful. Following a presentation on developing multicultural awareness and cultural identity, the chapter concludes with some thoughts on future directions in the study of cross-cultural human development.

◇ SPECIAL FEATURES

In an effort to make this book interesting and readable, we have included a number of pedagogical aids to assist readers in learning, remembering, and making practical use of the material covered.

Opening Vignettes. Each chapter opens with vignettes of two individuals from different geographical areas of the world who illustrate one or more of the behaviors described in the chapter. Since one of our major goals is to familiarize the reader with as many cultures as possible, we decided to open each chapter with stories of different individuals living in more than fifteen different cultures around the globe. The development of these individuals is integrated into each chapter in which they appear.

Recurring Themes. Throughout each chapter, the principal themes (e.g., ecological and contextual approaches, developmental niche, and developmental and cross-cultural perspectives) are continually interwoven into the narrative to provide a comprehensive and cohesive understanding of development.

Key Ideas. Every effort has been taken to make concepts easy to understand by placing them in bold type the first time they appear, immediately defining them, and providing numerous examples to illustrate their cultural relevance. For a quick review or preview, each chapter ends with a concise summary of important points.

Cultural Diversity. Unlike some books that claim to focus on culture but only sprinkle a few selected boxes or features in several chapters, this book contains scores of examples of cross-cultural research and findings in every chapter.

Practical Applications. Each chapter concludes with a section on "Things to Do and Think About"—thought-provoking questions and simple projects to encourage readers to engage in active observation of developmental principles, frequently from a cross-cultural perspective.

Further Readings. Each chapter closes with an annotated listing of recommendations for further reading. The books suggested have been selected for their ability to expand on topics covered in each chapter as well as for their interesting and often amusing writing style.

◇ NOTE TO INSTRUCTORS

Lives Across Cultures can be used as a core text in a course focusing on cultural similarities and differences in human development, whether it is in psychology, anthropology, or sociology. It can also be effectively used as a supplement to basic courses such as General Psychology, Child and Adolescent Development, Lifespan Development, Cross-Cultural Psychology, Social Psychology, Cultural Anthropology, Sociology of the Family, and similar courses in which the instructor might want to provide a cultural focus not represented in standard textbooks.

◇ NOTE TO READERS

The epigraph facing Chapter 1 is from *The Prophet* written by the Lebanese philosopher and poet Kahlil Gibran noting that parents may house the bodies of their children but not their souls, "for their souls dwell in the house of tomorrow" and "life goes not backward nor tarries with yesterday." In many respects, this most fittingly refers to you and your life's journey. You will indeed live in the world of tomorrow, where understanding and interacting with people of diverse cultural backgrounds will be a prerequisite for success in the family, school, workplace, and society. It is for you that this book has been written. We hope it will develop an appreciation for and sensitivity to the cultural similarities and differences that characterize those of us who live on this planet Earth today, including your parents and grandparents, and those who will call it home in future generations, including your children and grandchildren. We hope you will find this book enjoyable and informative reading.

◇ SUPPLEMENTS

The *Instructor's Manual*, containing suggestions for teaching, ideas for student projects, guide to films and videos, and test items, is available. Allyn & Bacon's World Wide Web site is: http://www.abacon.com.

◇ A FINAL COMMENT

We have spent more than two exciting and busy years working on this book. In the final analysis, there are certainly many more topics we might have included and a few we might have left out, but the "fun" had to stop sometime. It has now passed from our hands to yours. We began this project because all three of us felt there was a need for a book like this. We hope we have made a contribution to better understanding of development across cultures. Only you, the readers of our words, can tell us if we have succeeded or how we might do better in the future. Let us know how we did by writing or e-mailing us at the addresses listed below. We'd love to hear from you.

◇ ACKNOWLEDGMENTS

To complete a book like this would be impossible without the generous assistance of a great many people. To those who reviewed our manuscript and offered suggestions and revisions we owe a debt of gratitude. These include D. John Lee, Orellana Institute; Judith L. Gibbons, Saint Louis University; Thomas J. Berndt, Purdue University; Granville L. Sydnor, San Jacinto College; Alan Keniston, University of Wisconsin–Eau Claire; Deborah Stiles, Webster University; Michael Cole, University of California–San Diego; Walter Lonner, Western Washington University; K. Robert Bridges, Pennsylvania State–New Kensington; Vernon Hall, Syracuse University; Steven Kirsch, Washburn University; Stephen Buggie, University of New Mexico–Gallup.

We are also grateful to the editorial, production, and marketing staff at Allyn & Bacon who contributed their time and talent to moving this project from an idea to the finished product you now hold in your hands.

Finally, we thank our families for understanding why we spent so many hours in front of our computers late into the night or early in the morning trying to put words to the page. Special thanks to Ormsin Gardiner for understanding that creativity does not always follow a convenient schedule; to Alisa, Alan, Alexina, and Aldric Gardiner, whose bicultural lives provided many of the examples in this book; to Pat Mutter for her infinite patience; to the Mutter and Low families; to Larry Luttmers for his friendship and encouragement; and to Gloria Solomon for her support as well as her many intellectually stimulating discussions about issues represented in this work. Perhaps now we can catch up on our sleep and see more of each of you.

Harry W. Gardiner
Psychology Department
University of Wisconsin–La Crosse
La Crosse, WI 54601
harry_gardiner@uwlax.edu

Jay D. Mutter
Psychology Department
Saint Mary's University of Minnesota
Winona, MN 55987
jmutter@rex.smumn.edu

Corinne Kosmitzki
Evening, Summer, and Continuing Studies
P.O. Box 750382
Southern Methodist University
Dallas, TX 75275-0382

ABOUT THE AUTHORS

Harry Gardiner. I am a professor at the University of Wisconsin–La Crosse, where I designed and currently teach a course in cross-cultural human development. It was the inability to find a textbook for this course that led to the writing of this volume. I also offer courses in child development, cross-cultural psychology, the hurried child, and humor in education for teachers. My interest in culture has also led me to teach a course entitled "Orientation to Study Abroad" for students planning extended study and research at foreign universities. I also help orient international students to the university campus and serve as faculty adviser to the International Student Organization. My M.A. is from the University of Hawaii, where the seeds of my interest in cross-cultural psychology were first planted. I completed my Ph.D. at Manchester University in England, where my personal journey into culture was forever changed when I met a young lady from Thailand, Ormsin Sornmoonpin, who was studying to be an electrical engineer. I followed her to Asia, where we were married in Buddhist and Christian wedding ceremonies. I taught in the graduate program at Chulalongkorn University in Bangkok for two years before we moved to the United States. I live in an Asian-American family, consisting of two sons (Alan and Aldric) and two daughters (Alisa and Alexina), in which I am a minority—"the one with the blond hair and the blue eyes!" I was a charter member of the International Association for Cross-Cultural Psychology and currently serve as secretary/treasurer of the Society for Cross-Cultural Research. In addition, I serve as consulting editor for the *Journal of Cross Cultural Psychology* and assistant editor for teaching for the *Cross-Cultural Psychology Bulletin*. In addition to publishing articles in a wide variety of journals and participating in national and international meetings, I recently coauthored a chapter with my wife on "Women in Thailand" and am currently revising a chapter on "Child and Adolescent Development" for a book on cross-cultural topics in psychology. I have engaged in training, teaching, and research in Europe, Asia, and the United States for more years than I will admit. As my children frequently remind me, I have been celebrating my thirty-ninth birthday annually for as long as they can remember. In my "spare time" I enjoy writing for *Cobblestone*, a history magazine for young children, and have contributed interviews with Supreme Court Justice Sandra Day O'Connor and muppet creator Jim Henson, among others.

Jay Mutter.   I am a professor at Saint Mary's University of Minnesota, where I teach a variety of undergraduate courses, including courses in cross-cultural psychology, cross-cultural human development, lifespan psychology, cognition, and learning and memory, and cultural awareness in the Master of Arts in International Business Program. My interest in cross-cultural psychology began as a Peace Corps Volunteer in Malaysia in 1976, following my undergraduate and graduate school education at Central Michigan University. For two years, I taught at Universiti Kebangsaan Malaysia (National University of Malaysia) in Kuala Lumpur. During this time, I also served on a number of government task forces aimed at reforming the general education curriculum at Malaysia's five universities, expanding off-campus regional and statewide educational programs, and standardizing the assessment of undergraduate student performance. On completion of my Peace Corps responsibilities, I enrolled in a doctoral program at the University of Malaya under the auspices of the Malaysian-American Commission on Educational Exchange and studied categorization strategies among science students, receiving my degree in 1981. In addition, I served on a team of international researchers that coauthored the first manuscript of the ASEAN Development Education Project, sponsored by the Government of Australia to survey the philosophy of teacher education in Malaysia and other ASEAN Nations. This research required fluency in Bahasa Malaysia (the national language of Malaysia), substantial knowledge of Malaysian culture, and extensive travel throughout Southeast Asia, including Malaysia, Singapore, Indonesia, Thailand, and the Philippines. I continued teaching courses in human development at the University of Malaya until 1983. Since 1985, I have been developing and teaching curricula that promote racial and ethnic diversity, multicultural understanding, and cultural awareness at Saint Mary's University. In 1994, I participated in the Eighth Annual Workshop on Developing Courses in Multi-Cultural Studies at the East-West Center in Honolulu. Over the past five years, I have coauthored presentations with Harry Gardiner and Corinne Kosmitzki at a number of national and international meetings.

Corinne Kosmitzki.   I am originally from Germany, where I completed my first graduate degree in clinical psychology. All of my family still live in Germany, and I would like to visit them more often. I have traveled in almost every Western European country and now want to explore countries in Eastern Europe, which were not accessible before the end of the Cold War. I received my Ph.D. in psychology from the University of California at Berkeley. Berkeley and its surroundings are unique in their cultural and ethnic diversity and provided many challenges as well as novel experiences. Living and working in this environment and meeting people with a wide range of backgrounds and beliefs taught me what cross-cultural psychology really means. After teaching in Virginia and at Drew University in New Jersey, I am now the Director of Evening Studies and a teacher at Southern Methodist University in Texas. Much of my recent research has focused on social and cultural identity in relation to acculturation.

Your children are not your children.
They are the sons and daughters of Life's longing for itself.
They come through you but not from you,
And though they are with you yet they belong not to you.
You may give them your love but not your thoughts,
For they have their own thoughts.
You may house their bodies but not their souls,
For their souls dwell in the house of tomorrow, which you cannot visit,
    not even in your dreams.
You may strive to be like them, but seek not to make them like you.
For life goes not backward nor tarries with yesterday.

—Kahlil Gibran, *The Prophet*

CHAPTER ONE

INTRODUCTION

Many authors begin a book by introducing their readers to the history of the field. This is certainly essential (and sometimes boring) and will be done in this book as well (you can always skip it if you don't find it very interesting), but this will come later. As one of the authors (Gardiner), I would like to begin this book as I begin most of my classes in cross-cultural human development, cross-cultural psychology, and child development by relating a few of my humorous cross-cultural experiences.

In the Preface, I mentioned that my wife is from Thailand and we have raised our four children in an Asian-American family, where I am the minority—the one with the blond hair and blue eyes. I don't like to admit it, but I'm also the shortest, making me a double minority! As you might imagine, raising children in a cross-cultural and bilingual home has resulted in many interesting developmental experiences, some of which may help you to understand what we mean by developmental niche and ecological setting.

One experience concerned our eldest daughter, Alisa, and the way in which she became bilingual. Our cross-cultural family setting provided a unique opportunity for this to occur. We had been advised that the best approach to helping her become bilingual was to let her hear and speak both languages without emphasizing that they *were* two languages. So, when she was an infant and young child, my wife spent much of the day speaking to her in Thai, while I spoke with her in English. Then, one evening, when she was about three years old, one of my Chinese students came to babysit. Alisa opened the door, saw an Asian face, and began speaking to the student in Thai. The young lady patiently listened to her and then said, "I'm Chinese and I understand English, but I bet you were speaking to me in Thai, weren't you?" I watched as she thought about this and then turned to me and said, "I speak two languages, don't I? Daddy, I speak two languages!" I told her that indeed she did and asked, "What did you think was happening?" Her reply, based on what she had experienced as part of her unique developmental niche in a bilingual home was, "I thought it was all one big language and Mommy understood some words and you understood others and I understood them all!"

Throughout the chapters that follow, we will make reference to how important it is to understand another culture and realize that not everyone everywhere has the same understanding of topics and events. Sometimes, when traveling, studying, or working in another culture, our experiences are frustrating, scary, or humorous. I had an opportunity to live in England for three years while completing my doctoral studies at the University of Manchester. During that time, there was one food craving I found nearly impossible to fulfill (the one addiction to which I will admit)—*popcorn!* My roommate and I searched everywhere for it. The only place anything resembling it was available was at the cinema. The only problem was it was sticky, caramel-covered goop, not the white, fluffy kernels sprinkled with salt and hot butter with which we were familiar. Eventually, using the skills of Sherlock Holmes and Doctor Watson, we discovered small (tiny, actually) thirty-kernel bags of popping corn at the airport and bought the entire stock! A few days later, we visited a British family that had befriended these two "Yanks from across the pond" and took some with us. When we asked the husband if we could make some popcorn, he replied (much to our surprise), "No, that's impossible." When we asked why, he said, "Popcorn grows on bushes. You pick it and put caramel on it." We told him he might be confusing this with cotton, which grows on bushes but you don't eat it. Nevertheless, he supplied us with a pot, and we put in some oil and threw in some kernels. When it began to make noise, we tried to explain that this was the corn popping. When it was done, we showed him. He took one look and disappeared out the back door! A few minutes later, he returned with his neighbors, looked at us, and said, "Do it again!" When I retire, I think I'll open a popcorn stand on a street corner in London and surprise and amaze the public with the wonders of popcorn! Now, if I could only get it to grow on bushes! The moral of this story: we all grow up in cultures where we understand what happens around us because the experiences are a familiar part of our developmental niche. These experiences are not always easily understood by those living in different ecological settings.

Nearly two decades ago the anthropologist T. Schwartz, writing about the acquisition of culture, declared that "anthropologists had ignored children in culture while developmental psychologists had ignored culture in children" (1981, p. 4). Just two years later, John Berry, a Canadian psychologist and pioneering researcher in cross-cultural psychology, noted that the discipline was "so culture-bound and culture-blind . . . [that] . . . it should not be employed as it is" (1983, p. 449). Shortly thereafter, Gustav Jahoda, a well-known European psychologist and early contributor to the developing discipline, was able to express a more optimistic view and point out that cross-cultural studies of human development had been steadily increasing (1986). Yet, at the same time, he also criticized the field for being "too parochial in its orientation" (p. 418).

These were once serious criticisms of the newly emerging field of cross-cultural psychology. Fortunately, in recent years, great strides have been made in our approaches to, and understanding of, cross-cultural human development. Throughout this book, we hope to show the progress, excitement, and promise of this increasingly important area of study.

In this first chapter we set the stage for the rest of the book by introducing some historical perspective and expanding on some of the major concepts, themes, and issues briefly presented in the Preface. Let us begin by exploring the origins of cross-cultural human development.

○ WHAT IS CROSS-CULTURAL HUMAN DEVELOPMENT?

The field of cross-cultural psychology is remarkably diverse, and those who contribute to it bring with them a variety of viewpoints, including different definitions of the field itself. In volume 1 of the newly revised *Handbook of Cross-Cultural Psychology*, Berry, Poortinga, and Pandey (1997) define **cross-cultural psychology** as *"the systematic study of relationships between the cultural context of human development and the behaviors that become established in the repertoire of individuals growing up in a particular culture"* (p. x). This definition clearly states that this is a scientific endeavor that shares with more familiar disciplines the use of theories, scientific methodologies, statistical procedures, and data analysis.

The term *human development* has also been defined in a variety of ways. For the purpose of this book, we will view **human development** as *changes in physical, psychological, and social behavior as experienced by individuals across the lifespan from conception to death*. Although this definition encompasses a wide range of experiences, the intention of this book is not to provide exhaustive and comprehensive coverage of all aspects of human development (aren't you glad to hear that!). Instead, our goal is more limited, focusing on a number of selected topics that provide insight and understanding into how individuals develop and live their lives in different cultural settings. In doing this, we provide examples from literally scores of societies throughout the world.

Since we just mentioned the term **culture,** it should be pointed out that most researchers agree that this is one of the most difficult terms in the social sciences to define. Almost everyone who studies culture has a different way of looking at it. According to Berry, Poortinga, Segall, and Dasen (1992), E. B. Tylor was the first anthropologist to use the term in his two-volume work titled *Primitive Culture* (1871). He defined *culture* as *"that complex whole which includes knowledge, belief, art, morals, laws, customs and any other capabilities and habits acquired by man as a member of society"* (p. 42). More than forty years ago, two other anthropologists, Kroeber and Kluckhohn (1952), compiled a list of 164 definitions of the term. (We have no intention of listing all these definitions here, so if you are disappointed and would like to know what they are, we recommend you look them up yourself.)

When we use the term *culture,* we will be referring to a number of characteristics, including what Herskovits (1948) called *"the man-made part of the environment"* (Segall et al., 1990, p. 5) as well as *"the collective programming of the mind which distinguishes the members of one group from another"* (Hofstede, 1980, p. 21).

As the field of cross-cultural psychology has evolved, concerns in the area of development have undergone a number of significant shifts. Parke, Ornstein, Rieser, and Zahn-Waxler (1994) have succinctly summarized and discussed the changes in developmental focus over the past hundred years by looking at three periods. One hundred years ago, five major areas were of interest: emotional development, the biological basis of behavior, cognitive development, conscious and unconscious processes, and the role of self in development. During the 1950s and 1960s, the focus shifted to learning theory, the rise of experimental child psychology, interest in operant analysis of children's behavior, the emergence of investigations of infant sensory and perceptual development, and the objective measurement of cognitive understanding among preverbal infants. Today, there is a revitalized interest in emotional development and cognitive abilities of children, the biological bases of behavior, and social relationships. According to the authors, the "most unanticipated theme is the continuing discovery of the precocity of infants and young children—not only cognitively but also socially and emotionally" (p. 8). We shall see this point illustrated numerous times throughout this book.

◇ SOME IMPORTANT THEMES

This book differs in a number of significant ways from most other volumes that focus on cross-cultural aspects of human behavior, most notably in its efforts to integrate a variety of important themes. Let us look at these in some detail and discover how they will weave through future chapters.

A Cross-Cultural Perspective

Over the past two decades, and especially within the last five years, social scientists have become increasingly aware of the contributions that cross-cultural research findings can make to our understanding of human development. A review of recently published developmental books, compared with those of just a few years ago, reveals that references to cross-cultural topics and findings have grown tremendously (Best & Ruther, 1994; Gardiner, 1996).

Any attempt to include all or even the majority of these findings in a book of this length would be difficult, if not impossible. Therefore, we have decided to be selective and discuss representative areas of interest using a chronological-within-topics approach. For those readers desiring a more comprehensive view of cross-cultural human development, or for those wishing to explore particular topics in greater depth, we refer you to the "Further Readings" section at the close of each chapter as well as the references listed at the end of this book. If you are eager to get started, you might consider looking at such classics as *Two Worlds of Childhood: U.S. and U.S.S.R.* (1970) by Urie Bronfenbrenner and a series of volumes on *Six Cultures* by Whiting (1963), Whiting and Whiting (1975), and Whiting and Edwards (1988). Finally, there is the recently revised three-volume *Handbook of Cross-Cultural Psychology* (1997), edited by John Berry and others, which contains several chapters relevant to the study of cross-cultural development as well as the role of cross-cultural theory and methodology.

Goals for the Field

As to the nature and purpose of the cross-cultural method, Berry, Poortinga, Segall, and Dasen (1992), in a comprehensive overview of cross-cultural psychology, set forth three goals for the field. The first goal involves *testing or extending the generalizability of existing theories and findings.* In earlier writings, Berry and Dasen (1974) referred to this as the "transport and test goal" in which hypotheses and findings from one culture are transported to another so that their validity can be tested in other cultural settings. For example, are parental speech patterns in English-speaking families similar or dissimilar to those in Spanish-speaking families? Are the stages of cognitive development proposed by Jean Piaget specific to certain types of cultures, or are they universal?

The second goal focuses on *exploring other cultures in order to discover variations in behavior that may not be part of one's own cultural experience.* In other words, if findings cannot be generalized, what are the reasons for this, and are there behaviors unique to these other cultures? A good example is a study by Jablensky et al. (1992) that successfully demonstrates that a number of symptoms characteristic of schizophrenia (a serious psychological disorder) exist in ten very different cultures but that there is no single factor to explain differences in the formation or outcome of the disorder. At the same time, other psychological conditions appear to be "culture-bound" and occur only among certain groups of people. One example is *pibloktoq*, found only among specific groups of Eskimos, in which individuals, with little or no warning, perform any of a number of irrational acts (e.g., ripping off clothes, shouting obscenities, throwing objects, and running wildly into snowdrifts, from which they are often rescued by others) lasting a few minutes or as long as an hour (Wallace, 1961).

The third goal, which follows from the first two, is aimed at *integrating findings in such a way as to generate a more universal psychology applicable to a wider range of cultural settings and societies.* Examples of this include efforts by many cross-cultural researchers to refine and expand the usefulness of a number of theories, including the various ecological approaches cited in the present book.

At this point, you might be wondering, "How can a cross-cultural perspective contribute to our understanding of human development?" In answer to this question, Gardiner (1994) has pointed to a number of important benefits. First, looking at behavior from this perspective compels researchers to seriously reflect on the variety of ways in which their cultural beliefs and values affect the development of their theories and research designs. Increased awareness of cross-cultural findings provides an opportunity to extend or restrict the implications of research conducted in a single cultural group, most notably the United States and similar Western societies. Nothing helps to reduce **ethnocentrism,** or *the belief that one's culture is superior to others,* as quickly as looking at behavior as it occurs in another culture. Second, the number of independent and dependent variables to be investigated can be greatly increased in a cross-cultural design. Examples of studies in which this has been done include investigations of gender differences (Gibbons, Stiles, & Shkodriani, 1991; Morinaga, Frieze, & Ferligoj, 1993), aggression (Scott, 1992), and the effects of parent-child relationships in diverse cultures (Roopnarine & Carter, 1992b). We generally think of an **independent variable (IV)** as *the condition introduced into or systematically manipulated in an experiment by the researcher* and a **dependent variable (DV)** as *the subject's response or the behavior being measured in an experiment.* Without getting too complicated, it should be noted that in the context of cross-cultural research, these are really quasi-IVs and DVs, representing both a strength (more "real worldly") as well as a weakness (some loss of control and/or increased ambiguity). For an excellent discussion of culture as an antecedent, dependent, independent, or intervening variable, the reader is referred to several chapters in volume 1 of the recently published *Handbook of Cross-Cultural Psychology* (Berry, Poortinga, & Pandey, 1997). Third, cross-cultural studies help us to separate **emics,** or *culture-specific concepts,* from **etics,** or *universal or culture-general concepts.* According to Berry (1969), the emic approach focuses on a single culture, using criteria that are thought to be relative to it, and studies behavior from within the system itself. An example is an anthropological field study in which a researcher lives with a group of people and tries to understand the culture through their eyes and experiences, avoiding the ethnocentrism of his own cultural background. The etic approach, on the other hand, looks at several cultures, comparing and contrasting them using criteria thought to be absolute or universal, and studies behavior from outside the system. An example, which (happily) we don't see as often as we once did in cross-cultural psychology, involves an investigator conducting what has been called "safari research." An example is a professor (not very familiar with the field) who goes on vacation to several countries, taking along a favorite questionnaire concerning _____ (you fill in the blank). She visits a number of universities, collects data from available students (who may or may not understand many of the colloquial English language terms), returns home, and publishes the findings as "universal" attitudes of those living in cultures X, Y, and Z.

Separating emics from etics is better accomplished by testing theories or principles developed in one cultural context in another. The work of Freud, Piaget, and Kohlberg are examples. In some cases, findings lend support to the universality of behaviors in vastly different cultural settings (e.g., stages in language development and the sequence and timing of such behaviors as smiling, walking, stranger and separation anxiety, and pubertal development). On the other hand, results have sometimes suggested a need for modification of certain culture-bound concepts (e.g., intelligence, medical diagnosis, and, sometimes, gender behavior).

By focusing throughout this book on cross-cultural material, we hope to provide readers with opportunities to expand their awareness and sensitivity to global similarities and differences in human development and to reduce any ethnocentric thinking. The cross-cultural perspective complements and extends the work of earlier researchers who successfully presented the more traditional, but often culture-specific, approach to understanding lifespan development by offering a broader world view. By allowing readers to experience variations in behavior not normally found in their own societies (e.g., accelerated formal operational thought among some Asian populations, decreased susceptibility to visual illusions among certain African groups, and highly developed mathematical skills among Dutch children), this perspective contributes to our understanding of human adaptation. Perhaps most important, it encourages a closer look at the interconnections among culture, development, and behavior—a major theme in contemporary developmental psychology (Parke, Ornstein, Rieser, & Zahn-Waxler, 1994).

Can you find the Western anthropologist in this picture? (David R. Austen/Stock Boston)

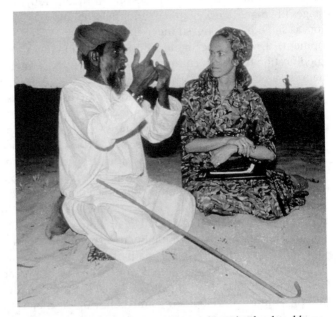

Noted anthropologist Dr. Dawn Chatty, discussing local problems with Harsous tribal member in Sahmah, Oman, in the Arabian Peninsula. (James L. Stanfield/National Geographic Society)

While we certainly are not the first to stress the importance of looking at cross-cultural data, we believe we give it greater emphasis because, as Segall so aptly stated more than a decade and a half ago, "It is to . . . theories of ecological, cultural, and socialization forces that we must turn for the most promising insights into why different peoples develop different . . . skills or develop the same skills at different rates" (1979, p. 129).

The mention of socialization practices, and the variety of ways in which we are influenced by ecological factors, leads us to another of our major themes.

An Ecological Systems Approach

The importance of viewing behavior within its social setting was first recognized not by psychologists but by sociologists, who stressed the importance of the individual's subjective view. Among the early proponents of this view were C. H. Cooley (1902), W. I. Thomas and F. Znaniecki (1927), and G. H. Mead (1934). When psychologists became interested in the topic, they tended to ignore the social context in favor of the cognitive processes (Koffka, 1935; Kohler, 1938; Piaget, 1954). Such analysis was extended beyond the individual to the study of the environment with the introduction of the concepts of "psychological field" and "life space" by Kurt Lewin (1935). Explicit recognition of the need to study an individual's subjective view of social reality came with the pioneering work of MacLeod (1947).

One of the most important contributions to these evolving ideas, and the one on which much of our presentation is based, is the ecological systems approach presented in the work of Urie Bronfenbrenner (1975, 1977, 1979, 1986a, 1989, 1993). This approach allows us to clearly see and understand the connection between culture and development.

The **ecology of human development,** as defined by Bronfenbrenner, involves *"the scientific study of the progressive, mutual accommodation between an active, growing human being and the changing properties of the immediate settings in which the developing person lives, as this process is affected by relations between these settings, and by the larger contexts in which the settings are embedded"* (1979, p. 21). In short, an individual is seen, not as a passive and static entity on which the environment exerts great influence (much like a *tabula rasa,* or blank slate) but as a dynamic and evolving being that interacts with, and thereby restructures, the many environments with which it comes into contact. These interactions between individual and environment are viewed as two-directional, or characterized by reciprocity. For example, while a child's development is being influenced and molded by parents, family, school, and peers, she is, at the same time, influencing and molding the behavior of others.

Building on Bronfenbrenner's definition, the concept of environment is expanded to include increasingly complex interconnections among settings and is a considerably broader and more differentiated view than those previously presented in psychology in general and in developmental psychology in particular.

Bronfenbrenner has suggested that an individual's perception of the environment is often more important than "objective reality" and that this perception will influence one's expectations and activities. A recognition and acceptance of the critical role played by the cultural or environmental context seem particularly suited to the study of human behavior and development.

In his critique of traditional research carried out on children, Bronfenbrenner has stated, "Much of contemporary developmental psychology is the science of the strange behaviors of children in strange situations with strange adults for the briefest possible periods of time" (1977, p. 513). In other words, while striving to achieve experimental rigor and control, we have often lost sight of the scientific and practical relevance of our findings by ignoring how the same phenomena might occur outside such artificial environments. One of the other major goals of this book is to stress the relevance and practicality of such findings.

The ecological systems approach allows us to go beyond the setting being immediately experienced—whether in a laboratory, a classroom, or a backyard—and permits the incorporation of indirect, but nevertheless very real, effects from other settings as well as from the culture as a whole.

Bronfenbrenner divides the ecological environment into four levels: microsystem, mesosystem, exosystem, and macrosystem (see Figure 1.1).

The Microsystem.   In Figure 1.1, the first level, the microsystem, represents the interactions between the child and her immediate environment (e.g., family or preschool) and resulting behaviors such as dependence or independence and cooperation or competition. This is the most basic level, the one at which individuals engage in face-to-face interactions, and their behaviors frequently reflect social position. Bronfenbrenner (1993) has recently expanded his original definition of the **microsystem** to include *"a pattern of activities, roles, and interpersonal relations experienced by the developing person in a given face-to-face setting with particular physical, social, and symbolic features that invite, permit, or inhibit engagement in sustained, progressively more complex interaction with, and activity in the immediate environment"* (p. 15). Examples would include home, church, school, hospital, or day-care center. Other factors to be considered include the effects of the physical environment on behavior, including background noise, crowding, and the number and types of toys available to a child (Wachs, 1987).

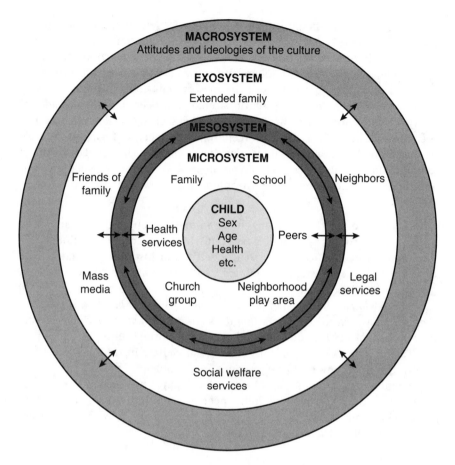

FIGURE 1.1   Bronfenbrenner's Ecological Model of Human Development

Source: From *The Child* (p. 648) by C. B. Kopp and J. B. Kaslow, 1982. Reading, MA: Addison-Wesley. Copyright © 1982 by Addison-Wesley Publishing Co., Inc. Reprinted by permission of Addison-Wesley Longman, Inc.

The Mesosystem.   The second level, the mesosystem, recognizes that the individual microsystems in which a child functions are not independent but are closely interrelated and influence each other. According to Bronfenbrenner's newly revised definition, the **mesosystem** *"comprises the linkages and processes taking place between two or more settings containing the developing person"* (1993, p. 22). This is a system made up of two or more microsystems (e.g., home and day care, day care and school, or family and peer group). It is the mesosystem that links or ties together information, knowledge, and attitudes from one setting that help to shape behavior or development in another setting. For example, while parents emphasize the importance of learning at home, preschool teachers provide stimulating activities at school that motivate a child to learn more. Steinberg and Brown (1989), in an effort to define and demonstrate the properties of the mesosystem, took this idea one step further by investigating the effect of parental and peer support of academic activities on performance of high school adolescents. At the conclusion of their investigation, they argued forcefully for the need to focus on multiple environmental influences as they affect development. They suggested that a failure to do so contributes to "the typically low proportion of explained variance in developmental research" (Bronfenbrenner, 1993).

The Exosystem. Beyond the child's immediate environment are social settings of which he may not be a part but which, nevertheless, influence his development in significant ways. These settings or institutions make up the third level—the exosystem. As defined by Bronfenbrenner, the **exosystem** *"comprises the linkages and processes taking place between two or more settings, at least one of which does not contain the developing person, but in which events occur that indirectly influence processes within the immediate setting in which the developing person lives"* (1993, p. 22). Included here are formal settings such as parents' place of work or community health and welfare institutions (e.g., hospitals). Bronfenbrenner (1993) provides an example of the link between the home and a parent's workplace for the developing child and of the link between the home and her children's peer group for the developing adult. Other less formal settings might include the extended family (aunts, uncles, cousins) as well as friends and neighbors.

The Macrosystem. The final level, the macrosystem, is the most complex system and is found in the outermost circle and consists of the customs, values, and laws considered important in the child's culture. Bronfenbrenner (1993), in an expanded definition, states that the **macrosystem** *"consists of the overarching pattern of micro-, meso-, and exosystems characteristic of a given culture, subculture, or other extended social structure, with particular reference to the . . . belief systems, resources, hazards, lifestyles, opportunity structures, life course options and patterns of social interchange that are embedded in such overarching systems"* (p. 25). The focus is on the consistencies among a wide variety of settings within a given society or culture. For example, in many countries there are striking similarities in the form and function of such familiar settings as school playgrounds, post-offices, shopping malls, and even fast food restaurants.

The ecological point of view, with its emphasis on the analysis of specific behaviors in increasingly complex settings, nicely complements our other themes. In fact, such a multilevel approach significantly expands the possibilities for explaining a variety of behaviors. This approach provides the central theme around which each of the remaining themes cluster.

The Developmental Niche

If Bronfenbrenner is correct in his view that culture and environment make significant contributions to one's development (and we, as well as others—e.g., Brislin, 1993—believe that they do), one might ask, "How does this happen and how can we better understand the processes taking place?"

One possible answer is provided by an exciting and promising idea emerging from the cross-cultural developmental work of Super and Harkness (1986, 1994). Based on an extensive series of studies among Kipsigis-speaking communities in western Kenya, Super and Harkness, a psychologist-anthropologist research team, have presented a way of bringing together and integrating findings from the two disciplines (Gardiner, 1994). Called the **developmental niche,** it provides *a framework for understanding how various aspects of a culture guide the developmental process by focusing on the child as the unit of analysis within her sociocultural setting or context.* In this regard, it is compatible with the ideas put forth by Bronfenbrenner and, in combination with it, comprises another major theme of this book.

It should be noted that the concept of the developmental niche (at least the "niche" part) was originally borrowed from the field of biological ecology, in which *niche* describes the combined features of a particular animal's, or species's of animal, environment or habitat (Super & Harkness, 1994). They use the example of a robin and a pigeon, both of which might live in the same section of a city park but differ in where they build their nests, the kinds of materials they use, and the kind of food they eat from the surrounding environment. The birds create a distinct niche for themselves based on each of these behaviors. The fact that this concept of a niche can be employed in biology, as well as in psychology, demonstrates, as we indicated earlier, that there is some unity to scientific efforts.

In applying the term to psychology, Super and Harkness (1994a) state that "at the center of the developmental niche, therefore, is a particular child, of a certain age and sex, with certain temperamental and psychological dispositions. By virtue of these and other characteristics, this child will inhabit a different cultural 'world' than the worlds inhabited by other members of his family—and further, the child's world will also change as the child grows and changes" (pp. 96–97).

Every child's developmental niche consists of three components, including (1) the physical and social settings or contexts of everyday life (e.g., one's family), (2) the culturally determined customs of child care and child-rearing (e.g., interactions with siblings), and (3) the psychology of the care-takers or characteristics of a child's parents (e.g., belief systems and develop-mental expectations). Super and Harkness propose that these components interact and function as a coordinated system in which the individual and the developmental niche adapt and are mutually influential. For an interest-ing example of the developmental niche in Somalia, see Box 1.1.

Consider, for a moment, two very different developmental niches and the effects each has on a child raised in different parts of the world. A young child in rural Kenya more than likely lives in a large family, often with eight or more brothers and sisters. Older siblings customarily serve as substitute caretakers for the younger child. When even younger siblings come along, this child will then take over the same role. Because Kenyan children fre-quently sleep with their parents for several years, they tend to show a great deal of dependent behavior first as children and later as adults. Examples of such dependent behaviors include obedience, cooperation, introversion, with an emphasis on group goals, togetherness, and security. Contrast this with a British child, who grows up in a much smaller family that often con-sists of one or two children. This child would likely begin sleeping in his own room shortly after birth. Parents would encourage and train him from an early age to be independent. Examples of independent behaviors include in-dividual decision making, competitiveness, and extroversion, with an em-phasis on development of individual capabilities, privacy, and achievement of personal goals. These examples illustrate different cultures, different de-velopmental niches, different lives.

A Developmental Orientation

It is well recognized that most of our behavior does not take place at isolated periods in our lives but rather evolves and continually develops throughout the lifespan. Although the body of cross-cultural research literature is signifi-cant, it frequently resembles "a confused mosaic of contradictory findings" (Gardiner, 1994). This may explain, in part, why none of the books that cur-rently examine cross-cultural topics systematically presents a developmental perspective as we will attempt to do here. Not all of the behaviors covered in this book will always fit neatly into this orientation or be easily explained by some of the other themes or approaches. However, many do and, where ap-propriate, we shall attempt to demonstrate how these behaviors evolve and change as individuals develop across the lifespan and across cultures.

To illustrate the importance of looking at behavior from a developmen-tal orientation, let us briefly consider the development of memory and atten-

BOX 1.1

 CHILDHOOD IN SOMALIA: AN EXAMPLE
OF THE DEVELOPMENTAL NICHE

In an extremely informative and detailed study, Norwegian psychologist Ragnhild Dybdahl explored childhood within the Somali sociocultural context, using the concept of the developmental niche. As part of her study, she conducted open-ended interviews in Mogadishu, Somalia, with twenty mothers, ranging in age from twenty-two to forty (mean age equals thirty), and twenty-three children (mean age equals ten). Most of the women lived with their husbands, and about one-fourth of them had been raised as nomads. The average number of family members was 7.5 and included various combinations of parents, children, grandparents, parents' siblings, and distant relatives staying as long-term guests. Topics of interest included reasons for having children, normative child care, and the roles played by parents and children in the Somali culture.

According to Dybdahl, the first component of the Somali developmental niche is characterized by the culture's economic and health problems; the nomadic way of life, with its emphasis on the extended family and clan; and the child's social and physical settings organized around school and Quaranic school, play, work, and household chores, especially care of younger siblings. The second component is characterized by socialization practices in which the infant, initially spending all its time with its mother, is gradually "distanced from the mother's back, breast and bed to be cared for by someone else." Although formal schooling plays a role, informal education is far more important and is the means by which children are taught such activities as household chores. Quaranic school serves as a mode of traditional education. The third component, based on interview comments from mothers, is characterized by mothers' focus on "physical health, obedience, resourcefulness, helpfulness and hard work," with expectations differing according to a child's age.

Dybdahl reported on the emergence of several themes associated with Somali childhood: (1) a clear responsibility for family and relatives; (2) the importance of such values as pride, hard work, loyalty, and obedience; (3) a constant struggle for survival and good physical health; and (4) the emotional importance attached to children as sources of short- and long-term security.

As a result of her interviews and observations, Dybdahl argues that Somali society represents a mix of "traditionalism and modernism, and collectivism and individualism." According to Dybdahl, her interviews with chil-

(continued)

BOX 1.1 CONTINUED

dren provided a look at "the niche from the inside." She points out that "in spite of the difficult living conditions at the time . . . [just before 'Operation Restore Hope' in 1989] . . . with war breaking out and relatively poor health conditions, beliefs in the future and in the possibility to change and improve one's life were recurring themes." She suggests that this may be due to a combination of factors, including the nomadic tradition of "moving on to another place," stoicism, and the belief that family and relatives will provide help if needed.

Dybdahl concludes that children must be studied in the "context and culture in which they live, and of which they are a part." Since developmental outcomes in Western societies have often come to be the norm for many of the world's children, "to avoid ethnocentrism and develop a global psychology, it is necessary to do cross-cultural research." Dybdahl is further convinced that, in order to make what she calls the "person-setting interaction" the focus of investigation, anthropologists and psychologists need to combine their efforts and that the developmental niche "might be a fruitful concept for this purpose."

Source: Adapted from "The Child in Context: Exploring Childhood in Somalia," paper presented by Ragnhild Dybdahl at the Twenty-Sixth International Congress of Psychology, Montreal, August 1996. Reprinted by permission.

tion, or the increased ability to organize information. As children we begin to think, attend, and store away memories. As adolescents and adults we develop the ability to make inferences, understand reversibility, and make use of abstract thought. Information that may have been remembered in childhood as a list can now be recalled in adulthood as a total pattern.

The implications of studying this topic from a lifespan developmental perspective have been nicely summarized by Forman and Sigel (1979), who write that "it is not clear whether the decline in memory and attention that occurs in old age is a function of reduced general cognitive competence or an inadequate problem-solving attitude due to social isolation, fear of failure, and other factors. But it is clear that the error rate of the elderly decreases when tests are not timed and social acceptance is reinforced. We can venture the tentative conclusion that poor performance in the 4-year-old is probably due to lack of a general cognitive competence, while poor performance in the 70-year-old is likely the result of an attitude toward solving problems (provided, of course, that the person shows no pathological signs of neurological deterioration)" (p. 89).

This brings us to another theme that will occur throughout this book—the chronological-within-topics approach.

A Chronological-Within-Topics Approach

In a book of this size, it is impossible to do all things—that is, provide a comprehensive view of development in all the necessary detail and also focus on all the important cross-cultural findings. Recognizing this, we have decided to look at selected topics for which a large literature of cross-cultural research exists and discuss these topics chronologically—from the early beginnings of development through the last years of life.

Using this *chronological-within-topics approach,* we hope to effectively demonstrate how behavioral processes evolve and change as individuals pass from infancy and childhood through adolescence and into adulthood. As a result, it should become clear that our behavior is dynamic and involves change, that it is at times orderly and predictable and at other times chaotic and unreliable, that both individual and cultural similarities and differences exist, and that specific cultural influences become important at different times and in different cultures. This approach will include basic concepts, principles, and theories that describe physical, psychological, cognitive, social, and personality changes that occur across the lifespan in a variety of cultural contexts.

✧ PRACTICAL APPLICATIONS

We believe that a book emphasizing process, content, and skill (at understanding and interpreting cross-cultural behavior), but avoiding unnecessary jargon and seeking a broad perspective, will provide a number of benefits to readers. Therefore, part of our focus will be on the *everyday experiences* encountered by individuals of differing ethnic backgrounds within their own society as well as between individuals of different cultural settings. We further believe that if readers come to understand the processes involved, they will begin to understand how to apply these principles for a deeper insight into the events and issues that touch their lives beyond the boundaries of their home, neighborhood, classroom, community, and nation. Throughout this book, material is continually related to issues and concerns that are important and relevant to all of us. Efforts are made to encourage critical thinking by using exercises that allow one to examine, question, explore, analyze, and evaluate a variety of everyday situations within diverse cultural contexts.

There is an adage that states "Tell me and I'll forget . . . show me and I'll probably remember . . . involve me and I'll never forget." Simply stated, this is another of our important themes—practical application. Many of today's texts are written for social science majors planning graduate study and frequently emphasize laboratory research—a shortcoming already recognized in our earlier comments on the need for an ecological point of view. While we feel a developmental text should be grounded in carefully researched theory, we also believe that if it is to be maximally useful, it should avoid jargon and focus on readers' "real-life" experiences and ultimately assist them to relate more effectively with other individuals and in diverse environments. This is especially true today as our world, even at the local neighborhood level, becomes increasingly multicultural.

These goals will be accomplished in several ways. First, in writing this book we have selected topics that have meaning for one's daily living: socialization (Chapter 2), physical development (Chapter 3), cognition and language (Chapter 4), personality (Chapter 5), issues of sex and gender (Chapter 6), social behavior (Chapter 7), the family (Chapter 8), and health issues (Chapter 9).

We don't expect, and indeed don't want, you to accept what we say without question. We believe in the adage mentioned above, and we try to practice what we preach by providing opportunities for you to question, explore, and analyze each of the topics presented. In doing this, we hope you will arrive at a better understanding of your own behavior, modifying it where necessary and desirable and developing and improving your cross-cultural interactions with others, now and in the future.

◇ DESIGN OF THE BOOK
AND SUGGESTIONS FOR ITS USE

Since the transition from theory to practice cannot be accomplished simply by reading about applications, we make an effort to present the material in each chapter in such a way that it explicitly encourages your active involvement.

First, as you notice, each chapter opens with vignettes focusing on issues and behaviors to be addressed by the material presented in a particular chapter. Not only does this give you an idea of what will be covered in each chapter, but it also allows you to formulate your own ideas as you read the material. For example, "What are the benefits of studying development cross-culturally?" "What are the effects of culture on socialization?" "How does children's play differ from one culture to another?" "In what ways are adolescents similar or different throughout the world?" "How do cultures treat their elders or older adults?"

Second, within the narrative, each new idea is defined, highlighted, and illustrated with cultural examples (many from the authors' own experiences) that, hopefully, you will find both relevant and entertaining.

Third, you will find real-life examples of cultural variations in childbirth, effects of culture on learning styles, growing old in different cultures, cultural variations in adolescent identity, and other important topics.

Finally, each chapter will close with a section on "Things to Do and Think About." Included are simple projects to encourage you to engage in active observation of developmental principles. For example, you may be asked to present a series of objects to children of different cultural backgrounds and observe the categories they use to organize them. You could be asked to keep a log of cross-cultural stories appearing in the media. You might be called on to visit with relatives and ask questions about their development at different periods in their lives.

◇ SOME CROSS-CULTURAL TEASERS

As we bring this chapter to a close, we'd like to leave you with a few "cross-cultural teasers," or questions for which we provide partial answers. Each of these will receive further attention in future chapters.

- Is there a unifying concept that might explain reasons for cultural variations in development? The answer lies in the area of adaptation, or the various ways in which peoples of diverse cultures have adapted or adjusted to the events occurring in their lives.

- Are there any universals in human development? If so, what are they? One example of a universal is gender-role assignment. All societies appear to socialize boys and girls into gender roles (e.g., allowing more aggressive behavior among boys and encouraging more caring behavior among girls).

- How can we explain cross-cultural differences in such behaviors as dependence and independence? Part of the answer depends on where infants sleep after they are born. The United States is known as a culture that greatly emphasizes individual achievement; parents generally place babies in their own cribs in their own rooms. Japan, a collectivist culture, encourages dependence; children are allowed to sleep with parents, often for many years. How does this affect development?

- Adolescents in many of the world's cultures confront the problem of identity, or trying to answer the question "Who am I?" For some, living in Nigeria, it is a relatively easy task. For others, growing up bicultural in New York City, it is more difficult.

- Eating disorders such as anorexia and bulimia are common in many Western societies. Do young people throughout the world all strive to attain the ideal body image? You may be surprised by some of the answers found in Japan, Australia, and other countries.

- How do different cultures view their elderly? Is grandparenting the same everywhere? We'll give you some answers to these questions from China, Japan, and the United States.

- How does family life differ from one culture to another? In some societies, the roles of mothers and fathers may surprise you. Did you know children in some cultures become more closely attached to their fathers than to their mothers? Why would this be the case? We'll find out later in this book.

- An increasingly common disorder among older adults today is Alzheimer's disease. Did you know that people suffering from this disease are treated differently by their caregivers if the patient and caregiver are Hispanic, Native American, or Anglo?

- What's important in selecting a marriage partner—money, good looks, security, health? You'll be surprised at some of the views expressed by men and women from cultures around the world. How many chickens or cows do you think you're worth on the bride market?

Have we gotten your attention? Do you want to know the answers to these and other interesting cross-cultural questions? Would you like to know some of the similarities and differences in human behavior and how people live their "lives across cultures?" Then turn the page and read on.

◇ SUMMARY

This chapter introduced the topic of cross-cultural human development and provided definitions of important terms and concepts. Discussion centered on a number of themes to be used in organizing developmental topics in a variety of cultural settings. These themes included a cross-cultural perspective, an ecological systems approach, the developmental niche, a developmental orientation, a chronological-within-topics approach, and an emphasis on practical applications. Suggestions were given for using the material in ways that will help readers develop a greater understanding of, and sensitivity to, those of a different cultural background than their own and develop and improve any cross-cultural interactions they might experience.

◇ THINGS TO DO
AND THINK ABOUT

1. Keep a log or diary for two weeks noting the variety of cultural topics reported in the media. Include any relevant newspaper or magazine articles as examples. Analyze these incidents in terms of the various themes presented in this chapter.

2. Consider your own development and how your developmental niche was established. What are some of the characteristics of your ecological subsystems (micro-, meso-, exo-, and macro-), and how did they contribute to the person you are today? In what ways were these different for each of your parents or for older or younger siblings? You might find it interesting to discuss this with a friend and compare and contrast your development up to this point in your lives and consider how it might change in the future.

3. Interview someone of a cultural background different than your own. Ask about family structure and relationships, educational settings, social activities, foods, and other topics you may find interesting. Compare and contrast this person's culture with your own. In what ways does the material in this chapter help to explain these similarities and differences?

◇ FURTHER READINGS

Dave Barry. (1992). *Dave Barry Does Japan.* New York: Fawcett Columbine.
An irreverent view of Japanese culture by one of America's premiere humorists. Witty and sometimes insightful. Contains discussion of such topics as "Failing to Learn Japanese in Only Five Minutes (Very much good morning, Sir)," "Lost in Tokyo (Looking for plastic squid)," and "Humor in Japan (Take my tofu! Please!)."

Bill Holm. (1990). *Coming Home Crazy.* Minneapolis, MN: Milkweed Editions.
In the words of the author, "This is a book about what happened to an American in China, about adventures in daily life and on the road, and about what America looked like to me—both its inner and its outer lives—after I got home."

Walter J. Lonner and Roy Malpass. (1994). *Psychology and Culture.* Boston: Allyn
& Bacon.

>A collection of forty-three short (five- to six-page), easy-to-read chap-
>ters on various aspects of cross-cultural psychology. A sampling of chap-
>ter titles includes "Continuing Encounters with Hong Kong," "A Multi-
>cultural View of Stereotyping," "Mate Preferences in 37 Cultures," and
>"Community Health in Ethiopia."

CHAPTER TWO

CULTURE AND SOCIALIZATION

Kamuzu Mathebula is fourteen years old and lives in Diepkloof, a section of Soweto, an all-black township outside Johannesburg, South Africa. He lives with his mother, aged grandmother, two brothers, and a sister in a shack made of discarded plastic sheeting and wood with a corrugated iron roof. There is no electricity or running water. Diarrhea and tuberculosis are common here. His mother, a widow, works as a maid for the Martins, an Afrikaner (white South African) family, five miles away. Kamuzu has attended poorly funded segregated schools most of his life. With the end of apartheid (the white-government-enforced system of "separateness") in 1990 his future has been looking better. Rather than working long hours for meager wages in one of the local textile factories, Kamuzu hopes to attend the University of Witwatersrand in Johannesburg and become a doctor and help his people.

◇ ◇ ◇

Hendrik and Patricia Martin, the Dutch-descended Afrikaner family that Kamuzu's mother works for, have a son named Jeremy who is also fourteen years old. He and his younger sister, Yvonne, live in a wealthy neighborhood of large well-kept homes. Jeremy's father is president of an import-export company, started by his grandfather, and his mother teaches science at the exclusive private school he and his sister attend. His goal, like Kamuzu's, is to attend the university in Johannesburg and study medicine.

◇ ◇ ◇

Two young South African boys—the same age, residing just a few miles apart near the tip of the African continent—supposedly live in the same society but have been raised in clearly different environments (developmental niches) by very different families, yet they share a common desire of becoming doctors.

How can we account for the similarities and differences in the development of these two young adolescents? While it is true that Kamuzu and Jeremy share a number of characteristics, in large measure, they are a reflection of two distinct cultures—different social contexts, parental belief systems, societal values, and cultural perspectives. Every one of us, like each of them, is influenced by a unique combination of factors, including the genetic material inherited from our ancestors, the family in which we are raised and the style of parenting to which we are exposed, the friends we make and the schools we attend, the historical period in which we are born, and (of pivotal importance) the culture and ecological context in which we live out our lives. As Sigel et al. (1992) noted, "Since it is a culture which serves to define values, beliefs, and actions of families, it is imperative and in fact a virtual necessity for the applied developmental psychologist to develop a knowledge base of cultures" (Roopnarine and Carter, 1992b, p. ix.).

Indeed, while this is essential, a knowledge of cultures is not enough. To genuinely understand and explain cultural differences in development, we first need to look at the way in which a culture defines these values, beliefs, and actions, and this requires an understanding of the crucial process of socialization.

◇ WHAT IS SOCIALIZATION?

Like many concepts in developmental psychology, socialization can be variously defined. For our purposes, we will view **socialization** as *the process by which an individual becomes a member of a particular culture and takes on its values, beliefs, and other behaviors in order to function within it.* According to Elkin and Handel (1989), it is this process that "helps to explain how a person becomes capable of participating in society . . . [as well as] . . . how society is possible at all" (p. 4). It is through the process of socialization that society teaches desirable behavior while inhibiting undesirable behavior, prepares individuals to become successfully functioning members in its principal institutional settings (family, school, community, and workplace), and guarantees that important traditions (although sometimes modified) will be passed to future members of the culture.

It is far from easy to describe or explain cultural socialization. Chamberlain and Patterson (1995) put this dilemma into focus when they state that "in a very real sense . . . socialization . . . is something that emerges from thousands of exchanges between the child and family members spread out over a period of many years. During these exchanges, the child is altering the behavior of the parent at the same time that the parent is presumably 'socializing' the child. It is this mutuality of effects that makes it very difficult to analyze cause and effect relations" (pp. 211–212).

With the steady increase in cross-cultural findings, our understanding of socialization has undergone significant change over the past several decades. According to Maccoby (1992), contemporary theories of socialization place greater stress on the interactive exchanges between parent and child as contributors to behavior. In addition, explanations have become more complex and multidimensional than those offered by earlier approaches.

Edwards (1996) has noted that socialization theories have also undergone substantial revision as theorists and researchers have recognized the cultural limitations of these theories. For far too long, theories and their proponents were ethnocentric (e.g., proposing that explanations of behavior in one society applied equally well in others). As we will frequently note throughout this book, such theories relied heavily on research and assumptions based in Western societies, with the result that theories were either nongeneralizable to other cultures or failed to take into account the richness of human diversity. In a sense, theorists were victims of their own socialization and were promoting what Kagitcibasi (1996) has called "an indigenous psychology of the Western world." As evidence, Edwards (1989) cites some of her own earlier work in which Mayan children in Zinacantan, Mexico, learned toilet training and other self-care skills by means of imitation and thereby made a relatively easy transition from infancy to early childhood, compared with other cultures in which these activities are characterized by resistance and great difficulty. There would appear to be an entirely different cultural context operating in this Mayan culture than what we tend to see in North America and some cultures of Western Europe. Values important to the successful functioning of these Mayan children are being transmitted in a way that provides a foundation for the development of infants and toddlers, who closely observe and carefully imitate and respond to their elders and others, rather than expecting others to respond to them (Greenfield, Brazelton, & Childs, 1989).

A researcher who has made significant contributions to our understanding of socialization, particularly in the area of cognition, is Barbara Rogoff. Her book *Apprenticeship in Thinking* (1990) is recommended in Chapter 4 as a source for additional reading in this area. Rogoff's approach to this topic has been greatly influenced by the work of the Soviet psychologist Lev Vygotsky, whose work on culture and cognitive development is discussed in detail in the same chapter. Both Vygotsky and Rogoff use the term *guided participation* to emphasize the bidirectional, or two-way, nature of socialization and the fact that children are active participants in their own socialization. In describing this concept, Brislin (1993) provides an example familiar to those who have lived in or conducted research in many of the countries in South and Southeast Asia—namely, the cultural requirement that children learn that the right (clean) hand is for eating and the left (unclean) hand is to be used for personal hygiene. If children do not learn this behavior through participation in daily home activities, parents, other adults, or even older siblings will guide the children in the appropriate way. For example, while eating, one of these "teachers" might be seen inhibiting use of the left hand while gently guiding the right toward the food. The point, Brislin says, is "that the children's behavior directs the teacher's behavior. If children learn through simple observation, there is no need for the more active intervention of holding down and guiding hands" (p. 130). Contrast this more directive approach with the observational approach of Mayan child training cited above.

Let us now consider how the socialization process relates to two of our major themes: the ecological systems approach and the developmental niche.

◇ ECOLOGICAL SYSTEMS AND THE DEVELOPMENTAL NICHE

As we have noted, socialization is a lifelong process, occurring within a variety of environments or social contexts in which we live, influencing the activities in which we participate, and significantly contributing to our development across the lifespan.

In the previous chapter, we introduced two important themes that will be interwoven throughout this book: Bronfenbrenner's (1979) **ecological systems approach** and the concept of the **developmental niche** (Super & Harkness, 1986, 1994a). The ecological systems approach allows us to look at human development as it occurs in its real-world settings or ecology and is composed of four interrelated systems. It is within these interconnected contexts that socialization takes place and in which we begin to see the development of "lives across cultures."

This approach, combined with elements of the developmental niche (a theoretical framework for looking at how a child's daily life is culturally shaped), creates a useful structure for better understanding the bidirectional nature of socialization and its effects on human development. According to Harkness and Super (1995), there are three major components of the developmental niche, each of which is directly related to parents. First, there are the **physical and social settings in which a child lives** (e.g., nuclear family living typically found in many Western cultures versus extended family arrangements found in many Asian or African countries). Aspects of this component include (1) the kind of company a child keeps (e.g., in rural Kenya families frequently consist of eight or more children, who serve as ready-made playmates and caretakers); (2) the size and shape of one's living space (e.g., in a large North American home children have their own rooms, compared with families living in overcrowded apartments in Tokyo, where small rooms sometimes serve as living, dining, and sleeping areas); and (3) eating and sleeping schedules (e.g., in many North American and European homes there are three meals a day at specified times versus the five to six small meals at unscheduled times customary in many Asian cultures). The differences in these components are clearly observable in the case of Kamuzu and Jeremy described in the opening vignette of this chapter.

The second component of the developmental niche focuses on **culturally regulated customs and childrearing practices** (e.g., informal versus formal schooling and independence versus dependence training). Again, consider and contrast the educational experiences of Jeremy and Kamuzu mentioned above. Other examples include the customary use of playpens in Holland to keep infants happy and safe and the care of younger siblings by older ones in Kenya (Super & Harkness, 1994a).

Finally, there is the third component relating to the **psychological characteristics of a child's parents** (e.g., developmental expectations or parental cultural belief systems). According to Super and Harkness (1994a) this component "is an important channel for communicating general cultural belief systems to children, through very specific context-based customs and settings" (p. 98). These authors, like us, see a connection between the developmental niche and Bronfenbrenner's approach when they comment: "Drawing from ecological and systems theory, we suggest that the three components interact with each other as a system . . . to maintain consonance among them. The niche is an 'open system,' however, in that each component interacts independently with elements in the larger culture" (Harkness & Super, 1995, p. 227).

The various aspects of the ecological approach and the developmental niche are illustrated in Box 2.1, which describes some of the ways in which Japanese children become socialized into their culture.

To further illustrate this point, we provide three brief examples that will receive detailed attention at a later time. First, if a child is doing poorly in school, this can have an impact on behavior within the family and affect the parent-child relationship in a variety of ways (e.g., neglect or abuse). Baca Zinn and Eitzen (1993) have pointed out that a home situation involving neglect or abuse can have effects on a child's relationships with parents, peers, teachers, and other family members. In addition, a child's temperament within a particular cultural context (e.g., Malaysia or Japan) may affect the way parents interact with that child and, in turn, influence the development of personality and self-concept. Finally, a sick, fussy, or light-sleeping child may keep parents awake at night, making them less effective at work or in their relationship with each other. (Variations in sleep patterns and their relationship to the approaches mentioned above will be discussed in the next section.)

BOX 2.1

BECOMING JAPANESE: AN ECOLOGICAL VIEW OF SOCIALIZATION

In her insightful book on Japanese culture, Joy Hendry (1986) has provided a delightful picture of the organization and function of three of the most important microsystems of early childhood development: family, neighborhood, and preschool. Using everyday examples, she shows how these contexts are connected with some of the most important cultural values found in the mesosystem, which, in turn, have significant effects on the surrounding exosystem. In addition, Hendry discusses the strong emphasis the culture places on cooperative behavior; academic achievement; indulgent attitudes toward infants; and the hierarchical nature of parent-child, sibling, and neighbor-child relationships. These fall within the setting of the macrosystem and deepen our understanding of how, accompanied by a traditional respect for age and seniority, these behaviors effectively combine to produce characteristics that are uniquely Japanese.

Hendry describes the family microsystem and the influence of those within it in this way: "The child . . . is in close contact with one set of grandparents and possibly one or two sets of great-grandparents, as well as its parents. . . . Other close relatives are likely to be frequent visitors . . . [and] may well play quite an important part in their early rearing" (p. 36). However, unlike recent developments in Western societies, Japanese fathers tend to play a relatively minor role in early childrearing because "many men [return] . . . home each evening after the children are asleep, and [leave] . . . in the morning before they get up" (p. 38).

According to Hendry, relationships within the neighborhood microsystem are much more institutionalized than in many other countries. For example, "Informal aid is usually given between houses popularly delineated as 'the three opposite and one on either side' (*mukosangen ryodonari*). . . . In this context, mothers of young children meet at the local swings, discuss problems with each other, and occasionally look after each other's children" (pp. 40–41). These neighbors are frequently the first people outside the family with whom the children interact and from which they acquire their first friends. When they enter school, children are organized into a children's group (*kodomogumi*) based on neighborhoods, which arrange "sporting activities, outings and school disciplinary groups [and] . . . gather at a meeting point every morning in order to walk to school together. Thus, the relations established informally at an early age are likely to continue, and even for children whose families move, there are similar groups for them to join in other areas" (p. 42).

BOX 2.1 CONTINUED

The third microsystem, that of the kindergarten or day nursery, is also a highly structured setting in which children are separated according to age "so that most of their contact with other children will be with peers, great emphasis being placed on the ideal that all children should be friends (*to-modachi*) and get on well with one another. . . . Conflict and competition is discouraged [and] . . . every child has a turn eventually to serve and to discipline the others" (p. 43). Later, "after-school classes in English and music provide excellent opportunities for kindergarten classmates to maintain their friendships throughout their school lives" (p. 45).

This short excerpt provides only a glimpse into the complex but interrelated ecological world of Japanese children and their families; we highly recommend that the reader look at Hendry's book for a fuller picture.

Source: Adapted from "Becoming Japanese: The Arenas and Agents of Socialization" by J. Hendry (1993) in R. W. Wozniak (Ed.), *Worlds of Childhood Reader* (pp. 34–47), New York: HarperCollins.

Before we get to the examples, let us introduce Richard Lerner, known for his theory of developmental contextualism—in which the central idea is that "changing, reciprocal relations . . . between individuals and the multiple contexts within which they live comprise the essential process of human development" (Lerner et al., 1995, p. 287). Does this sound familiar? It should, since it owes much to the work of Bronfenbrenner and, in some respects, expands on his ideas. In fact, Lerner and his colleagues (1995) provide us with Figure 2.1. When you first look at this figure don't panic and think "What is that?" or turn the page and ignore it altogether. If you take a few minutes and carefully study its components, you'll find (believe it or not) that it clearly describes most of the major points made in this chapter.

Did you understand the figure? Let us give you some help. First, it divides the child and parent into components reflecting some of the multiple dimensions of individuality (e.g., cognition, personality, temperament, and health—topics discussed in succeeding chapters). The arrows represent the bidirectional relationships or reciprocal influences that exist between parent and child across the lifespan (e.g., our discussion of the socialization process above). Lerner and his colleagues (1995) also make the point in Figure 2.1 that "the parent-child relationship, and the social networks in which it is located, are embedded in still larger community, societal, cultural, and historical levels of organization" (p. 296). Each of these rings can be seen to correspond to the systems set forth by Bronfenbrenner: the microsystem, meso-

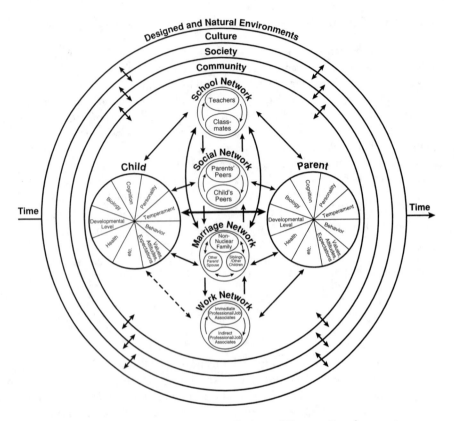

FIGURE 2.1   Developmental Contextual View of Human Development

Source: From "Developmental Contextual Perspective on Parenting" (p. 297) by R. M. Lerner, D. R. Castellino, P. A. Terry, F. A. Villarruel, and M. H. McKinney, 1995, in M. H. Bornstein (Ed.), *Handbook of Parenting*, vol. 2, Hillsdale, NJ: Erlbaum. Copyright © 1995 by Lawrence Erlbaum Publishing Co. Reprinted by permission.

system, exosystem, and macrosystem. One extremely important point made in this figure is that people are continually experiencing change (e.g., the family unit begins with infants and young children, changes to having adolescents, changes again when adult children leave their parents to establish their own families, and may change again when parents need to take care of their own aging parents). It also suggests that cultures undergo change as well, and the system illustrated in this figure provides an organized view of the contextual approach to human development.

All of this may appear highly complex (and it is) but as Lerner and his colleagues (1995) accurately point out, unless we address this complexity, "then—given the diversity of parent-child relationships that is both a product and a producer of multilevel person-context relations—neither research nor applications will be adequate" (p. 297). In short, while there certainly are cultural differences in human development, we need also to recognize individual and familial differences as well.

With (hopefully) a clear understanding of the developmental contextual perspective, combining the ecological systems approach with the developmental niche, and throwing in the cross-cultural theme for good measure, we are prepared to look at some cultural variations in socialized behavior.

◇ SOME CULTURAL VARIATIONS IN THE SOCIALIZATION OF BEHAVIOR

As pointed out in Chapter 1, in a book of this type, with its major focus on cultural similarities and differences, it is impossible to provide as comprehensive a view of human development as do some more traditional developmental books. For a general overview of human development principles, we direct the reader to one of these books. Our goal is to consider selected topics for which a large or growing body of cross-cultural research evidence exists and discuss these topics chronologically—from the early beginnings of infancy through the later years of adulthood. Another aspect, unique to this discussion, will be the incorporation (and suggested modification) of Erik Erikson's psychosocial theory of development in an effort to place these behaviors within a cross-cultural perspective. Before doing this, let us say a few words about this theory.

Erikson's **psychosocial theory** provides a useful framework for attempting to define and unravel some of the major changes in social behavior that take place at various points in the lifespan. He views development as a series of **psychosocial crises** requiring resolution if an individual is to successfully move from one period to the next. These crises or periods of increased vulnerability and heightened potential involve conflicts between newly developing competencies and a desire to maintain the status quo (see Table 2.1).

Before looking at Erikson's theory, keep the following in mind. First, although he assigns an age range to each of his eight stages, these should be considered only as a descriptive guide. Second, successful resolution of a crisis will depend on how a particular culture views the crisis, the sequence in which a particular stage occurs, and the solution evolving from it. Third, while many of Erikson's original ideas were based on development in Western societies, we attempt to modify some of these to show their increased applicability in other cultural and ecological settings.

We begin our discussion of selected topics, which will be followed in a similar fashion in subsequent chapters, with a consideration of some of the principal behaviors socialized by most parents across cultures. We turn first to socialization during infancy.

TABLE 2.1   Erikson's Stages of Psychosocial Development

STAGE	CRISIS	PSYCHOSOCIAL TASK
Infancy	Trust vs. mistrust	Develop first social relationship with primary caretaker(s); develop a fundamental trust in life and the world
Toddlerhood	Autonomy vs. shame and doubt	Explore the social environment outside the primary relationship; recognize self as an individual being
Early childhood	Initiative vs. guilt	Negotiate one's place within social relationships; learn about the impact of one's social behavior on others; develop a sense of power
Middle childhood	Industry vs. inferiority	Learn the importance of social norms and the personal consequences of conformity and nonconformity; develop a sense of competence
Adolescence	Identity vs. role confusion	Find social roles and social environments that correspond to one's identity and principles; form one's own identity
Young adulthood	Intimacy vs. isolation	Negotiate one's own identity within the context of intimate relationships
Middle adulthood	Generativity vs. stagnation	Make a contribution to the larger society; acquire a sense of accomplishment and a place in the world
Late adulthood	Integrity vs. despair	Become an integral and active part of one's family and community; come to terms with one's life and choices

Infancy

When a newborn arrives in the world, independent of its particular culture, it has a number of basic needs that require immediate attention. How these needs are met and the manner in which they are socialized varies considerably across cultures and often among ethnic groups within a single society.

In fact, as we shall see frequently throughout this book, there is often more variability in certain behaviors within cultures than between or among cultures.

It is clear that culture influences patterns of parenting from the first hours of infancy (e.g., when and how parents care for infants, the extent to which they allow them to explore their surroundings, how nurturant or restrictive they might be, and which behaviors they value and socialize). Bornstein (1995) has expressed it very succinctly when he says, "With the birth of a baby, a parent's life is forever changed. The pattern that those changes assume, in turn, shapes the experiences of infants and, with time, the people they become. Parent and infant chart the course together. Infancy is a starting point of life for both infant and parent" (p. 30).

Sleep

While all babies require sleep, psychological, anthropological, and even pediatric literature reveals considerable variation in cultural sleeping arrangements (Morelli, Rogoff, Oppenheim, & Goldsmith, 1992; Super & Harkness, 1997; Super, Harkness, & Blom, 1997; Wolf, Lozoff, Latz, & Pauladetto, 1996). According to Harkness and Super (1995), the way sleep is organized, including where and with whom, is an intriguing aspect of culture because, although it is a private rather than public behavior, it is highly structured by different societies and tends to be relatively resistant to change. As these researchers point out, "Parents play a primary role in the assignment of settings and routines for sleep, thus perpetuating a cycle of culture transmission within the privileged context of the family" (p. 227). For example, in a 1981 study of Kipsigis farming families in the highlands of rural Kenya in East Africa, Harkness and Super noted that, although the next-to-youngest child continues to sleep with its mother and other siblings after the birth of a younger child, it no longer sleeps at the mother's front but rather at her back. This change, along with the termination of breast-feeding and back-carrying, results in a "fundamental shift in the child's physical and social settings of life" (1995, p. 227).

Characterizing sleep management as one of the earliest culturally determined parent-child interactions, Wolf and his colleagues (1996) suggest that their study may provide a useful framework for interpreting cross-cultural differences in the varying emphases placed on such behaviors as autonomy and dependence.

While it is common practice among middle-class families in the United States and Canada to put young infants in their own room to sleep (in part, to give them an early start down the road to independence), many Mayan mothers (American Indian peoples of Mexico and Central America) view this custom as "tantamount to child neglect" (Morelli et al., 1992, p. 608). On the other hand, interdependence—a prominent personality and cultural characteristic among Japanese—can be attributable, at least in some measure, to the fact that Japanese children (sometimes due to an overcrowded microsystem) frequently sleep with their parents until the age of six or even, in some cases, to the beginning of puberty, when independent sleeping marks a culturally recognized change in one's developmental niche (Caudill & Plath, 1966, in LeVine, 1988).

According to Erikson's model, which, as we have cautioned, tends to present a predominantly Westernized perspective, social maturation during the first year of infancy is reflected in the development of a feeling of *trust versus mistrust* (e.g., the world is good and comfortable—trust—or threatening and uncomfortable—mistrust). Whichever view develops will depend largely on the parent-infant relationship. For example, many infants learn to trust that if they cry because they are hungry, someone will pick them up and feed them. Parents, on the other hand, learn to trust that their infants will be quieted and comforted when they are fed because the pattern of interaction is consistent.

Similar patterns develop near the end of infancy (during the second and third year) with regard to the second crisis of *autonomy versus shame and doubt*. For example, children will either begin to explore their surroundings on their own (sometimes getting into trouble) and decide for themselves what they want to wear, eat, or do, or they will obediently follow the demands of parents and develop doubts about their abilities and feel incapable of making decisions and governing their own behavior.

If we look at trust and independence, as illustrated in the Kipsigis and Japanese examples mentioned above, the Western bias inherent in Erikson's theory becomes obvious. In these cultural contexts, social maturation is not associated with increased independence but rather with increased interdependence within the family. In both cultures, infants first develop trust and attachment as a result of sleeping with parents. Some degree of autonomy in Kipsigi infants is achieved when breast-feeding ends and the older child is moved from the mother's front to her back to accommodate the arrival of a new baby. In the case of Japanese culture, in which a mother sleeps with the child for an even longer period, interdependence would appear to be even stronger than in Kipsigi society. Consideration of these examples strongly suggests that we may need to make adaptations in Erikson's theory when attempting to apply it in another cultural context.

The practice of cosleeping (a child sleeping with the parent) is, in fact, routine in most of the world's cultures and was the practice in the United States until shortly after the beginning of the last century. Studies have suggested that the United States and other parts of North America are nearly alone in their expectation that children sleep in their own beds, in their own rooms, apart from their parents (Barry & Paxson, 1971; McKenna, 1993).

The well-known pediatrician Benjamin Spock, to whom generations of American parents have turned for advice on raising their children, has stated that "it's a sensible rule not to take a child into the parents' bed for any reason" (Spock & Rothenberg, 1992, p. 213). Super and Harkness (1982), on the other hand, have suggested that the expectation that infants will be able to sleep through the night without some contact or involvement with parents may be "pushing the limits of infants' adaptability" (p. 52). Again, we see the importance of cultural as well as individual and familial differences in the determination of a particular behavior such as sleep patterns.

In an examination of sleep practices among parents in Japan, Italy, and the United States, Wolf and others (1996) conclude that "as in other child-rearing practices, it may not be the specific practice itself, but rather the context and values that are the most important factors" (p. 382). This view supports the ecological and developmental niche themes expressed throughout this book and leads us to another basic infant need requiring socialization— feeding.

Feeding

When infants are not sleeping, much of their time is spent eating. Just ask any new parent! How, what, and when to feed a child is another socialized behavior heavily influenced by the developmental niche, social context, parental beliefs, and values of one's culture.

Children need adequate nutrition, before birth as well as during infancy, if they are to grow properly and develop into healthy children and adults. The effects of nutritional deficiencies in infancy can be carried into adulthood and even affect another generation in terms of a mother's poor diet, inability to carry a baby to full term, or delivery of a low-birth-weight infant. According to figures gathered by the United Nations International Children's Emergency Fund (UNICEF, 1993), undernutrition is a major problem in many nonindustrialized or recently industrialized countries. It can have an impact on an individual's resistance to disease as well as normal development of intellectual or cognitive abilities. In fact, Pollitt, Gorman, Engle, Martorell, and Rivera (1993) report finding a link between inadequate nutrition in infancy and cognitive functioning in adolescence, notably among those living in poor socioeconomic circumstances. In a recent study among low-income Nicaraguan mothers, findings revealed a clear relationship between maternal beliefs about infant feeding and a child's nutritional level during the first year (Engle, Zeitlin, Medrano, & Garcia, 1996). The authors conclude their study by stating that "behavioral encouragement to eat as observed here did not reflect the sense of responsibility of the mother about feeding [and that] . . . further work is needed to determine the ways in which mothers translate their belief in helping children to eat into feeding behaviors" (p. 443).

For a long time, mothers around the world have been told that breast-feeding is the ideal method for providing nourishment to babies. The reasons most frequently mentioned include the fact that breast milk is more easily digested than other types of milk (e.g., milk from goats or cows), it protects against disease by providing natural immunization, and it is (obviously) immediately available. In most non-Western cultures, it is the method most preferred by mothers, although one study has suggested a recent decline among mothers in Third World or Majority World (a term suggested by Kagitcibasi, 1996) countries and an accompanying increase, at least on a short-term basis, among mothers in the United States (Ryan, Rush, Krieger, & Lewandowski, 1991). This topic will receive additional attention in Chapter 3.

As you might expect, cultural attitudes play a significant role in whether babies are breast-fed or bottle-fed (Van Esterik, 1989). Some cultures, many of them in the West, tend to make a woman feel embarrassed about engaging in this natural function in public. When mothers return to work shortly after their child's birth, as many tend to do in North American and European countries, they may be unable to continue breast-feeding. On the other hand, if bottle-feeding is the method of choice, more fathers are able to participate in feeding and bonding with their infants.

At this point, we would like to emphasize that research findings have not yet clearly demonstrated that one method has long-term benefits over the other (Van Esterik, 1989). If both options are equally available, we would support the opinion of most experts and recommend breast-feeding for the reasons mentioned above. However, we stress that the method is not as important as what happens during the feeding process. The feeding situation provides an excellent opportunity, through socialization, for parents to establish an emotional connection with their infant (attachment or bonding) that has been shown to have important implications for interpersonal relationships throughout the remainder of the lifespan. (For an excellent overview of this topic, see the book by Virgina Colin mentioned in the Further Readings section of this chapter.)

As one moves through the lifespan, these early cultural experiences with food strongly influence what, when, and how much an individual will eat. For example, which would you rather eat right now—a hamburger with french fries, a bowl of rice with spicy flavored beef, snake on crackers, octopus, grasshoppers, or (perhaps) nothing? Depending on your cultural training, the mention of any one of these meals might make you hungry or completely suppress your desire to eat. While hunger and the feeding process begin biologically, they are individually socialized by cognitive, learning, and experiential factors deeply rooted in the culture and often within the immediate family. As with other behaviors, eating preferences may show greater variability within families or within cultural subgroups than they do across cultures.

Crying

All babies cry. But what does their crying mean, and is it responded to in the same way in all cultures? Crying is the newborn's earliest form of communication with those in its immediate surroundings—the world of the micro- and mesosystems. Through crying, a baby lets others know that it is hungry, is not feeling well, has a wet diaper, wants attention, would like its older brother to stop annoying it, or conveys other information about its condition. In a sense, when newborns and infants cry, they are bringing their parents and others into their world and socializing them into understanding what their feelings are when they have no other way of expressing them. Although most parents in diverse cultures around the world can clearly differentiate these cries and distinguish one from another, it is almost impossible to teach this skill to others (Gustafson & Harris, 1990); experience seems to be the best teacher.

In addition, numerous studies have shown that infants with various disorders (cystic fibrosis, Down syndrome, and others) cry differently than normal babies and that individuals across cultures can recognize and differentiate among these various cries (Lester, 1984; Molitor & Eckerman, 1992; Zeskind, 1983; Zeskind, Klein, & Marshall, 1992; Zeskind, Sale, Maio, Huntington, & Weiseman, 1985). Research also shows that fathers and other males respond in as nurturing a way to an infant's crying as do mothers and other women (Rosenblith, 1992).

When and how often should a caregiver respond to a child's crying? If it is responded to frequently, will the child be spoiled? If crying is ignored, will insecurity be the result? These are difficult questions, and not all experts agree as to the answers. Bowlby (1989) believes that crying should be responded to frequently, especially during the first year, and will not result in spoiling but rather will greatly assist in promoting secure attachment. In terms of Erikson's theory, frequent responding to crying appears to promote attachment as well as assist in resolving the crisis of trust versus mistrust mentioned earlier.

Childhood

When we use the term **childhood,** we are referring to *the period extending from the end of infancy, about one and a half to two years of age, to just before the beginning of adolescence, typically about the age of eleven or twelve,* depending on the particular culture.

Edwards (1996), in a discussion of the parenting of toddlers, has outlined the developmental tasks she believes children are confronted with during their second and third years. We view each of these as an area of behavior in need of socialization and indicate, in parentheses, the chapters in this book in which they receive extensive discussion. These include, but are not limited to, learning to function independently or interdependently (discussed earlier in this chapter), developing the beginnings of a self-concept (Chapter 5) as well as a moral conscience (Chapter 7), understanding sex roles and establishing gender identity (Chapter 6), becoming a functioning member of a society (Chapter 2), and taking a place in the larger family grouping (Chapter 8).

Edwards (1996) points out that "although socialization processes in the field of toddler development are by no means fully understood . . . bidirectional, multicausational, and transactional models have become the goal" (p. 59). She goes on to say that "toddler development cannot be adequately described without introducing further theoretical perspectives based on Vygotsky's (1978) writings and using naturalistic observations that clarify the meaning systems and communication processes involved in socialization" (p. 49). Since these topics, in fact, provide the basis for a large part of the discussion on culture and cognition covered in Chapter 4, we will forgo any further mention of it at this time and direct your attention to that chapter. For the remainder of this section, let us consider some other behaviors that cultures socialize in one way or another during the years of childhood.

Aggression

Most children in most cultures fight, argue, or aggress against one another (peers or siblings) as well as against adults (especially parents) at some time during the years of childhood. Learning the differences between appropriate and inappropriate behavior and how to handle hostility and aggression fall within the realm of socialization.

Let us begin by distinguishing between two often misunderstood terms that are frequently used incorrectly to mean the same thing. **Hostility** is *a motive or desire to cause damage or injury.* If someone calls me a name or insults me, I may feel like I want to strike back by returning the insult or by taking something away from that person. **Aggression,** on the other hand, is *an overt action or behavior intended to cause harm, damage, or injury.* If I follow through on my feeling and actually use an insult, hit the person, or take something away, I am acting aggressively.

The form and extent to which such feelings and actions are exhibited depend on many factors including culture and gender. Research generally shows boys, in most cultures, exhibiting more aggression than do girls. Although there is not a great deal of agreement as to why this may be the case, socialization plays a major role, and differences appear to become particularly noticeable between the ages of two and three (Legault & Strayer, 1990). At least one study (Fagot & Leinbach, 1989) has suggested that an observed increase in aggressive behavior among boys and a corresponding decrease among girls may be related to a greater awareness of one's sex role and a culture's rules regarding the expression of this behavior. (See Chapter 6 for a detailed discussion of the relationship between gender and the development of aggression.)

What causes a particular child to be aggressive? We wish there were a simple answer to this question but none seems readily available. Some say the cause lies in the evolution of the human species; others, in a child's models (siblings, peers, and parents); still others, in the methods by which one's culture rewards or punishes the expression of aggression. Rather than attempt to do what others have been unable to do (adequately explain the causes of childhood aggression), we would prefer to view the topic within a cross-cultural context and discuss similarities and differences across cultures with some detailed illustrations.

Bourguignon (1979) gives an example of two children, a girl of seven or eight and a boy of about six, walking along a path in the mountains of Haiti. The girl is hitting the boy and calling him names. He complains loudly but makes no effort to hit back. Why? We learn that the girl's mother has put her in charge of her younger brother and, modeling her mother's behavior, she is punishing him for being disobedient. Bourguignon explains, "We are dealing with an example of child socialization. Children are beaten to enforce obedience toward elders, a central concern in this society. . . . Haitian society is based on a hierarchy of age [and] . . . places less stress on differences in sex" (p. 3). The girl is older and so her brother must obey her and pay her respect. She is permitted to hit him, if necessary, to discipline him, and he is not allowed to hit back. In another example, Bourguignon describes a quarrel between two boys in a village in southern France, who are seen insulting and threatening each other. One boy hits the other, runs away, but is not chased. According to Wylie (1974), who studied the village in which this incident occurred, "If two children start to fight they are immediately separated by any adult who may happen to witness the scene. . . . If it is relatives who separate fighting children, both children are punished. No inquiry is made into the question of which child started the fight or which was in the right. They are both fighting and consequently they are both guilty" (pp. 49–50). Wylie further notes that while French parents discourage physical aggression, they do permit verbal aggression (e.g., insults) as a socially accepted way to deal with anger. According to Bourguignon (1979), adults tend to model this behavior and may themselves "on occasion make a great public show of anger in words and threats, but physical fighting is said to be rare" (p. 2).

As these examples illustrate, there are certainly considerable cross-cultural differences in the amount of aggressiveness various societies will tolerate, first among its young people, and later among its adult members. With

some effort, it would be possible to draw a continuum with the least aggressive cultures on one end and the most aggressive on the other. Among the
least aggressive would be the Inuit of the North American Arctic, the Pyg-
mies of Africa, and the characteristically tranquil and polite Amerindian
tribes of Zuni and Blackfoot (Moghaddam, Taylor, & Wright, 1993). At the
other end would have to be the Yanomamo, living in the Amazon region of
Brazil and Venezuela, often described in anthropological literature as the
"most fierce and violent people in the world."

According to Chagnon (1983), the first anthropologist to report on
Yanomamo society, aggressiveness is the major determinant of status within
the group, and learning the aggressive ways of the society begins at an early
age. He relates an example involving a four-year-old boy named Ariwari,
whose father encourages him to "beat him on the face and head to express
his anger and temper, laughing and commenting on his ferocity. . . . He has
already learned that the appropriate response to a flash of anger is to strike
someone with his hand or with an object, and it is not uncommon for him to
give his father a healthy smack in the face whenever something displeases
him [and he is] . . . rewarded by gleeful cheers of assent from his mother and
from the other adults in the household" (p. 115).

In contrast, Ember and Ember (1993) cite an example from the Semai
of central Malaya, a group known for its timidity, who say, "We do not get
angry" (Dentan, 1968). The Semai raise their children to be nonviolent and,
on the rare occasion that one of them may show anger, do not use physical
punishment. As Dentan points out, with this kind of socialization, children
are seldom exposed to aggressive models and, as a result, have no aggressive
behavior to imitate.

Finally, we would be remiss if we did not mention the findings of the
six cultures studies (Whiting, 1963; Whiting & Edwards, 1988; Whiting &
Whiting, 1975). These studies examined, in great detail, a wide range of behavior in children ranging from three to eleven years of age in India, Japan,
Kenya, Mexico, the Philippines, and the United States. In an analysis of this
data, Lambert (1971) reported that American parents were fairly tolerant of
displays of aggression against other children, whereas Mexican parents were
the most punitive. Lambert attributes these differences, in part, to a higher
level of interdependence within extended Mexican families, which leads, as
we saw earlier, to more adult supervision and greater management of children's behavior. As far as American parents' greater tolerance of peer-di-
rected aggression is concerned, Moghaddam and his colleagues (1993) quote
one mother as saying, "If he can't get along with one child, he can always
play with someone else. There are plenty of children around to choose from"
(p. 126). They conclude with the observation that "this statement clearly reflects the attitude that interpersonal relationships are the product of choice
and can be terminated. Given this element of choice and impermanence, it is

less consequential to be aggressive against those around you" (p. 126). Once again, we see the intermingling of cultural and individual differences as influences on behavior.

We hope, after reading these examples, you are able to see how early socialization (occurring as part of one's unique developmental niche and place within a culture's ecological system) helps to determine the definition and expression of aggressive behavior. It is only by looking at a topic like this from a cross-cultural and developmental perspective that the richness and diversity of human behavior can be fully observed.

For an especially useful discussion and approach to studying aggression within a cross-cultural framework, see Chapter 12 in the book by Segall, Dasen, Berry, and Poortinga (1990). They end their presentation on a positive note, stating that "because the evidence reviewed in this chapter does not support the view that it is inevitable that male adolescents will aggress, there is hope that the pervasive amount of aggression that presently characterizes the world may be reduced, but only if we become more knowledgeable about the experiential factors, rooted in culture, that presently encourage so many people to aggress" (p. 285). We can only hope that they are right.

How children learn aggressive, as well as other, behaviors is very frequently embedded in a variety of environmental settings, including specific types of learning environments. Depending on the culture, these may be formal settings (e.g., a public or private school) or informal settings (e.g., a desert or jungle area). We will consider these settings in more detail in the following section.

Formal Versus Informal Learning

Most of the socialization experiences of children in nonindustrialized countries take place in informal settings (e.g., within the family or among peers and siblings) and are a fundamental part of one's daily activities. **Informal learning** is not characterized by a defined curriculum and is *generally picked up by means of observation and imitation.* According to Cushner (1990), "The responsibility for learning falls mainly on the learner, making it rather personal, with extended family members often playing a critical role in the act of instruction. . . . Change, discontinuity, and innovation are highly valued" (p. 100). For example, in certain African and South American tribal groups, young boys learn hunting and fishing skills as well as methods for navigating their way through jungles and rivers by observing and imitating adult males in their culture. Girls learn cooking and child-care techniques, not in school, but by helping their mothers, aunts, and other women in the daily activities of family and village life. Traditions change very little in some cultures; this is the way it has been for centuries and the way it is almost certain to be long into the future.

In other countries, the majority of children learn important cultural skills as part of their society's formal education system. As Cushner (1990) points out, **formal learning** is "set apart from the context of everyday life and is typically carried out in the institution we know as school [and is characterized by] . . . an explicit and highly structured curriculum [in which] . . . material is learned from a book that may or may not be useful at a later time" (p. 100). For a particularly insightful discussion of the failures of formal schooling, in what Kagitcibasi (1996) calls the Majority World, see Serpell's (1993) work on Zambia.

The issue of formal versus informal schooling gives us another opportunity to look at the two crises Erikson says are characteristic of the stage of childhood. As shown in Table 2.1, these are initiative versus guilt and industry versus inferiority. To put these crises into perspective, let us consider the case of Tamiko and Alexina. Tamiko, age ten, lives and goes to school in Akita, Japan. Like most children in her country, her success or failure depends more on her effort and character than on her innate ability. She is learning and working productively and harmoniously in mixed-ability groups similar to what she will encounter when she is an adult. Cooperation is seen as essential to the success of the group as well as the individual, and formal instruction occurs with this in mind. In this case, the developmental niche in which early learning takes place will share certain characteristics with the adult niche in which Tamiko will later live and work. The Japanese believe that parents and teachers must coordinate their efforts so that there is a high level of contact between the school and the home throughout a child's formal schooling. For Tamiko and her parents, academic work comes before everything else and involves long hours of study. There is a Japanese expression—"Pass with four, fail with five"—referring to how many hours of sleep are needed in order to succeed. Tamiko's education actually began prior to entering formal preschool when her mother taught her to read, write, and perform simple mathematics. She spends more hours in school each year than almost any other children anywhere else in the world. This includes her regular classes, followed by several hours in a "juku" (cram school), and finally her studying and doing homework at home until the early morning hours. While the latter is not formal in the strict sense of the word, it is nevertheless very serious and regimented. Alexina, also ten years old, lives in Minnesota in the midwestern part of the United States and is equally serious about her education. However, in her case the focus is more on independence and self-expression. She has learned that autonomy and individual achievement are valued over group collaboration. Getting ahead is a personal goal, as characterized by Alexina's ability to take the initiative to complete assignments on her own. As with Tamiko, there will be a certain consistency between the values and behaviors present in the developmental niches of childhood and adulthood. Unlike the Japanese, Americans believe education is to be provided in the school, not in the home. This again points out the distinction between formal and informal schooling mentioned above. If you think about the opening chapter vignettes, Kamuzu's educational experience, while not as rich in opportunities, would be similar in many ways to that of Tamiko (e.g., more cooperative or group learning and more informal home schooling). Jeremy, like Alexina, would be expected to show greater independence, autonomy, and self-expression. Again, in the case of Jeremy and Kamuzu, we observe more variability in their individual educational experiences within the South African culture than we do between the experiences of Jeremy in his culture and Alexina in the United States.

How might we apply Erikson's model and resolution of crises to these four children? In Tamiko's case, *initiative* and *industry* are achieved only after successfully recognizing the need for others to assist in the learning process. The same is somewhat less true in Kamuzu's situation, since his school is underfunded and he had to learn more in the informal settings of his home and community. In Alexina's case, industry is achieved when she is able to take initiative independently and become a "self-starter." Her success in this area is reflected in her school report card, which has a category for "industriousness." In this respect, Jeremy behaves similarly to Alexina. In short, Alexina's culture and Jeremy's subculture view initiative and industry in independent terms, whereas Tamiko's culture and Kamuzu's subculture, to a lesser extent, look at these qualities in interdependent terms. Again, when applying Erikson's theory to non-Western cultures, it is of crucial importance to consider the relevance and cultural definitions of his concepts (e.g., independence and autonomy, initiative and industry). If this is not done, a researcher is liable to make serious misinterpretations of cultural behavior.

Let us now turn our attention to another aspect of formal versus informal learning—the socialization of mathematical skills—and to the current argument that American schoolchildren lag far behind children of other nations, particularly Japan and China, in math achievement (Gardiner, 1994). In a study of parents' beliefs, cultural values, and children's math achievement, Chen and Uttal (1988) report that it is more common for Chinese parents to set higher standards for their children and to work more closely with them on homework assignments than for American parents. In a cross-cultural study comparing performance among Thai and American students, Gardiner and Gardiner (1991) reported similar conclusions. A cross-cultural study by White (1987) reinforces our earlier comments (on sleeping and feeding) as to the differential emphasis cultures place on the socialization of such values as cooperation versus competition and dependence versus independence. Specifically, White reported that Japanese "mothers spend many hours in cooperative games and pursuits with their children, such as drawing, reading storybooks, and playing writing and counting games," whereas American mothers give their children materials and games they can enjoy and play with independently (p. 97). On several occasions, the present authors, in their role as teachers, have observed Asian and Asian-American adolescents working cooperatively on solving math problems. Such group behavior has sometimes been proffered as a contributing factor in these ethnic groups' superior achievement in math courses (Gardiner, 1994). At the same time, Gardiner, Gardiner, and Gardiner (1994) reported that while such students were more likely to major in science and mathematics than many other ethnic groups, significant numbers did not graduate, had relatively low grade point averages, and were more likely to withdraw for medical reasons or be placed on academic probation. In cases such as these, individual differences in behavior are more important than cultural differences and should be recognized as such.

Summarizing the themes and results of these and several other studies of mathematical achievement, Gardiner (1994) states, "First, there is recognition of the dominant role in this process played by mothers. Second, cross-cultural evidence strongly suggests that an informal learning style, like that found in Asian cultures, focused on building interest, is a more effective way to teach children a variety of skills, including math" (p. 71).

Support for this last statement, particularly with reference to informal math learning, can be found among some of Brazil's more than two hundred thousand *Mennios de Rua* and Colombia's *Gamines* or *Chupagruesos*—street children (Aptekar, 1989). Many of these children survive by selling fruits and vegetables on street corners. Most of them dropped out of school by the time they were ten, before learning good math skills. Although they conduct scores of informal financial transactions each day without making a mistake, the majority of them are unable to complete a formal, written math problem requiring them to calculate change (not unlike what they do every day) without making numerous errors. Their school (ecological setting) is the street, and it is here that they have been socialized and have learned functional math skills that allow them to survive in the street culture of large Latin American cities where they live.

Adolescence

We know that adolescence begins in biology, when hormones that bring about physical changes and prepare the body for sexual reproduction are released into the bloodstream. But adolescent development ends in culture, where one's status is defined by the new role played in society and the transition to adulthood begins. From an ecological or cultural contextual perspective, adolescence is seen as a developmental stage in some, but not all, cultures (Burbank, 1988; Hollos & Leis, 1989; Whiting, Burbank, & Ratner, 1986). According to Cole and Cole (1996), its distinctiveness as a stage depends in large measure on whether or not "young people reach biological maturity before they have acquired the knowledge and skills needed to ensure cultural reproduction" (p. 629). For example, in the United States and

Canada, there sometimes are young adolescents (ages twelve and up) with children of their own who, without a job or educational training, are totally incapable of providing for the welfare of their children or of themselves. Contrast this with the !Kung San living in the Kalahari Desert in Botswana and parts of Namibia and South Africa. Even before reaching the years of adolescence, older children have learned through socialization to hunt animals and gather wild plants as part of their nomadic life. They, like their North American counterparts, are biologically capable of reproduction but already know their developmental niche and have the skills to economically support themselves and a family if necessary (Draper & Cashdan, 1988).

Adolescence provides another opportunity to dramatically illustrate how the major themes of this book can be used to describe and explain how cultures structure and teach the kinds of activities that Cole and Cole (1996) say need to be mastered in order to "carry out the full process of human reproduction [and how these] . . . shape the psychological characteristics that one develops at the end of childhood" (p. 629). It is at this point in the lifespan that we can again clearly observe the development of "lives across cultures." For example, compare two fourteen-year-old girls growing up in cultures separated by both time and space. Mankushai is a member of the Masai tribe and lives on a flat grassy plain in southern Kenya. Her days are spent in her husband's village working side by side with her mother-in-law cooking and taking care of her young daughter, Consolata. Far away, in the United States, in California, Alisa spends her days in school studying chemistry, calculus, and world history so that she will be able to attend college and prepare for a career as an economist. Each lives in a developmental niche within an ecological system, surrounded by family, peers, and teachers, learning her culture's values, and being socialized into an adult role. But how different their lives are and how different they will continue to be as they move through the lifespan. At least part of their development will be influenced by the presence or absence of rites of passage.

Rites of Passage

In many cultures, the transition from childhood to adolescence is marked by some sort of public recognition. Called **rites of passage,** these are *ceremonies or rituals that recognize or symbolize an individual's movement from one status to another* (Gander & Gardiner, 1981, p. 498). These "coming-of-age" experiences vary significantly from one culture to another but, according to a study by Schlegal and Barry (1991), are found in most nonindustrialized societies where nearly 80 percent of girls and close to 70 percent of boys go through some form of initiation.

Frequently, these rituals can be harsh and painful. Consider the following passage from Alex Haley's novel *Roots* (1974), which describes the beginning of Kunta Kinte's journey from adolescence into manhood: "Hands knocked him down and feet kicked him. Kunta thought desperately of bolting away somehow, but just as he was about to try, a firm but gentle hand gripped one of his. Breathing hoarsely under his hood, Kunta realized he was no longer being hit and kicked and that the screaming of the crowd was suddenly no longer near by. The people, he guessed, had moved along to another boy's hut, and the guiding hand that held his must be a slave Omoro would have hired, as every father did, to lead his hooded son to *jujuo*" (p. 104). Enduring this painful and abusive four-month journey would teach Kunta the skills he needed to survive and be successful in the Mandinka village of Juffree.

In eastern Africa, ten- to twelve-year-old boys in the Kaguru tribe are led into the bush, stripped of all clothing, and ritually circumcised while being taught the sexual practices of adulthood by male members of the community. Later, they return to their village, are celebrated at a large feast, receive new names, and are expected to become responsible adult members of their society (Beidelman, 1971). Passage for a Kaguru girl is not as complex as for boys and occurs when she experiences first menstruation and is taught the ways of womanhood by her grandmother or older women in the tribe. She is fortunate in escaping the very painful and widespread practice of female circumcision already experienced by as many as 114 million women in twenty-eight countries in Africa, India, the Middle East, and Southeast Asia (Armstrong, 1991; Kelso, 1994).

The transition from adolescence to adulthood in North America and many other Western countries is not marked by such clearly defined rituals. In fact, many would say there are no true rites of passage experienced by all members of these societies at this particular stage in the lifespan, and if there ever were, they have disappeared (Elkind, 1984). Among certain ethnic groups within the larger society, there may be some fairly commonly experienced ceremonies, such as the Bar or Bas Mitzvah for Jewish boys and girls, that may come close to being a rite of passage. On the other hand, while not experienced by all adolescents at the same time, or by many at all, the following are frequently mentioned as possible rites of passage in North American society: graduation from high school or college, successful passing of a driver's test, marriage, or the first job.

Age certainly is not a very helpful marker in cultures like the United States, since there are several criteria by which individuals are considered adults (e.g., age sixteen for driving, eighteen for voting, and twenty-one for drinking). American adolescents, and their counterparts in many other countries, often linger in a kind of "cultural limbo" between the ages of twelve to the early twenties when they may (or may not) one day be considered adults.

An exception to the comments made above is the **Vision Quest,** an experience common to many of the more than five hundred culturally diverse Native American tribes in North America. Performed primarily as a rite of passage for adolescent males, it begins with the taking of a boy, age fourteen or fifteen, into a "sweat lodge," where his body and spirit are purified by the heat given off by burning cedar. Sitting with the boy is a medicine man, who advises him and assists him with ritual prayers. Later, he is taken to an isolated location and left alone to fast for four days. He prays, contemplates the words of the medicine man, and waits for a vision that will reveal to him his path in life as a member of his tribal culture (Delaney, 1995). As another example, Navajo girls at the time of menarche take part in a rite of passage that involves morning running and the baking of a ceremonial cake.

It is clear from this discussion that different cultures treat their young people very differently. Some provide a clearly defined niche within the microsystem of the family where the parents, elders, and others initiate and prepare their young people to move into the wider realms of the mesosystem, exosystem, and macrosystem and be ready to deal with the challenges and opportunities available to them as recognized adults. Other cultures, such as many Western societies, could do more to prepare their young people for the often difficult transition to adulthood.

In discussing rites of passage, it is important to keep in mind that each culture uses these as a way of helping their adolescents arrive at an understanding of their **identity,** or *self-definition as a separate individual in terms of roles, attitudes, beliefs, and values.* In the case of the Kaguru mentioned above, adult male identity is achieved when young boys undergo circumcision, and adult female identity is attained when young girls experience their first menstruation. Identity and adulthood are defined and achieved in terms of tribal customs and beliefs. In North American societies, identity is achieved when adolescents demonstrate some measure of independence, initiative, and industriousness, although these qualities are not always clearly defined.

The differences between these cultures can be considered in terms of Erikson's fifth crisis—*identity versus role confusion.* Failure to achieve identity in these cultures results in what Erikson refers to as role confusion. The difficulty in terms of this crisis lies in how each of these cultures defines identity and marks the onset of adulthood. In many respects, achievement of identity is less ambiguous in traditional, nonindustrialized societies because rites of passage are clearly defined and adolescents know what is expected of them in order to become an adult. Conversely, in many industrialized societies, true rites of passage (which apply to all members of a given society) do not exist; as a result, there is ambiguity in how identity is defined and achieved. The result is that many adolescents do not know who they are or how they are supposed to behave as adults. Erikson refers to this dilemma as role confusion.

Some theorists and researchers imply that Erikson's theory also applies to preindustrial societies. However, when used to explain such behaviors as identity versus role confusion, the theory contains Western biases (e.g., viewing successful identity achievement as rooted in autonomous judgments). (For an extended discussion of identity formation, see Chapter 5.)

Adulthood

Developmentalists have historically devoted most of their attention to the earlier part of the lifespan, particularly the years from birth through adolescence. As a result, there is a great deal of research, many findings, and a host of theories describing, explaining, and predicting the events during the first two decades of life. A similar situation applies with regard to cross-cultural human development: only recently have the last three quarters of the lifespan received serious attention. Even so, treatment of topics has been sparse and inconsistent (Birren & Schaie, 1995; Zarit & Eggebeen, 1995). Cole and Cole (1993) explain it well: "Since psychologists are sharply divided over the relative roles of biology and culture in the process of development, it is only natural that they should be sharply divided on the question of whether development continues into adulthood and old age" (p. 656).

We know from casual observation that the experience of adulthood varies dramatically across and even within cultures and depends on a variety of factors, including age, gender, socioeconomic status, occupation, family structure, and timing of life events (e.g., marriage, parenthood, grandparenthood, and retirement).

Many psychologists (whose research you will become familiar with in subsequent chapters) have paid little attention to developmental changes after adolescence. For example, G. Stanley Hall, who wrote the first book on adolescence in 1904, believed that senescence (old age) began shortly after adolescence ended, generally when one reached the late thirties or early forties (Hall, 1904, 1922). Of course, he based this assumption partly on the fact that life expectancy was much shorter at that time. Jean Piaget, in his theory of cognitive development, proposed that individuals reached the final stage of formal operations during their late adolescence or early adulthood years. Only recently have attempts been made to explain cognitive changes in later adulthood through the establishment of a stage of post-formal operations (see Chapter 4).

Two psychologists who did attribute significant developmental changes to the years of adulthood, and some of whose ideas have been subjected to cross-cultural examination, are Lev Vygotsky and Erik Erikson. Vygotsky, a Russian psychologist and one of the founders of the cultural-historical viewpoint, made some of the earliest contributions to our understanding of cognitive development within social settings, or cultures. (His ideas, many of which are similar to those expressed in our major themes, receive extended attention in Chapter 4.) Erikson, as we have previously noted, is one of a small number of theorists who emphasize cultural and social development across the entire lifespan, separating the years following adolescence into early, middle, and later adulthood. It is in this area that his views coincide most closely with those of the ecological, or cultural context, approach. Limited findings from anthropological, sociological, and cross-cultural studies, particularly those looking at adolescence, tend to lend support to his theoretical assumptions (Erikson, 1963, 1982; Ferrante, 1992; Ochse & Plug, 1986; Rosenthal, Moore, & Taylor, 1983).

Early and Middle Adulthood

During early adulthood (early twenties to mid-thirties), in cultures throughout the world, a majority of adults are dealing with the crisis of *intimacy versus isolation* (see Table 2.1). Decisions are made about establishing a close, intimate relationship with another person, or individuals go their way alone and fail to achieve an intimate relationship. Chapter 6 looks in detail at intimate relationships in a variety of cultures and at the impact of this crisis on one's life.

Lefrancois's earlier comment that age ranges be used only as descriptive guidelines is relevant here in terms of the cultural example we provided in the section on adolescence. Confronting the crisis of intimacy versus isolation usually requires that the individual has achieved a sense of identity, probably is self-supporting, and is involved in a long-term and interdependent relationship. With this in mind, consider fourteen-year-old Mankushai of the Masai tribe in Kenya, East Africa, mentioned earlier. Mankushai lives in her husband's village, cooks his meals, and takes care of her daughter, Consolata. Except for her age, she would appear to be in the stage of early adulthood. What about other cultures, like those parts of India where child marriages are common? In which stage do we put these individuals? Compared with earlier stages of development, there is less cross-cultural research on this stage and the crisis contained within it. This raises additional questions and problems about applying this theory beyond Western societies. We clearly need more critical analysis of ideas and concepts, as well as additional research to extend the cross-cultural usefulness of theories such as these.

For example, consider Catholic nuns and priests, Buddhist monks, or Hindu holy men, all of whom choose a religious life involving vows of chastity and, in some cases, isolation in cloistered settings. Have they failed to resolve the intimacy versus isolation crisis in a positive way? According to Erikson, they have done so only if they have resolved the earlier identity crisis. But we need to look further. Erikson might suggest that these individuals are not necessarily isolated but rather that they have defined intimacy differently. For example, Catholic nuns or priests who have devoted their lives to the service of others in the name of Christ would see themselves as married to and intimate with God. In fact, nuns are considered "brides of Christ." Buddhist monks experience intimacy with nature, Buddha, and the Sangha (membership of monks). In applying Erikson's theory, additional cross-cultural research and modification are recommended.

When one reaches middle adulthood (mid-thirties to mid-sixties), a new crisis appears that involves *generativity versus stagnation* (see Table 2.1). Middle-aged adults make work and career decisions, raise children, and show concern by guiding the next generation, or they become stagnant, self-absorbed, and self-centered. Some of our earlier comments regarding the role parents play in socialization would appear to be relevant here. It is through socialization within their ecological settings that individuals have the kinds of experiences that help them as adults find a balance between their self-interests and the interests of others. Unfortunately, as with some other areas, there is a lack of cross-cultural findings related to this stage crisis; the need for additional theorizing and research is clear.

Late Adulthood

During the last period in the lifespan (mid-sixties and after), older adults find themselves dealing with the crisis of *integrity versus despair* (see Table 2.1). According to Erikson, when individuals reach this stage they tend to reflect on their lives. They find that they are either generally happy and satisfied with their choices, having fulfilled many of their goals and having made their best efforts (integrity), or they find themselves filled with despair over missed opportunities or mistakes made, which leaves them unhappy and dissatisfied.

Considering the example of the nuns, monks, and holy men in the last section, will these individuals look back at their lives from this final crisis and feel unhappy and unsatisfied? Unlike Erikson, who would take this position, we suggest the opposite. In our thinking, most of these individuals will, in fact, feel their lives have been very satisfying and fulfilling and will have feelings of hopefulness and integrity.

In the final analysis, the manner in which this crisis is resolved and the reasons for the outcomes appear to involve a significant cultural component. Consider a nonindustrialized, collectivist, and extended family-based culture in which respect and recognition are given the elderly for their wisdom and accomplishments. For example, most Native American tribes have a hierarchy of elders who are held in high respect for their knowledge of tribal rituals and ceremonies and who pass this heritage on through socialization of the future generation of tribal members.

We hypothesize that a negative outcome to this crisis might be more often found in some Western societies, which place great emphasis on economic and career success and in which nuclear families are the norm. In these cultures, parents or other relatives in their later years are sometimes seen as burdens to be moved from the microsystem of the family to rest homes in the mesosystem or exosystem. In societies in which young people enjoy the greatest status the elderly are more often rejected. Contemporary

Four generations of a Mexican family enjoy an afternoon together in Vera Cruz. (Spencer Grant/Photo Researchers)

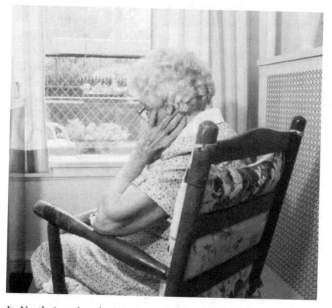

In North America, the elderly often feel isolated and lonely living in institutional settings like nursing homes rather than within extended families. (David Spratt/The Image Works)

North American society is currently such a society, but given rapid increases in its older population, the ecological setting will soon undergo dramatic changes. An ecological setting that focuses on youth rather than age places an older person in a developmental niche where either they have few contributions to make or their contributions are not highly valued. In these circumstances, individuals might well feel despair and regret about the past and a real fear of aging. Contrast this with an Asian or African culture in which intergenerational families are the norm and older relatives are looked after by their family or by the village community. These differences are sharply distinguished in Photographs 2.1a and b.

It is interesting to note that when Erikson reached the eighth decade of his life, he reviewed his theory and suggested that increases in life expectancy might require a rethinking of his ideas, especially those related to development during adulthood (Erikson, Erikson, & Kivnik, 1986). We encourage others to begin this careful rethinking and, in the process, attempt to apply these new ideas to cross-cultural human development.

◇ SUMMARY

It should be clear after reading this chapter that universally accepted generalizations about the complex relationships among family, culture, and socialization are sometimes difficult. Numerous variables contribute to cultural differences, including cultural contexts, societal beliefs and values, individual views of children and their place in society, rural versus urban living, family structure, and parenting styles, to mention only a few. However, cross-cultural research on human development also shows that we are gaining a much better understanding of the significant role culture plays in socialization at all levels, from birth through the last years of the lifespan. Traditional, primarily Western, theoretical explanations of human development are, in large part, obsolete and were never very accurate when transported to other cultures in an effort to describe, explain, and predict behavior for which they were never intended.

You are reading this at a time when many societies are undergoing dramatic change in the way they and their family structures operate. In China, the "one-child policy" is having striking effects on traditional family practices; in the former Soviet Union, political and social changes are affecting parental goals and behavior; in Sweden, children's rights have taken center stage; in the United States, high divorce and remarriage rates and large numbers of working mothers are reshaping family relationships. In countries throughout the world, we have seen major changes in the roles played by children and their parents and yet, as Roopnarine and Carter (1992a) have pointed out, "Perceptions of children and how a culture manages to mesh those perceptions with children's own birthright and value to members of a society, its rituals, functions, and expectations, are not well understood" (p. 251). We have only started the journey toward understanding; much lies ahead of us.

◇ THINGS TO DO AND THINK ABOUT

1. Using the material in this chapter, show how the concepts of the developmental niche and ecological system apply to your own development. Think of examples from your childhood or adolescence that illustrate the various points made by Super and Harkness and by Bronfenbrenner.

2. Borrow a videotape from your school, public library, or other source that focuses on life in a culture different than your own. View it in terms of the concepts discussed in this chapter (e.g., the ecological systems approach, cultural beliefs, and developmental niche). Make a list of some of the behaviors and values the society sees as important and indicate how these are socialized by that culture. If available, programs in the *Nova* and *National Geographic* television series are good choices for this activity.

3. Read several selections from *Into the Widening World* (in the following Further Readings). Write your own fictionalized coming-of-age story based on a critical incident from your adolescent experience. This story should be between three to five pages in length.

◇ FURTHER READINGS

Virginia L. Colin. (1996). *Human Attachment.* New York: McGraw-Hill.
    Without question, the most comprehensive, introductory review of attachment research and its implications for development throughout the lifespan. Easy to read and containing a cornucopia of cross-cultural studies and findings related to the topic.

Walter J. Lonner and Roy Malpass. (1994). *Psychology and Culture.* Boston: Allyn & Bacon.
    A collection of forty-three short (five to six pages), clearly written, easily understood, informative, and enjoyable chapters by sixty experts in cross-cultural psychology, many of whose work is mentioned in the present book.

John Loughery. (1995). *Into the Widening World: International Coming-of-Age Stories.* New York: Persea Books.

An edited anthology of twenty-six short stories from twenty-two countries focusing on the adolescent experience and emergence of adulthood. Visit the sun-baked alleys of Cairo, the terrifying forests of wartime Nigeria, a hidden grove in Jamaica, a turkey farm in Canada, a young woman facing an arranged marriage in Malaysia. Fascinating, insightful, and informative reading.

Dana Raphael and Flora Davis. (1985). *Only Mothers Know.* Westport, CT: Greenwood Press.

A fun book in which the authors describe patterns of infant feeding in seven traditional cultures, including an Egyptian village, a Sardinian shepherd mountain community, a Moslem town in Trinidad, and a Mexican family. An engrossing narrative based on women's stories "about hardships and courage and fun and the wisdom of mothers who know—as their own mothers knew—what keeps babies alive."

Mark Salzman. *Iron and Silk.* (1987). New York: Vantage Books.

A delightful book by a young American graduate in Chinese language and literature who documents his experiences and cultural adventures as a teacher in China. Has a lot to say about cultural socialization and how "Teacher Mark" learns valuable lessons about Chinese culture from his students at the same time he is teaching them about the United States and the English language.

CHAPTER THREE

CULTURAL ASPECTS OF PHYSICAL GROWTH AND DEVELOPMENT

A widow of twenty-five years, Madam Foo Mei Yin is approaching seventy years of age and lives with her eldest son, Kit Seng, in Petaling Jaya, a suburb of Kuala Lumpur, Malaysia. Her husband, Boon Seng, died of heart failure at the relatively young age of fifty. Madam Foo, as matriarch of the family, is much respected and well cared for by her four sons and two daughters. She receives frequent visits from her eighteen grand-children, six great-grandchildren, and other relatives. Since old age is seen as a wel-come milestone denoting wisdom, knowledge, and experience, preparations for her birthday celebration have been taking place for months and almost two hundred rela-tives and friends are invited. A troupe of Lion Dance performers will arrive to the sound of banging drums and firecrackers, bringing prosperity and good luck to the family. Food will be offered to the household gods, and a red cloth will adorn the en-tryway, symbolizing good health and prosperity and warding off evil spirits. Each member of her extended family will wish her good health and a long life. After a din-ner, which includes long-life noodles and sweet bean paste dessert, everyone will toast "Yum seng"—"To your health and success"—to Madam Foo.

◇ ◇ ◇

On Saturday night, Sarah Lawson will turn seventy in Melbourne, Australia. She is planning her own birthday celebration and hopes her two sons, three grandchildren, and great-granddaughter will be able to come. She lives alone in a three-bedroom house her husband built forty-five years ago. Five years ago, her husband, Patrick, died after a long battle with cancer. Her two sons, who live in the adjoining state of New South Wales, try to visit as often as they can, although distance prevents them from doing so on a regular basis. Mrs. Lawson is very independent and is actively in-volved in her church and senior citizens' association. She enjoyed good health until a recent stroke left her in need of a cane. Each Tuesday, she drives thirty miles to get her allergy shots and to volunteer at the regional Red Cross office. She also swims every other morning on the advice of her physical therapist. It's been a tradition in the Lawson household to celebrate birthdays with a barbie (barbecue) in the backyard. A few neighbors and long-time friends will be there to help Sarah usher in the new decade. She has bought the meat; prepared the salads and vegetables; made sure there's plenty of beer, soda, and iced tea; and bought party favors for the guests. Her best friend, Mildred, who lives next door, has promised to bake a cake. Sarah is looking forward to seeing her old friends, some of whom she hasn't seen in years. Eventually, the guests will gather around the piano and retell stories of growing up in the outback.

◇ ◇ ◇

Madam Foo and Sarah are both approaching their seventieth birthdays, but the way in which each has lived her life up until now, and will live the remainder of it, differs in many ways. Their developmental niches, family settings, relationships, and health concerns illustrate the many ways in which lives are lived across cultures.

◇ CROSS-CULTURAL PERSPECTIVES ON PHYSICAL DEVELOPMENT

When we talk about **physical development** we are referring to *changes in an individual's size and body structure* (e.g., variations in height and weight, increases in muscle size, specialization of brain and sense organ functions, improved motor skills, and various effects of nutrition and physical health). Changes such as these do not take place in a vacuum separate from one's cognitive experience, social and emotional development, or cultural context. Each realm interconnects with the others and influences one's development throughout the lifespan. For example, when studying child development, we explore the maturation of gross and fine motor skills together with cognitive abilities, social and emotional development, and cultural orientation. While muscle coordination is taking place, a child is also acquiring the language skills necessary for improvements in perceptual and memory processes. At the same time, social and emotional development is laying the foundation for the development of the child's interactions with others in the increasingly complex ecological settings in which we live. While there are many similarities in the manner in which these skills and abilities develop, the timing of changes varies across cultures and depends, in part, on the norms prescribed by each society.

Likewise, during the years of adolescence, we look at the physical changes of puberty as well as young people's abilities to make decisions and to prepare for adulthood in a way that reflects their culture's expectations as exhibited in their **rites of passage,** or *ceremonies recognizing or symbolizing movement from one status to another.* North American adolescents and those of the !Kung living in the Kalahari Desert of southwestern Africa (primarily in Namibia) provide an interesting example of cultural contrast. When young adolescents in North America become parents, they frequently encounter severe hardships because they typically are unable to support themselves or their children. They are often too young to work and do not have the skills for gaining employment. As a result, they often become dependent on their families or the welfare system. On the other hand, !Kung children are taught from an early age the hunting and gathering skills that will allow them to support themselves and a family (Lee & Devore, 1976). When puberty makes its appearance, !Kung adolescents are biologically prepared to have children and are also economically equipped to take care of them (Shostak, 1981).

At the other end of the lifespan, adult women experience another important physical change—**menopause,** or *the cessation of menstrual periods and childbearing capability.* Several researchers (Voda, Dinnerstein, & O'Donnell, 1982) have shown how responses to this event are affected by physiological factors as well as differences in culture and immediate physical and social environments (what we described earlier as the developmental niche and the various levels of the ecological system). For example, Mayan women in Central America and southern Mexico, no longer restricted by concern about pregnancy, tend to become increasingly active socially.

In this chapter, we will be focusing on cultural influences on physical development across the lifespan. We begin with the prenatal period following conception.

The Prenatal Period

While we will not discuss prenatal development in great detail (you can find this information in any number of good developmental books), let us point out that **conception,** or **fertilization,** takes place when a sperm and an egg unite and form a **zygote,** or *fertilized egg.* The zygote then goes through a process of rapid cell division, duplicating the genetic composition provided by the mother and father. This cluster of increasing complex cells moves down the Fallopian tube into the uterus, where it penetrates the uterine wall and becomes implanted. It will progress through the embryonic and fetal periods until birth takes place.

The **prenatal period,** *the time between conception and birth,* generally lasts about 266 days, or thirty-eight weeks. Yet, the physical growth and development at this time can influence individuals' behavior for the remainder of their lives.

Physical development during the prenatal period is critical, and any number of environmental factors can adversely affect this development and increase the odds of giving birth to a child with birth defects (Jacobson, Jacobson, & Humphrey, 1990). Environmental toxins (aluminum, lead, carbon dioxide) or **teratogens** (agents such as chemicals or diseases) can contribute to the development of prenatal abnormalities. For example, recent research suggests that even a small amount of alcohol consumed during a critical period of pregnancy may increase chances of giving birth to a child with physical and cognitive abnormalities (Waterson & Murray-Lyon, 1990). Known as **fetal alcohol syndrome (FAS),** these abnormalities include an unusually small head, low birth weight, facial deformities, neurological impairments, and signs of mental retardation. While it is difficult to know the precise number of cases of FAS throughout the world, Abel and Sokol (1987) report that in comparative studies conducted in Australia, North America, and several European countries, approximately one in every five hundred infants is born with the disorder. The result is that FAS contributes significantly to the number of children suffering from mental retardation. Along these same lines, other studies have shown that if an expectant mother uses **crack cocaine** (*a concentrated form of cocaine*), or another addictive drug such as heroin or methadone, it will have the same effect on her fetus that it has on her (Hutchinson, 1991). The developing fetus is most vulnerable to teratogens during the third to sixth week after conception (the critical period), when the central nervous system, heart, arms, and legs are developing.

As many of the world's cultures move toward increased industrialization, the dangers of pollution to pregnant women and their children can sometimes be carried to horrifying extremes. A particularly graphic example comes from the former Soviet Union, where Tamara Kapanadze, the mother of a child with a birth defect, made a shocking discovery. Acting on her own, she put together a map using data derived from hospital records and a factory producing artificial limbs. She found that over a twenty-year period, at least ninety children in Moscow had been born with the same birth defect as her child—namely, terminal-limb deficiency, which consists most often of a missing forearm. Her figures showed that more than half the children lived in neighborhoods heavily contaminated by industrial emissions. While no definitive link could be made between the incidence of the birth defect and pollution, the number of children with the deformity was higher in these areas than in Russia as a whole (Edwards, 1994).

To turn to another aspect of this topic, two widely studied concepts discussed in cross-cultural psychology are **individualism** and **collectivism** (Hofstede, 1980; Triandis, Brislin, & Hui, 1988; Brislin & Yoshida, 1994; Kim et al., 1994). We first introduced these concepts in the last chapter. At that time, we pointed out that in individualistic cultures, the individual frequently pursues autonomy, independence, and personal achievement, often

Russian children from two Moscow neighborhoods, born with terminal-limb deficiency, possibly the result of industrial pollutants. (Gerd Ludwig/National Geographic Society)

at the expense of the group. On the other hand, in collectivist cultures, emphasis is on group success, and individual ambitions are generally set aside for the attainment of group goals (Hofstede, 1980).

You might be asking "How are these cultural concepts related to the issue of prenatal care?" In traditional collectivist countries such as Malaysia, Singapore, Indonesia, the Philippines, and Thailand, where childbirth is more family centered, expectant mothers can rely on a large number of individuals to ensure the safe delivery of a healthy child. In a sense, the entire extended family acts as a midwife preparing a woman for childbirth. In fact, in such cultures, it is customary for a young mother to yield to the elders in the family when it comes to decisions regarding diet and other matters. In contrast, in individualistic cultures such as the United States and Canada, childbirth is a more private affair, and precautions taken to avoid environmental hazards are the primary responsibility of the expectant mother.

Interestingly, research shows that more babies die at or soon after birth in the United States than in many western European countries (which, like the United States, are individualistic) and Pacific Rim countries, which have collectivist cultures (Behrman, 1985; Miller, 1987). One possible explanation for reduced infant mortality in these two different cultures may lie in the additional assistance given by extended family members in Pacific Rim countries during the prenatal period and at birth and also in the fact that pre- and postnatal health care is provided without cost in both western Europe and

Pacific Rim countries. These cultural and medical practices appear to significantly reduce rates of infant death, low birth weight, and other birth complications (Brown, 1985; Ingram, Makuc, & Kleinman, 1986; Singh, Forrest, &
Torres, 1989).

Infancy and Early Childhood

During infancy, enormous changes take place in physical growth and development. In just two years, many infants make the transition from dependent, almost helpless babies to independent, curious children. As their bodies
grow and respond to social and cultural cues, their nervous systems mature,
and their cognitive experiences are enhanced. They quickly adapt to the
world outside the womb, slowly begin to imagine a future involving themselves and others, and discover methods for storing away memories of past
and present events.

    While parents help their children to develop these and other abilities,
individual styles of parenting can vary considerably from one culture to another, and infants raised in these differing ecological settings sometimes
show significant variations in physical development. For example, it has
been well documented that the motor skills of African infants in such activities as sitting, walking, and running develop several months before they do
in Caucasian infants. In Uganda, for example, infants begin to walk at about
ten months (earlier than in most countries); in France, fifteen months is
more typical; in the United States, the average is around twelve months.

    What accounts for these differences? In most cases, it is likely to be the
result of a combination of factors, including genetics, activity level, body
type, and physical maturation. Genetic factors obviously play a major role in
this early motor development. However, cultural and environmental factors
(e.g., interactions between the child and others in his micro- and mesosystems and his unique developmental niche) are also extremely influential.
For example, in many African and West Indian cultures, parents and extended family members place considerable importance on sitting and walking and actually provide early "formal handling" experiences that stimulate
these behaviors. Examples of formal handling practices used by West Indian
mothers in Jamaica for helping their infants develop their motor skills are
shown in Figure 3.1.

    Beginning with stretching exercises shortly after birth, parents gradu-
ally introduce other activities (e.g., placing infants in a sitting position or
playing games that allow them to practice jumping and walking skills) (Hopkins & Westra, 1988; Super, 1981). !Kung infants of the Kalahari Desert also
walk earlier than Western infants. In this case, it may be because they spend

FIGURE 3.1   Handling Practices Used by West Indian Mothers

Source: Adapted from "Maternal Handling and Motor Development: An Intracultural Study" by B. Hopkins and T. Westra, 1988, *Genetic, Social and General Psychology Monographs, 14*, pp. 385, 388, 389. Adapted with permission of the Helen Dwight Reid Educational Foundation. Published by Heldref Publications, 1319 Eighteenth St., N.W., Washington, DC 20036-1802. Copyright © 1988. Reprinted by permission.

a great deal of time in slings that keep them upright and give them considerable freedom of movement (Konner, 1976).

Several of these handling practices have been found to be associated with maternal expectations. For example, in a study of Jamaican mothers and their infants, Hopkins and Westra (1990) asked mothers to estimate when they felt their one-month-old infants would be able to sit, crawl, and walk without assistance. Most reported that they planned to provide their infants with a variety of formal handling routines ranging from gentle massage to vigorous bouncing and stepping exercises. Results were compared with those of English mothers, who provided no formal handling for their infants.

Findings supported a self-fulfilling prophecy—that is, when handling practices were conducted daily, Jamaican mothers' predictions were accurate as
to when these motor skills would develop. English infants, on the other
hand, learned to sit and walk somewhat later than did Jamaican infants.
Time of crawling did not differ significantly between the two groups.

Dennis and Dennis (1940), in a classic study of infant motor development, disclosed that Hopi Indian children, though traditionally strapped to a
cradleboard for much of their first year, still walked at approximately the
same time as did children in other countries (e.g., early in their second year).
In related research, conducted by Hindley, Filliozat, Klackenberg, Nicolet-
Neister, and Sand (1966), infants reared in several European cities generally
started walking at about twelve to fifteen months, in spite of any significant
differences in the assistance they received for this activity.

*Native American children strapped to cradleboards during
their first year walk at about the same time as other children.*
(Lionel Delevingne/Stock Boston)

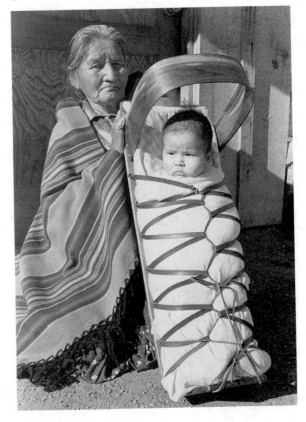

On the other hand, African infants do not crawl any sooner than Western infants. There would appear to be at least two possible cultural explanations for this. First, African children are seldom placed on their stomachs and therefore do not receive the practice in crawling that Western infants do (Hopkins, 1991; Super, 1976). Second, African parents do not tend to encourage or value this behavior. In fact, it is generally regarded as dirty and potentially dangerous (Rogoff & Morelli, 1989).

Lack of stimulation or encouragement may also result in a delay in walking. For example, Dennis (1960) observed orphans in two Iranian institutions who spent the majority of their time lying on their backs in their cribs and were never propped upright. The infants rarely interacted with adults and when taken from their cribs were usually placed on the floor and left by themselves. Findings indicated that very few of them ever crawled in the typical hands-and-knees fashion. Instead, they tended to move themselves along the floor in a sitting position. None of the one- and two-year-olds could walk, and among the three- and four-year-olds, only 15 percent were able to walk at all without help.

The most observable changes during this time are in height and weight. Typically, if well nourished, babies triple their birth weight by the time they are one year old and increase their height by nearly 50 percent in the same time period (Wardlaw & Insel, 1993). However, differences do exist. For example, by the time they reach four years of age, some children in Africa and Asia weigh as much as thirteen pounds less than their European and American counterparts and may even be as much as seven inches shorter (Hendrick, 1990).

In this regard, the importance of nutrition during infancy cannot be overemphasized. Nutrition affects changes in physical stature, brain development, and motor skill mastery as well as other developments. Most of us have seen photographs or news reports of chronic malnutrition in many parts of the world. Recent figures indicate that of all deaths throughout the world, one in every three involves the death of a child five years of age or younger (Grant, 1994). More than 250,000 children die each week in developing countries from infection and malnutrition. In fact, the major cause of child mortality is the malnutrition and dehydration caused by diarrhea. Yet, nearly three-quarters of the children who died from diarrhea in 1989, estimated at 40 million, might have survived if their parents had had access to an inexpensive procedure known as **oral rehydration therapy (ORT),** *a treatment that prevents dehydration.* According to Grant (1993), in 1986 the highest mortality rates for children five and younger occurred in Afghanistan (325 per 1,000 births) and Ethiopia (225 per 1,000). During the same year, the countries with the lowest mortality rates were Finland and Sweden (7 per 1,000 births). Although the mortality rate in the United States was lower than in many other countries (13 per 1,000), twenty countries ranked higher. For more recent rankings, see Figure 3.2.

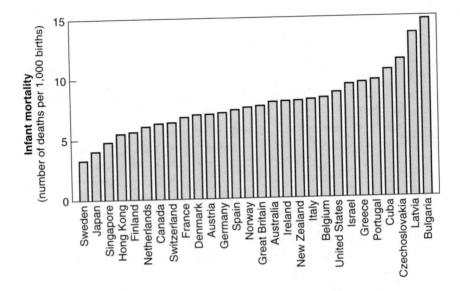

FIGURE 3.2   Incidence of Infant Mortality in Selected Countries, 1993

Source: Adapted from *Annual Survey of Vital Statistics—1993,* by M. E. Wegman, 1994, *Pediatrics, 94,* 792–803. As seen in *Child Development,* 3rd ed. (p. 117) by L. Berk, 1994, Needham Heights, MA: Allyn & Bacon. Copyright © 1994 by Allyn & Bacon Publishing Co. Reprinted/adapted by permission.

In industrialized countries, bottle-feeding is frequently preferred to breast-feeding, in part, because it allows women to pursue individualistic goals and to engage in professional activities. As developing nations become more technologically advanced and increasingly industrialized, there is a reduction in breast-feeding. In some situations this has resulted in many mothers, especially those living at the poverty level, diluting baby formulas and contributing to their infants' already deficient nourishment.

The nutritional status of children and the effects of poverty on physical growth and development have been studied in a number of countries, and the United States ranks fairly high in comparison to other countries (see Figure 3.3).

In the United States, several government programs have proven successful. These incude the Supplemental Food Program for Women, Infants, and Children (WIC), the National School Breakfast and Lunch programs, and Food Stamps. Even so, instances of inadequate nutrition are still found among low-income families and children (National Center for Children in Poverty, 1990; Wardlaw & Insel, 1993).

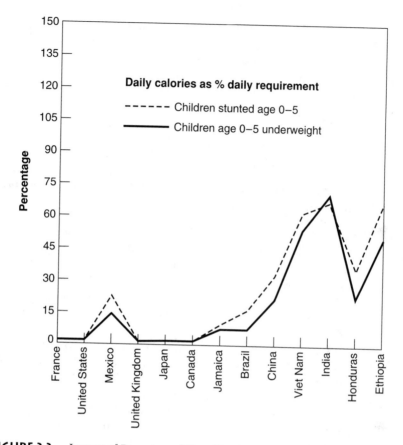

FIGURE 3.3 Impact of Poverty and Poor Nutrition on Physical Growth and Development

Source: From *Child Malnutrition: Progress Toward the World Summit for Children Goal* by United Nations International Children's Emergency Fund, 1995, New York: UNICEF.

On a more positive note, the early effects of malnutrition can, in some cases, be lessened and even turned back. For example, Barrett, Radke-Yarrow, and Klein (1982) conducted a follow-up study on a group of Guatemalan children who had been participants in an earlier investigation carried out by the Institute of Nutrition of Central America and Panama (INCAP). These children, suffering from the effects of severe malnutrition, were provided with caloric or nutritional supplements during the first several years of their development. As a result, they were significantly more active, physically as well as socially, than children who did not receive such supplements. In a related study involving malnourished Colombian infants, those who received regular food supplements along with home visits were taller and heavier than a comparable group who had not been given such treatment. The former group also demonstrated slightly higher ability in cognitive and social areas (Super, Herrena, & Mora, 1990).

During early childhood, young children also show improvements in the development of gross motor skills, especially as a result of their mastery of play (Whitall, 1991).

Play and Physical Development

While play may look like a simple activity to adults, it is a highly complex and intricate achievement for a young child. For example, physical play builds on the relationship among a child's cognitive abilities, social experiences, and cultural context. The simplest, least developed form of play is called **functional play** and consists of a child making *simple, repetitive movements with or without an object*. In **constructive play,** children learn how to *physically manipulate objects in order to construct or create something*. For example, in most cultures, young children are encouraged to play with blocks or similar objects; in addition to being fun, this play also teaches children how to approach and solve problems.

In a study of Kpelle children in Sierra Leone, Lancy (1980) noted that families found a variety of ways to combine constructive play with physical work involving *nee-pele* (make-believe), *sua-kpe-pele* (hunting play), *mana-pele* (dancing and playing musical instruments), and *kppa-kolo-pele* (adult play). As in many other countries, play was used by adults to teach children the importance of play and work, while stimulating coordination, encouraging imagination, and fostering interpersonal relationships.

It is apparent that play is a necessary part of a child's normal physical development and an important expression of cultural heritage. In addition to developing gross motor skills through play and other activities, children also acquire fine motor skills (e.g., tying shoelaces, buttoning shirts, making towers out of blocks, cutting paper, coloring within the lines, and putting together simple jigsaw puzzles). Play is also a critical part of a child's social development and receives extended treatment in Chapter 7.

Another topic associated with the development of fine and gross motor skills during infancy and early childhood is hand preference.

Handedness

Handedness refers to *the tendency to use one hand in preference to the other in writing and other activities*. Most children tend to show such a preference by about six months, with this tendency becoming stronger in early childhood

(Shucard & Shucard, 1990; McManus, Sik, Cole, Mellon, Wong, & Kloss, 1988).

Right-handedness appears to be historically dominant in most of the world's cultures (Coren & Halpern, 1991). In fact, ultrasound images and interuterine photographs have vividly demonstrated that even before culture and parental training can possibly have an effect, more fetuses suck the thumb on their right hand than on the left. In addition, the fact that infants between the ages of five months and two years show a universal preference for the right hand suggests a strong genetic factor (Fischer, 1987; Michel, 1981).

Why might this be the case? When we look at different languages, we find that many meanings for the word *left* involve negative connotations or stereotypes. For example, the French word *gauche* means both "left" and "clumsy" (Coren, 1992).

While more left-handers are reported to suffer from migraine headaches and are diagnosed with reading disabilities, they are also more likely to be musicians, mathematicians, professional baseball and basketball players, architects, and artists than are right-handers (Geschwind & Behan, 1984; Coren & Halpern, 1991).

In a recent review of the handedness literature, Halpern (1996) cited earlier research (Casey, 1996) that supports the link between handedness and genetic predispositions. Halpern reports on a model developed by Annett (1985) that demonstrated that handedness is associated with a single gene believed responsible for both right-handedness and the lateralization, or specialization, of language in the left cerebral hemisphere of the brain. As each society adapts to different ecocultural settings, they develop specific spatial orientations (ways of viewing and understanding dimensions—e.g., horizonal and vertical—within their physical world) and corresponding preferences for right- and left-handedness. Since most people are right-handed (Coren & Halpern, 1991), on the basis of the approach we take in this book, we would suggest that ecocultural systems (including physical settings, family customs, and cultural traditions) tend to establish developmental niches that nurture a genetic predisposition toward left hemispheric dominance, or right-handedness. This presents an interesting area for future cross-cultural investigation.

Not only is there a universal preference for right-handedness, but children in some countries are deliberately discouraged from using their left hand at all. In Africa, the Middle East, India, and Asia, there is strong social pressure against using the left hand for many activities, because it is used in personal cleansing and other use is viewed as unhygienic. Thus, it would be considered rude to extend one's left hand to a merchant when waiting for change or to pass a drink to a friend or relative with the left hand. Likewise, in some of the areas of the world just mentioned, it would be unwise to use your left hand to pass your driver's license to a police officer about to cite you for a traffic violation. Such insensitivity may cause your fine to increase substantially!

Middle Childhood

Throughout the world, individuals passing through **middle childhood** (*approximately ages four to eleven*) experience changes in physical development that seem slower and less uneventful than in some periods of the lifespan (e.g., early childhood and adolescence). In most societies, school occupies most of children's time and energy, enabling them to build on existing patterns of physical and motor development. However, this does not mean they are any less active. Just watch children between the ages of six and twelve in almost any city or village in the world as they leave school at the end of the day. You will see young people running onto playgrounds, riding bicycles, climbing trees, wrestling, and playing tag and other games. Outside of school, they often take private lessons to learn how to play musical instruments, dance, swim competitively, or participate in group sports like soccer, baseball, and badminton. While possessing a seemingly unlimited supply of energy and excitement, their rapidly growing and changing bodies soon move them from the isolated world of the nursery and day care to the world of the schoolchild.

Physical Growth and Change

During middle childhood, the growth rate begins to slow down a little. Baby fat gradually disappears, and children become slimmer and more muscular. They can run faster, fly a kite higher, and throw a ball farther and with greater accuracy than they once did. As a result of mastering new skills, children are able to compete more effectively against their peers in such board games as chess, backgammon, and mah-jongg.

According to Engels (1993), the average six-year-old child adds about fourteen inches and thirty-five pounds by the time she or he reaches the age of twelve. For both boys and girls, this results in an average gain of two to three inches in height and seven pounds in weight per year during middle childhood. This pattern continues until the adolescent growth spurt, which typically begins at about age ten or so for girls and twelve for boys.

In addition, in middle childhood growth rates vary with ethnicity and socioeconomic level. For example, in a worldwide sample of eight-year-olds, the mean height of the shortest children, those from South America, Southeast Asia, and Oceania, differed by about nine inches from the tallest children, those in North America, northern and central Europe, and eastern Australia (Meredith, 1978). While some of this variance results from differences in genetics, an important factor is also environmental influences (see Figure 3.4).

While underweight and malnourished children encounter considerable health risks and obstacles to normal physical, social, and cognitive development, overweight children experience unique problems too, particularly as regards childhood obesity.

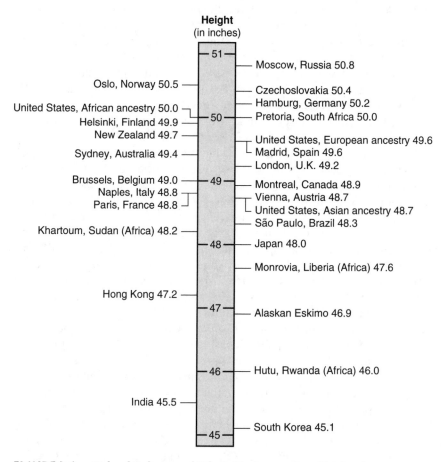

FIGURE 3.4   Role of Culture and Ethnic Background on Height of Eight-Year-Old Girls

Source: Adapted from "Research Between 1960 and 1970 on the Standing Height of Young Children in Different Parts of the World" by H. V. Meredith, 1978, in H. W. Reese (Ed.), *Advances in Child Development and Behavior,* Vol. 20, New York: Academic Press.

Childhood Obesity

Over the past three decades, health care professionals in the United States have become alarmed about the growing problem of obesity in middle childhood. This topic has important implications for the consideration of physical growth and development, and more discussion of obesity will follow when we address cultural variations in eating disorders among adolescents and young adults.

Obesity in middle childhood can lead to serious physical and emotional problems later in life. It can cause considerable respiratory and cardiovascular problems and can trigger excessive dieting and consequent complications. In addition, children often reject and ridicule their overweight peers, which negatively affects their self-esteem. **Obesity** is generally considered to be *body weight that is 20 percent or more over the recommended weight for one's age, gender, and body type* (Epstein, 1985). Based on this definition, about 10 percent of American children have been classified as overweight (Lamb, 1984).

What causes obesity? Many researchers believe it is caused by a combination of genetic and sociocultural factors. For example, Zhang and others (1994) have reported the results of research with mice that suggests that a specific obesity gene may be linked to obesity. However, this genetic explanation cannot explain obesity entirely; various social factors must also be taken into consideration. For one thing, children often get mixed signals in their culture. In North American society, there is a preoccupation with physical appearance, and being tall and slim are seen as acceptable forms of beauty. Furthermore, children are likely to observe their parents worrying about overeating and gaining weight. This, in turn, can add to children's confusion about how much food they should eat. There is also a tendency in some cultures for parents to overfeed their children in infancy and early childhood. This is often done in an effort to pacify restless children and as a way to cope with parents' busy schedules. Given the amount of food served in many family restaurants—the "all you can eat" specials—it is not surprising that many overweight children exist, particularly in North America.

Another social factor that contributes to obesity is lack of exercise (Epstein, 1992). This may seem paradoxical, since we think of children as running around and being involved in the activities mentioned earlier. But while many children are active, there are a substantial number of children who stay at home spending many hours taking care of younger siblings, playing video games, watching television, or, more recently, "surfing" the Internet. As a result, many school-age children do not get nearly enough exercise. For example, Wolf and colleagues (1993) reported that nearly half of North American boys between six and twelve years of age in their study could do no more than one pull-up and that 25 percent were unable to do even one. Clearly, when children are inactive—spending many hours watching television (with its large number of food-oriented commercials) and snacking the while on junk food—they take in far more calories than they are able to burn off. The result is that obesity becomes a major problem.

Motor Skill Development

During the school years, children become better coordinated. They are able to master many of the skills they could not manage when they were younger. This is due, in part, to increased levels of myelin in the brain, which is manufactured at a faster rate between the ages of six and eight (Lecours, 1982). Thus, in many Western societies, eight- and nine-year-olds are able to ride a bike, skip rope, draw, write or print, type at a computer keyboard, and play a variety of sports. In other parts of the world, a particular child's eco-cultural system and developmental niche emphasize different skills. For instance, in Malaysia children engage in many of the same activities just mentioned but are also taught how to perform a variety of ethnic dances; weave intricate baskets; spin colorful tops; build and fly their own kites; and play soccer, cricket, or *sepak-takrow* with a bamboo ball.

Are physical activities like these dependent on age, experience, and gender—or a combination of all three? Does culture influence the types of motor skills taught to children of one gender or the other? Unfortunately, there is relatively little cross-cultural research focusing on such questions; this suggests the need for future investigation.

Adolescence

Much of the change associated with physical development during adolescence centers on **puberty,** *a period of biological transition between childhood and adulthood lasting approximately one to two years.* While the age at which puberty begins varies from one culture to another, it represents a milestone in most individuals' lives (Rice, 1992).

Cultural Variations in Puberty

In the previous chapter, we introduced the topic of rites of passage and how cultures use these to prepare young people for the responsibilities of adulthood. According to Weisfeld (1997), in many traditional societies, these rites provide insight into how cultures view differences in physical development between boys and girls as well as how cultures mark the beginning of marriage eligibility.

As an example, let us consider how adolescents in eastern Africa make the transition from childhood to adulthood. Ten- to twelve-year-old Kagura boys are taken into the wild and circumcised. They are taught about sexuality and learn ritual songs and riddles that initiate them into adulthood Beidelman (1971). After several days in isolation, they are led back to the community by village elders and reintegrated into Kagura society. In contrast, a Kagura girl, when she experiences her first menstruation, is initiated by herself apart from the community. Her clitoris is not surgically removed, as it is in many non-Western cultures, although her genitals are seared with a hot knife to indicate her new status. It is then her responsibility to seek out the advice of parents and grandparents in the selection of a prearranged marriage partner.

One of the most important pubertal changes among girls, regardless of culture, is **menarche,** or *first menstruation.* In a study of ninety-five women from twenty-three countries, Logan (1980) reported that large numbers of Asian women had limited knowledge and understanding about the process of menstruation and that half of these women indicated they were embarrassed by its onset. Fifty percent of Japanese women also stated they were surprised when menstruation began. Furthermore, only about half of the Asian mothers said they spoke to their daughters prior to menarche, and more than half of the daughters reported feeling surprised when menstruation began. In addition, less than half of these mothers had given their daughters any information about the topic, and over half the daughters said they felt unprepared for their first menstruation. Clearly, each culture views menarche differently and, as a result of the unique interactions between a specific young woman and her developmental niche and ecological setting, has a variety of norms for dealing with it.

The importance of viewing menarche within the cultural context and the ecocultural system is illustrated in a study of young girls living at low and high altitudes in Peru. Gonzales and Villena (1996) compared ten- to nineteen-year-old Peruvian girls living in the mountainous regions of Lima with girls of similar age in Cerro de Pasco. Results indicated that those living at higher elevations, where food sources are more limited, experienced the onset of menarche later than those living at sea level in Cerro de Pasco. The authors concluded that although nutrition is an important factor in determining the age at which menarche occurs, one's physical surroundings and developmental niche also need to be considered.

In recent years, some cross-cultural researchers have focused on the extent to which exposure to modernization alters the menstrual experience of young girls. In one such study, Fitzgerald (1990) examined three Samoan communities as part of an ongoing stress and health project at the University of Hawaii. One community consisted of residents living in remote traditional villages on the island of Savaii in Western Samoa. A second community, experiencing rapid modernization, was made up of seven villages on the southern coast of the island of Tutuila in American Samoa. The third community was composed of individuals living in affluent neighborhoods in Honolulu, Hawaii. Ninety-three young girls reported on their family medical history, menstrual symptoms, menstrual beliefs and practices, and menstrual experiences. According to Fitzgerald, although the literal translation of the Samoan word for "menstruation" (*ma'imasina*) means "monthly illness," most Samoans view menstruation as a natural part of life—something given to them by God in order to prepare them for motherhood—over which they have no control. Findings revealed that the more exposed Samoans were to the influences of modernization, the more likely they were to report severe menstrual symptoms. This suggests that as cultures come into greater contact with each other, the values and beliefs of one tend to influence the behaviors of the other. In this case, the values and beliefs characteristic of the more modern society (Honolulu) tended to affect the menstrual experience of the Samoan islanders. Once again, this tends to lend support to the validity of studying behavior from the perspective of the recurring themes of the ecological systems approach and the developmental niche.

Early and Middle Adulthood

Although the process of aging actually begins early in the lifespan, physical growth nears completion by the end of adolescence or the beginning of the early adulthood years.

Physical Changes

As we have seen in earlier periods, biological processes occur slowly at first but then advance more quickly. For example, around the age of twenty-one, slow, continuous changes begin to affect the functioning of the human body (Spence, 1989). Muscular strength, reaction time, sensory acuity, and heart function approach their peak through the mid-twenties and then, depending on diet and exercise, slowly decline thereafter. By the time people reach their forties, they are well aware of the age-related changes affecting them and their bodies. (Doesn't this discussion make you feel good?)

The Experience of Menopause

A major event for women during these years is the experience of menopause. Since menopause, like menarche, is a universal event, it would be easy to assume that all women experience it in the same way. However, based on our earlier discussions of Bronfenbrenner's ecological systems theory, we would expect that cultural values, expectations, and context would contribute strongly to shaping the experience—and they do. For example, in previous decades, Europeans and North Americans, among others, frequently described menopause as a "change of life." Many early television programs stereotyped elderly and middle-aged women as moody, unpredictable, and depressed.

Today, most North Americans and, in fact, people in many other countries view menopause very differently. Women's own expectations have changed, and for some, menopause is seen as a liberating experience (Matthews, 1992). Part of this new view can be attributed to changing cultural views of aging.

In Israel, interviews conducted among five groups of Israeli women reveal different reactions to menopause (Datan, Antonovsky, & Moaz, 1984). These researchers interviewed four groups of middle-aged Israeli women from central Europe, Turkey, Persia, and North Africa and a fifth group of Moslem Arab women. The women from European and Arab cultures reported experiencing the fewest problems, viewing menopause as simply one more event in their lives. By comparison, women raised in the three remaining cultures reported greater stress related to menopause.

In a cross-sectional study of Japanese women between forty-four and fifty-five years of age, Lock (1991) indicated that only about 12 percent reported experiencing hot flashes, compared with 47 percent of Canadian women. Less than one-fifth of Japanese women had experienced a hot flash, compared with nearly three quarters of Canadian women. In fact, there is no specific word or phrase in the Japanese language for "hot flash." However, Japanese subjects reported more physical discomforts (e.g., headaches, ringing in the ears, dizziness, and other complaints not usually associated with menopause).

In an interesting cultural interpretation, some Japanese government officials have suggested that such complaints occur more often among women with little to occupy their time (e.g., no children or work) and even went as far as proposing that caring for elderly parents would fill this idle time and thereby minimize such complaints (Lock, 1991). This topic would certainly make an interesting cross-cultural study.

Later Adulthood

The term **senescence** is used to describe *the process of biological change associated with normal aging*. While the rate of senescence varies individually, socially, and culturally, few people (if they live long enough) can escape the aging process.

A better understanding of lifespan development, along with advances in medical technology, has helped to expand the life expectancy of the world's people. For example, in the United States, nearly 14 percent of the population is sixty-five or older. When the so-called "baby-boom generation" (those born between 1946 and 1960) turns sixty-five, this figure is expected to climb to nearly 20 percent.

Cultural Images of Aging

What images do we have of people when they grow old? What role does culture play in shaping the way we think about aging? Certainly in many Western cultures, notably North America, stereotypes have portrayed the elderly as frail individuals, usually in poor health and unable to take care of themselves. We now know that these stereotypes do not fit the current population of elderly, many of whom remain active, independent, and in good health well into their eighties and nineties and beyond.

It is interesting to note how North American stereotypes of the elderly have influenced societal views of the aging process, especially when we consider how the elderly are perceived and treated in other countries. For example, in Brazil, Colombia, Japan, China, and many other collectivist societies, elderly people are revered and given high social status. Family members look to them as wise and knowledgeable members of the society with much to offer. Rather than attempting to push back the aging process and appear young, many look forward to aging. In traditional Native American culture, old age represents an important time of life, a time when a number of milestones have been attained. Old age is given prominence; elders teach tribal customs to children through the use of campfire stories, songs, games, and dances.

Aging—A Positive View

People are living longer than ever before, many over the age of one hundred, and this number is expected to rise dramatically in the next century. In fact, several remote areas of the world have become known for having large numbers of people who live unusually long lives. In parts of China and the former Soviet Union, senescence is postponed well into late adulthood, and a disciplined, highly active lifestyle is routine. Why do these people live to such advanced ages? Some commonly cited reasons for longevity include diet (lots of fresh vegetables, little meat and fat), mutual interdependence, family and neighborhood cohesiveness, and regular exercise. Whether it be regular morning tai chi exercises, meditation, walks, or hobbies, maintaining an active lifestyle is a way of life for most of these elderly persons (Pitskhelauri, 1982).

Tai chi, the popular Chinese method of exercise and self-defense, emphasizes coordination, balance, and effortlessness. (Fritz Hoffman/ The Image Works)

Tse and Bailey (1992) designed a study to investigate the value of tai chi in promoting postural control (balance) among elderly, but healthy, adults. Tai chi is a Chinese method of exercise and self-defense emphasizing balance, coordination, and effortlessness. Their subjects consisted of six men and three women (aged sixty-five to eighty-four years) who practiced tai chi and a similar group of six men and three women (aged sixty-six to eighty-six years) who did not practice the Chinese method. Each participant completed a series of balance tests and a questionnaire concerning wellness issues and was measured for posture control. The tests included being able to maintain one's balance while standing on a single right and then left leg with eyes open, standing on a single right and then left leg with eyes closed, and doing a heel-to-toe walking exercise with both eyes open. Findings supported the researchers' hypothesis that those who practiced tai chi would perform better on the tests than those who did not practice such exercises. The better performance was attributed to a long-established connection between tai chi, improved balance, and self-control. It was suggested that tai chi practice might have therapeutic value in helping to fight disease, lethargy, and listlessness.

Studies like these and others suggest that contrary to many myths, aging is not synonymous with disease. We should not assume that illness is a necessary outcome of living longer. What is important to remember is that each culture has its own prescription for growing old and that although it may be different from our own, no one particular approach is necessarily right or wrong, it's simply different. If we look closely at other cultures and the way in which their societies function, we may learn many lessons that could be positively applied to our own lives.

◇ SUMMARY

This chapter discussed cultural similarities and differences in physical development at various stages of the lifespan. Attention was given to important issues of prenatal care, including exposure to environmental toxins and to alcohol (fetal alcohol syndrome) as potential causes of birth defects. Cultural differences in the role of nutrition and its relationship to health and physical development were also considered. Special emphasis was devoted to the interactions between culture and the development of motor skills, play, and coordination, including hand preference, in early childhood. The physical changes of adolescence, especially puberty and menarche, were viewed from a cross-cultural perspective. Cultural reactions to changes associated with the transition to middle and later adulthood, including menopause and senescence, were also explored. As in previous chapters, our discussion placed these topics within the context of our recurring themes: the cultural-ecological model, developmental niche, and individualism-collectivism.

◇ THINGS TO DO AND THINK ABOUT

1. What impact does age have on self-esteem? In this chapter we addressed the notion that Western cultures identify age in different ways than do non-Western cultures and that these differences play key roles in physical development and personal well-being. Interview two groups of elderly persons, one group from your own culture and the other from a different culture in your community (e.g., Latin American, Southeast Asian, or European). Ask how age is interpreted in each of these cultures. When you have enough information, share it with your class and possibly with community organizations.

2. It is common practice for infants raised in North America and other Western societies to sleep in separate beds and separate rooms from their parents. Yet in many other cultures, children sleep with their mothers for the first few years of life. Think about the advantages and disadvantages of these different sleeping arrangements. Comment on how each could affect physical, psychological, emotional, and social development.

◇ FURTHER READINGS

Frederick W. Bozett and Shirley M. H. Hanson. (1991). *Fatherhood and Families in Cultural Context*. New York: Springer.
   A collection of articles by scholars of cross-cultural human development examining the interactions among different ecocultural systems; the sociocultural and historical context of fatherhood; and the development of physical, cognitive, and social maturation across the lifespan.

Jaipaul L. Roopnarine, James E. Johnson, and Frank H. Hooper. (Eds.). (1994). *Children's Play in Diverse Cultures*. Albany: State University of New York.
   An extremely interesting and engaging illustration of children's play around the world. An added feature is the way the authors relate play to the cultural-ecological concepts in Bronfenbrenner's model.

Robin W. Winks and James R. Rush. (Eds.). (1990). *Asia in Western Fiction*. Honolulu: University of Hawaii Press.
   A collection of comparative essays offering insights into Asian cultures and behaviors. Contains references to important novels and short stories depicting life in India, the Himalayas, China, Hong Kong, Japan, Indonesia, Vietnam, and the Philippines.

CHAPTER FOUR

CULTURE AND COGNITION

Deratu lives in one of the oldest nations in Africa—Ethiopia, a Greek word meaning "sunburned faces." Like almost 80 percent of the people in this nation in northeastern Africa, she lives in a rural village where her family grows sugarcane and raises goats and chickens. Deratu, like more than half the children in the country, does not attend school nor does she have many toys. What she needs to know, she learns in an informal manner from the work she has been assigned according to her age and gender, since this is the way new members of each generation learn what is expected of them. At five years of age, she helped her mother fetch water and gather wood for the fire. Now, at the age of eleven, she helps with the cooking and cares for her younger brothers and sisters. In just a few years, at about fifteen, she will start a family of her own. Deratu's learning is very much a social activity guided by her mother, who teaches her the important cultural and practical lessons she will need in order to survive in her rural Ethiopian village.

◇ ◇ ◇

Maria, two weeks away from her twelfth birthday, lives in Brazil, in São Paulo, the seventh most populated city in the world. Brazil is the largest country in South America, occupying almost half the continent. She has attended the country's free public schools since she was six years old. Maria's parents and teachers have always described her as a naturally curious child who seems to have enjoyed learning languages and trying to solve mathematical problems on her own. As a newly emerging adolescent, she is beginning to look more abstractly at the world and is using more logical problem-solving skills than she would have been able to use just two years ago.

◇ ◇ ◇

Deratu and Maria live worlds apart physically as well as psychologically. In this chapter, we will look at culture and cognition and their effects on development. We will consider two opposing theoretical viewpoints and some of the cross-cultural evidence that supports or refutes these views. As you progress through this chapter, you will be better able to understand and explain the cognitive behavior of these two young women using key concepts from these theories.

First, let us explain what we mean when we use the term *cognition*. **Cognition** can be thought of as *the act or process of obtaining knowledge, including perceiving, recognizing, reasoning, and judging* (Gander & Gardiner, 1981). Cognition involves thinking, knowing, remembering, categorizing, and problem solving. We'll begin with a presentation of the theories of Piaget and Vygotsky, two pioneers who have helped shape our contemporary understanding of cognition and the role that cultural factors play in it as well as how cognitive development affects lives across cultures.

◇ PIAGET'S THEORY OF COGNITIVE DEVELOPMENT

Jean Piaget (1896–1980), the Swiss-born psychologist, first developed an interest in cognitive development while working with Alfred Binet on intelligence testing in Paris. Piaget gradually became curious about children's thinking and problem solving and why children of the same age made similar mistakes when trying to solve problems. For years, he carefully recorded the cognitive changes he observed in his three children in their home in Geneva. From these and other observations, he theorized that individuals learn by actively constructing their own cognitive world. To Piaget, development is a dynamic process that results from an individual's ability to adapt thinking to meet the demands of an ever-changing environment and, as a result, to formulate new ideas.

According to Piaget's view, normal cognitive growth passes through four distinct periods: infancy, early childhood, middle childhood, and adolescence (see Table 4.1). Although Piaget provided age ranges for these various developmental periods, he recognized that the exact age at which a particular individual enters a specified period could be significantly affected by that person's physical, cognitive, or cultural experience—what Bronfenbrenner has referred to as the *ecological setting*.

Piaget's term for the first period of cognitive development (birth to two years) is the **sensorimotor period,** characterized by *coordination of sensory abilities and motor skills* when a child understands the world largely through immediate action and sensation. The highlight of this period is the achieve-

TABLE 4.1 Piaget's Periods of Cognitive Development

PERIOD	APPROXIMATE AGE	DESCRIPTION
Infancy	Birth to 2 years	Sensorimotor
Early childhood	2 to 6 years	Preoperational
Middle childhood	6 to 12 years	Concrete operations
Adolescence	12 years and older	Formal operations

ment of **object permanence,** *the awareness that objects remain the same or continue to exist even when they cannot be seen* (e.g., a doll not visible because it is covered by a blanket still exists). Piaget's term for the second period of cognitive development (two to six years) is the **preoperational period,** characterized by *development of language, use of symbols, and egocentric thinking* (e.g., failure to distinguish between one's own point of view and that of another individual). From ages six to approximately twelve, children are in the third period of **concrete operations,** characterized by *performance of tasks involving conservation, in which thinking is governed by fundamental rules of logic.* **Conservation** refers to the *ability to recognize that specific properties of an object, such as amount or number, do not change in spite of rearrangement or superficial modification in their appearance* (e.g., when a child thinks one sandwich cut into four slices is more than another sandwich cut into two slices). Piaget's term for the fourth and final period (age twelve through adulthood) is the **formal operational period,** characterized by the *ability to deal with hypothetical problems and abstract thinking* (e.g., mentally thinking about two different routes that could be taken to the same destination).

Core Structures

It was Piaget's belief that cognitive development occurs as a result of children's attempts to adapt to their environments and to make sense of the many experiences taking place around them. The ability to do this requires the systematic development of progressively more complex mechanisms or structures. At the center of this activity lies the scheme. A **scheme** is *an organized pattern of thought or action applied to persons, objects, or events in an effort to make sense of them.* In short, it is a mental picture of the world and those things in it. For example, infants develop a wide variety of schemes during the first few months, including schemes for mother, breast, bottle, and father's voice. Over the years, increased interactions with the environment result in these schemes becoming more sophisticated and better coordinated, so that by the time an individual reaches formal operations, they are capable of thinking about behaviors and imagining their consequences.

According to Piaget, cognitive development and the ability to adapt to the environment depends on the processes of assimilation and accommodation. **Assimilation** is *the process by which new information and ideas are incorporated or fitted into existing knowledge or schemes.* **Accommodation** is *the process of adjusting or modifying existing schemes to account for new ideas and information.* For example, when four-year-old Juanita, on the island of Mindoro in the Philippines, sees a coconut, she may call it a "furry rock" and play with it accordingly. She deals with this object by assimilating it into her present scheme of toys and other objects. If she were to modify her understanding of what a nut is after she sees and plays with the coconut, she would be accommodating to the object (e.g., developing a new scheme or category for this object). Anyone who has traveled abroad and attempted to make sense of new surroundings or tried to explain new objects or words to a foreign visitor has engaged in assimilation and accommodation—sometimes with success, sometimes with failure, and sometimes with humor! For example, what happens when Hakon from Norway tries to explain the making of a snowman to Yang, who lives in Malaysia and has never seen or touched snow? In this situation, Yang must make use of accommodation and adjust an existing scheme with which Yang is familiar (perhaps shaved ice) or create a new scheme (snow) to explain this new idea of a snowman. Another illustration of how assimilation and accommodation result in the development of cognitive operations can be seen in Piaget's classic conservation of liquid task.

Children in the preoperational period usually think that a tall, thin glass contains more liquid than a short, fat glass, since the level is higher, although they correctly say the amounts were initially the same. The problem is beyond younger children's capabilities, and they are unable to accommodate their thinking enough to understand that while the shape of the glass may be different, the amount of liquid remains the same. They simply assimilate what they see into their existing scheme, believe it to fit well, and feel no disequilibrium or imbalance in their perception of the situation. With the change in cognitive development that comes with increasing age and experience, children in the concrete operational period are able to consider the differences in the width, as well as the height, of the glasses and are no longer satisfied with their original answer, correctly recognizing that the liquid remains the same. At this point, they have achieved the concept of conservation. It is through active and open interaction with one's environment or surroundings that individuals learn to balance these twin processes of assimilation and accommodation. In terms of Bronfenbrenner's ecological systems approach, these cognitive processes can be said to begin in the family (microsystem); gradually extend to increasingly complex situations that arise in the neighborhood, at day care, or at school (mesosystem); and eventually, as the individual moves into adolescence and adulthood, operate in the workplace (exosystem) and the culture at large (macrosystem).

Evaluation of Piaget's Theory

While there is no doubt that Piaget's theory has had a significant impact on the study and understanding of cognitive development in mainstream Western psychology, his ideas have been challenged on several points. First, some have criticized his emphasis on individual activity occurring apart from social interaction. Such a focus reflects a more individualistic cultural perspective, such as that found in North America and Western Europe, and thereby fails to consider similarities or differences in cognitive development in traditional collectivistic cultures (e.g., China, Japan, and the islands of the South Pacific). Second, some have suggested that Piaget may have overestimated the contribution of motor activity and underestimated the ages at which children are capable of learning and performing a variety of behaviors by themselves. Third, Piaget's claim that once a person moves to a new period of cognitive development, the competencies mastered at that level will be exhibited in other phases of that individual's thinking do not appear to be fully supported by cross-cultural research findings. While advances may be apparent in some domains of a person's thinking processes, this may not be true in other domains (Wellman & Gelman, 1992). For a defense of Piaget's theory, as well as a response to common criticisms, see Box 4.1. Whatever one's position is regarding Piaget's theory, it continues to have considerable influence on contemporary research and practice and has, as we shall see shortly, been applied to the study of cognitive development in a large number of cultures throughout the world—with varying success.

◇ VYGOTSKY'S SOCIOCULTURAL THEORY OF DEVELOPMENT

As we have already noted, Piaget's position was that cognitive development is largely an individual accomplishment, directed and shaped, in part, by the environment. However, he said little about the importance of the social context in learning. This view was challenged by the Soviet psychologist Lev Semyonovich Vygotsky.

BOX 4.1

IN DEFENSE OF PIAGET'S THEORY

Piaget's theory of cognitive development has often been criticized. Two researchers, Lourenco and Machado (1996), have recently discussed the most common criticisms and provided ten reasons for supporting or defending Piaget's claims. This box considers these arguments.

1. *Piaget's theory underestimates children's competence.* While some researchers agree with this statement, recent evidence suggests children's competencies are indeed revealed in the way Piaget speculated when certain factors are taken into consideration (e.g., language, context, memory, nature of the task, number of objects present, and type of questions asked). Few people have changed our understanding of the cognitive potential of children more than has Piaget.

2. *Piaget's theory establishes age norms disconfirmed by the data.* Piaget believed the key element in understanding cognitive development in children to be sequencing rather than age. If a child is able to solve a task earlier than anticipated, so what? Does this pose serious conceptual damage to his theory? Probably not.

3. *Piaget characterizes development negatively.* Piaget did not argue for evidence of cognitive incompetence in children but rather for the lack of evidence for the advance of a cognitive gain. When referring to a child's inability to conserve, he was referring to a child's lack of logical competence in one area, not a lack of any logical abilities.

4. *Piaget's theory is an extreme competence theory.* Some investigators have criticized Piaget for ignoring the role performance plays in solving operational tasks. However, it was never Piaget's contention that performance depends exclusively on cognitive competencies. Instead, he insisted that performance requires the discovery of new ways of knowing as they emerge in the course of development.

5. *Piaget's theory neglects the role of social factors in development.* Piaget believed cognitive development is best described in a series of fixed stages that are indeed influenced by surrounding social and cultural circumstances.

BOX 4.1 CONTINUED

6. *Piaget's theory predicts developmental synchronies not corroborated by the data.* This criticism stems from Piaget's prediction of homogenous performance across developmental tasks. This critique is ill-founded because Piaget never suggested that structural change in cognitive development represents a holistic representative characteristic of everyone.

7. *Piaget's theory describes, but does not explain, behavior.* Piaget's theory does describe the structure and sequencing of qualitative and quantitative change and does not purport to prescribe the process of cognitive development.

8. *Piaget's theory is paradoxical because it assesses thinking through language.* While the relationship between thought and language has long been debated, Piaget's early writings indicate that he conceptualized these two processes in the acquisition of knowledge as interactive and interdependent.

9. *Piaget's theory ignores postadolescent development.* In Piaget's original theory, he believed the stage of formal operations begins at approximately the age of eleven or twelve and reaches its peak shortly thereafter. While Riegel, Basseches, Labouvie-Vief, and others were among the first to propose a fifth stage (post-formal operations), Piaget never suggested that cognitive development stops after adolescence. He believed that adult cognition takes on different forms and simply represents variations on the theme of formal operations.

10. *Piaget's theory appeals to inappropriate models of logic.* Piaget used logic to characterize the evolution of intelligence over time. He did so because he believed that psychological explanations should describe, coordinate, and synthesize behavior into a coherent theory that warrants immediate application. Theory should provide a language that helps psychologists achieve the goals of description, explanation, and prediction. Despite this criticism, Piaget revised his models of logic to include pragmatic implications of cognitive change.

Lev Vygotsky (1896–1934) was one of several children raised in an orthodox Jewish family in Russia. As a young man, he frequently wrote critically about Soviet government policies, with which he did not agree. As a result, his scientific writings were banned, although his highly acclaimed and influential book *Thought and Language* was finally published in 1934, the year he died of tuberculosis.

Core Structures

Vygotsky suggested that development is the result of interaction between cultural and historical factors. He believed that the key feature of development lies in matching a child's demands with the requirements of her culture. Vygotsky suggested that there were three major components in this process: the role played by culture, the use of language, and the child's zone of proximal development (Kozulin, 1990). Briefly, the **zone of proximal (nearby) development (ZPD)** refers to the distance between a child's actual developmental level and the higher-level potential (Vygotsky, 1978). It is *the difference between what children can achieve independently and what their potential level of development might be if given help or guidance.* This concept of the ZPD emphasizes Vygotsky's view that social influences contribute significantly to children's development of cognitive abilities and that mentoring or guidance strengthens their growth (Steward, 1994).

To tie this into the major themes cited in previous chapters, let us consider the case of twelve-year-old Dabir, a young Saudi adolescent. We might say that the process of learning, which takes place through mentoring in a number of Dabir's diverse ecological settings (home, mosque, school), defines his developmental niche at a particular time in his life. As Vygotsky would view it, Dabir does not have his own ZPD but participates in a shared ZPD with those around him. This is also true with regard to Deratu (introduced in this chapter's opening vignette), who does not go to school but learns the important cultural and practical lessons necessary for living in rural Ethiopia from the daily guidance provided by her mother.

From Vygotsky's point of view, culture is a social construction, and cognition is rooted in language and cultural experience. He describes three sequential stages in the evolution of speech that are considered essential in language and cognitive development. The first is **social speech,** which is *designed primarily to gain the attention of others or to express simple ideas* and lasts until approximately three years of age. **Egocentric speech** is the second; this occurs between the ages of three and seven, *serves to control the child's own behavior, and is usually verbalized.* The third is **inner speech;** this develops around the age of seven, and *consists of self-talk, during which children rehearse* *what they are going to say before actually saying it* (Vygotsky, 1978). According to Vygotsky, early use of language helps children reflect on their behavior and thus plays a major role in cognitive development.

Evaluation of Vygotsky's Theory

While much of Vygotsky's work has been praised for its originality and usefulness, like the pioneering ideas of Piaget, it has its critics. For example, some argue that the zone of proximal development is vague and cannot be adequately measured (Paris & Cross, 1988). Others believe that parts of Vygotsky's theory have been lost or misunderstood in translation and therefore are confusing and incomplete (Nicolopoulou, 1993). Nevertheless, the theory still represents an increasingly important contribution to cross-cultural human development. Now that we are familiar with the fundamental concepts in the theories of Piaget and Vygotsky, let us examine how these and other theories contribute to our understanding of cognitive development from a cross-cultural perspective and how all of this meshes with our major themes.

◇ SOME CULTURAL VARIATIONS IN COGNITION

Infancy

Piaget's and Vygotsky's interest in children's intellectual development as a focus for understanding how ideas change over time has drawn attention to several important issues related to the study of cultural differences. Over a period of thirty years, hundreds of researchers throughout the world have subjected these theories to careful scrutiny, with the result that the cross-cultural literature is immense and cannot be given here anything approaching the full attention it deserves. However, there are a number of excellent reviews that we recommend to those who would like to pursue the topic further. These include the work of Rogoff and Chavajay (1995); Gielen (1994); Dasen (1994); Bronfenbrenner (1993); Segall, Dasen, Berry, and Poortinga (1990); D'Andrade (1990); and Cole (1992a, 1992b).

Of all Piaget's periods, the sensorimotor (occurring during infancy) has been the least studied from a cross-cultural perspective. A major reason is that observation methods and data-collecting techniques based on Piagetian concepts have only recently been standardized (Cole, 1995). According to Dasen, the first cross-cultural study of sensorimotor intelligence, using a scale developed by Corman and Escalona (1969), was conducted in Zambia (Goldberg, 1972). In general, while minor differences in behavior were noted (a slight advance for African infants over American at six months and a slight lag at nine and twelve months), Goldberg's findings tend to support Piaget's observations. A later study, conducted by Dasen and his colleagues (1978) on the Ivory Coast, suggested that African infants are advanced in their development of object permanency and other object-related cognitive behaviors. In yet another African study, this one conducted in Nigeria, Mundy-Castle & Okonji (1976) reported that while early manipulation of objects is similar for English and Igbo infants, important differences emerge in later interactions. What they have to say about these differences lends support to our emphasis on the importance of looking at cognitive behavior from an ecological point of view. Specifically, Mundy-Castle (1974) proposed that, after a certain age, European and American infants develop increased experiences in the handling of objects, with their attention "more often deliberately focused on objective properties of reality," whereas "African babies receive more social stimulation and early emotional support than European babies. The issue here is whether in the long run this divergent stimulation brings about a differential patterning of cognitive development, with Africans acquiring an intelligence that is more socially oriented, while Europeans acquire one that is more technologically oriented" (pp. 19–20). Although not specifically mentioned, since this was not the concern, the microsystem (family) and macrosystem (cultural values) have an important effect on the development of these cognitive behaviors.

In an early review of the cross-cultural literature, Dasen and Heron (1981) recognized that differences in the ages at which the substages of this period are attained do occur. However, they go on to stress that "in emphasizing these cultural differences, we may overlook the amazing commonality reported by all these studies: in fact, the qualitative characteristics of sensorimotor development remain nearly identical in all infants studied so far, despite vast differences in their cultural environments" (p. 305). Werner (1979), however, concluded that "even in the first stage of cognitive development, that of sensorimotor intelligence, culture seems to influence the rate of development to some extent, although admittedly, the similarity of structure and process is more striking than the differences. Content seems to have little relevance to the activation of sensorimotor schemata" (p. 216).

An example of Vygotsky's contextualist research during the sensorimotor period is seen in the work carried out by Bornstein and his colleagues (Bornstein, Toda, Azuma, Tamis-LeMonda, & Ogino, 1990; Bornstein, Tal, & Tamis-LeMonda, 1991; Bornstein & Tamis-LeMonda, 1989). They studied infant cognition by observing patterns of interaction between American and Japanese mothers and their infants. Interestingly, it was noted that American mothers responded more favorably to their babies' requests when the infants were playing with physical objects. Japanese mothers, on the other hand, were more responsive when their babies were engaged in play with them. The researchers also noted how often mothers responded to their infants' vocalizations. Interestingly, maternal responsiveness appeared to be positively related to the IQ scores of Japanese children when they were about two and a half years of age and to scores of American children at the age of four years. At five months of age, infants in both cultures showed early signs of object permanence and were equally likely to engage in goal-directed behavior. This example clearly demonstrates Vygotsky's claim that culture plays an active role in directing cognitive activity, even in infancy.

More recently, Uzgiris and Raeff (1995), in a study of parent-child play interactions, stated that "the cognitive representations, communicative formats, and affective explorations inherent in play ensure that through the matrix of play interactions available to them, children work to become adept members of their societies" (p. 372). In other words, the variety of activities involved in play (e.g., talking, touching, and interacting) help children to learn skills that will enable them to be active participants in later cultural interactions. You can probably see how these ideas fit into and support our major themes. For example, it is within the family context (mesosystem) that early parent-child interactions take place. It is here that infants are introduced to activities (e.g., play and the use of language) that help prepare them for successful participation in the broader cultural contexts of the workplace (exosystem) and understanding of important values and attitudes (macrosystem).

Along similar lines, Bornstein and his colleagues (1992) looked at the various ways in which young infants in Argentina, France, Japan, and the United States were engaged in conversation by their mothers. In each of these cultures, mothers were more conversant with older children (thirteen-month-olds) than they were with younger children (five-month-olds) and exhibited a variety of cultural differences in speech patterns when talking with them. For example, expressive speech was employed more often by Japanese mothers than it was by French, Argentinean, or American mothers. This behavior on the part of Japanese mothers is compatible with their culture's stress on interdependence as an important value. (You may recall our earlier discussion in Chapter 2 of interdependence and Japanese childrearing practices as they relate to socialization.)

French, American, and Argentinean mothers, on the other hand, gave greater attention to speech that communicated information to their infant or child. This is consistent with other findings in cultures characterized by individualistic behavior, such as the three Western societies represented in this study (Barratt et al., 1993). Still, not all of these mothers communicated the same kind of information to their children. For example, American mothers asked lots of questions, reflecting, in part, the view within American society that children are active participants in the learning process and often (as we saw in our earlier theoretical discussion) construct their own knowledge. In contrast, French mothers provided their infants and children with less stimulation but greater emotional support. Finally, Argentinean mothers appeared to be the most direct in their interactions with their children, which is indicative of a more authoritarian approach to dealing with children (Bornstein et al., 1992).

Childhood

As we move from the infancy and early childhood periods to the school-age period, the majority of cross-cultural Piagetian studies have focused on the transition from the preoperational period to the concrete operational period and the attainment of conservation (Gardiner, 1994). These studies show great variability in their findings (Dasen, 1994; Rogoff, 1990). Fishbein (1984) points out that the research literature on these topics, published during the 1960s and early 1970s, reports consistently large differences (as much as seven years) in the favor of children in Westernized cultures when compared with children from developing cultures. However, Kamara (1977) has drawn attention to what he feels are three serious faults with the majority of this work. He makes the following criticisms: (1) The study of thinking in both of these periods depends heavily on the use of language, yet most of the researchers who conducted these early studies had little knowledge of either the culture or the language of their subjects. (2) Although Piaget favored the use of clinical interviews for gathering information about children's thinking processes, many of these investigators attempted to employ various types of standardized measures that required little use of language. (3) Accurate birth dates of subjects were not always available, and attempts to approximate ages were frequently off by as much as two years. These are serious criticisms still deserving of further attention on the part of cross-cultural researchers.

In an extremely interesting and creative cross-cultural study, Nyiti (1982) attempted to avoid the pitfalls mentioned by Kamara by varying the languages used and by employing three of Piaget's well-known conservation tasks for substance, weight, and volume. Subjects consisted of ten- to eleven-year-old Micmac Indian children from Cape Breton Island in Canada and white English-speaking European-Canadians. The European-Canadian children were interviewed in English by an English-speaking European, while the Indian children were divided into two groups. In the first group, children were initially interviewed in English by an English-speaking European and later in Micmac by a Micmac-speaking Indian. In the second group, the order of interviewing was reversed. When the white European-Canadians and

Micmac Indian children were tested in their native languages, their performances on conservation tasks were nearly identical and were comparable to those of other European, Canadian, and American children. However, when tested in English, Micmac Indian children performed at a significantly lower level than the other two groups. More important, the results indicated that nearly twice as many children at both age levels, when interviewed in their native language, were more capable of solving each of the three conservation tasks than were the Micmac Indian children interviewed in English. Nyiti concludes his study by stating that "it appears that cognitive structures described by Piaget are universal and represent a necessary condition for any successful acculturation [and] . . . while children in different cultures may have to deal with different realities, they all apply the same operations or processes of thought" (p. 165).

In an important and exhaustive review of cross-cultural findings on conservation task performance, Dasen (1972) sorted results into four types, each supported by a large number of studies. These included (1) cultural groups in which conservation appears at about the same time as it does in American and European children (i.e., Nigerians, Zambians, Hong Kong Chinese, Iranians, and Australian Aborigines), (2) groups in which conservation generally develops earlier (i.e., Asians), (3) cultures in which conservation appears as much as two to six years later (i.e., African and lower-socioeconomic-status Americans and Europeans), and (4) groups in which some individuals fail to engage in concrete operations even when they reach adolescence (i.e., Algerians, Nepalese, Amazon Indians, and Senegalese). What can we conclude from this vast amount of cross-cultural data? First, support for the universality of the structures or operations underlying the preoperational period is highly convincing. Second, whether or not these structures become functional and the rate at which this might take place appear strongly influenced by factors within one's culture—further validation of the importance of looking at cognitive development from the ecological systems approach.

Based on cross-cultural findings accumulated over many years, using the Piagetian approach, Dasen (1994) has recently suggested that the qualitative characteristics of concrete operational development (e.g., stage sequences and reasoning styles) appear to be universal and the rate of cognitive development in certain domains (e.g., quantification and spatial reasoning) is not uniform but depends on ecocultural factors. He implies that it is impossible to characterize an individual as being in a single period of cognitive development or to attribute any single period to an entire group. Finally, Dasen points out that "the eco-cultural framework within which the data are interpreted precludes attributing value judgements to developmental sequences" (p. 148). To use his example, it is not necessarily "better" for an Australian Aborigine living in his traditional setting in the bush "to give a conservation rather than a non-conservation answer. . . . In the new settings brought about by acculturation (for example, at school), it may indeed be more adaptive to handle quantification concepts with ease; in this case, they could be taught explicitly—and the more materialistic value system at the same time!" (p. 148).

Finally, it appears that although the rate and level of performance at which children move through Piaget's concrete operational period depend on cultural experience, children in diverse societies still proceed in the same sequence he predicted (Dasen, 1977; Mwamwenda, 1992; Segall, Dasen, Berry, & Poortinga, 1990). The work of Price-Williams, Gordon, and Ramirez (1969) supports this view. For example, in one of their studies, conservation tasks were administered to two groups of Mexican children—half from pottery-making families and half from non-pottery-making families. Those children who had helped their families by working with clay showed signs of conservation at earlier ages than those without such experience.

These young Mexican girls take great pleasure in making traditional pottery figures. (D. Donne Bryant)

In a further review of cross-cultural studies of concrete operational behavior, Dasen concludes that while parental ethnotheories or cultural beliefs and daily activities of children are closely related, psychological tests (those indigenous to cultures as well as those adapted for them) often fail to measure behaviors other than those valued in North American or European societies (Segall, Dasen, Berry, & Poortinga, 1990). For example, in one study, Dasen (1984) looked at the developmental niche of concrete operational thought among the Baoule of Cote d'Ivoire in Africa and in a follow-up study used observations to document the relevant learning contexts within this cultural group (Dasen, 1988). His findings further support the view we take here—that the belief systems of parents are deeply rooted in culture and, through a system of reciprocal socialization, reflect and reinforce the values considered necessary for functioning successfully in a variety of ecological settings, whether this be within the family (mesosystem), community or school (exosystem), or wider culture (macrosystem). (We have provided numerous examples of this thesis in our earlier discussion of socialization in Chapter 2.)

What is Vygotsky's position on these issues? He claimed that cultural influence, mental processes, and language are dynamic processes that occur simultaneously (Wertsch & Tulviste, 1994). He further believed that the continuous interaction between language and thought, embedded in a particular cultural context, results in dialogue between individuals, especially a mother and her child. It is this social interaction that helps shape the quality of mental abilities at various ages across the lifespan (Philip & Kelly, 1992). With this theoretical perspective in mind, Vygotsky coined the expression, *"Talking to Learn."* By this he meant that as children verbally interact with others, they internalize language and use it to organize their thoughts (Vygotsky, 1978).

According to Greenfield and Cocking (1994), as parents interact with their children, they become socialized into a particular set of cultural values and beliefs. Consequently, as children pass through Vygotsky's zone of proximal development, they acquire specific cognitive skills at the same time they are becoming enculturated into a way of life. An effective method for achieving this is **scaffolding,** which refers to *the temporary support or guidance provided to a child by parents, older siblings, peers, or other adults in the process of solving a problem.* In construction, scaffolding is placed around a building to provide temporary support. Once completed, the scaffolding is removed, and the building is left to stand on its own. Similarly, the amount of scaffolding, in the form of guidance and support, a child may need depends on his ability to solve a problem alone. When the problem has been solved, the parent or others can remove the temporary scaffold (guidance) until help is again needed. An example of this guidance, or scaffolding, is illustrated on the next page.

Here a mother is shown mentoring her young son as he learns shapes of objects and how to place them in the right arrangement. As with recipro-

*A mother using scaffolding to help her child learn a
new skill.* (Courtesy of the authors)

cal socialization (Chapter 2), parents carefully observe their children's behavior to determine how much help they may need in completing a task or
activity. As the activity continues, parents become increasingly sensitive to
their children's needs, with the result that children do better on subsequent
tasks (Pratt, Kerig, Cowan, & Cowan, 1988).

As we mentioned earlier in this chapter, Vygotsky died in 1934, the
same year that his sociocultural theory was published. At that time, his theory was still being developed. However, in recent years his theory has been
receiving increased attention. Clearly, there is a need for additional research,
and we predict that once cross-cultural scholars recognize how closely the
sociocultural theory of Vygotsky and the ecological systems theory of Bronfenbrenner complement each other, a variety of interesting and significant
studies will begin to appear.

This lack of available findings is one reason that you will seldom find
reference to Vygotsky's theory and ideas in the last three sections of this
chapter. Another reason is that, unlike Piaget, Vygotsky did not characterize
his theory in terms of periods but rather as a continuous process of interaction between individuals and sociocultural factors. With this in mind, let us
move on to the period of adolescence and look at some cross-cultural findings related to Piaget's stage of formal operations.

Adolescence

Piaget's stage of formal operations also has been studied cross-culturally, and it is the view of some researchers that individuals in many societies never achieve this type of thinking (Byrnes, 1988; Shea, 1985). In fact, a study recently conducted among Nigerian adolescents by Hollos and Richards (1993), using Piagetian tasks, revealed little use of formal operational thinking.

One of several tasks frequently used to measure cognitive development in the stage of formal operations is the pendulum problem. In the pendulum problem, individuals are shown several pendulums of different weights that are attached to different lengths of string. When the pendulums are swung, individuals are asked to figure out what determines the speed at which the pendulums swing back and forth. For example, is it the weight, the height from which it is dropped, the force with which it is pushed, the string's length, or perhaps a combination of all of these? According to Inhelder and Piaget (1959), children in the stage of formal operations should be able to solve the pendulum problem through the process of elimination. Several cross-cultural studies have utilized this problem to observe cognitive changes in formal operations. For example, in studies carried out among adolescents in New Guinea, no subjects performed at the formal operational level (Philip & Kelly, 1974; Kelly, 1977). Similarly, few adolescents showed formal operational thought when tested in Rwanda (Laurendeau-Bendavid, 1977). On the other hand, among Chinese children exposed to the British education system in Hong Kong, formal operational performance was found to be equal to or better than the performance of American or European children (Goodnow & Bethon, 1966). Some formal operational thinking was also found among schoolchildren in Central Java and New South Wales (Philip & Kelly, 1974). Based on these and similar findings, Piaget (1972) proposed that development of formal operational thinking is influenced by experience as well as by culture (Rogoff & Chavajay, 1995). As we have seen before, events taking place within one's ecological niche frequently determine how one will perceive and behave in a particular ecological setting.

These examples provide added impetus for considering the ecological setting in understanding why behavior, including cognitive activity, is expressed as it is. For example, Cole and Cole (1996) point out that "a lawyer might think in a formal manner about law cases but not when sorting the laundry . . . a baseball manager might employ formal operational thinking to choose his batting lineup but [not when doing] . . . the combination-of-chemicals task" (p. 674). As evidence, they cite a study by Retschitzki (1989) showing that when African men and older boys play a popular board game involving the capture of seeds from opponents, they make use of complex rules, complicated offensive and defensive moves, and skilled calculations. Interviews with skilled Baoule players from Cote d'Ivoire revealed that their strategies in playing this game made use of the types of logical thinking we usually attribute to formal operations.

The inability to show evidence for the universality of formal operational thinking among adolescents and adults is not confined to non-Western areas. In fact, earlier studies (Modgil & Modgil, 1976) demonstrated that not all adolescents or adults living in Western technological cultures achieve this type of thinking and that they frequently show low levels of success on formal operational tasks (Modgil & Modgil, 1976). Even earlier studies conducted by Kohlberg & Gilligan (1971) with subjects in late adolescence reported that only between 30 and 50 percent of such individuals perform successfully on formal operational tasks. Werner (1979) sums this up by stating, "Formal-operational thinking might not appear at all or might appear in less-generalized form among cultures and individuals whose experience is limited to one or a few specialized or technical occupations. In other words, survival in a particular culture may not call for, nor be influenced by, formal logical thinking. Thus formal thought processes are probably cultural alternatives that can be learned. Humans have the capacity for it, but may not have realized it in order to 'get by' in their particular society" (p. 224). More recently, Shea (1985) has suggested that formal operational thinking (i.e., scientific reasoning) may not be valued in all cultures.

Finally, in a discussion of the socialization of cognition, Goodnow (1990) concludes that Piagetian theory can be effectively applied to the conservation of weight, amount, and volume. However, she goes on to say that "if one's goal is to go beyond these domains—to construct an account of cognitive development that cuts across many domains or that takes place in everyday life—then classical Piagetian theory will certainly need some additions" (pp. 277–278). This, of course, is a position with which we certainly agree and which we encourage other researchers to take into account when conducting future cross-cultural studies in the area of cognition.

Early Adulthood

Most of the research in the area of cross-cultural human development has emphasized cognitive growth in childhood and adolescence. By comparison, few cross-cultural studies have examined cognitive development in adulthood. Piaget believed that formal operational thinking represented the highest level of cognitive development and proposed no additional stages in adulthood. He believed that an adolescent and an adult would think in the same way. However, some developmental psychologists have challenged this belief, arguing for a post-formal stage of cognitive development in adulthood. For example, Labouvie-Vief (1986) has suggested that in early adulthood, a change in thinking occurs in which individuals begin to recognize cognitive limitations and may adapt their thinking to the demands of their environment. This process is called **adaptive logic** and involves *balancing critical analyses of objective observations with one's subjective reactions to these observations.* For example, when performing a memory task, older subjects may make a conscious decision to exclude much of the detailed information they remember, believing it may be uninteresting to the researcher or to other listeners. If this is the case, Salthouse (1987) suggests that when measuring cognitive abilities of middle-aged adults, we need to employ strategies different than those used with young adults (e.g., experience and expertise). This represents one more challenge for researchers interested in the study of cognitive development.

According to some theorists (Basseches, 1984, 1989; Riegel, 1975), the highest level of post-formal cognition is what is called dialectical thinking. **Dialectical thinking** *suggests that for every viewpoint there is an opposing viewpoint and these two can be considered simultaneously.* The ability to synthesize and deal with such opposing ideas represents a new level of cognitive flexibility and a deepening of thought, which, in turn, facilitates developmental growth.

The developmental psychologist, K. Warner Schaie (1977–1978) has proposed that near the end of adolescence or during the early twenties, individuals advance from the **acquisition stage,** in which emphasis is placed on *attaining concepts for solving problems,* to the **achievement stage,** which involves *goal-directed behavior.* In middle adulthood, Schaie has proposed that individuals enter a third stage, the **responsible stage,** in which *long-term goals and family responsibility take precedence over the goal-directed behavior of young adulthood.* This attention to family responsibilities lays the foundation for the **executive stage,** in which emphasis is placed on *larger social systems and civic involvement* (e.g., serving on a school board or running for local political office). Finally, in late adulthood, there is the **reintegrative stage,** when individuals begin *a review of accomplishments and failures* and put their lives in perspective. While you may see some similarities between Schaie's description of adult cognition and Bronfenbrenner's ecological systems approach, the ideas of Schaie are more general and therefore may not account for much of the diversity found among adults in non-Western or nonindustrialized societies. However, these proposed stages do provide a useful framework for describing changes in adult cognition and are worthy of cross-cultural investigation, especially since little is known about adult cognition from this perspective.

Middle and Later Adulthood

As one gets older, one supposedly gets wiser. At middle age and late adulthood, one has greater experience, becomes more sensitive to inconsistencies, and responds differently to social, political, and economic changes. These are generally the years of greatest productivity and self-satisfaction in one's career, avocation, or family.

Studying and understanding cognition during the middle and late adult years presents unique challenges, in part due to a confounding or intermingling of age and experience. Since the majority of research efforts have been conducted in Western cultures, which are youth oriented, the focus has tended to be on cognitive development among children and adolescents, not on the later years of adulthood. As a result, we know very little about changes in cognitive abilities among adults and even less from a cross-cultural perspective.

In their efforts to investigate changes in cognitive development during middle and late adulthood, Cattell (1965) and Horn (1967, 1968, 1970) proposed a distinction between fluid and crystallized intelligence.

Fluid intelligence involves *the ability to form concepts, reason abstractly, and apply material to new situations.* It is thought to be biological or intuitive and to be uninfluenced by culture. It is reflected in an individual's ability to make inferences, draw analogies, solve problems, and understand relationships among concepts. **Crystallized intelligence** refers to *an individual's accumulated knowledge and experience in a particular culture* (e.g., ability to react to social situations or respond to classroom tests).

Previous research in developmental psychology indicates that these two types of intelligence unfold in different directions. While fluid intelligence stays the same or declines somewhat throughout adulthood, crystallized intelligence may actually improve (Horn & Donaldson, 1980; Horn & Hofer, 1992; Lerner, 1990). Over the years, this view has been disputed on the basis of research conceptualization and methodology (Baltes, 1987; Schaie, 1984).

How might the ideas of fluid and crystallized intelligence apply across different cultures? To apply this view would require an understanding of how different cultures value speed, experience, youth, and age. For instance, it has been shown that the speed of cognitive functioning tends to slow down in late adulthood (Salthouse & Coon, 1993; Sternberg & McGrane, 1993), but it is important to consider other factors when addressing this issue cross-culturally. For example, it is not clear how the cultural environment will react to or even notice an individual's cognitive slowdown. In some cases, a lack of speed might be compensated for by experience. Individuals who are admired for their experience (or wisdom) are often expected to be more reflective in matters requiring wise decisions. For example, Yang Tsu, an eighty-four-year-old master of martial arts in China, exhibits great discipline and patience (which took many years to cultivate), when teaching his young, impulsive apprentice, Low Chi Tho, who wants to learn everything very quickly. After some time, Low Chi has come to admire Yang Tsu and to realize the need to develop a more reflective approach to learning. In short, what might be negatively viewed by some cultures as a slowdown or decline in cognitive response is positively viewed in this case as a necessary quality for achieving success. Our familiarity with cross-cultural research suggests that there are many instances in which a behavior in one culture is viewed quite differently in another. This richness of differences (as well as similarities) provides many opportunities for those interested in pursuing the study of behavior from a cross-cultural, ecological, or sociocultural perspective.

In Western societies, speed is often more highly valued, and the ability to think quickly and make rapid decisions is seen as an indicator of high intelligence. In many non-Western societies, time and speed are less valued, since individuals are encouraged to first view themselves as part of a group and to concentrate their efforts on the well-being of the family. In these societies, experience is more valuable than quick action. For example, when asked what advice he would give incoming American managers, a Japanese executive who had worked in Tokyo for fifteen years replied, "I'd tell him not to do anything for the first six months." He continued, "I've seen a lot more problems caused by Americans trying to do things too quickly than waiting too long to act." In America, it is often said, "Don't just stand there, do something." In Japan, they say, "Don't just do something, stand there" (Condon, 1984, p. 62).

In Western societies, youth is idolized, and displays of fluid intelligence are often synonymous with quick-mindedness. This attribute is often preferred over experience, or crystallized intelligence. Today, many corporations in the United States actively look for young employees who possess a fresh perspective and demonstrate the characteristics associated with fluid intelligence. At the same time, many senior employees, who have devoted several decades to their employers and have years of accumulated experience, find themselves confronted by the loss of their jobs or by offers of early retirement.

The issue of accumulated experience over time has been associated with wisdom (Smith & Baltes, 1990). But does age alone make an individual wiser? Not necessarily. Smith and Baltes investigated sixty German professionals and divided them into three age groups of twenty-five to thirty-five, forty to fifty, and sixty to eighty-one. Each group was presented with four made-up examples of demanding situations and was asked to prepare solutions for these problems. Their approaches and solutions were rated by a panel of human services professionals. Of the 240 respondents, eleven scored in the "wise" category but were not necessarily older. In fact, they were found in almost equal numbers in each of the three groups. Wisdom, then, would not appear to be characteristic of any particular age group. In short, individuals do not become wiser simply because they get older. Wisdom takes many forms and varies according to each culture's orientation. In this study the criterion for determining what constituted wisdom was set by the researchers, who represent a specific cultural orientation that may or may not apply to all cultures. Replication of this study in a variety of other cultures might produce some interesting findings.

More recent research on this topic has led Baltes and his colleagues to propose a number of general characteristics associated with wisdom, including the ability to focus on important issues and to exercise good judgment, the development of a broad base of experiences, and recognition of one's wisdom by others (Baltes, 1993).

In the final analysis, it is important to realize that although some aspects of cognitive functioning decline with age, how this change is viewed and evaluated depends largely on one's culture, ecological surroundings, and developmental niche.

◇ SUMMARY

Cognition is a general term referring to thinking, reasoning, decision making, remembering, categorizing, and problem solving. Cultural factors and beliefs found in the interaction among Bronfenbrenner's ecological systems—the microsystem, mesosystem, exosystem, and macrosystem—the developmental niche, and the sociocultural orientation contribute in a variety of ways to cognitive development across the lifespan.

The theories of Piaget, Vygotsky, and others provide a useful framework for conceptualizing cognitive growth and development. According to Piaget, children's thinking differs significantly from that of adults, which is acquired only after successfully passing through a series of discrete stages. In the sensorimotor stage, infants acquire coordination, begin to understand that their behavior produces a reaction, and eventually realize that objects exist even when they can no longer be seen (object permanence). In the preoperational stage, schemes develop and provide the foundation for language acquisition. During this time, young children find it difficult to understand that others perceive the world differently than they do (egocentrism). In the stage of concrete operations, children begin to understand logical connections and realize that items remain the same despite superficial changes in their physical appearance (conservation). Finally, in the stage of formal operations, school-age children and adolescents develop the ability to manipulate concepts and formulate abstractions. These stages have been studied from a cross-cultural perspective, and research evidence suggests that some aspects may be universal (the sequence of stages) while others (the stage of formal operations) may not.

Vygotsky's sociocultural theory emphasizes the strong influence of social and cultural factors on both cognitive and language development. He introduced the zone of proximal development, which refers to what a child is presently capable of doing and what she could potentially be able to do if guided by adults or capable peers. Vygotsky argued that cognitive development is enhanced when instruction is focused on an individual's potential rather than on the level of actual development. According to Vygotsky, the development of egocentric speech, inner speech, and external speech is grounded in one's social and cultural orientation. Vygotsky also emphasized the need for guided instruction (scaffolding), in which adults provide assistance (scaffolds) for children as they attempt to solve difficult problems.

Cross-cultural investigations of human development have tended to focus primarily on children and adolescents and devote less attention to middle and late adulthood. At the same time, research in adult cognition has revealed that a fifth stage of cognitive development (post-formal thought) may emerge after formal operations. This new thinking allows an individual to move beyond abstract conceptualization and to integrate diverse reasoning abilities with pragmatic problem-solving strategies. The work of several researchers suggests that adult cognition is characterized by adaptive logic and dialectical thinking. The ability to synthesize new ideas and to realize that there are at least two sides to every point of view provides adults with more flexibility, effective problem-solving skills, and a broadening of thought.

The developmental psychologist K. Warner Schaie has proposed that adult cognition passes through five stages, beginning with a period of acquisition in childhood and adolescence. In adulthood, an individual advances to the achievement, responsible, executive, and reintegrative stages. While these stages may provide a reasonably accurate description of adult cognitive development in Europe and North America, there has been little effort to examine these stages from a cross-cultural perspective to learn if they apply equally well to other, non-Western societies.

Cognitive development in middle and late adulthood follows a different pattern than in childhood and adolescence. Cattell and Horn have suggested that a distinction be made between fluid and crystallized intelligence. Fluid intelligence is a person's ability to solve problems, think abstractly, and to apply new material in creative ways. Crystallized intelligence is learning that is based on experience. Early cross-cultural research indicates that as we get older, fluid intelligence declines, whereas crystallized intelligence increases. More recent research by Baltes and Schaie disputes this claim and suggests the need to consider cultural and contextual factors when attempting to explain individual differences in cognitive decline during late adulthood.

◇ THINGS TO DO AND THINK ABOUT

1. Return to the opening vignettes and identify the major developmental principles discussed in the chapter. Explain how these apply to the lives of Deratu and Maria.

2. After reviewing Vygotsky's sociocultural theory, try to teach or coach another person (friend, sibling, teammate) to learn a new skill by providing guidance, or scaffolding, to move through the zone of proximal development. To obtain optimal results, focus your instruction on that person's potential rather than his level of actual development.

3. Now that you understand the basic nature of cognitive processes and the factors that influence them (e.g., one's ecological systems, developmental niche, and sociocultural orientation), think of how you might use this knowledge to improve your understanding of your own and other cultures.

4. *Sesame Street* is one of the most successful and widely watched children's television programs in the United States, having several international versions in other countries. Watch one or two episodes and identify developmental principles discussed by Piaget and Vygotsky and cultural values unique to Western and non-Western societies. Indicate in what ways these values differ.

◇ FURTHER READINGS

John Korte. (1995). *White Gloves: How We Create Ourselves Through Memory*. New York: Free Press.

Drawing on the latest research on cognition and clinical psychology, the author, in an intriguing, readable, and jargon-free manner, illustrates the nature of memory from childhood to old age. Using personal narratives, he covers such topics as first memories, photographic memories, memories of dreams, and repressed memory.

John Naisbitt. (1996). *Megatrends Asia: Eight Asian Megatrends That Are Reshaping Our World*. New York: Simon & Schuster.

One of the world's leading trend forecasters describes the significant political, social, business, and cultural values and beliefs that will change the world as we know it into the next century. A "new Asian way" of thinking is emerging that reflects increased individualism and urbanization and a more modern role for women.

Barbara Rogoff. (1990). *Apprenticeship in Thinking*. New York: Oxford University Press.

This book overflows with examples of parents leading their children through rough and calm cognitive seas to new levels of thinking. Illustrations of daily activities performed in scores of cultures fill almost every page of this book, which was written by one of the most prominent proponents of the cultural context perspective.

CHAPTER FIVE

CULTURE, SELF, AND PERSONALITY

Sergej was happy, agreeable, and easy to care for as a child. He grew up on a kolkhozy (collective farm) in the Ukraine, one of the fifteen republics in the former Soviet Union. Sergej was quiet, and even his adolescent years were not characterized by the confusion and psychological turmoil experienced by so many young people. Sergej did well in school, completed an apprenticeship, and following the breakup of the Soviet Union, now works on his family's small farm. He has been married for several years, and his wife Tamara describes him as a "good husband" who works hard, stays at home, and cares for his family.

⬦ ⬦ ⬦

Yuen, born in Guizhou province in south central China, was what her mother considered a difficult child. Her moods were unpredictable and when upset, she took a long time to calm down. Yuen never developed a regular sleeping and feeding schedule, making it difficult for her mother to coordinate her work and child care. Her adolescent years were equally challenging. Yuen had few friends and struggled with discipline problems at school. Now in her mid-thirties, she has assumed a leadership position in her work. Occasionally, she has to be reprimanded for her creative and sometimes radical ideas.

⬦ ⬦ ⬦

Sergej and Yuen clearly are very different people and showed very distinct character traits as children and as adults. Were they born with different personalities? Are these differences due to innate cultural patterns of personality? How much do cultural expectations about the course of one's life influence adult personality? We will address these and other questions in this chapter by examining issues of personality, self, and individual differences and their embeddedness in a cultural context.

✧ INFANCY AND TEMPERAMENT

Many of the childhood behaviors exhibited by Sergej and Yuen can be explained according to differences in **temperament,** or *a person's characteristic behavioral style or typical pattern of responding to events in the environment.* Individual differences in temperament can be observed in the earliest hours following birth. For example, while some newborns and infants are irritable and cry frequently, others appear to be good-natured and calm. During the first few months of life, some infants are extremely expressive and react to people and events by making sounds and waving their arms; others are less active, may hardly respond to their environment, and appear withdrawn and uninvolved. Frequently, the differences we see in temperament among infants tend to be characteristically consistent throughout individual lives. In fact, some researchers maintain that infant temperament reliably predicts adult personality (Buss & Plomin, 1984). The infant who is shy and anxious around strangers is more likely to be a shy adult than is an infant who curiously approaches strangers (Cheek, 1989). The potentially powerful relationship between infant temperament and adult personality has led many researchers to the conclusion that traits of temperament are, to a significant extent, inherited. They argue that environment and socialization can influence temperament only within the limits initially defined by heredity.

The concept of heritability of temperament has received support from careful studies of twins (identical and fraternal) reared together and apart (Plomin, DeFries, & McClearn, 1980; Rushton, Fulker, Neale, Nias, & Eysenck, 1986). These studies are based on the hypothesis that identical twins share 100 percent of their genes and therefore should be identical in their temperamental dispositions at birth. In contrast, fraternal twins, like other siblings, share only 50 percent of their genetic makeup and therefore should be less similar in their temperament. Studies such as these should be able to provide answers to such questions as the following: (1) Are identical twins more similar in their temperament than fraternal twins? (2) Are identical twins raised in different environments more similar in temperament than are fraternal twins reared together? and (3) Are fraternal twins (who share half of their genes) more similar to each other than are adopted siblings (who do not share any genes)?

If the answer to all of these questions is "yes," we can conclude that genetic disposition, rather than environment, is responsible for the differences in temperament observed among people. However, in order to accurately assess the results of twin studies, it is important to understand the way heritability is measured. In general, the degree of heritability is expressed by the **heritability quotient,** which is *an estimate of the percentage of the variability in a given trait that can be attributed to genetic differences.* For example, a heritability quotient of 50 percent for trait X means that approximately half of the variation, or individual difference, found in a sample is due to genetic differences among those subjects in the sample. The remaining half of the variation is assumed to be the result of complex environmental factors or, possibly, unexplained errors in measurement. With this in mind, let us consider some twin research and what it tells us about the inheritability of temperament.

In general, twin studies have produced moderately high heritability quotients. For example, a study of 13,000 sets of Swedish twins showed a heritability quotient of about 50 percent for the traits of extraversion and neuroticism (Floderus-Myrhed, Pedersen, & Rasmuson, 1980). Similarly, a study of 350 twins in Minnesota revealed that approximately 40 percent of variability among subjects in such traits as stress reaction (related to neuroticism and general anxiousness) and aggression could be attributed to genetics (Bouchard, Lykken, McGue, Segal, & Tellegen, 1990).

While results like these suggest that certain temperamental traits are genetically transmitted, they also suggest that in specific instances other traits are heavily influenced by socialization within the family environment. After all, a heritability quotient of 40 to 50 percent also means that 50 to 60 percent of variation is due to environmental rather than genetic factors. The issue of environmental and genetic influences on temperament continues to be controversial, and researchers are not yet able to provide a definitive answer as to which plays the most significant role in determining differences in temperament. Most researchers recognize the existence of an intricate relationship between individual temperament and the larger sociocultural environment. In the next section we will discuss some theoretical perspectives that attempt to explain that relationship.

Temperament and the Developmental Niche

As we pointed out in Chapter 1, a child's developmental environment consists of four subsystems: (1) the microsystem, consisting of interactions between the child and her immediate environment (e.g., home or day-care center); (2) the mesosystem, made up of individual microsystems (e.g., family and preschool); (3) the exosystem, consisting of influential social settings (e.g., parents' place of work); and (4) the macrosystem, consisting of customs, values, and laws important to the child's culture. Together, these subsystems provide the individual child with her developmental niche, or unique combination of socialization experiences. Each of these subsystems is influenced by, and in turn influences, a child's individual temperament. A child's behavior will initiate a specific response from a caretaker in a particular setting (home or preschool). However, these responses differ from one environmental setting to another. For example, a mother's reaction to a child who exhibits irregular sleep and eating patterns differs from North America to East Africa. A North American mother typically pays more attention to an infant who is unpredictable in eating and sleeping patterns, and she arranges her schedule to take care of the child's needs. In contrast, Super and Harkness (1994) report that mothers in Kokwet, a small farming town in Kenya, interact more with children who operate on a regular daily schedule. Knowing when her baby will be awake and alert, the mother can more easily arrange her many other duties and activities. Kokwet infants who are less predictable in their daily patterns are more often left to the care of an older sister or another caretaker.

This example illustrates how a child's temperament influences the environment. At the same time, however, specific patterns of response exhibited by others in the child's environment may facilitate or inhibit particular behavioral styles on the part of the child, thus making the child-environment relationship a two-way interaction. A fussy child receives more attention from the primary caretaker in most Western cultures, thus potentially rewarding and facilitating the child's dependency on the caretaker. In non-Western cultures, dependency and emotional attachment to the mother are often less pronounced because mothers may not be available to respond with immediate emotional attention to fussy children.

Temperament and "Goodness of Fit"

Another theoretical explanation that contributes considerably to the understanding of how temperament, development, and culture relate to one another is that of **goodness of fit**—*the quality of the adaptation, or "match," between a child's temperament and the demands of his immediate environment.* This concept was introduced by Thomas and Chess (1977) in an elaborate longitudinal study of children's temperament that eventually included a wide range of environmental factors. The researchers began by interviewing and observing middle-class families of European background living in New York.

They were able to identify clusters of traits that characterized three different temperament types among infants: (1) the "easy" child, (2) the "difficult" child, and (3) the "slow-to-warm-up" child.

An **easy child** was *characterized by a good mood, regular sleeping and eating cycles, and general calmness.* Mothers considered these babies unproblematic and easy to raise. On the other hand, temperament traits of a **difficult child** included a *negative mood, slow adaptation to and withdrawal from new experiences and people, irregular sleep and feeding patterns, and high emotional intensity.* More-over, these "difficult" infants were found in later childhood to be less well adjusted and prone to more behavioral problems. A **slow-to-warm-up child** generally *shows few intense reactions, positive or negative, and tends to be mild and low in activity level.* Thomas and Chess assert that it is not the individual child's temperament itself that is related to future maladjustment but rather the match or mismatch of the child's temperament with the environment that predicts problematic behavior. If "difficult" temperament disrupts family routine and leads to negative parental reactions, negative developmental outcome is likely.

A follow-up study by Korn and Gannon (1983) with Puerto Rican families in New York provided additional support for the goodness-of-fit concept

Differences in infant temperament can often be observed side-by-side within the same cultural context. (Gary Buss/FPG International)

but sounded a note of caution as well. For example, early "difficult" temperament did not predict poor adjustment and behavioral difficulties in later childhood. The researchers point out that in these families characteristics that were originally classified as "difficult" were not perceived as necessarily problematic and therefore did not disrupt family life or evoke negative parental reactions toward the child. These studies and others provide convincing evidence that culture is a critical determinant of the "goodness of fit" between an individual child (temperament) and her environment.

DeVries (1994) and DeVries and Sameroff (1984) further illustrate this concept by describing two individual cases encountered in the study of infants from different parts of Kenya. The case of Hamadi, a Digo boy, demonstrates how an "easy" temperament can lead to poor adjustment due to a mismatch between the boy's temperament and his environment. For example, as an infant, Hamadi was energetic and active and exhibited healthy approach tendencies. He was described as one of the most advanced infants in the entire study. However, after starting school, Hamadi began to withdraw, became shy, and showed clear signs of distress through acting-out behavior.

What caused this transition? The researchers interviewed Hamadi's parents and teachers and were told that Hamadi's temperament did not fit with the cultural expectations of how a Digo boy his age should behave. The efforts of teachers and parents to control his energetic temperament and discourage his curiosity, instead of rewarding his enthusiasm and challenging his intellect, led Hamadi to withdraw and become angry and fearful.

The second case reported by DeVries introduces Enkeri, a Masai boy born in the same year as Hamadi. According to traditional temperament measures, Enkeri scored as "difficult." He was the classic "fussy" child—very intense, persistent, overactive, irregular in his daily behavior patterns and not easily distracted or consolable. In a Western culture, these temperament traits would place Enkeri at risk for future adjustment problems. However, the behaviors that Western mothers dislike and describe as undesirable and difficult are valued highly in Masai society.

The Masai are an agricultural society and often have to struggle for survival in an extremely hostile environment. In times of drought, when herds of cattle and goats are destroyed, infant mortality is high because families cannot rely on the usual supply of milk. Under these kinds of conditions, infants who show "difficult" behavior tend to survive at a higher rate than infants who are quiet and undemanding. Why? Because infants who cry are fed and attended to, whereas those who don't are assumed to be content. Consequently, infants who cry a lot are fed more and are in better physical condition, which contributes to their survival.

Finally, Meijer, Super, and Harkness (1997) have recently attempted to further clarify the nature of "goodness of fit" and find a systematic relationship between maternal judgments of "difficult" and specific dimensions of child behavior. In a comparative study of mothers in Bloemenheim, Holland, and towns near Cambridge, Massachusetts, the researchers reported that parents in the two different cultural settings systematically interpreted the causes of difficult behavior differently. For example, while more American parents viewed difficulty as inherent in a child, more Dutch parents viewed it as a result of environmental factors. Clearly, the interaction of culture and individuality are different in these two ecological settings, and the resulting behavior and the interpretation of it are strongly influenced by the presence of different developmental niches.

Individual Temperament Within Different Cultural Contexts

Are there cross-cultural differences in temperament? A number of studies have attempted to answer this question. In this section, we will present two examples of cultural differences in temperament and explanations for these differences.

Children in Malaysia

Banks (1989) interviewed parents of forty infants and preschool children in a Malay village not far from the capital city of Kuala Lumpur. The interviews were based on translated versions of Carey's Infant Temperament Questionnaire (Carey, 1970) and Thomas and Chess's Parent and Teacher Questionnaire (Thomas & Chess, 1977), both originally used with children and parents in the United States. When Malay infants were compared with the infants in Carey's (1970) study, differences emerged on four temperament dimensions. Malay parents described their babies as less regular in their daily patterns, less adaptable, less eager to approach new experiences, and as having a lower threshold for responses to stimuli.

Banks argues that these differences can be explained by cultural variations in values and in childrearing practices. She points out that Malay babies have a lower threshold in responding to stimuli because Malay parents actively encourage their children to be aware of sensations such as pain, heat, and cold as well as sounds, lights, and scents, particularly if the sensations are uncomfortable. For example, Malay children immediately indicate when a diaper needs to be changed even if it means interruption of playtime. A delay in diaper changing on the part of the parents would be considered very neglectful by others.

The lower adaptability to new situations in Malay children, compared with American children, may also have its roots in the different beliefs and values of Malay parents. As pointed out earlier in this chapter, based on American values, a child who is slow to adapt to new situations is considered difficult and fussy because the expectation is that parents know what is best for their child and the child adapts to parents' wishes. In contrast, Malay culture expects that parents will consider all factors in a situation and, to a greater extent than in American culture, respect the child's wishes and decisions. Since Malay children rarely face situations in which they need to show much adaptability, their adaptability is generally lower.

Children in Japan

Shwalb, Shwalb, and Shoji (1994) took a different approach in identifying dimensions of infant temperament in Japan. Rather than simply translating existing temperament measures into Japanese, they developed the Japanese Temperament Questionnaire and asked 469 mothers to describe their infants' temperament when the children were one, three, and six months of age. They found that Japanese infant temperament could be described along nine different dimensions, which were fairly consistent during the first six months of life. These dimensions are as follows:

1. Easy/difficult of care
2. Intensity of emotions/reactions
3. Sociability/social responsiveness
4. Motoric activity
5. Stability/gentleness
6. Willfulness
7. Reactivity to change/cautiousness
8. Sensitivity to physical contact
9. Indulgence/dependency

Several of these dimensions appear closely related to concepts derived by some Western researchers. Most notable are the dimensions "easy/difficult of care," "intensity of emotions/reactions," and "reactivity to change/cautiousness," which resemble the dimensions reported in the original research of Thomas and Chess (1977). However, Shwalb, Shwalb, and Shoji caution that even though the broad dimensions seem to be very similar across cultures, the content of the statements that comprise the dimensions may differ considerably and are worthy of further cross-cultural study.

For a humorous view of how temperament or personality characteristics are sometimes associated with those living in different cultures, see Box 5.1.

BOX 5.1

 CULTURAL CHARACTER
OR STEREOTYPE?

Heaven
The cooks are French,
the mechanics are German,
the lovers are Italian,
the police are British,
and it's all organized by the Swiss.

Hell
The cooks are British
the mechanics are French,
the lovers are Swiss,
the police are German,
and it's all organized by the Italians.

Anyone who can see the humor in the above understands how personality traits are associated with different cultures. The question is "Are these characteristics based on real differences in the biological bases of temperament and personality, or are they the result of persistent and inaccurate stereotyping?" Are Italians really more impulsive and passionate? Are Swiss truly inhibited and rational?

There is a large body of research literature exploring national and cultural stereotypes (Katz & Braly, 1933; Peabody, 1985). In several of these studies, members of different national groups were asked to characterize one another. Not surprisingly, findings reveal a consensus as to which characteristics are perceived as typical of a particular national group. For example, French, British, Germans, and Russians show strong agreement with regard to their stereotype of North Americans. Likewise, North Americans also agree with the stereotype assigned to them (the only difference being that they see the attributes more positively). These results suggest that cultural character traits, as they are reflected in stereotypes, may not only be in the eye of the beholder but in some cases may represent actual differences between cultural groups.

This raises another question: "Are these characteristics based on different gene pools (as Freedman, 1974, suggests), or are they merely a reflection of different cultural values facilitating the development of some characteristics and not others, not unlike the cases illustrated by the Masai and Digo children discussed earlier in this chapter?"

◇ CHILDHOOD AND THE EMERGENCE OF THE SELF-CONCEPT

If you were asked to draw a picture of your mother, what would your picture look like? Would it show a single figure in the middle of the page? Would you attempt to portray the most typical features of your mother (e.g., her hairstyle, her clothes, her facial features)? Or would you show your mother at work, at home, with her friends, or with her family? The way we think about persons, as individual entities or in a social context, is influenced by the cultural understanding of what a person is and what characterizes her.

◇ CULTURAL VIEWS OF THE INDIVIDUAL

After decades of research, anthropologists, psychologists, and sociologists have determined that cultural views of the person frequently fall into one of two main categories: cultures with either a collectivist view or cultures with an individualistic view of the person. (You will recall our discussion of these dimensions in Chapter 2.) Not surprisingly, the collectivist/individualist distinction coincides with the distinction between Asian and Western cultures. How does the Asian/collectivist concept of the person differ from the Western/individualistic view? Perhaps this distinction can be best understood by using several of our themes (cross-cultural perspective, ecological systems approach, and the developmental niche) as a way of looking at life within a number of culturally diverse environments.

Individualism and Collectivism in a Balinese Village

Anthropologist Clifford Geertz (1973) spent years studying the lives of people in a small Balinese village. Among his many observations were those involving cultural customs related to the manner in which individuals describe and address another person. He found that the Balinese use six distinct labels to address another person and to identify him as a unique individual: (1) personal names, (2) birth-order names (first child, second child), (3) kinship terms (sister, aunt), (4) tekonyms, (5) status titles or cast names, and (6) public titles or occupational titles.

Personal names are rarely used among the Balinese. These and birth-order names are principally applied to children or adolescents. Kinship names are also used sparingly. Balinese most frequently use tekonyms when referring to or addressing each other. **Tekonyms** describe the relationship between two people, typically *the relationship between older and younger family members.* Geertz points out that as soon as the first child is born and named, the parents will be referred to as "mother-of" and "father-of" that particular child. These terms then take on the function of personal names. Only after the first grandchild is born will the parents be addressed as "grandmother-of" and "grandfather-of" a child. This approach to identifying individuals is quite different from practices found in Western cultures and denotes a very different understanding of the person, emphasizing the connectedness of the individual with the family—what Bronfenbrenner would view as part of the microsystem. On the other hand, individuals in Western cultures are designated by personal names, and their personhood is not usually derived from their relationship to others. The only comparable practice in Western culture may be the custom of the bride giving up her personal name and taking on her husband's family name. She may then be referred to as "Mrs. John Smith," creating a new identity that reflects her relationship to her husband. However, this practice is not as common as it once was, and married women are finding new ways of both retaining their premarriage identity and denoting their new relationship. Some women continue to be known by their maiden name, some place a hyphen between their maiden name and their husband's last name, and many find other ways to express their individuality.

Personhood in China, Japan, and the United States

Hsu (1985) has presented an interesting description and analysis of the concepts of personality and self in three very different cultures—China, Japan, and the United States. We chose this exemplary study to illustrate some of the existing cultural differences in conceiving of what defines a "person." We should note, however, that Hsu's study is not exhaustive, and thus we cannot draw conclusions about many other cultural concepts that exist. Hsu emphasizes the similarities between the two Asian cultures and their dissimilarity with North American culture. For example, the Asian concept of *jen* (Chinese for *"man,"* used also in the Japanese language) is defined by a person's place within her system of relationships (again reminiscent of the microsystem in the ecological systems approach). According to Hsu, personal wishes, motives, and feelings are only important to the individual in relation to their consequences for interpersonal relationships.

In China, the immediate family provides a place for the person and a framework for his sense of personhood. Similarly, in Japan an individual's personhood is also tied to one's relationship with others and not to oneself as an individual. However, in Japanese culture it is not exclusively kin members that provide a consistent system of social relationships. Japanese families are more willing to accept unrelated individuals into their family circle. Hsu concludes that in general, Japanese tend to form larger social networks than do Chinese because they have fewer ties to their kin and need to seek their social network outside the immediate kinship group.

In contrast, American culture subscribes to the belief that a person is defined by her innermost feelings, thoughts, and motives. The individual's behavior as it relates to others is only an expression of these personal attributes. Personal boundaries are generally defined by the physical body (i.e., a person ends and the environment begins at the outer layer of one's skin). Personhood, therefore, is not directly tied to relationships with others. People in the environment are not considered a consistent feature of the person and thus seem readily exchangeable. For example, Hsu points out that the parent-child relationship in Western cultures is more voluntary than it is in Asian cultures, particularly after an individual is recognized as an adult. An individual can decide whether or not she wants to continue a relationship.

This brief discussion of personhood raises an interesting question: "What impact do these different conceptions have on individuals' perceptions of themselves?" After all, when I speak about myself, I am speaking about a person. My understanding of what it means to be a person must also apply to the special case of myself as a person.

◇ CULTURAL VIEWS OF THE SELF AS A PERSON

Before discussing culture-specific aspects of the self, we should point out that there are considerable similarities among humans in terms of the development of their sense of self. For example, psychologists generally agree that in many cultures individuals develop an understanding of themselves as distinct and separate from others. In addition, some developmental researchers argue that the sense of oneself as distinct from others develops within the first year of life (Mahler & Pine, 1975).

These processes help to lay the foundation for development of the **self-concept**—*the perception of oneself as a person with desires, preferences, attributes, and abilities.* The unique structure and content of the self-concept, as well as some of the psychological processes related to it, are largely influenced by one's developmental niche and the level of the ecological system (microsystem, mesosystem, exosystem, or macrosystem) in which one finds oneself at a particular time in the lifespan.

Culture-Specific Aspects of Self

As with the concept of the person, the concept of self differs, depending on the cultural context. Since the self can be seen as a special case of the concept "person," it is not surprising that cultural differences in self-concept parallel differences in the person concept. Those who write most frequently about the topic of self-concept tend to discuss cultural variations in relation to the dimension of individualism-collectivism.

Triandis (1989), who has written extensively about individualism-collectivism, suggests that culture-specific views of the self result from early exposure to differing values and beliefs about the person in general. For example, childrearing patterns in collectivist cultures tend to introduce and reinforce the welfare of the collective over the welfare of the individual. In contrast, parents in individualistic cultures teach their children that the individual's primary goal is independence and the establishment of a unique self. Based on these fundamentally different approaches it seems logical that collectivist and individualistic cultures should vary in how they view themselves. Some authors make a distinction between interdependent and independent selves (Markus & Kitayama, 1991; Gardiner & Mutter, 1994), whereas others look at Asian and Western conceptions of self (Page & Berkow, 1991; Spiro, 1993).

Figure 5.1 shows both the collectivist and the individualist conceptions of the person. The collectivistic/interdependent conception of self is defined by the individual's relationships with members of groups significant in that person's life. The larger circle of self touches each group, illustrating the situational flexibility of the self-concept: the self must change if relationships change. In contrast, the individualistic/independent self-concept remains relatively stable and consistent, because interrelations with others are not defining elements of one's identity. This is represented in the figure as a smaller circle that does not contact the groups that surround the person.

The Self in Buddhism

The Singhalese monk Walpola Rahula (1959), explaining the role of self in Theravada Buddhism, has written: "Buddhism stands unique in the history of human thought in denying the existence of such a Soul, Self, or Atman. According to the teaching of Buddha, the idea of the self is an imaginary, false belief which has no corresponding reality. . . . To this false view can be traced all the evil in the world" (p. 51).

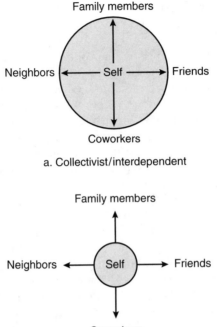

a. Collectivist/interdependent

b. Individualistic/independent

FIGURE 5.1 Collectivistic and Individualistic Conceptions of the Person

The self in Buddhism, which is more a psychological system than a religion, is thought of as an imaginary construct that limits the experience of total reality. Page and Berkow (1991) compare the sense of self to a "powerful belief" that results from the "desire to achieve an [illusory] sense of permanence within the ongoing flux of reality" (p. 89). The focus on "self" clouds a person's perception and experience of reality because one organizes experiences according to this limited belief (self) and is unaware of the reality beyond. Once this belief is abandoned and the self "ends," the perception and experience of reality are thought to be more comprehensive and unified. The loss of self, according to Buddhist teachings, is not the loss of identity. In fact, individuals continue to refer to themselves by name and are aware of themselves as individuals. Rather, the loss of self provides a new way of perceiving the world characterized by empathy, awareness, and deepened experience of reality (Beck, 1995).

These ideas are quite unlike what we find in Western thought, in which the self is viewed as a distinct and functional construct that psychologists have even succeeded in "assessing" and "measuring." Individuals are taught from an early age to become aware of, express, and satisfy their own wishes and needs. In fact, in Western societies, any significant or unusual change in the typically consistent and unitary entity called the self is considered pathological. When a person is "just not himself" or is "beside himself," he is frequently thought to suffer from disturbed perceptions, thinking, and behavior. Moreover, a person with multiple individual selves (or personalities) is considered severely mentally ill and highly dysfunctional.

Buddhist thinking exerts a very strong influence in many Asian cultures (Gardiner, 1995). How do Buddhist ideas regarding the self translate into the beliefs of the people in these cultures? Are conceptions of self the same in all Asian societies? Do individuals really deny the existence of self and strive to dissolve it in order to achieve a more complete understanding of reality?

Spiro (1993), while conducting field work in Burma, discovered that the cultural norm or ideal represents only one aspect of a culture's concept of self. Interviewing Burmese villagers, Spiro determined that the cultural ideal of the selfless person is not generally reflected in the personal beliefs of

Wearing his ceremonial robe, this Buddhist monk finds peacefulness in meditation. (Topham/The Image Works)

many people nor does this ideal fit the personal understanding of their spiritual aspirations. In short, at least in Burmese Buddhist society, the ideal of the selfless person does not make sense to many people. For example, the idea of a selfless person appears to conflict with other strongly held beliefs, such as those related to reincarnation or rebirth in a different physical body. According to Buddhist thinking, the form rebirth takes depends on an accumulation of actions and behaviors performed in previous lives. Several of Spiro's subjects expressed the following reservations: If there is no self and it is not me who is reborn, then why should I be concerned about my actions in my present life? After all, it is not me who would benefit from my virtues or suffer from my misdeeds in the next life. The inference, from these statements, is that contrary to this particular society's cultural ideal, a very strong sense of self exists among individuals. Yet the selfless being remains an ideal and a norm in this culture. The occasional conflict of cultural ideal with personal beliefs is integrated into the person's identity without causing overt emotional distress or other psychological discomfort. Those familiar with Asian thinking do not find this unusual. In fact, Asians have generally been much more pragmatic in their thinking than Westerners and quite capable of resolving what for others would appear to be serious contradictions in beliefs or behavior. For example, in Japan, couples are married according to Shinto traditions (which celebrate life) but perform their funerals according to Buddhist practices (which celebrate death). In contrast, Western families often are seriously divided by issues centering on religious differences among its members.

◇ CONTENT AND CONTEXT OF THE SELF-CONCEPT

Numerous comparative studies have revealed distinct cultural patterns in the way individuals conceptualize the self as well as in the content of the self-concept. In a cross-cultural study of self-concept in Japan and the United States, Cousins (1989) reported that subjects differed in the way they described themselves as individuals. Cousins used the Twenty Statements Test, which asks individuals to write twenty responses to the question "Who am I?" Results indicated that Americans used more psychological attributes, such as traits or dispositions, to describe themselves. In contrast, Japanese subjects frequently included the larger context when describing who they were. For example, Japanese subjects used more preferences and wishes, social categories, and activities in their self-descriptions.

Interestingly, the results from this study support several of the major themes we discussed in Chapter 1. For example, in terms of Bronfenbrenner's ecological systems approach, Americans can be said to view the self as part of the microsystem. The individual selects characteristics derived from early interactions between the child and the immediate environment, most notably the family. This conception reflects the individualistic nature of the American culture. The Japanese, on the other hand, select characteristics that emerge from interactions in social settings or institutions—that is, in the exosystem or even the macrosystem—where they have come into contact with the customs, values, and laws of their culture. Such behavior refelcts a collectivist society. This contrast can be seen in the examples of Sergej and Yuen in the opening vignettes of this chapter.

In another study using the same methodology (the Twenty Statement Test), Bochner (1994) reported similar results when comparing adults from Malaysia (a collectivist culture) with adults from Australia and Britain (individualist cultures). Interestingly, unlike Cousins's study cited above, Malaysians gave more responses referring to personal traits and dispositions than responses associated with social groups, and members of the two other cultures (Australia and Britain) gave more socially oriented responses. However, overall Bochner's cross-cultural comparison showed significantly fewer personal responses and significantly more group-related responses among Malaysians than in either the Australian or British samples.

In yet another study, Miller (1984) found similar differences in perceptions between Americans and Hindus in India. When adults in these two cultures were compared, Indians attributed their actions more to contextual factors, whereas Americans explained actions in terms of personal dispositions. Miller suggests that these differences are developmental in nature (another theme weaving through our topical discussions). For example, self-descriptions among young American and Hindu children (eight to eleven years of age) did not differ in any significant way; both groups referred more to context than to personal characteristics. This suggests that Americans, with age, may learn to focus more on the person than on the context when perceiving and evaluating behavior. This might be an interesting area for future research.

Additional evidence for the early influence of culture comes from a study conducted in the Netherlands (Van den Heuvel, Tellegen, & Koomen, 1992). Moroccan, Turkish, and Dutch children in grades six through eight were asked to describe five things about themselves, about one classmate who is like them, and about one classmate who is different from them. As hypothesized by the researchers, children from the two more collectivist cultures (Morocco and Turkey) used more social statements indicating group memberships, social activities, or clearly interpersonal traits (e.g., friendly toward others) when describing themselves or a similar classmate. Dutch children used significantly more psychological attributes, such as traits and personal preferences, in their description of themselves or a similar classmate. The authors conclude that the significant psychological differences found between individuals with an individualistic cultural background and those with a collectivistic background emerge at an early age and continue to develop across the lifespan.

Development of self-concept is greatly aided by language development and the words we use to describe ourselves. Pronouns such as *me, mine, you, us,* and *them* distinguish between self and others. Through the use of such words we learn to understand ourselves as unique and different from others (Sheriff & Cantril, 1947). In an early study, Mead (1934) suggested that personal names were at the center of self-concept development. Personal names help identify the self and distinguish oneself from others who are not referred to by that name. In many cultures in which names are carefully selected for their meaning, the person is thought to adopt characteristics associated with that name. These attributes become part of their self-concept (Olowu, 1990). How often have we met someone with the same name as someone else we know and compared the characteristics of the two individuals?

Self-Esteem

A recurring question in the study of self-concept is whether or not we can and should separate how we *think* about ourselves from how we *feel* about ourselves. Some contend that the content of the self-concept and its evaluation, which results in self-esteem, are virtually inseparable (Shavelson & Bolus, 1982). However, recent developments in self-concept research increasingly demonstrate that self-esteem may indeed be a distinct aspect of self-concept (Markus & Wurf, 1987). From a developmental perspective, Harter (1982) has shown that a global sense of self-esteem (perceived competence), distinguishable from the descriptive aspects of self, emerges around the age of eight.

Watkins and Dhawan (1989) argue that the distinction or lack of distinction between self-esteem and self-concept may be a cultural phenomenon. In several studies, these investigators examined aspects of the self-concept and self-esteem of children and adults from diverse cultural groups. As before, they found distinct differences between members of Western and Asian cultures. For example, in one study, Dhawan and Roseman (1988) reported that 62 percent of responses of American young adults were classified as self-evaluations, compared with 35 percent of responses among Indians of the same age group. In addition, most of the self-evaluations made by Western subjects were positive rather than negative.

These results, along with others, suggest that the distinction between self-concept and self-evaluation is more pronounced in Asian cultures, whereas both aspects of self are intertwined in Western cultures. As before, the explanation seems to lie in the individualistic or collectivistic orientation of the cultures involved. If an individual is independent and responsible for her success or failure, a focus on specific positive aspects of the self is an efficient protection against low self-esteem (Gardiner & Mutter, 1994). In contrast, in cultures in which individual success and enhancement are less important, personal attributes and accomplishments are not an immediate source of self-esteem and their value need not be emphasized.

As we noted previously, particularly in our discussion of the developmental niche and the ecological systems approach, childrearing practices and family environment are major contributors to cultural differences. These factors are also believed to be very influential in the development of personality and self-esteem, especially during the first years of life (Maccoby, 1980). Therefore, the fact that cultural differences in self-esteem are related to cultural differences in childrearing should not be surprising. Childrearing that emphasizes warmth and acceptance, together with consistent rules and achievement expectations, is clearly related to high self-esteem. For example, Olowu (1990) argues that many African children have higher self-esteem than children in Western countries because they enjoy the warmth and acceptance of an extended family. Such parental warmth can be provided by aunts and uncles as well as grandparents (Jegede & Bamgboye, 1981). Western children, on the other hand, frequently rely on one or two caretakers for their self-esteem needs.

Another example of the direct influence of the family atmosphere on self-esteem can be found in Jamaica. Phillips (1973) notes that it is common for Jamaican parents to separate and remarry several times. Children from previous marriages are expected to adapt to new environments and form relationships with new family members. While the family structures are very loose, children experience strict and authoritarian discipline from both parents and teachers. According to several researchers, this combination of unstable family dynamics and overly strict discipline results in a lack of self-esteem and self-worth in Jamaican children (Phillips, 1973; Smith & Reynolds, 1992).

Methodological Issues

Most research on the self is based on self-reports gained from interviews or questionnaires that represent variations on the question "How do you see yourself?" In contrast to objective information (age, household income, occupation), self-reports are subjective and cannot be tested for their accuracy. Therefore, uncertainties in the interpretation of self-reports cannot be resolved by consulting a neutral source or by gathering "objective" information (Omoluabi, 1990). In cross-cultural research, interpretations of self-reports present particular difficulty because they can be influenced by a variety of factors. Thus, those who use self-reports as a source need to consider several questions before interpreting their results.

First, is the methodology appropriate? For example, in a culture with a high rate of illiteracy, it would not make sense to conduct a study using a paper-and-pencil questionnaire. It is good to determine how much prior experience subjects have had with interview or questionnaire methodology. Researchers also need to be aware of cultural factors that might influence responses. For example, in cultures with very strict rules concerning interactions between members of the opposite sex, a female interviewer may receive very different responses to questions than might a male interviewer, or vice versa.

Second, is the wording of the questions appropriate? If another language is used, do questions have the same meaning after being translated? Frequently, questions cannot be directly translated from one language to another. Even if direct translation is possible, the meaning of a question needs to be carefully checked. While the words may appear to be the same in the second language, the context in which they are used may cause questions to differ in intensity or tone. For example, in McNabb's (1990) study of several Eskimo populations, the same response category had different meanings in different dialects. He reports that the Kotzebu Sound Eskimos used the item "not satisfied" to express strong and outright rejection, whereas in other dialects the same item merely represented dislike or disapproval.

Third, what are the cultural norms regarding self-disclosure and the revelation of personal information? Are there specific conventions regarding how personal opinions and inner states are expressed and communicated? In order to emphasize the importance of this point, McNabb (1990) reports his experience with Eskimo populations in Alaska, which place great value on self-control and restraint. The public expression of emotions or opinions is considered annoying or even a sign of psychological instability. As a result, McNabb found a high percentage of nonresponses overall and a low variability within responses. Subjects were very cautious in expressing their opinion and did not use extreme judgments such as "completely satisfied" or "not at all satisfied." Instead, they seemed to prefer less extreme options such as "mostly satisfied" or "somewhat satisfied."

◇ ADOLESCENCE: THRESHOLD TO THE ADULT WORLD

Adolescence is a particularly interesting period of transition in the lifespan. It begins with biological maturation and ends with society's acceptance of the young person as an adult. In many cultures a young person is considered an adult when she becomes sexually mature. A girl's first menarche is a celebrated event that signifies her transition to womanhood. She is now physically able to conceive and bear children and fulfill a variety of adult roles. In Western cultures, adolescents may be sexually mature but not considered emotionally mature enough to take on full adult status. Most Western societies have clear social markers that define the time at which a young person is considered mature enough to assume adult responsibilities (voting in elections) and adult privileges (driving a car or consuming alcohol). In contrast to many nonindustrialized cultures, adolescence generally lasts several years in most modern Western cultures. According to Kett (1977), adolescents in non-Western societies assume adult responsibilities much earlier because these societies cannot afford to let their young people be "nonproductive" and engage in idle "self-discovery" for an extended period of time.

Identity Formation

During the adolescent years, young people encounter one of the most important developmental tasks of their lives—the establishment of an individual identity. **Identity** is *a person's self-definition as a separate and distinct individual including behaviors, beliefs, and attitudes.* Simply stated, the individual is trying to answer the question "Who am I?" Finding the answer isn't always easy and involves many of those within one's various ecological systems, including family and friends, members of peer groups, and teachers. Some adolescents find the journey particularly difficult and have to deal with a variety of serious issues, including antisocial or delinquent behavior. These topics receive attention in the section that follows.

Psychologist Erik Erikson is generally credited with the first complete analysis of identity development (Erikson's stage theory is discussed in detail in Chapter 2; see Table 2.1). Furthermore, he proposed the integration of identity, social roles, and the broader cultural context (Erikson, 1963). In his cross-cultural research he collected evidence for the universal existence of identity development, yet the exact process by which individuals achieve an adult identity is influenced by specific contextual factors. The basic premise of identity development across cultures is that it is rooted in the physical and psychological developmental changes an individual experiences during the adolescent period. Achievement of physical and sexual maturity is regarded as a prerequisite for fulfilling adult tasks and roles (Marcia, 1980).

According to Erikson, finding one's identity depends to a large degree on the manner in which four earlier childhood issues or crises have been resolved. These issues center on developing *trust,* establishing *autonomy,* taking *initiative,* and developing a sense of *competency.* However, as the individual matures and develops socially and cognitively, these issues take on a different meaning, and previous solutions may no longer fit the adolescent's view of himself. For example, while autonomy for a three-year-old may mean exploring the neighborhood or village without telling parents, autonomy for an adolescent takes on larger meaning (e.g., making one's own decisions or choosing one's own lifestyle). If the four issues of trust, autonomy, initiative, and competence are successfully revised and integrated, the young person will be able to resolve the identity crisis and achieve a healthy adult identity (Erikson, 1968).

What makes this task of **identity formation** even more challenging is the fact that individuals must take into account not only their own view of themselves but also the views of others and of society (Erikson, 1968, p. 22). In other words, *identity is achieved through a complex process of judging oneself (1) as an individual, (2) in comparison with others' judgments, and (3) in comparison to social and cultural norms.* It is this last sociocultural aspect that is primarily responsible for cultural differences in identity formation among adolescents.

Empirical evidence of cross-cultural differences or similarities in identity formation is surprisingly scarce. Only a small number of studies have explicitly addressed adolescents' identity development in relation to their sociocultural environment (e.g., Stiles, de Silva, & Gibbons, 1996). Two studies shall serve as examples of this type of research. The first discusses the implications of living in a collective context on identity formation. Wiseman and Lieblich (1992) learned, through in-depth interviews in an Israeli kibbutz, that these Israeli adolescents were concerned with issues of autonomy. In particular, they were struggling to integrate their own individual identity with the norms of the collective, which emphasized conformity, communal rules and control, and close relationships. Asserting their own individuality and still fitting into the adult world of the collective were challenges for these adolescents not shared in exactly the same way by their counterparts growing up in more urban areas (Sharabany & Wiseman, 1993).

A second study examines identity conflict in two cultural groups within the same nation—Israeli Jews and Israeli Arabs. Tzuriel (1992) was interested in knowing whether adolescents exposed to multiple (and sometimes conflicting) sets of norms and expectations experience more identity conflict than adolescents with a less ambiguous environment. Israeli Arabs, who represent a relatively small minority in Israel, grow up experiencing elements of both their traditional culture and the Jewish majority culture. Would they have a more negative view of themselves or express more confusion regarding their identity? Among the six factors of identity examined in this study, Arabs scored higher on three and lower on the other three, showing no difference between the two groups in the total identity score. In particular, Arab youths expressed more self-confidence, a stronger sense of ideological and vocational commitment, and more genuineness. In contrast, Jewish adolescents reported more feelings of alienation and discontent with their appearance and behavior. However, they also recognized that others valued them and their abilities.

These findings suggest that Jewish adolescents experienced a greater struggle in their identity formation than did Arabs. Tzuriel speculates that the ambiguous environment, especially among Israeli Arabs, may actually facilitate identity exploration and self-awareness in relation to identity issues.

Thus, a seemingly ambiguous environment may have a more positive influence on identity formation than common sense would suggest. With the resolution of the identity conflict, most adolescents achieve an identity with which they are comfortable and adjust their behavior accordingly.

It has long been assumed, particularly in Western societies and most notably in the United States, that the transition to adulthood is a rather painful and psychologically challenging event (Hall, 1904). However, recent research shows that the experience of stress during adolescence varies cross-culturally (Offer, Ostrov, Howard, & Atkinson, 1988). Some writers suggest that adolescence is more stressful when individuals are confronted by a large number of choices, as they frequently are in Western cultures. In non-Western societies, in which roles are frequently more clearly defined and choices are more limited, the transition to adulthood appears to be much smoother. For example, if the firstborn child is expected to take over the family business and assume care of the aging parents, it is not necessary for him to explore a variety of social roles in order to find a suitable adult identity. The important decisions have already been made for him. In contrast, those societies that value independence offer adolescents numerous opportunities to explore a variety of different social roles, making the search for identity more difficult and of longer duration (see Box 5.2).

◇ ADULTHOOD AND AGING: A TIME OF STABILITY AND CHANGE

Given a secure identity by the early to mid-twenties, along with a set of relatively stable personality dispositions, one might assume that personality would not change much after that time. Indeed, some psychologists argue that most aspects of personality are set by the age of thirty (McCrae & Costa, 1984). This appears consistent with traits that are related to temperament, such as extraversion/introversion, proneness to anxiety, energy level, or risk taking. However, other aspects of personality are strongly influenced by changes that occur over the lifespan. Among these are self-concept, self-esteem, intellectual abilities, caring, and competence.

Social Clocks

Every individual experiences unique changes in his life such as moving to a different location or experiencing an illness, but some life transitions are culturally defined. All cultures have defined times at which certain life events are supposed to take place. For example, at some point in their lives individuals in most cultures are expected to find a partner, start a family, produce offspring, and retire. These age-related milestones and the times at which

BOX 5.2

 ## CULTURAL VARIATIONS IN BODY IMAGE AND SELF-CONCEPT

Body image refers to *one's concept of one's physical appearance.* Initially, the self-concept is characterized by such clearly noticeable physical characteristics as skin color, primary sex attributes, and body size and shape. Later, significant individuals in one's exosystem or macrosystem, such as parents, peers, or teachers, respond to physical appearance in particular ways. To a large extent, this social feedback influences how individuals see and feel about themselves. For example, many individuals with physical disabilities are sometimes considered weak and helpless and are even ridiculed. It is easy to understand how potentially harmful this could be to one's self-concept.

One's body image and the satisfaction with it result from comparisons with an implicit cultural ideal or standard. This ideal may vary considerably from one culture to another. For example, females in Western cultures frequently compare themselves with the "tall and thin" ideal considered desirable in these cultures. Such an ideal appears to be associated with high socioeconomic status, youth, health, and success (Anderson, Crawford, Nadeau, & Lindberg, 1989). In these cultures, young women are constantly exposed to images of slender (and often severely underweight) models (e.g., models used in advertising "Virginia Slims" cigarettes or Calvin Klein products to young women). Through these means, women are encouraged to attain a thin body shape in order to appear young and healthy. Only after accomplishing this image will they receive the admiration and praise that positively influences their view of themselves as desirable and attractive. Attitudes toward overweight women in Western cultures are generally negative, and obesity is associated with a negative self-concept.

This cultural ideal of thinness leads to distortions in body perception in young women in several Western countries. The underweight "ideal" is mistakenly perceived as a "normal" standard, with the result that women who fail to attain the norm tend to perceive themselves as "abnormally" overweight (Stroz & Greene, 1983).

Are these distortions in body image less pronounced in cultures with a more "realistic" body ideal? Jamaican culture promotes the image of the "curvy and plump" female as desirable and attractive (Smith & Cogswell, 1994). At the same time, Jamaica is a popular destination for tourists from Europe and North America, who bring with them their cultural values and beauty ideals. Smith and Cogswell (1994) wondered if the Jamaican body image ideal would be strong enough to counteract the Western body image ideal. In their study of young Jamaican women, they reported that only 13

BOX 5.2 CONTINUED

percent of all adolescents within normal weight range considered themselves overweight, compared with 30 percent of Australian and 43 percent of American female adolescents (Paxton et al., 1991; Desmond, Price, Gray, & O'Connell, 1986). This finding suggests that for Jamaican young women, the Jamaican ideal of the heavier woman dominates as a standard for young women's physical identity, at least as far as body shape and weight are concerned. Nonetheless, earlier studies of other aspects of physical appearance (Miller, 1975) suggest that Jamaican adolescents prefer Caucasian features and express dissatisfaction with their own skin tone, eye color, and hair texture, thus demonstrating that contact with Western culture has affected the Jamaican cultural definition of beauty. Although it was not explicitly examined in these studies, it is likely that young women who were dissatisfied with their body image also had a more negative overall attitude toward themselves.

In contrast to girls' ideal of thinness, boys in Western cultures strive for a large, muscular body (Jourard & Secord, 1955; MacKinnon, 1987). Austin, Champion, and Tzeng (1989) found strong evidence for the relation between perceived strength and activity and positive self-concept among adolescent boys from thirty different cultures.

In his study of Nigerian and British adolescents of both genders, Olowu (1983) noted that a heavier, well-built body was traditionally associated with wealth and prosperity among Yoruba adolescents in Nigeria. However, he also found that overall, Nigerian adolescents paid less attention to the enhancement of physical appearance than did British adolescents.

various cultures expect them to occur are referred to as the **social clock**— *the schedule by which individuals are presumed to complete the major tasks within the lifespan* (Neugarten, 1979).

It has been suggested that these markers affect the adult personality in several ways. First, people adjust more easily to transitions that occur according to the social clock than to transitions that are "not on time." The unexpected death of a child represents an "off-time" event, because parents are supposed to be survived by their children. However, the same event, while unexpected, is not considered off-time in societies with high infant mortality rates. Second, a new stage of life requires changes in behavior that frequently result in personality changes. For example, new parents develop their nurturing skills, become less independent, and take fewer risks than they once did. Similarly, on entering the work force, an individual's competence in a particular area tends to improve and is accompanied by a change in self-concept related to that competence. Finally, certain personality traits appear to be associated with adherence or nonadherence to the normative social clock. Helson and her colleagues (1984) examined 141 women over a period of several decades and found that those whose lives followed the cultural expectations of women at that time (e.g., prescribed role of wife and mother) displayed an increase in tolerance, responsibility, nurturance, and self-control but also a decrease in self-confidence and feelings of competence. Those women who chose a career path and departed from their prescribed roles as mothers and wives and who adhered to the "masculine occupational clock" adapted to this role by developing high levels of confidence, initiative, and intellectual independence. Finally, those who did not adhere to any normative social clock (feminine social clock or masculine occupational clock) appropriate for their cohort suffered from self-doubt and low self-esteem. These findings demonstrate that the women in Helson and others' study have defined a developmental niche for themselves. Women responded to the feminine social clock by developing attributes that would benefit them in their roles as wives and mothers. In contrast, women who chose a different niche, namely the masculine occupational clock, developed skills and abilities that would help them succeed in that environment. Social clocks are the result of cultural expectations, and thus social clocks in different cultures vary.

The Female Normative Social Clock in Samoa

Margaret Mead (1928), in her well-known book *Coming of Age in Samoa*, presents a description of important normative transitions in a Samoan woman's life and the changes that follow. Mead's work focused mainly on girls and young women but she also discusses the lives of adult women. Although her work has been criticized for its potential biases, it is still a rich source of information about the lives of women in Samoa (Freeman, 1983). Before puberty, girls are assigned light household chores, and their primary role consists of caring for younger children. With the onset of adolescence, around the age of twelve or thirteen, girls are expected to assume more demanding tasks and responsibilities almost equal to those of adult women. Adolescence also is the time of first sexual explorations and experiences. A young Samoan woman is expected to be married by the time she is twenty-two years old. Although marriage is an important event, not much changes in a woman's life. She may move into the house of her husband's family, but her status and her tasks do not differ markedly from those of unmarried women her age.

A much more important transition is the first pregnancy and the birth of the first child. During pregnancy, a woman's life is limited by a number of rules. For health reasons, she is discouraged from doing work that is too physical or from exposing herself to the cold or the heat. At the same time, there are many social taboos for pregnant women. For example, they are prohibited from doing anything alone. This is based on the belief that most activities that are considered "wrong" are committed when one is alone. Any wrongdoing by the mother may hurt the unborn child; therefore, the mother is expected to be around others at all times. With the birth of a child the woman and her family gain status in the community, and the birth is a celebrated event. The arrival of other children is taken for granted and does not represent a significant life event. After this, women settle into their lives without having to fulfill any other specific social expectation. Some may become more influential in the political and social organizations of their village by virtue of the rank of their family, but their participation is a voluntary choice rather than a normative expectation.

Women who do not adhere to this social clock, who are not married, or who do not have children later in life are looked down on. Nevertheless, they usually enjoy some status in the community because they have developed valuable skills and knowledge that compensate for their lack of children. Figure 5.2 directly compares the normative expectations of Samoan women in the earlier part of this century and North American women in the latter part of this century.

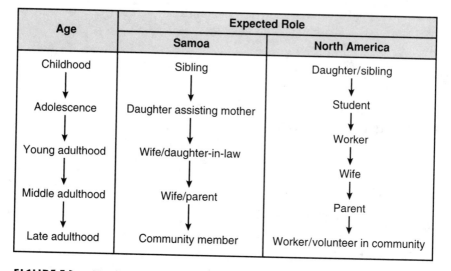

Age	Expected Role	
	Samoa	North America
Childhood	Sibling	Daughter/sibling
↓	↓	↓
Adolescence	Daughter assisting mother	Student
↓	↓	↓
		Worker
Young adulthood	Wife/daughter-in-law	↓
↓	↓	Wife
Middle adulthood	Wife/parent	↓
↓	↓	Parent
Late adulthood	Community member	↓
		Worker/volunteer in community

FIGURE 5.2 Normative Social Clocks of Samoan Women and North American Women

Source: Adapted from *Coming of Age in Samoa* by M. Mead, 1973 [1928], New York: American Museum of Natural History; and "Personality Patterns of Adherence and Nonadherence to the Social Clock" by R. Helson, V. Mitchell, and G. Moane, 1984, *Journal of Personality and Social Psychology, 46,* pp. 1079–1096.

Life Themes

Specific periods in the lifespan are often characterized by certain life themes. **Life themes** are *general issues or concerns that provide a structure according to which one organizes events and perceptions of self and others* (Csikszentmihalyi & Beattie, 1979; Kaufman, 1986). The study of individual life themes may also reveal the cultural influences that guide individuals' behavior throughout the lifespan. This is demonstrated by the work of Mokuau and Browne (1994), who interviewed six native Hawaiian *kapuna* (female elders) and asked them simply to "tell their story." From the interview materials, the researchers systematically extracted three themes that were particularly important in the cultural lives of these women. First, the interviews revealed a continuing emphasis on their relationships with other people, particularly with other family members. Second, the women spoke of their close relationship with nature, making statements about the beauty of the land and its value as a food source. They also acknowledged their appreciation and respect for natural phenomena and emphasized that exploitation of nature can be dangerous. Finally, spiritual and religious beliefs played an integral part in these *kapunas'* lives. They subscribed to a unique combination of their own indigenous spiritual beliefs and beliefs adopted from Christian traditions. For example, although the traditional Hawaiian belief in good or bad spirits and their supernatural powers is very much a part of everyday thinking, the *kapuna* often referred in the interviews to Christian beliefs (e.g., "God made me" and "pray and ask the Lord's help").

◇ SUMMARY

This chapter discussed the development of individual, self, and personality across cultures and in specific cultural contexts. It was pointed out that some aspects of personality and behavior are clearly influenced by innate temperamental dispositions. The ways in which individual temperament is expressed and what is considered acceptable were shown to be largely dependent on cultural values and practices. Discussion also focused on cultural variations in the concept of person and self and their relationship to the early development of self-concept. While adolescents in most cultures experience the need to establish an identity, the manner in which they accomplish this and the specific issues and behaviors related to it show great cultural variation. Finally, examples from a variety of environmental settings illustrated how cultural expectations influence the development of life themes and patterns that continue to affect development in adulthood and beyond.

◇ THINGS TO DO
AND THINK ABOUT

1. Write the question "Who am I?" at the top of a blank piece of paper. Reflect about yourself for a moment, then write down twenty statements, each beginning with "I am . . ." that describe yourself. Review your statements and sort them according to content. Which statements describe unique personal attributes, such as physical appearance or personality traits? Which statements reflect relationships with others, such as family roles and associations with peers? Which statements reflect memberships in groups or organizations, such as nationality, religion, or scouting?

    After reviewing these statements, assess how "independent" or "interdependent" your self-concept is. Based on the discussion of culture and self in this chapter, which statements would you most likely not find in the self-descriptions of people of different cultural backgrounds? Can you think of statements you might find instead?

2. In the popular television series *Star Trek—The Next Generation,* the crew of the starship "Enterprise" repeatedly encounters an alien civilization called the "Borg." Although this society appears to consist of individual entities, half human, half machine in their appearance, the Borg society is a true collective. All individuals share the same pool of knowledge, thoughts, and experiences. If an individual Borg experiences a new situation, the information is immediately distributed to all other "individuals" in the society. In this way, every member of the culture shares the experience of the one Borg as if it were their own experience. An individual Borg does not think as an individual or have a sense of individual self. It only thinks of itself in relation to the larger collective. It does not have a personal name and refers to itself as "we" rather than "I."

    Imagine you are a cross-cultural scientist on the starship "Enterprise" and your task is to explore the psychological and social dynamics of this alien society. In particular, you are interested in the issue of self and identity, since this seems to be a striking attribute of this particular culture. You are planning to examine how the Borg self differs from the human self. How would you go about researching this question? Which methods would you use? What difficulties might you anticipate in conducting your research? How do you think your knowledge about cultural differences on Earth could aid you in this research? What results do you expect to find?

3. Arrange a visit with your parents, grandparents, or an older acquaintance who would be willing to tell you about their lives. Ask them to tell you about important events that they feel changed their lives. Ask them how old they were at the time and how their life changed as a result of each event. Ask them what was expected of them at certain ages (17, 21, 25, 30, 35, 45, 55, etc.). Plot out the person's life events and transitions and consider the following questions:
- How many of the important events were social clock events?
- How many were uniquely individual events (e.g., accidents, personal achievements)?
- Did their lives follow the normative social clock, or were they generally unaffected by cultural expectations?
- Did the person follow the social clock expected of someone of their gender or their culture, or did this person choose a different reference group?

◇ FURTHER READINGS

B. Blauner. (1989). *Black Lives, White Lives.* Berkeley: University of California Press.
An interesting study of cultural and ethnic differences within the American culture.

Sigmund Freud. (1961). *Civilization and Its Discontents* (Vol. 21). London: Hogarth.
One of the most important writings on the interaction between personality and culture by one of the most creative and influential contributors to the field of psychology.

D. J. Levinson, C. M. Darrow, E. B. Klein, M. H. Levinson, and B. McKee. (1978). *The Seasons of a Man's Life.* New York: Knopf.
Presents a framework for defining and understanding phases in the life-span development of adult men. Represents a good opportunity to identify "ecological systems" that may contribute to aspects of development shared by men in American society.

Margaret Mead. (1973). *Coming of Age in Samoa.* New York: American Museum of Natural History.
The author's best-known book; compares the lives of Samoan adolescents with adolescents in Western cultures. The accuracy of the comparisons have been seriously challenged, causing anthropologists to give greater attention to multiple interpretation of findings gathered by field research. Nevertheless, a classic and worth reading.

CHAPTER SIX

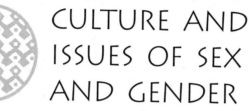

CULTURE AND ISSUES OF SEX AND GENDER

Jessica and Jarrat are middle-aged adult siblings who grew up in a small town in the midwestern United States. As young children, they lived in a single-parent home with their mother, who worked as a secretary. Growing up, they experienced typical gender socialization for that time. Jessica, dressed in her favorite frilly pink party dress, enjoyed playing with her dolls and stuffed animals in her room, while Jarrat, in his sturdy jeans and T-shirt, played rough-and-tumble games outside. During their school years, Jarrat was encouraged to study science and went on to become an engineer. Jessica, who did well in school, hoped to have a career too but was raised to see her future role as a wife and mother. Both Jessica and Jarrat married and had children. One of Jessica's daughters is an astronaut in the American space program and another is a surgeon. Now divorced, Jessica takes care of her elderly mother since Jarrat lives and works in Germany.

◇ ◇ ◇

Harin and Tippa, also in their middle adult years, grew up in rural Thailand with their parents, two brothers, two sisters, and various aunts, uncles, and cousins. As children, they played the same games, took care of their younger siblings, and worked in the rice fields. They both went to the same schools and enjoyed studying together. After graduation from high school, they went to Chulalongkorn University in Bangkok, where Harin studied to be an elementary school teacher and Tippa became an electrical engineer. Both are married today with families of their own.

◇ ◇ ◇

These two pairs of mixed-sex siblings experienced childhood in very different ways. Harin and Tippa shared most of their activities and interests; Jessica and Jarrat grew up in two different worlds. Did Jessica and Jarrat deliberately "choose" different interests or were they "assigned" those interests? Was Harin and Tippa's experience really that similar? Did the upbringing experienced by these children influence the choices and preferences all four made in later life? How did culture contribute to these differences in upbringing?

Many introductory textbooks in psychology carefully differentiate the concepts "sex" and "gender." **Sex** is usually defined as *biological aspects of femaleness and maleness;* **gender,** as *acquired behavioral and psychological aspects of being a woman or a man* (Ashmore, 1990). This nature-nurture distinction provides the illusion of two nearly independent sources of behavior. However, on further review, it becomes clear that the two are not as independent as these definitions might suggest. Rather, it is essential to understand that the relationship between biological sex characteristics and gendered social behavior is much more complex.

West and Zimmerman (1987) argue that a person's sex is initially determined by applying culturally agreed-on biological criteria, such as external genitalia at birth. Depending on the evaluation of these criteria, the person is placed in one of two sex categories: female or male. This sex category represents the person's biological sex, even though the biological characteristics greatly vary from person to person and sometimes the classification as male or female is ambiguous at best.

A person's sex is determined by four different criteria: chromosomes, hormones, gonads, and external genitalia. In most cases, all variables correspond with each other and with the designation of female or male. Yet, there are exceptions. For example, one female may carry the XY chromosomes usually occurring in males yet show all "female" physical characteristics. In contrast, a female with the "normal" XX chromosomes may have a naturally occurring hormonal imbalance (e.g., adrenal hyperplasia) that causes her to develop muscle patterns and genitals similar to those of males (Nelson, 1994). In short, culture creates an artificial dichotomy of two mutually exclusive groups, "female" and "male," while disregarding the wide range and variety of biological variables. Once the nurse or doctor announces "It's a girl" or "It's a boy," the first major decision in a child's life has been made for her or him.

A great deal of social behavior is determined by one's assigned membership in one or another such exclusive category. For example, there are distinctly different sets of normative expectations associated with each category that guide the interaction between people in most situations. West and Zimmerman (1987) even suggest that gendered behavior is a necessary social requirement, since it helps identify a person as a member of one or the other gender, even if biological characteristics are ambiguous or lacking. For example, some traditional Islamic societies demand that women not reveal their faces to strange men. In this case, a woman needs to know if a stranger who approaches her is a woman or a man so that she may dress accordingly. Identifying another person as male or female provides us with one of the most basic social clues as to how this person is likely to behave toward us and how we are expected to behave toward that person. In this chapter, we will discuss the developmental challenges involved in growing up female or male in different cultures.

Before we reflect on the role gender plays in every stage of a person's life, we will introduce some of the issues and theoretical perspectives relevant in gender research today.

◇ DIFFERENCES BETWEEN THE GENDERS

Decades of psychological and anthropological research have produced evidence showing that differences between women and men appear in many known cultures. How many consistent differences exist and to what degree they can be rendered truly "universal" is the subject of much discussion in the field. We selected two aspects of behavior that are likely to vary along gender lines—activity level and aggression—in order to illustrate the relationship between gender and social behavior. Female children typically engage in limited behavior involving fine-motor movements, whereas male children engage in more exploratory behavior involving gross-motor movements (Rogoff, 1990). At the same time, young boys are encouraged more frequently by adults to engage in high-activity behaviors. Rogoff (1990) further argues that boys' behavior is more often noticed by adults and therefore attracts more attention and encouragement than does the behavior of quietly playing girls. Consider, for example, Brazilian children living near Rio de Janeiro. Girls might huddle together in a small group, stringing seashells to be worn as necklaces, while boys chase an escaped chicken through the village.

Cross-cultural research reports a convincing contrast between male aggressiveness/dominance and female nurturance/submissiveness (Block, 1983; Khan & Cataio, 1984; Maccoby, 1990; for a discussion of female aggression, see Bjorqvist & Niemela, 1992). For example, girls tend to engage more in interactive games involving cooperation and large amounts of verbal interaction, whereas boys tend to take part in more physical activities, often

Gender-specific play in childhood is often characterized by competition and aggression among boys. (Suzanne Szasz/ Photo Researchers)

testing their strength or their skills in competitive games. Jessica and Jarrat, in our vignette at the beginning of the chapter, experienced these differences in their childhood play. In this connection, Salamone (1983) has described differences in the games played by girls and boys in Yauri, Nigeria. A popular girls' game is called *sunana bojo ne* (My name is Bojo). Ten to fifteen players, holding hands, form a half circle and move clockwise while singing and dancing. They dance around one girl in the middle, who serves as the song leader. Eventually, and without warning, this girl falls backward into the circle, trusting her playmates to catch her. Girls will take turns playing the role of the lead singer. In contrast, a popular boys' game is ring toss, where each boy tosses a rubber ring at a bottle or a stick with the goal being to get the ring to land around the neck of the bottle. This game involves a great deal of competition, since none of the players wants to be the last one to score and be teased by his playmates as the loser. These gender-specific games illustrate the interaction of individuals within their specific developmental niche. The traditional games played by girls reinforce behaviors considered desirable for females in that particular culture. By playing *sunana bojo ne* girls practice co-operation and interpersonal skills rather than focusing on their physical and motor skills. The reverse is true for the boys. At the same time, girls would probably not think of playing ring toss, because they would be teased by the boys for their lack of skill.

Nonetheless, not all games are gender segregated, as illustrated by Harin and Tippa, the Thai siblings in the chapter vignette. However, even in mixed-gender groups we find evidence showing gender differences in interpersonal behavior. Based on elaborate observations of same-gender and mixed-gender play groups, Maccoby (1990) observed that girls' groups have a more egalitarian structure and girls are more likely to make polite suggestions to each other. Boys, on the other hand, interact with each other by making demands or issuing direct orders. In mixed-gender groups, the interactional style common to girls was ineffective when dominant boys were involved. As a result, girls dropped out of the game, reinforcing male dominant behavior in the context of this particular game. Unfortunately, there are few cross-cultural studies of this type and therefore little concrete evidence to support the universality of this pattern of behavior. However, Weisfeld, Weisfeld, and Callaghan (1982) did find interaction patterns similar to those observed by Maccoby in their studies of African-American children in Chicago and Hopi Indian children in Arizona. In mixed-gender competition (dodgeball), girls in both groups tended to be noncompetitive and passive and ultimately lost interest in the game.

◇ THEORETICAL PERSPECTIVES ON GENDER DIFFERENCES

Biological Perspectives

It is generally accepted that females and males of any species exhibit distinct biological and physiological differences. These include differences in chromosomes, hormonal production, and reproductive capabilities. It is unclear, however, how directly connected these physiological differences may be to differences in social behavior. For example, there is evidence that testosterone level is related to aggressiveness (Wilson & Herrnstein, 1985). Since men are known to have higher average levels of testosterone than do women, they should be expected to exhibit more aggressive behavior than do women. However, it is entirely possible that in cultures that encourage aggressive behavior in both genders, women will be more aggressive than men in cultures that discourage aggressive behaviors in general. Consequently, we can only assume that physiological makeup may predispose women and men toward different behaviors (Lee & Daly, 1987).

The extent to which these behaviors are actually expressed depends in large part on environmental expectations and restrictions. Viewed from Bronfenbrenner's ecological systems approach, the degree to which a child's behavior becomes gender appropriate in a given society depends heavily on the ecological system surrounding that particular child. The macrosystem (or larger outer ring) provides general customs and values regarding gender. For example, it is customary in most cultures for men and women to wear clothes and hairstyles appropriate for their respective gender. At the microsystem level, girls and boys may be assigned different roles in the family depending on their gender and may be given different rights and responsibilities (e.g., taking care of siblings, helping with household chores, or working in the garden).

Evolutionary Perspectives

Proponents of the evolutionary perspective suggest that a number of gender differences may be explained by an organism's motivation to pass on genes by producing offspring (Buss, 1994a, b; Low, 1989). The particular way in which this is accomplished appears to differ among men and women. Women, who have the ability to produce a limited number of children over a lifetime, put their energy into creating an environment that ensures the survival of a maximum number of children. Such an environment requires food, drink, shelter, and protection from enemies. To accomplish this, a large number of a woman's activities are directed toward the family and involve food preparation, home maintenance, and creation of a protective network of other people who will assist in larger tasks and also help protect against enemies (a part of the microsystem). At the same time, women need to let suitable mates know that they are interested in having children. In other words, the woman creates a developmental niche (or a microsystem) that will be most favorable for the development of her children.

In contrast, men can produce an almost unlimited number of children, given the availability of women. According to the evolutionary perspective, men strive to produce as many children as possible because the more they have, the more will be likely to survive. In order to do this, they have to compete with other men. Under these circumstances, much of their energy is devoted to competing with other men for available women and the focus is on physical strength and aggressiveness.

Despite these different reproductive strategies, women and men have a common goal; this ensures that their children have the greatest possible chance of survival. According to Darwin's "survival of the fittest" doctrine, children have a greater chance of survival if both parents have healthy genes. Consequently, men and women can increase the chances of their children's survival if they mate with a healthy partner. Therefore, the goal is for both men and women to enhance those characteristics that are evolutionarily attractive in order to be chosen as mates. According to this perspective, men tend to exhibit behavior that conveys strength and sexual prowess, such as engaging in challenging sports and games or displaying symbols of wealth and status (ranging from a Mercedes Benz in Europe to camels in Egypt) (Buss, 1988). Women, on the other hand, tend to reinforce symbols of youthfulness and health, such as smooth skin, healthy teeth and hair, and a strong body, to communicate that they are young and fit enough to bear many children (Buss, 1988). Women in most cultures draw attention to these characteristics by artificially enhancing these attributes. If one accepts this evolutionary view of reproductive strategies, it may help explain those social behaviors that are considered specific to women and men in most societies. Regardless of the universality of reproductive strategies, culture-specific ecological systems determine the manner in which these behaviors are expressed. For example, women in one society may strengthen their youthful appearance by wearing clothes that reveal the leanness of their bodies and smoothness of their skin. This approach may not be appropriate in cultures in environments with harsher climates; in these cases women may color their hair or wear it in elaborate styles, since long and healthy hair may be viewed as a symbol of youth.

Socialization and Learning Perspectives

Beginning at birth, individuals are socialized into their particular culture and taught the values, beliefs, and behaviors that will permit them to successfully function within it (see Chapter 2). From an early age, as part of the socialization process, children learn to conform to the roles that culture considers consistent with their biological sex. In general, girls are rewarded and praised for exhibiting behavior considered desirable for a woman in that culture and discouraged from showing undesirable, or gender-inappropriate, behavior. In turn, boys are rewarded for male behavior and ridiculed if they exhibit behaviors reserved for girls or women.

By no means are "feminine" and "masculine" behaviors consistent across cultures. Occasionally, gender-specific norms may interact with cultural norms and modify gender roles. For example, while modesty and humility are viewed in China as culturally important values for all individuals, in other cultures these traits are more desirable, and more expected, in women than in men. For example, Chinese women have been found to be more self-effacing, modest, and less likely to take personal credit for accomplishments than are men, even though the cultural norm requires modesty from both genders (Crittenden, 1991). However, other sources suggest that these values, as well as gender socialization, are undergoing significant change in China as well as in other Asian countries (Ruan, 1991; Smith, 1992; Yi, 1993).

In addition to direct reinforcement and punishment, children in most cultures also observe same-sex adult role models and imitate the gender-appropriate behavior exhibited by these models. These behaviors are further reinforced and become internalized as attributes of gender-appropriate behavior patterns.

Another value differentially socialized by one's culture in terms of gender is related to work or career. For example, based on findings from a study of work-related values in forty countries, Hofstede (1980) suggests that some countries subscribe to work-related values that are more representative of a feminine style, whereas other countries promote more masculine values as part of the structure and experience in the work and business world. According to Hofstede, feminine work values are generally associated with belief in group decisions, service-oriented managers, an emphasis on quality of private life and human contact, lower job stress, and gender equality in the workplace. The five countries he found that most preferred a "feminine" approach to work were Sweden, Norway, the Netherlands, Denmark, and Finland. Countries that considered "masculine" work-related values most effective were Japan, Austria, Venezuela, Italy, and Switzerland. In these latter countries, the workplace is characterized by strong managers who make independent decisions and operate in a highly competitive atmosphere. In general, work is more central to people's lives, and achievement is defined in terms of recognition and wealth. Power and status differences between men and women are greater in these countries.

As we can see from these findings, work-related values and preferences will determine, at least in part, the general roles women and men are permitted to play in a culture. Hofstede's findings illustrate the influence of what Bronfenbrenner calls the exosystem. In "feminine" cultures such as Norway, which are characterized by equality and cooperation, women's work contributions are equally valued, and positions of power are held by both men and women. As a result, women are able to influence public policies that address women's concerns, such as child care and maternity leave, making it possible for them to successfully engage in a wider variety of roles. As Gibbons, Stiles, and their associates have demonstrated, these cultural "systems" in turn influence the gender socialization of children (Gibbons, Stiles, Perez-Prada, Shkodriani, & Medina, 1996).

In their studies, the researchers obtained drawings of the "ideal" woman and the "ideal" man from children and adolescents in several different countries (see Figure 6.1 a–d). Although they found a common tendency for the children to portray women as caring for children and the men as occupied in work roles outside the home, the researchers also found a number of specific cultural differences. For instance, adolescents were more likely to draw the ideal woman in a nontraditional role as businesswoman in cultures with "masculine" work values, and the ideal man in a nontraditional role as caretaker in "feminine" cultures. The latter was the case in Norway, where adolescents more often expect the "ideal" man to participate in housework (Stiles & Gibbons, 1995). The researchers explain this finding by pointing out that Norwegians hold very egalitarian beliefs about the roles and status of women and men in their society and convey these beliefs to their children. Ideals may not always reflect social reality. Loscocco and Kalleberg (1988) point out that in highly "masculine" cultures such as Japan, positions of power are largely held by men, and women have only limited opportunity to achieve status and power and tend to remain in subordinate positions, both in the workplace and in private life. However, there is evidence that the role of Japanese women is slowly changing, affecting the image of women throughout Asia (Smith, 1992).

In summary, these different perspectives all propose a slightly different explanation for why some behaviors seem to vary with gender. The biological perspective considers gendered behavior a result of underlying biological and physiological processes. The evolutionary perspective describes gendered behavior as the result of evolutionary processes. Gendered behaviors represent behaviors that have evolved as most adaptive, considering both biological attributes and environmental challenges. Finally, socialization and learning theories see gendered behaviors as the result of a person's individual learning history within a specific sociocultural context. None of these perspectives can explain the phenomenon of gender differences and how they originated. Nonetheless, they show clearly that gender, like many other concepts in this book cannot be viewed just from one perspective. Keep that in mind when we now turn our attention to how issues of sex and gender relate to development in each of the stages of the lifespan.

a. Drawing by fourteen-year-old girl from Mexico

b. Drawing by fifteen-year-old girl from the Netherlands

FIGURE 6.1 Drawings of Ideal Men and Women by Children of Various Cultures

Source: From material from J. L. Gibbons and D. A. Stiles. Reprinted by permission.

c. Drawing by thirteen-year-old boy from Guatemala

d. Drawing by eleven-year-old boy from Spain

FIGURE 6.1   Continued

◇ INFANCY AND CHILDHOOD

As we pointed out in Chapter 2, parents are the primary source of socialization in the lives of young children, and it is they who introduce the important knowledge, values, beliefs, and expected behaviors of the culture. One aspect of this concerns society's expectations regarding appropriate behavior for women and men, or gender-role stereotypes.

Gender Socialization

One of the most exhaustive investigations of gender stereotypes and attitudes was conducted by Williams and Best (1990), who found significant differences between male and female stereotypes in each of the twenty-five countries studied. In general, passivity, submissiveness, affiliation, and nurturance were seen as more typical in descriptions of women, whereas activity, dominance, achievement, and aggressiveness were more typical of men. In this study, Williams and Best also found fascinating evidence related to differences in the socialization of gender stereotypes among children five to eleven years of age. For example, across all age groups, children in most countries were more familiar with the male stereotype than with the female, suggesting that male stereotypes are more dominant in their lives and are learned earlier. Only in Brazil, Portugal, and Germany did five-year-old children clearly identify more items associated with the female stereotype. Overall, Williams and Best suggest that gender stereotypes are well established in children by the time they are eight years old. After that age, they serve as powerful "blueprints" for behaviors that are reinforced throughout life. Gender-role stereotypes not only promote overt behavior and prescribe types of clothing and social rituals but also influence the way in which men and women in a given society view themselves and others. According to these researchers, by the age of nine, children are already applying gender stereotypes in their descriptions of themselves. In the case of the midwestern siblings Jessica and Jarrat, both did well in school and both wanted a career. Yet, Jessica was raised according to the cultural stereotype of women as caretakers. She cared for her husband and two children, and even after her divorce she continues her role as the caretaker of her elderly mother.

Feminist scholars (Chodorow, 1978; Rhode, 1990) argue that these gender blueprints socialize women into lower-status roles and dependency due to the differential positions of power either group holds in society. Since, in most known societies, men tend to hold positions of power and to distribute available resources, they frequently have the opportunity to define social roles for both women and men (Johnson, 1988). They also have the potential to use resources and status as rewards. In order to preserve male social dominance, younger men are rewarded for conforming to the type of behavior that later enables them to achieve positions of power in society. Among these desirable behaviors are competitiveness, aggressiveness, and dominance. If men conform successfully and "play by the rules," they will gain power, status, and access to resources.

Women, on the other hand, are usually discouraged from exhibiting behaviors that are reserved for men. Instead, an entirely different set of normative behaviors is defined for them. In many cultures, they are expected to be submissive, nurturing, and weak. This feminine ideal is defined by men in order to preserve male privilege. The idea is that weak and submissive individuals are not likely to compete for resources and power (Johnson, 1988). By conforming to this feminine ideal, women become attractive and gain the recognition of powerful men. In turn, they may be rewarded by receiving indirect access to power and resources. Women who refuse to conform to the female gender role will be denied these resources and status. In this case, the differing social status and power of women and men represent an important part of the ecological system in which children grow up. Power differences between women and men are related to their differential treatment by society as well as gender differences in behavior.

Low (1989) examined the training of children in relation to different reproductive strategies prevalent in several cultures. In polygynous societies, in which it is customary for men to have multiple reproductive partners, the competition among men for women is very strong. In polygynous societies like those of sub-Saharan Africa, young boys are taught to be aggressive and competitive. In societies in which monogamy or even polyandry prevails, the number of reproductive partners is restricted, and men are not engaged in competition to the same extent. For example, the role and socialization of boys in Nyinba, Tibet, are quite different. They are taught cooperation and sharing rather than competition and aggressiveness, since they will one day share a common wife and children with one or more men (Levine, 1980). In addition, polyandrous societies grant women more control over resources and more independence from one particular man. Consequently, socialization of girls focuses more on independence and assertiveness and less on obedience and submissiveness.

Cultural Influences on Female and Male Socialization

In spite of the widespread similarities in gender-role expectations across cultures, there are distinct differences in how gender-related behaviors are transmitted to young girls and boys (Davenport & Yurich, 1991). Depending on availability of role models, displays of expected role behavior, or influence of socialization agents, children in different cultures experience their socialization differently. Examples from Russia and New Guinea will serve as illustrations of this point.

Socialization in Russia

Kerig, Alyoshina, and Volovich (1993) present a revealing description of male and female socialization and the conflicts that sometimes result from socialization practices running contrary to gender-role expectations. In Russian society, children are surrounded by female caretakers (mothers, teachers, doctors, day-care workers), whereas men are relatively little involved in family and household matters. This situation provides a young girl with a large number of female role models in different familial and professional roles. She is presented with an image of women that is versatile and active, and she has the opportunity to practice behavior appropriate for her gender, following that of her mother or other female role models. As a consequence, she is socialized into a very active and dominant role. This socialization pattern is continued in adolescence and adulthood.

Russian society expects women to be as involved in the work force as are men and to also take over most of the housework. This dual identity reinforces the image of the woman as active and dominant. However, the Russian stereotype expects women to be passive and obedient; active, masculine behaviors are viewed as highly undesirable. This apparent contradiction between stereotype and social norm provides a dilemma for Russian women unless they are very flexible in their behavior and adjust to the demands of different situations. At home and at work, they need to be able to be active and energetic, but in their social interactions with men they need to be feminine (i.e., passive and weak). In this way, Russian society has created an ecological system for women in which the values and norms representative of the microsystem (interactions with men in the immediate environment) are at odds with the values and norms of the exosystem (expected economic contribution and role as the head of household).

Russian boys, on the other hand, have few opportunities to practice active, dominant behavior. They are surrounded by female authority figures and caretakers involved in female activities. At the same time, Russian culture strongly disapproves of aggressiveness and emphasizes cooperation and caring. As a result of these social constraints, a young boy frequently withdraws and responds with passivity, which represents highly unmasculine behavior. Understandably, a young boy experiences a certain amount of confusion trying to define his gender identity in a context in which he is not able to observe or practice masculine behavior. Only later in adolescence do many young men compensate for their lack of practice of masculine behavior by becoming involved in motorcycle gangs or even engaging in antisocial

BOX 6.1

 ## VIOLENCE AGAINST WOMEN

Physical and sexual abuse of women exists and has existed in all societies. Cultures differ in the degree to which intergender violence falls within culturally accepted behavior. Physical violence toward women is accepted in Sambian culture and condoned as a part of male socialization. While generally viewed negatively in China, it is justified in certain instances (e.g., when resulting from alcohol use or as "punishment" of one's wife). In Russia, aggression against women is socially unacceptable but does occur frequently when men "act out" their masculinity as a reaction to their "demasculinizing" socialization.

In a cross-cultural examination of variations in the occurrence and meaning of rape, Rozee (1993) randomly selected thirty-five world societies and analyzed available data. She found that rape, defined as sexual contact against a woman's will, occurred in all of these societies. In 97 percent of these cultures, some form of rape existed that fell within social norms for acceptable behavior. These types of rape included marital rape, ceremonial rape, exchange rape (in which guests or friends are granted access to one's wife as a friendly gesture), or punitive rape (done to reprimand a woman). Not unlike other aspects of gender relations, violence against women, and rape in particular, is also directly related to social stratification. Rozee argues that "in every known society, women and men have different status, with males having authority over females. Rape legitimizes male authority, assures the right of sexual access to females, confirms entitlement, and demonstrates male dominance. Rape is prevalent precisely because it is so intimately tied to the meaning of gender in all societies, including our own" (p. 512).

activities such as vandalism, substance abuse, and physical and sexual abuse of women. (See Box 6.1 for more on violence against women.)

Socialization in New Guinea

In Sambia culture in Papua New Guinea, male aggression plays a salient role in the development of men and women over the lifespan (Herdt, 1986). For example, during childhood boys often are treated in aggressive ways by older men in order to teach them obedience and to serve as punishment for "unmanly" behavior. Young boys direct their aggression toward peers, younger siblings, and women in their families. At the same time, women and girls are discouraged from showing any aggressive behavior. Instead, they are expected to show the qualities of passivity and subordination.

After their first initiation ritual, which customarily consists of physical thrashing and ritualized nose bleeding, boys are separated from their families and go to live in the "men's house," where they are under the constant supervision of elders who also serve as powerful role models. Boys are encouraged to act aggressively toward their peers in competition to attain status; occasionally, aggressive behavior is even directed toward an elder for this same purpose. However, at this stage, boys are still the main target of aggressive treatment by their elders. Separation from boys also represents a change in the lives of girls. They are introduced to a more active role, namely taking responsibility for many household tasks. During this time, they are frequently victims of aggressive attacks by younger brothers or older boys who are attempting to establish their warrior status.

By the time of puberty, young men have learned to express their aggression toward women in their tribe as well as women of other tribes as evidence of their dominance as warriors and for the sake of aggression itself. Yet, elders still use nose bleeding and other aggressive rituals to instill a strong sense of obedience and discipline in young men, because the ultimate goal of male socialization is controlled aggressiveness. Impulsiveness and self-indulgent aggression are undesirable in warriors and tribal leaders and are occasionally punished with death. The only socially recognized expression of aggression by Sambia women lies in their acknowledged powers of sorcery. Since sorcery is greatly feared by men, female shamans are used in rituals in order to keep male aggressiveness in balance and provide peace within the village.

In conclusion, one cannot view the socialization of certain behaviors independently from the cultural context. Cultures define the basic values and ideals as well as the agents who teach the values and the settings in which they are taught. In turn, individuals growing up in this developmental niche will shape their environment by adding individual characteristics to that setting. As a consequence, the socialization experiences of youngsters in Russia and Papua New Guinea take very different paths.

Gender Relationships in Childhood

Apart from parents and caretakers, the role of peers in childhood socialization cannot be underestimated. In fact, Hartup (1983) points out that "in most cultures, the significance of peer relations as a socialization context is rivaled only by the family" (p. 103). Consequently, same-sex and mixed-sex peer groups provide an effective context for the observation and practice of gender-role behaviors. For example, it could be argued that early gender segregation indicates very large differences in normative expectations for women and men in that society; these differences need to be reinforced early. On the other hand, mixed-sex peer groups throughout childhood and the relative lack of differential treatment of the two genders may indicate greater equality between the genders in adulthood. The examples of our two pairs of siblings in the chapter vignettes may suggest that this is indeed the case. Harin and Tippa shared many of their childhood activities and did not experience much gender segregation. As adults, they have chosen professions that appear to contradict the stereotype associated with many occupations, suggesting greater flexibility of gender roles. However, a look at different cultures shows that the relationship between gender relations in childhood and adult gender-role behavior is not always as linear.

Overall, there is a large range of cultural variation in the extent to which children's playmates are of both genders or predominantly of the same gender (Whiting & Whiting, 1975). Gender relations in play groups range from completely segregated, to segregated for part of the time, to intergender relations. The makeup of play groups can be more or less dictated by cultural conventions that include the gender constellation of the groups.

As an example, there seems to be clear evidence that even though most activities are not gender segregated by definition in early childhood, children in North America prefer to interact with peers of their own gender (Maccoby, 1990). On the other hand, Harkness and Super (1985) report that rural Kenyan children are segregated by gender starting at about six years due to gender-specific duties expected from boys and girls. However, regardless of this culturally imposed segregation, the authors argue that there is evidence that children do not interact more with same-sex peers than with opposite-sex peers, even when more of them are present. According to an early description of Truk society in Oceania, children there associate with playmates of both sexes without distinction until the age of about six, when groups tend to become more structured according to gender (Gladwin & Sarason, 1953). Similarly, Sambia culture in Papua New Guinea (mentioned in the previous section) does not formally segregate girls and boys until they are six or seven years old. However, expectations for girls differ greatly in this mixed-gender setting. While boys are expected to assert their dominance toward younger siblings and female peers, girls are expected to be passive and endure the often hostile behavior expressed by boys without complaining. Beginning in middle childhood, girls and boys are strictly segregated and are taught gender-appropriate tasks and behaviors by their peers and their elders. (This mentoring or teaching of gender roles is a good example of children passing through Vygotsky's zone of proximal development, being guided by adults and capable peers; see the discussion in Chapter 4.) Gender relations are nearly taboo until marriage, when submissive women and aggressive men practice their now well-socialized behavior patterns in their relationships with each other (Herdt, 1986).

Another example of gender segregation in childhood and its consequences for gender relations later on is reported in an early study from Taiwan (Wolf, 1972). In childhood, relationships between girls and boys are characterized by competition, especially in schools that are coed but separate girls and boys within the classroom and during other activities. Interactions between girls and boys are characterized by heated exchanges in which it is the goal to insult the other group. Wolf reports that this hostile attitude is often carried into adulthood, during which time women and men are expected to cooperate in usually mixed-gender work settings. These examples demonstrate the different arrangements for gender interactions during childhood (and beyond) in various cultures. However, even when culturally determined arrangements are seemingly similar, there are variations in how gender relations develop. For example, even lacking cultural demands for gender segregation, younger children nonetheless may prefer to interact more with same-sex peers (Farver & Howes, 1988; Maccoby, 1990; Super & Harkness, 1994).

Harkness and Super (1985) explain these differences in terms of the developmental niche, in which children actively explore and define gender relations within the parameters set by cultural expectations. For example, the girls in Yauri (discussed in an earlier section) may enjoy the playful and musical interaction with other girls while playing "My name is Bojo" more than the teasing, competitive atmosphere boys thrive on during their ring toss game. Yet, there may be "androgynous" children who feel comfortable with either gender role and create their own developmental niche within the confines of their culture. These children may engage in activities with both genders or create suitable variations of existing gender-specific activities. For example, playing baseball may not be appropriate for a girl in the United States, but playing a variation of the game, such as softball, is entirely acceptable.

◇ ADOLESCENCE

Markers of Sexual Maturation

In addition to clear biological markers of sexual maturity, such as menarche and development of breasts in girls and growth of facial hair and change of voice in boys, there are distinct cultural markers that indicate a readiness among women and men to find a sexual partner. Biological and cultural markers may or may not coincide, depending on cultural norms. For example, Hindus consider a girl sexually mature with the onset of menstruation.

However, a sexually mature unmarried woman living in her father's house is considered unfortunate for all involved, and it is the duty of the father to marry off his daughter as soon as she reaches puberty or even before (Kumari, 1988).

The transition from adolescence to adulthood is often considered a highly spiritual event that is celebrated with elaborate initiation ceremonies. These ceremonies often involve a ritual change of hairstyle, clothing, tattoos, or even circumcision in order to make the newly gained status as adult visible to all. However, transition to adulthood is not always marked by one single event. Mayan culture, for example, considers young women and men sexually mature and allows them to find a mate when they begin to feel sexual desire (Bertrand, Ward, & Pauc, 1992). Parents or other members of the community do not get involved in the young person's decisions about who or when to marry. Bertrand and others (1992) report that this generally does not happen until the ages of sixteen to eighteen for women and twenty for men.

Sexual Activity and Cultural Taboos

Once young women and young men are considered sexually mature, they are prepared to experience their first initial sexual encounter. Across cultures, these experiences vary greatly in terms of how strictly they are guided by cultural norms and which forms they take. The expectation of chastity until marriage (particularly for women) is a norm among many cultures. Patriarchal societies and those based on traditional Catholic or Islamic values generally have very strict chastity norms. Consequently, young women have little or no sexual experience or instruction until they marry. In societies in which girls are allowed to explore their sexuality more or less freely, such as the Masai of Kenya or the Hopi Indians of North America, there are some legal or normative rules about the age at which a girl may become sexually active. Usually, the minimum age is no younger than thirteen or fourteen. Chastity norms rarely apply in the same way to young men. Instead, boys are frequently encouraged to engage in various types of activity in order to practice sexual behavior, satisfy their sexual desires, or express their virility and dominance. Young men's sexual experience is seen as preparation for a long-term relationship or marriage. It is the practice in some cultures for older women, frequently prostitutes or unmarried women in the community, to instruct adolescent boys in sexual matters (Ruan, 1991).

In some cultures, such as the indigenous societies of North and South America, communication about sexual matters is largely taboo and surrounded by myths, so that adolescents are left to explore their sexuality on their own. In their study of Mayan culture in Guatemala, Bertrand, Ward, and Pauc (1992) report that adolescents receive little education or information about sex. Young girls do not learn about menstruation until they experience menarche and also have few sources from which to learn about sexual matters. In contrast, boys learn about physical development in school, from friends, or even from television or movies. While these are informal sources of information, culturally sanctioned information about marriage is conveyed during a traditional religious ceremony. However, according to Bertrand, Ward, and Pauc's findings, this ceremony is considered primarily a ritual and does not provide practical advice and instruction regarding sexual relations.

In addition to prohibiting sexual intercourse before marriage, some societies have strict taboos about a variety of sexual activities. In China "the only sexual behavior which is acknowledged to be legally and morally permissive is heterosexual intercourse within a monogamous marriage. Every imaginable variation is explicitly proscribed. Thus, prostitution, polygamy, premarital and extramarital intercourse (including cohabitation), homosexuality, and variant sexual behaviors are illegal" (Ruan, 1991, p. 159). Traditional Hinduism prescribes a very specific definition of sexuality, and following that definition is absolutely essential. Any unnatural sexual activity, including extramarital relations or homosexuality, results in losing one's caste, mutilation, or even death (Kumari, 1988). It should be noted that these norms refer to the most strict followers of traditional Hindu teachings. Within modern India, as in many other cultures, the norms themselves, as well as the consequences for breaking them, vary greatly.

Young adolescents in many other cultures are permitted to explore and express their sexuality in a variety of ways. For example, among the Maya in Guatemala, it is common to freely choose one's sexual partner. Parents do not have much to say regarding the selection of a mate or the age of marriage. Nonetheless, Mayan adolescents respect cultural traditions and generally abstain from sexual contact before marriage. Their interactions are typically limited to talking, holding hands, kissing, and embracing.

In cultures in which premarital relations between women and men are not prohibited by cultural norms, they are considered an expression of love and affection. Yet, how love and affection are perceived and expressed is, again, subject to wide cultural variations. In a comparison of college students of four different ethnic backgrounds, Dion and Dion (1993) found that Asian subjects of both genders view love relationships more in terms of friendship and caring than do women and men of European or Anglo-Celtic backgrounds. The authors argue that this view of love is consistent with the notion of self and others in cultures that emphasize collectivism (see also Ting-Toomey, 1991).

◇ EARLY AND MIDDLE ADULTHOOD

Cultural Views of Marriage and Other Long-Term Relationships

The motivation for marriage or other forms of cohabitation is multifaceted and strongly influenced by cultural values, rules, or beliefs. Children generally benefit from a stable system of primary caretakers, commonly including, but not limited to, the biological parents. Thus, heterosexual long-term relationships are facilitated, sanctioned, and protected in most societies. The motivation for marriage is to provide a stable environment for children. In fact, the cultural definition of "family" influences the ecological system on many levels. For example, it shapes the microsystem, in that it ensures that two parents are present, and also regulates the macrosystem, because it views this form of "family" as an important element of societal structure.

In addition to providing a good environment for the children, individuals may commit themselves to long-term relationships for other reasons. For example, Hindu religion considers marriage to be sacred and a symbol of the marriage between the sun goddess Surya and the moon god Soma. Without a wife a man is considered spiritually incomplete (Kumari, 1988). The motivation for marriage is the striving for spiritual growth. Chinese cultural philosophy proposes that all objects and events are the outcome of two interacting principles—**yin,** the *negative, passive, weak, and female*, and **yang,** the *positive, active, strong, and male*. Harmonious interaction of the female and male principle ensures the continuation of reality as we know it. Thus, in Chinese culture, long-term relationships between women and men are a spiritual necessity for the survival of humankind (Ruan, 1991).

Marriage may also be a means to gain or maintain status in one's society. In most cultures, simply the fact of being married gives married men and women a higher status than their unmarried counterparts (Sonko, 1994; Kumari, 1988). Unmarried adults may be stigmatized and denied full adult status. In addition to social status, marriage may result in higher economic status. The pooling of resources of two families or a dowry paid by the family of the bride can mean considerable financial gain for both spouses. Finally, individuals may be motivated to share their lives out of a desire for love and companionship.

Polygamy, Polyandry, and Same-Sex Relationships

People form many different types of long-term relationships throughout the world. Some of the concepts introduced in this chapter will reappear in Chapter 8, relating to family structure. This overlap is intended, and we will focus the discussion in this chapter mainly on how different types of cohabitation may affect social relations between the genders and perceptions of women and men.

Polygamy is a form of marriage found on every continent. It describes *the practice of one man being married to several women at the same time*. An abundance of wives of different ages not only represents wealth and power but it also ensures the reproductive success of the man. Polygamy is common in many Islamic countries, African societies, and parts of Asia, but is also found in North America (Sonko, 1994; Levine 1980).

It is less common for *a woman to be married to several husbands at a time* (**polyandry**). This practice occurs in different forms. In some regions of Tibet and Nepal, brothers may share the same wife. However, in most cultures in which polyandry is accepted, husbands do not share blood relations. In general, polyandry is associated with greater economic power of women. Men in polyandrous societies have to be more considerate of women's needs in order to prevent them from switching their attention to more generous and caring husbands. Thus, wives can rely on generous shares of their husbands' wealth or income and may acquire considerable wealth themselves (Sangree, 1992). Only a few societies allow both women and men to be married to multiple spouses. Sangree (1992) points out that these polyandrous-polygynous societies have been found only in some regions in Western Africa.

A number of cultures permit sexual relations of some sort between individuals of the same sex. The very few studies that address the subject in a cultural context mainly focus on homosexual relationships between men. In reviewing research conducted in many different cultures, Crapo (1995) distinguishes two main forms of long-term homosexual relationships that are socially recognized: mentorship and pathecism. **Mentorship** *refers to relationships between partners of different ages and social status*. Sexual relations by no means occur in all mentorships and when they do take place are only one aspect of the relationship. More important, the older man frequently serves as a socializing agent for the younger man and introduces him to the fundamentals of warfare, politics, and religion. **Pathic** (not to be confused with pathetic!) **relationships** *involve partners of similar age and status who commit themselves to a long-term partnership* comparable to heterosexual marriage.

Since cross-cultural studies of homosexual relationships are limited in number, it is difficult to know with certainty what percentage of societies accept, tolerate, or even support same-sex relationships. Nonetheless, Bolton (1994) concludes from a review of anthropological studies that male homosexual relations are common in 41 to 64 percent of societies studied. By comparison, data on lesbian relationships are not as readily available, but Bolton argues that "societies which are tolerant of homosexuality are consistent in expressing that tolerance across age and gender categories" (p. 162).

The presence or absence of homosexual relationships in a given society once again illustrates the concept of the developmental niche—namely how certain behaviors may develop or be inhibited in response to cultural conditions. In societies that tolerate or even support relationships between people of the same sex, there will be a greater number of gay and lesbian relationships. In contrast, societies that strictly prohibit homosexual relations report fewer instances of homosexuality. These differences do not occur as a result of a higher or lower percentage of gays and lesbians in the population but as a result of differential opportunities to develop a certain preference and behavior within one's ecological surroundings and to express it as part of one's developmental niche.

Status and the Division of Labor Within the Family

Based on universal gender-role stereotypes and gender-role socialization, the adult roles of women and men are very different. Throughout history, and in almost all known societies, women take primary responsibility for childrearing and housework, while men are responsible for work outside the home. Industrialization and increasing economic pressures have brought about drastic changes that have affected the exclusive nature of this arrangement. Today, agricultural communities can no longer sustain all their families, and many men have to leave their villages and towns to find work in larger cities. As a result, traditional family structure is disrupted and along with it traditional gender roles. Women then find it necessary to seek work outside the home in order to fulfill some of the tasks the departed men leave behind. Also, in highly industrialized countries, technology has made housework much easier and less time consuming, but sometimes more expensive. In many cases, these additional financial needs can only be met by an additional income provided by the woman.

Surprisingly (or maybe not so surprising to some), increased participation of women in the work force has not led to a significant change in gender roles at home. Numerous studies show that men tend to participate more in housework when their spouse works outside the home (Coverman, 1985). However, even if both spouses are employed fulltime, childrearing and housework are still the main responsibility of the woman. Similar patterns are found in families in the United States, Switzerland, Indonesia, the Philippines, Taiwan, and South Korea (Charles & Hoepflinger, 1992; Sanchez, 1993).

Kerig, Alyoshina, and Volovich (1993) describe some psychological and social consequences of these changing demands and unchanging gender roles within some Russian families. Russian policies strongly emphasize equality of men and women in the work force, and the large majority of families are two-income families. However, traditional gender-role socialization puts the burden of household chores and child care exclusively on women while men actively focus on their work and career. Women may request that their husbands take more responsibility for the family, but husbands are reluctant to become involved in gender-inappropriate activities and often respond by distancing themselves even further from the family. As a result, wives become more demanding and husbands withdraw more, causing great distress for all involved. The authors point out that "rates of divorce are higher in Russia than in any other industrialized nation except the United States, and that births among ethnic Russians have been rapidly declining" (p. 402).

Division of Labor in the Work Force

In addition to the gendered division of labor within the family, women and men are frequently segregated into different occupations within the labor force. Many occupational fields are either female dominated or male dominated. One possible explanation is that those occupations requiring female stereotyped attributes (e.g., nurturance) are female dominated because women have better skills for that work or simply prefer it. For many women and men, these gender-stereotyped occupations represent an important aspect of their developmental niche. Not surprisingly, in many cultures women tend to be teachers, nurses, or caregivers. Similarly, occupations requiring physical endurance, strength, or assertiveness (e.g., laborer jobs or executive positions) tend to be dominated by males. However, stereotypic gender roles are only one possible explanation for occupational gender segregation.

Occupational fields are also frequently segregated by status. For example, female-dominated occupations generally have a lower status than male-dominated occupations, regardless of the work involved. For example, activities that involve interpersonal communication and interaction are often associated with women because they tend to have stronger verbal and interpersonal skills. This helps to explain why more women than men become teachers, therapists, and social workers. Yet, few women are involved at the highest levels in international politics, business, or academia, all of which require a great deal of interpersonal and verbal skills (Blau & Ferber, 1986; Dexter, 1985; Reskin, 1988). Harin, mentioned in our opening vignette, who prepared to be an elementary school teacher in Thailand, probably has many more female colleagues than male colleagues, unless this occupation is highly regarded in his culture.

High-status occupations typically are better paid and are associated with access to greater resources, resulting in frequent wage and status gaps between some women and men (Blau & Ferber, 1986; Reskin, 1988). As a consequence, women are often economically disadvantaged and dependent

As his daughter plays with a baby goat, this Tibetan man grinds roasted barley into a flour called tsamba *that can be eaten dry, stirred into tea, or mixed with tea and butter to form patties.* (Dr. Melvyn C. Goldstein/National Geographic Society)

on their husbands or other men as financial providers. The following section discusses how this societal stratification may, as part of the ecological system, affect interpersonal relationships in some contemporary societies.

Gender Relations in Social Status, Religion, and Public Policy

Social and economic stratification is deeply rooted in culture (Lee & Daly, 1987), contributes to gender inequality, and is reflected in relationships within the family. Assuming that economic power equals social power, the family member with the greatest social power will be most dominant within the family and thus be a powerful influence within the microsystem. Asserting this power can mean making financial and social decisions, asserting one's needs, assigning tasks to other family members, and yielding or denying access to resources. Since men generally have more economic and social power than women, they are likely to control and shape interpersonal relationships with a spouse and within the family. While women may manage everyday financial or social affairs, the ultimate power of approval or disapproval for decisions often lies with men, who may choose or not choose to exercise this power. Since these status differences are so pervasive, they are often reinforced by the religious and political institutions present within a culture's various ecological settings. Traditional Christian and Islamic religious teachings present arguments for the "destructiveness" of women as justification for the superiority and dominance of men.

Similarly, traditional Hindu religious texts assert that women represent an inherently dangerous spiritual force that needs to be controlled and restrained through all stages of her life (Kumari, 1988). Thus, first the father and then the husband are assigned the religiously sanctioned task of subordinating and subduing the woman. In interpreting this philosophy, Kumari (1988) writes, "Thus, the ideal Hindu woman is one who sees her highest good in her husband, is devoted to him with a religious zeal and is good and chaste. In other words, she is under the control of her husband, and the wifely role is one of subordination and devotion whatever may be the circumstances. The woman's place is primarily confined to the home, her role limited to procreation and the bringing up of children and catering to the needs of her husband. Chastity and control of sexuality are the most important aspects of the role of a wife. The maintenance of chastity requires control of sexuality and a woman's sexuality should always be under the control of a man. Before marriage it is the father who controls her, and after marriage the husband" (p. 11).

Following these religious prescriptions is beneficial for women. Religious texts further command that the woman who meets this ideal is to be worshipped and held in the highest regard. Thus, her subordinate role to man is to be seen as an honorable subordination that contributes to spiritual salvation of both herself and the husband who successfully fulfills his task of controlling her "evil" powers. However, the modern Hindu woman would most likely have a very different image of her responsibilities and role in society.

In cultures where there is an absence of support for working mothers, policies that prevent women from managing their own financial affairs, and neglect of health issues, women frequently find themselves in a position of dependency. Making changes in such policies would reverse these situations and contribute to greater gender equality and a reduction in gender-role stereotypes. For example, in contemporary China, the government's practice of assigning individuals to selected work sites separates many married couples, who are only allowed to see each other for about two weeks in a given year (Ruan, 1991). As a result, husbands and wives have little opportunity to develop and practice traditional gender-role behavior in the home. In addition, China's one-child policy gives women the opportunity to make nontraditional career choices and increase their financial independence (Hong, 1987).

Furthermore, China has seen a dramatic change in sexual attitudes. Even though public policy explicitly prohibits any sexual relations between women and men outside of marriage, premarital and extramarital sexual activity has increased sharply in recent years (Ruan, 1991). While all of these factors may contribute to high divorce rates and marital dissatisfaction among Chinese couples, they also promote more egalitarian relationships between men and women.

Similarly, children's views of men and women have already begun to change in countries where public policies have addressed gender equity. For example, in one study, when asked to draw their image of the ideal woman and the ideal man, adolescents in North America depicted women as working at a job and men as caring for children (Stiles, Gibbons, & de la Garza-Schnellman, 1990). Williams and Best (1990) found the same trend in Norway, a country in which the government has promoted gender equity for many years.

◇ LATER ADULTHOOD AND OLD AGE

From our discussion so far, it should be clear that marriage is considered one of the highest sacraments in most cultures and religions. However, in any society there will be a number of individuals who do not have a spouse, either because they never married or because they lost their mate through divorce or death.

Divorce and Widowhood

According to traditional Hindu beliefs, divorce is unacceptable. If men are not content in their marriage, they are allowed to take a second wife. After their wife's death, men are also permitted to remarry immediately. Widowhood for women, on the other hand, carries a strong social stigma. Without her husband, she is considered incomplete and even sinful. She is not allowed to remarry, becomes a social outcast, and simply awaits her own death. As a result, some women choose to burn themselves at their husband's funeral in order to attain spiritual salvation. **Sati,** or *widow immolation,* is a sacred practice (Kumari, 1988). Although the current Indian government strongly discourages this practice, a widow's memory is still held in high regard if she dies within a reasonable time after her husband's death.

Among the Hausa of Northern Nigeria, marriage also plays an important spiritual role. Adults who die while still married are expected to move on to **Lahira,** or *paradise* (Smith, 1965). While divorced and widowed adults are stigmatized, they are not met with nearly as much resentment as adults who never marry. Previously married women can still acquire some status by becoming prostitutes and remarrying later, an option denied to women who were never married. Similarly, Wolf (1964) reports a surprisingly high number of divorced women who work as prostitutes in Hokkien society in Taiwan.

In many Native American societies, a widow secures her livelihood by remarrying one of her husband's brothers or another close relative (Niethammer, 1977). Divorced women may return to their parents or marry another man. Divorce proceedings are relatively uncomplicated unless wife and husband share a great deal of property or the wife's relatives want to negotiate the return of the bride price paid to the husband. These examples of women in different societies show that even in adulthood, individuals create their own developmental niche in response to cultural norms and expectations associated with, in this case, divorce and widowhood.

Gender Roles and Status in Old Age

In traditional societies, age is frequently associated with a gain in community status. Older adults are respected and accepted as leaders who bring with them a wealth of life experience. Furthermore, they are frequently thought to have supernatural powers, and they hold important spiritual and religious responsibilities. Finally, both female and male elders are considered important to the socialization process because they pass on the group's cultural heritage to the next generation.

Sangree (1992) examined two societies, with a particular focus on older men and women. The Tiriki of Kenya and the Irigwe of Nigeria are two societies that view their elders with great respect and appreciate the wisdom they bring to the society. On closer examination, Sangree discovered it is not seniority alone that leads to status and influence among these elders. A necessary condition for being recognized as an elder is grandparenthood. In order to achieve the highest respect as an older person, one has to have at least three living children. Being accepted as an elder represents a gain in status, particularly for Tiriki women. According to cultural norms, Tiriki women cannot be initiated as adults and are denied important positions in the clan or the village. Moreover, their activities are limited to domestic work and farming. As elders, women achieve considerable power and influence by being involved in community affairs, although their contributions are not publicly recognized.

Among the Irigwe, elder status derives from the cultural belief surrounding a mystical relation between death and birth. The Irigwe believe that the soul of a deceased person will eventually be reincarnated as a newborn. The departure of one soul is essential for the creation of a new life. Elders who are approaching death are held in high esteem because their death ensures the continuation of life.

Although Irigwe women are not granted formal leadership in the form of a public office, they nevertheless play a critically important role in community life. In contrast to Tiriki society, women have more opportunities to excel in certain areas and gain public recognition (e.g., as healers or craftswomen). As grandmothers, they achieve even more status and are held in high regard.

With changes brought about by modernization, the gender roles and status of older adults, as well as of younger adults, have changed, particularly in Irigwe society. Sangree (1992) describes how young educated men are taking over community activities formerly conducted by the male and female elders. Such changes are not characteristic of younger women. They are often too busy with their family responsibilities or limited by their lack of education to compete with men for jobs and status.

Among the Tiriki, male elders retain their influence in some local affairs. The culture has preserved the elder males' role as an essential agent in the socialization and initiation of younger males. They are also more involved in their sons' lives, since they manage their sons' property while they are away from home working. The influence and status of female elders are gradually disappearing, and there are fewer opportunities for them to be involved within the community. Overall, the status of Tiriki individuals in late adulthood and how they are viewed increasingly resemble the view held by other modern cultures.

◇ SUMMARY

This chapter discussed the development of women and men across the lifespan. Whereas some gender differences can be viewed from a biological perspective (see Chapter 3), the emphasis here was on social and cultural forces that contribute to the psychological development of men and women in different societies. In early childhood, prevailing gender stereotypes already influence the socialization of gendered behavior. Cultural customs and arrangements determine the structure and content of social interaction between boys and girls. These interactions become increasingly important during adolescence, when young people are preparing for their roles as adults. Aside from biological maturity, cultural norms determine when a youth may engage in sexual activity. In addition, cultural rules may dictate mate selection as well as acceptable or unacceptable sexual activities. The years of adulthood are characterized by clearly stipulated roles and obligations, many of which are defined by gender. Although many of these roles show great similarities across cultures, the status of men and women and their relationships may differ depending on their cultural environment and their unique developmental niche.

◇ THINGS TO DO
AND THINK ABOUT

1. Ask four people who are older than you and four people who are younger than you to draw their picture of the "ideal" woman or man. What do the pictures show? Are they similar within the same generation? Are they similar across generations? Can you identify beliefs about gender-specific roles that are prevalent in your culture? Compare those with the beliefs of other cultures described in the chapter.

2. Think about certain conventions of dress and decoration for women and men in different societies: for women, high heels in European and North American cultures, the veil in the Mideast, the sari in India; for men, long pants in Europe, the yarmulke in Jewish culture, elaborate scarring in many African cultures. How do these customs relate to beliefs about women and men in different cultures? How are they part of the ecological system that influences the development of women and men?

◇ FURTHER READINGS

Leslie Feinberg. (1995). *Transgender Warriors: Making History from Joan of Arc to RuPaul.* Boston: Beacon Press.
> A historical look at the social and cultural constructions of gender. The author's discussion of gender issues, ranging from pink and blue to bathroom taboos to transexuality/transgenderism, opens readers' eyes to the myriad of ways in which gender shapes everyday experience.

Carolyn J. Niethammer. (1977). *Daughters of the Earth: The Lives and Legends of American Indian Women.* New York: Macmillan.
> A collection of interviews with modern Native American women accompanied by historical accounts and anthropological research. Discusses the cultural settings and everyday experiences of Kiowa, Navajo, Hopi, and Taos women in different stages of life.

Deborah L. Rhode. (Ed.). (1990). *Theoretical Perspectives on Sexual Difference.* New Haven, CT: Yale University Press.
> A unique study of the nature, origins, and consequences of sexual differences by experts in a variety of disciplines including history, law, philosophy, biology, sociology, psychology, political science, and anthropology. The focus is on male-female differences as well as those among women and the ways in which these differences mediate gender relations and social change.

CHAPTER SEVEN

 CULTURE AND
SOCIAL BEHAVIOR

Shula grew up in a kibbutz not far from Haifa, Israel, where she lived with her parents and two siblings. Shortly after she was born, her mother returned to her job on the farm, leaving Shula in the care of the kibbutz day care. At day care, Shula built close relationships with the three or four women who were assigned to take care of her. When she was older, Shula spent her mornings in school and her afternoons at the communal area, where she and the other children played and worked under the supervision of adult kibbutz members. Even though her family expected her to stay in the kibbutz, she could not wait to leave to be on her own. She now attends Ben Gurion University in Beer-Sheva, where she dedicates most of her time to her studies and her political activities.

◇ ◇ ◇

Manami and her parents live in a small apartment on the outskirts of Sapporo, Japan. Even though her father is an engineer, his salary alone barely supports the family. Manami's mother, Midori, gave up her job as an architect when her daughter was born. As a woman who was raised in a traditional Japanese family, Midori decided it was best to stay at home and raise the child herself rather than leaving Manami in the care of someone else. Manami has no siblings, and the first year in school was very difficult for her. She missed the undivided attention of her mother and did not get along well with the other children. After a while she built a circle of friends with whom she stayed close all through college. Now in her early thirties, Manami is an independent woman with a career in the competitive business of real estate.

◇ ◇ ◇

Manami's and Shula's social and cultural environments were very different from the day they were born. How did these aspects influence their development as social beings? Did the emphasis on collectivism in the kibbutz instill values such as sharing and cooperation in Shula? How do single children like Manami fare in a collectivist culture? In this chapter we will examine psychological and cultural factors that influence how people relate to their social environment and develop as social beings.

◇ INFANCY

During the first year of life, children actively begin to explore their environment; their curiosity seems almost limitless. In order to ensure continued learning and growth, the caretaker must encourage this exploration. At the same time, the child must trust that the caretaker is nearby and provides a safe haven when needed. The emotional bond between child and caretakers that allows children to feel secure and to know to whom they can turn in threatening situations is known as **attachment** (Maccoby, 1980). Early studies with baby monkeys (Harlow & Zimmermann, 1959; Harlow & Harlow, 1962) showed that infant-caretaker attachment goes beyond the fulfillment of physical and security needs. In fact, Harlow and others argue that it is the social interaction that takes place within a secure infant-caretaker relationship that is necessary for the development of healthy social behavior.

Child-Caretaker Relationships and Attachment Patterns

The process of attachment over the first two years appears to be similar across different cultures. It is assumed that children have developed an attachment with their caretaker if they show distress when separated from the caretaker. As illustrated by Figure 7.1, most children in the four cultures studied by Kagan and his colleagues (1978) did not show behavior indicating attachment until about their seventh month of life. This does not necessarily mean that they were not attached to their caretaker earlier. Rather, they may not have had the psychological and social abilities to interpret the departure of the caretaker as threatening and to translate their attachment into social behavior. Toward the end of the first year, social development interacts with development in other areas and accounts for a dramatic change in the child's social behavior. At about seven to nine months, children first acquire **object permanence,** *recognition that objects and/or persons continue to exist even when they cannot be seen.* At the same time, infants begin to commu-

FIGURE 7.1   Cross-Cultural Comparison of Children Showing Distress in the Strange Situation

Source: Adapted from *Infancy: Its Place in Human Development* by J. Kagan, R. B. Kearsley, and P. Zealazo, 1978, Cambridge: Harvard University Press.

nicate and respond more by means of language rather than facial expressions (Bates, 1976), and they actively check for their caretaker's responses to their behavior (Campos & Stenberg, 1981).

In addition to the similarities of attachment across cultures, there are also differences. Caretaker-child interactions and relationships are influenced by the environment in which they take place. From the two examples at the beginning of this chapter, one may conclude that Manami and Shula had very different relationships with their mothers during their first years of life.

Ainsworth and her colleagues (Ainsworth & Wittig, 1969) are credited with developing a standardized event (the **strange situation**) that makes it possible to observe the type of bond a child has with her primary caretaker. In the strange situation, a mother and child are placed together in a room equipped with toys. A stranger enters the room and sits quietly in a chair. The stranger begins a conversation with the caretaker and, after a while slowly approaches the child. The mother leaves the room while the stranger keeps interacting with the child. After a few minutes, the mother returns, reunites with the child, and the stranger leaves the room. Another few minutes pass and the mother leaves the room again. Shortly thereafter, the stranger reenters and tries to distract the child. Finally, the mother returns and reunites with the child.

The child's responses are recorded at specific times during the situation. How close does the child stay to the mother during the initial period? How does she react when approached by a stranger in the presence of the mother? How distressed is the child when the mother leaves the room? How does she react when alone with the stranger? Is the child happy when reunited with the mother? Specific responses indicate the type of attachment the child has with the primary caretaker.

Ainsworth and her colleagues observed that children could be classified according to three categories of behavior patterns when faced with the strange situation (Ainsworth, 1982). Children classified as *anxious/avoidant* will not pay much attention to whether the primary caretaker is absent or not. If they experience distress, they may turn to a stranger for comfort. On the mother's return, these children do not actively strive to reunite and be close. Children classified as *anxious/resistant* tend to stay close to their caretaker and become very distressed when she leaves the room. Even when comforted after the caretaker's return, these children will take a long time to settle down and remain anxious about the caretaker's whereabouts. Finally, *securely attached* children will be calm and not threatened by strangers in the presence of the caretaker. When the caretaker departs, the distressed child is unlikely to be comforted by a stranger. When the caretaker returns, the child is eager to reunite and will settle down and relax very quickly.

Although cross-cultural comparability of the strange situation has been questioned (LeVine & Miller, 1990; Takahashi, 1990), findings from numerous studies in Europe, Asia, Africa, the Middle East, and North America demonstrate that these attachment patterns occur in a wide variety of cultures (Lamb et al., 1985; Grossman, Grossman, Huber, & Wartner, 1981; Miyake, Chen, & Campos, 1985). However, societies differ in the percentage of children falling into each of these categories. Table 7.1 shows the distribution of the three attachment styles in eight different cultures, according to Van Ijzendoorn and Kroonenberg (1988). Their findings reveal that the anxious/avoidant classification is relatively higher in West European countries and the anxious/resistant classification is relatively more prevalent in Japan and Israel. They also point out that the intracultural variation in classification is 1.5 times greater than the intercultural variation, indicating that the attachment patterns in various cultures are, in fact, more similar than different. It is important to keep in mind that similar behaviors in the strange situation may have very different meanings in different cultures. For example, while Westerners may interpret anxious/resistant behavior as "clingy," Chinese parents may interpret it as "bonded."

TABLE 7.1   Cross-Cultural Comparison of Children's
Attachment Classifications

	ANXIOUS/ AVOIDANT	ANXIOUS/ RESISTANT	SECURELY ATTACHED
Germany (3 studies; N = 136)	35.3%	8.6%	56.6%
Great Britain (1 study; N = 72)	22.2	2.7	75.0
Netherlands (4 studies; N = 251)	26.3	6.4	67.3
Sweden (1 study; N = 51)	21.5	4.0	74.5
Israel (2 studies; N = 118)	6.8	28.8	64.4
Japan (2 studies; N = 96)	5.2	27.1	67.7
China (1 study; N = 36)	25.0	25.0	50.0
United States (18 studies; N = 1,230)	21.1	14.1	64.8

Source: Complied from data from "Cross-Cultural Patterns of Attachment" by M. H. Van Ijzendoorn and P. M. Kroonenberg, 1988, *Child Development, 59,* 147–156.

Cultural Explanations for Variations in Attachment Patterns

The contexts in which early social interactions take place are characterized by different parameters that define the developmental niche, such as characteristics of the caretaker, general conditions of infant development, and the child-caretaker relationship itself. As these parameters vary from culture to culture, so does the developmental niche, providing unique developmental challenges and opportunities for each child in his first months of life.

Caretaker Characteristics

Both the infant and the caretaker bring certain characteristics to the caretaker-infant relationship that become a crucial part of the ecological system in which the child grows up. This happens when some of the behaviors and characteristics of the mother interact with the characteristics of her child to create a unique developmental niche. For example, Richman, Miller, and Levine (1992) studied the behaviors Mexican mothers showed in response to their infant's distress signals such as crying and worried facial expressions. One factor that influenced mothers' responsiveness was their level of education. Mothers with more schooling tended to respond with more talking and facial expressions than mothers with less schooling, who tended to hold their infants more. In explaining these findings, the researchers pointed to earlier research suggesting that mothers with more education generally tend to initiate more verbal interaction with the children.

Caretakers also bring their unique cultural beliefs about parenting to the relationship (Harkness & Super, 1996). These beliefs may be culturally influenced, but they are also based on the caretaker's unique experiences. For example, Grossman and colleagues (1985) noticed that mothers in their German sample appeared quite unresponsive to their children's crying. Closer observations revealed that this behavior resulted from a shared cultural belief that infants should become independent at an early age and learn that they cannot rely on the mother's comfort at all times. In contrast, traditional Japanese mothers instill a strong sense of dependence in their young children by being available at all times (Miyake et al., 1985).

General Conditions of Infant Development

The conditions under which a child experiences her first year are often determined by the specific cultural setting. These conditions may influence the relationship between caretaker and child considerably. Two of these conditions involve availability of the primary caretaker and the number of other individuals involved in child care. For example, parents' economic circumstances or the structure of the community may require them to work outside of the home, leaving the care of the children to family members or others in the community.

Sagi (1990) speculates that the high rate of insecurely attached children in the Israeli kibbutz may be a result of the specific childrearing arrangements. For example, caregivers in the kibbutz (metaplot) are often assigned to work with three or more infants during the day, while all of the infants are watched by a single caretaker at night (in kibbutzim with communal sleeping arrangements). Sagi argues that this "multiple mothering" leads to inconsistencies in maternal behavior and may result in different (possibly less secure) attachment patterns.

Tronick, Morelli, and Ivey (1992) describe a different childrearing arrangement among the Efe in Zaire. Here, children also enjoy multiple social relationships with other children and adults. However, particularly during the first year, the mother is involved in more than half of the child's social activities. This also means that children spend half of their time with individuals other than their mothers. For example, during the time the mother works away from the camp, her child is left in the exclusive care of other adults or older children. Even when the mother is present, other family members, the children's peers, or other adults are continually engaged in social interactions with the child. In fact, the authors point out that at a given time about ten people are within sight or close hearing range of the child. Unfortunately, there are no data available from this culture describing specific attachment patterns resulting either from these continuous multiple relationships with others or from the close relationship with the mother. However, the authors suggest that the children benefit from this setting in that they develop a multitude of social skills early in life; this leads to better adjustment in social situations later on.

Similarly, Indonesian children not only enjoy much attention from their mother but also from their older siblings. For example, Farver and Wibarti (1995) found that mothers and older siblings engage in different types of playing behavior with young children. In particular, older siblings were more active playing partners and facilitated pretend play more often than mothers, thus adding an important dimension of social interaction to the young child's microsystem.

In other settings, mothers keep their infants with them during work. Women in Madura, Indonesia, for example, systematically adjust their work patterns to accommodate their children (Launer, 1993). Several North American Indian societies utilize the cradleboard. Niethammer (1977) has written that "all [cradle boards] provide a firm, protective frame on which babies felt snug and secure. A baby in a cradle board could be propped up or even hung in a tree so it could see what was going on and feel part of family activities. After spending much time in their cradle board, Indian children became very attached to them. One Apache mother related that whenever her toddler son was tired or upset he would go and get his cradle board and walk around with it on his back" (p. 15).

Similarly, the Quechua use a **manta pouch** to carry their infants. This is a backpacklike device that protects the infant from the harsh elements in the Peruvian mountains and provides a secure environment close to the mother (Tronick, Thomas, & Daltabuit, 1994). These and similar devices allow parents to keep their infants near them and to provide the necessary restraint so that children's physical activity does not interfere with the mother's work.

According to Bronfenbrenner, these general child-care arrangements could be classified as part of the macro- or mesosystems in the child's ecological environment. In setting the stage for the microlevel aspects of parent-child interactions, these general settings are crucial in the development of social relationships and behavior in early childhood.

Specific Settings of Parent-Child
Social Relationships

As pointed out in earlier chapters, infants spend the majority of their time sleeping and eating. Thus, feeding practices and sleeping arrangements provide an important context for social interaction and bonding with caretakers during the first year of life. Consequently, these represent a central aspect of each child's developmental niche and his attachment with caretakers.

Although the sucking reflex represents a universal neonatal ability, mothers in different cultural settings respond with a variety of nursing behaviors (Cole, 1989). Depending on the mother's obligations, both within and outside of the family, she may nurse the infant herself, employ a wet nurse, or bottle-feed the child. It is easy to see how feeding practice may shape the early relationship of mother and child. For example, the child may develop a different relationship with the mother if a wet nurse is present during the first year. On the other hand, babies who are bottle-fed may have a similar social relationship with their mother as children who are nursed, simply because the social interaction between mother and child is regular and continuous, regardless of the mode of feeding.

The mode of nursing for infants is also guided by cultural norms or taboos. For example, while the use of a wet nurse is common in many cultures, Cosminsky, Mhlovi, and Ewbank (1993) report that wet nursing is generally not accepted among members of communities in rural Zimbabwe. They believe that a baby nursed by another woman would "make the child sick, or the child might die from it" because "the blood does not go hand in hand or the other person might be dirty" (p. 943). However, concessions are made if the woman is in any way related to the mother such as her sister, mother, sister-in-law, or the husband's cowife. The duration of nursing is also determined by several individual and cultural factors, such as the health of the mother and the child, availability of suitable nutritional supplements for the child, and cultural beliefs about the developmental adequacy of nursing (Cosminsky et al., 1993).

Even after the child is weaned, the context of eating continues to play a crucial role in the development of social relationships. Dettwyler (1989) argues that "who controls what and how much the child eats, how this control is achieved, and the basis for these decisions" shapes long-term power dynamics between child and parents (p. 696). For example, force feeding is a routine practice among Ibadan mothers in Nigeria. The mother pours liquid into the baby's mouth while simultaneously holding its nose (Meldrum, 1984). While force feeding is not a common practice, parents in England, Sweden, the United States, and Newfoundland routinely use techniques to coerce their children into eating (Dettwyler, 1989). These techniques include feeding games (e.g., the spoon represents an airplane transporting each bite into the mouth), rewards for finishing a meal (e.g., dessert), punishment for not finishing a meal (e.g., withholding privileges), and passive restraint (e.g., high chair).

In contrast, Raphael and Davis (1985) found that mothers in the Philippines, northern India, and Sardinia, Italy, allow their children much more control in deciding how much they want to eat and when they want to eat. Filipino mothers accept the child's refusal, Indian mothers may try to distract their children and offer them food again after a period of time, and Sardinian mothers use merely gentle coaxing to get their children to eat more.

Similar to feeding practices, sleeping arrangements influence early parent-child relationships and reflect cultural beliefs about infants' social development. Morelli and her colleagues (1992) observed that Mayan infants usually slept with their mothers, fathers, or siblings until the birth of a new sibling. In contrast, cosleeping is not very common among middle-class U.S. American families. In this culture, the newborn may sleep in the same room as the mother but not in the same bed. In such cases, an infant would eventually move into a different room when about three to six months old. The differences in these practices appear to be firmly rooted in parental beliefs and cultural values. According to Morelli and her coresearchers (1992), mothers in the United States believe that cosleeping interferes with their efforts to train their children early to become self-reliant and independent. In contrast, Mayan parents believe that the closeness that occurs as a result of cosleeping arrangements fosters the baby's social awareness and social learning. Japanese parents express similar views and consider cosleeping as a way to develop the child's interdependence with others (Caudill & Weinstein, 1969). Abbott (1992) observed a similar practice in a non-middle-class Eastern Kentucky community and, in a recent report (1997), indicated that 90 percent of children in her Appalachian samples either slept in the same bed with their parents or in the same room with them.

Sleeping arrangements and their implications for social development—the interaction between the child and the environment—represent a good example of the developmental niche. The presence or absence of the caretaker during the night may even facilitate and reward a certain attachment style (e.g., anxious/resistant). This attachment style involves social behavior patterns that are adaptive and desirable in certain cultures, since they tend to emphasize interdependence with others in a collectivist or group-oriented culture.

◇ CHILDHOOD

When children pass the stage of infancy, they begin to develop social relationships that extend beyond caretakers and the family context. These relationships include children in the immediate neighborhood or within the school context and frequently become quite complex and multifaceted. Corsaro and Eder (1990) refer to these expanding relationships as children's "peer culture."

Peer Culture and
Social Relationships

In their review of relevant research, Corsaro and Eder identify three central themes that characterize peer culture from early childhood to adolescence. These include (1) dealing with confusion, concerns, fears, and conflicts; (2) resisting and challenging adult rules and authority; and (3) sharing and social participation.

Dealing with Confusion, Concerns, Fears, and Conflicts

In the company of their peers, children learn to cope with everyday conflicts and fears through fantasy play (e.g., role-playing the defeat of a monster). Children also engage in fantasy play to deal with anxiety and violence. For example, children in several South African communities, where daily life was often interrupted by riots or police raids, played out the violence and aggression they saw around them (Dawes, 1990; Liddell, Kvalsvig, Qotyana, & Shabalala, 1994). In a related study, Kostelny and Garbarino (1994) explored the drawings of Palestine children living in Israeli-occupied territories. The drawings of the five- to eight-year-olds frequently showed themes of victimization (e.g., large soldiers with guns threatening small children).

Resisting and Challenging Adult Rules and Authority

Corsaro and Eder (1990) maintain that challenging adult rules serves to establish a sense of independence from parents. At the same time, children strengthen their peer group identity by developing rituals and routines that make fun of adult authority or challenge adult rules. Corsaro (1988) observed frequent violations of Italian and American nursery school rules prohibiting children from bringing toys from home to school. Children attempted to break this rule by bringing in concealed toys or candy, which were then shared with other children who gladly became coconspirators in the violation. Similarly, Marshall (1976) describes a game called "frogs" played by !Kung children. In this game one participant poses as the "mother," and the others are the "children." While the "mother" pretends to prepare "frogs" as food, the "children" openly refuse to perform tasks, disobey the orders of the "mother," steal the frogs and hide them, and so on. The game ends by the mother chasing the children, who run away in all directions in an effort to avoid being caught.

Aside from challenging rules and authority, it is through games and play that children come to understand concepts of creating and enforcing rules as well as cheating and breaking rules. Schwartzman (1983) provides a thoughtful analysis of the socializing function of children's play and includes examples of children in the kibbutz, Australian Aborigine children, Kpelle children in Liberia, and several more.

Sharing and Social Participation

As they get older, children begin to seek the company of other children and enjoy social activities. In interaction with other children and without the presence of adults, they acquire a sense of **cooperation** and sharing. One of the most important settings in which social interaction takes place is that of play and games, which represent a crucial element of the ecological system during childhood. Games like tag, hopscotch, and jacks as well as soccer and baseball are played in similar forms in many cultures (Avedon & Sutton-Smith, 1971; Duda & Allison, 1990; Reynolds, 1989). All these games facilitate taking turns, cooperation, and negotiation, yet the rules or content may vary with different contexts. Children in the United States may play soccer (what most of the world refers to as football) in an organized league governed by adults and consisting of set teams, coaches, scheduled match play, and so on. Soccer may also be played without adult participation and with makeshift goals and changing teams in a back alley of São Paulo, Brazil, or in a farmer's field in Nigeria. The social interactions taking place in each of these settings may be quite different. For example, organized sports and games tend to focus on competition, achievement, rules, and success, whereas free play activities tend to focus on participation, equality of players, and adapting or creating rules in order to ensure everyone's enjoyment of the game (Figler & Whitaker, 1995).

Games and play also introduce children to concepts of competition and differential status. Observers of children's peer culture have noted the cultural variation in competitiveness and cooperation in children's play. For example, children in North America generally appear to be more competitive than children in many other societies (Madsen, 1971). On the other hand, Domino (1992) found Chinese children to be more concerned than American children about group accomplishment. In this study, children were asked to complete a task in which tokens could be exchanged for various prizes. Depending on the task, tokens could be obtained by working alone or collaboratively. Most of the American children preferred to work individually, trying to accumulate as many tokens as possible for themselves. Chinese children tended to adopt strategies that emphasized collaboration with others rather than individual success.

In another example, Starkes (1991) used a dyadic (two-person) marble game in which children had the choice to play cooperatively or compete with each other. Findings showed that Chinese children were more competitive in this situation than American children in the comparison group. Starkes points out that these differences may be due to the different teaching styles practiced in these cultures. She suggests that the Chinese emphasis on teacher-directed large-group activities leaves little room for dyadic interactions. As a result, Chinese youngsters may have less experience in negotiating roles and taking turns with a partner. These selected examples demonstrate that cultural differences or similarities in competitive and cooperative behavior may depend on the definition of these concepts and the specific context in which the behavior takes place.

Studies in Africa provide additional cues for environmental factors that may influence cooperative and competitive behavior. Friedman, Todd, and Kariuki (1995) studied 120 Kenyan children from different backgrounds (a middle-class Westernized suburb of Nairobi, poor semiurban Kikuyu, and a poor rural mission village). Results showed that middle-class children behaved competitively, even when cooperation was the most adaptive strategy. Surprisingly, rural children also engaged in competitive behavior. Poor semiurban children from Kikuyu were the most cooperative of all groups. One could speculate that the degree of Westernization corresponds to the degree of individualism found in these settings (i.e., the more individualistic the environment, the greater the emphasis on competition).

Marshall (1976) reported a complete absence of competitive games among !Kung children living in tribal communities in Southwest Africa (tug-of-war being the exception because of its special historical meaning). The author suggests that the collectivist nature of !Kung society emphasizes group performance rather than individual achievement and success. Taken as a group, these studies suggest that the degree of collectivism-individualism may play a role in the social behavior of children since it is part of the ecological system in which social behavior develops.

Kagitcibasi (1990) has recently criticized the use of the collectivism-individualism dimension as a simplistic explanation of cultural differences in competitiveness and the health concern it may pose for children (see Box 7.1). As an alternative, Searle-White (1996) proposes a Vygotskian approach. As you may recall from our earlier discussion, this framework emphasizes socialization and language as "psychological tools" for mental growth and development. Depending on how these tools are used, children and adults view

BOX 7.1

 COMPETITIVE STRESS AND CHILDREN'S HEALTH

A common misconception of childhood is that it is an easy period of one's life with little to worry about. The reality is that children in nearly every culture have their share of stress and frustration. Parents' beliefs about children's academic success play an important role in how much competitive stress children may experience. Chao (1996) found that Chinese children are under greater pressure to achieve academically than are European-American children. Chinese mothers emphasize academic achievement and hard work, while European-American mothers want well-rounded children and place emphasis on social skills and self-esteem. For Chinese mothers, academic success results in upward mobility and family cohesiveness, whereas academic failure is associated with loss of face. At times, children may feel they have to outperform their peers in order to save face for their family name. In addition, many education models are based on competition and encourage a certain degree of competitive stress. Sometimes children find it difficult to handle all of the demands placed on them; this can lead to a variety of health problems, including migraine headaches, asthma, eczema, and others.

Prevention of the negative effects of competitive stress in children has been studied systematically by a number of investigators (Beck, 1976; Ellis, 1962; Seligman, 1990). In some cases, simple relaxation techniques such as deep breathing and imagery may help children cope with anxiety-producing events (Forman, 1993). In addition, adjusting cognitive strategies, known as "reattribution training," has been employed to help reduce children's test anxiety, impulsivity, and distractibility (Seligman, 1990). In India, children are taught yoga and other forms of meditation to help detach themselves from stressful events and self-defeating behaviors (Sinha, 1993).

themselves as being at a point along a continuum of interdependence, where cooperation reflects, in part, the inclination to stay socially connected to others.

This approach fits in with our themes of the developmental niche and the ecological systems approach. When children cooperate with others, they work within their developmental niche and recognize that they are interconnected with others. Likewise, in terms of Bronfenbrenner's model, the child interacts with other people within her microsystem. At first, this system may be small, involving just a few caregivers. However, as children get older, they do more things with others, expanding their social world. As they become socialized within the mesosystem of the school and the neighborhood, they recognize the benefits of working together to accomplish their academic and personal goals. They learn the rules of cooperative play and practice social behaviors. Later, as children express the cultural values of cooperation and interdependence through language and social behavior, they begin operating within the cultural context of the macrosystem.

Moral Development and Prosocial Orientation

With increased social participation in early childhood, children begin to understand how to relate to others in socially desirable ways. As they acquire the foundations of moral reasoning and behavior, they begin to understand concepts such as "right" and "wrong." Developmental psychologists have proposed that moral development progresses in stages, each stage representing more mature reasoning about moral thought and conduct (Kohlberg, 1981; Gilligan, 1982; for a detailed overview, see Shields & Bredemeier, 1995).

Moral reasoning refers to *the cognitive process by which individuals make decisions about moral issues and justify these decisions, regardless of the content of the issue.* One can reason in a morally mature (or less mature) manner about either side of a moral issue. For example, a person may decide that the death penalty for a homicide conviction is morally acceptable. Possible reasoning may be "the person has brought on his bad karma himself by killing another person" or "it's the law in this country." Another person may find the death penalty unacceptable because "two wrongs don't make a right" or "all life should be respected."

The most influential of theoretical models remains Kohlberg's theory of moral development (Kohlberg, 1981). He proposes six stages of moral reasoning, each stage representing a more sophisticated and complex orientation toward justice and normative moral principles. The six stages of moral development are summarized in Table 7.2. In the table, Kohlberg's model is compared with Damon's model, which is discussed in the later section on distributive justice.

One of the main assumptions underlying Kohlberg's theory is that the six stages are universal and are present in any culture. However, Kohlberg concedes that the stage at which individuals complete their development and the time it takes to be completed may vary. Kohlberg's definition and assessment of moral reasoning maturity has been challenged by several others (Eckensberger, 1994; Snarey, 1985; Shweder, Mahapatra, & Miller, 1987).

TABLE 7.2   Kohlberg's and Damon's Levels of Justice Reasoning

KOHLBERG *Moral reasoning is guided by . . .*	DAMON *Judgments about the fair distribution of goods are based on . . .*
1. Reward, punishment, and obedience: "One should not steal because one could end up in jail."	O-A The mere expression of a wish: "Whoever wants it most gets the most."
2. Own and others' immediate needs and interests: "One should not steal because the other person may need the item."	O-B External characteristics such as size, gender, age: "Whoever is older or bigger gets the most."
3. Expectations from people close to oneself; general social expectations about social roles: "One should not steal because that's not being a good child."	1-A Strict equality regardless of other attributes or actions: "Everyone gets the same."
4. Obligation to fulfill duties and follow consensual laws and rules: "One should not steal because it is against the law."	1-B Reciprocity for behavior or actions: "Whoever works hardest gets the most in return."
5. Values and rules relative to one's group and awareness of diversity of moral values: "One should not steal, unless there are extraordinary circumstances."	2-A Psychological or material need: "Whoever needs it most gets the most."
6. Self-chosen ethical principles that are considered universally valid, or social laws that are based on universal principles: "Stealing is the violation of someone else's rights, which should be honored."	2-B Compromise between need, reciprocity, and equality: "Everyone should get what she or he deserves, which may differ by person and situation."

Cultural Influences on Caring and Justice Orientation

A number of studies suggest that individuals in many non-European cultures, as well as women, exhibit moral reasoning equivalent to that of an adolescent in Kohlbergian terms. Critics argue that an Anglo male bias is built into the model because the highest level of moral development is based on interviews with a 1960s sample of Harvard male undergraduates. In addition, the hypothetical moral dilemmas Kohlberg created in order to elicit moral reasoning responses and the scoring of the responses may also be culturally biased. Carol Gilligan (1982) specifically pointed to the gender bias in Kohlberg's theory. In her own research, she learned that women's moral thought is *guided by caring and maintaining the welfare of others,* whereas men emphasize *more abstract principles of justice.* Gilligan concludes that women develop a different kind of morality altogether, due to their different socialization. Stack (1974) found a similar **caring orientation** (as opposed to a **justice orientation**) described as "what goes around comes around" in a midwestern African-American community.

Different socialization, parental beliefs, and customs of child care—that is, different aspects of the developmental niche—may explain many research findings in the cultural domain. For example, studies of Buddhist monks showed that young adolescent monks reasoned at stage 2 and even mature adults barely reached stage 4 in Kohlberg's schema (Huebner & Garrod, 1993). Can we conclude that the monks' moral reasoning is less highly developed compared with Western adolescent males? Huebner and Garrod (1993) argue that Kohlberg's model is only partially applicable in this context because the Buddhist conception of morality is different than the Western, Christian, liberal democratic view inherent in Kohlberg's theory.

According to the authors, the ideal moral person from a Western perspective is an autonomous individual with strong convictions who stands up for her own, as well as others', rights. She is an influential individual who uses her power to influence others in a "good" way. In contrast, among Buddhists, ideal moral individuals are those who are ultimately connected (to others, the environment, the cosmos) through their compassion and detachment from their own individuality. Buddhist morality is characterized by an understanding of interconnectedness and interdependence and is more reminiscent of Gilligan's caring orientation than Kohlberg's justice orientation. Similarly, Bersoff and Miller (1993) found that people from India were more likely to forgive moral violations if there were extenuating circumstances or emotional hardship.

In a comparative study of adolescents from China, Hong Kong, and England (Ma, 1989), both Chinese samples showed a stronger orientation toward abiding by the law as well as being altruistic or affective toward others. Ma concludes that this cultural difference may result from the Chinese practice of rearing their children in a more authoritative manner than the English, encouraging them to obey authority and follow norms. At the same time, Chinese cultural values are inherently collectivist, emphasizing human relationships and interdependence.

This discussion of various cultural influences on aspects of moral reasoning demonstrates that moral development may not strictly follow a universal psychological script, as suggested by Kohlberg. Instead, the ecological system in which early social participation takes place shapes individual development of moral thought and behavior.

Cultural Influences on Distributive Justice

Based on Kohlberg's broad model of moral reasoning, Damon (1975) focused specifically on children's understanding of one aspect of moral reasoning that has important implications for the development of social judgment and social behaviors, namely **distributive justice**—*the judgment of what constitutes criteria for the fair distribution of goods and resources in society.* Damon's five levels of distributive justice reasoning, which occur from early to middle childhood, are presented in Table 7.2 along with Kohlberg's stages.

In order to assess children's distributive justice capabilities, Enright, Franklin, and Manheim (1980) created the **Distributive Justice Scale (DJS),** which is *a pictorial instrument used as a tool in one-on-one interviews.* Researchers have since adapted the DJS for use in a variety of contexts. For example, Box 7.2 shows Solomon's (1996) Adapted Distributive Justice Scale, which is used to assess the thinking of children from different ethnic backgrounds within a sports context.

Cross-cultural studies have suggested that cultures may differ in their normative beliefs of what constitutes a "fair" distribution of resources. For example, Sweden is considered more of a need-based society (i.e., everyone receives according to his needs), whereas the Protestant work ethic (i.e., everyone receives according to his effort) still prevails in the United States (Enright et al., 1984). Similarly, the concept of reciprocity , a central concept in Damon's model, is conceptualized differently depending on cultural context. In Damon's model, mature reasoning about the just distribution of goods and resources in society is guided by two principles: equality and reciprocity. Equality refers to the judgment that people are equally deserving of receiving resources and goods. Reciprocity refers to the reception of resources, either in exchange for a behavior (e.g., work) or in order to meet a need. At the most mature level of reasoning, children are able to take both equality and reciprocity into account when making judgments about the fair distribution of resources. Miller and Bersoff (1994) point out that in India, exchanging helping behavior for money is considered a personal choice but exchanging helping behavior for previous helping behavior is a social obligation. In contrast, either type of reciprocity is considered a personal choice in the United States. Based on these differences in ecological systems, it would be easy to assume that developmental patterns of distributive justice reasoning may also vary for children in different cultures. Surprisingly, studies in Japan, Sweden, Germany, and the United States indicate that children show

BOX 7.2

THE ADAPTED DISTRIBUTIVE JUSTICE SCALE

The following example is from Solomon's (1996) Adapted Distributive Justice Scale:

All of these boys and girls are on the same baseball team. There is Clarice, the oldest one on the team; Jennifer, whose family does not have much money; Lamar, who is a hard-working ball player; and Matthew. One afternoon they thought it would be a good idea if they helped the younger

BOX 7.2 CONTINUED

children learn how to play baseball. When they were done, Clarice had helped for two hours, Jennifer had helped for two hours, Lamar had helped for four hours, and Matthew had helped for two hours. After they did this, the coach decided that the children were so nice to help the younger children that she gave them eight quarters. The children have to decide how to divide up the quarters. What is the best way to do this?

Answer options and corresponding levels of reasoning:

Matthew gets the most quarters because he wanted the quarter more than anything. (Level O-A)

Clarice gets the most because she is the oldest. (Level O-B)

All children get the same amount so there won't be any fights about who gets more. (Level 1-A)

Lamar gets the most quarters because he helped more than the other children. (Level 1-B)

Jennifer gets the most quarters because she is poor and needs them more than the other children. (Level 2-A)

Source: From *Fair Play in the Gymnasium: Enhancing Socio-moral Skills of Children at Risk* by G. B. Solomon, 1997, unpublished manuscript, Texas Christian University, Fort Worth. Reprinted by permission.

similar patterns of distributive justice reasoning corresponding to Damon's developmental model (Eisenberg, Boehnke, Schuhler, & Silbereisen, 1985; Enright et al., 1984; Watanabe, 1986). In this case of distributive justice reasoning, differences in ecological systems do not account for developmental differences.

◇ ADOLESCENCE

Social Identity Formation

We tend to think of identity as something that is very unique and represents the individual's personal history, experiences, and personality. However, our lives are inextricably connected with those around us, may it be our family, our peers, or our coworkers. Viewed from an ecological systems view, the groups of people in a given context show a great degree of overlap. Therefore, it is not surprising that part of what we like to think of as our self results from what we share with others. Psychologists call these shared aspects of self social identities. French psychologist H. Tajfel (1981) defines **social identity** as *"that part of an individual's self-concept which derives from his knowledge of his membership of a social group (or groups) together with the value and emotional significance attached to that membership"* (p. 255).

We tend to belong to multiple groups; some are assigned to us (e.g., gender, nationality), some we choose (e.g., political affiliation). Among these, ethnic or cultural identity has been singled out as particularly important to self-concept and psychological functioning of ethnic group members. Phinney (1990) and other researchers suggest that the formation of ethnic/cultural identity is very similar to the formation of ego-identity outlined by Erikson (Atkinson, Morten, & Sue, 1983; Cross, 1978).

In particular, ethnic/cultural identity formation progresses in three stages: the first stage, usually occuring in adolescence, is characterized by the lack of exploration of ethnic identity. The second stage involves becoming aware of one's ethnicity and actively exploring that ethnicity. At this stage, the person may engage in ethnic group activities, including reading and talking to people about the culture and participating in cultural events. The completion of this stage results in the final stage: ethnic identity achievement. This stage is characterized by a deeper understanding of one's ethnicity and the internalization of ethnic identity into the self. Since this understanding of ethnic identity varies from person to person according to personal history, the implications for the self-concept and, ultimately, social behavior may also vary. For example, one person may become deeply involved in the activities of her ethnic group by maintaining the language, wearing traditional garb, and practicing ethnic rituals and customs. For another person, ethnic identity achievement may result in a intrinsic confidence in his ethnicity and not necessarily require strong ethnic involvement.

Cultural Influences on Social Identity

Just as the larger cultural context influences the specific content of adolescents' self-concepts and personal identity (see Chapter 5), culture also plays an important role in the progression of social identity formation and its psychological consequences such as self-esteem. The position an ethnic group holds in the larger society (minority or majority status) and the relationships between ethnic groups are the most influential of these cultural factors (Phinney, Lochner, & Murphy, 1990).

Research in the West Indies (Gopaul-McNichol, 1995) shows how general cultural conditions and beliefs (i.e., macrosystem) shape the basis from which young people begin their ethnic identity formation. Gopaul-McNichol (1995) presented black and white preschool children with black dolls and white dolls. The investigator asked the children questions such as "Which doll would you like to play with?" "Which doll do you want to be?" "Which doll is rich, ugly, pretty?" Similar to research in the United States almost five decades earlier (Clark & Clark, 1947), most of the children chose the white doll in response to the positive questions. The author concludes that colonialism, along with the representation of blacks and whites in the media, has made a marked impact on attitudes toward and perceptions of ethnic groups in the West Indies. It is not far-fetched to assume that these attitudes and perceptions will later play an important role in the ethnic identity formation of the black children and white children who participated in the study.

The research examining the relationship between ethnic identification and self-esteem is inconclusive. Some studies indicate that stronger identification with one's ethnic group is related to higher self-esteem among adolescents (Paul & Fisher, 1980; Grossman, Wirt, & Davids, 1985). Other studies have failed to find a definitive link between these two concepts (Houston, 1984; White & Burke, 1987). On the other hand, Phinney (1990) points out that the role of ethnic identity and self-esteem becomes clearer when looking at stages of identity development. In fact, she and her colleagues have reported in several studies of African-American, Asian-American, Mexican-American, and European-American adolescents that lower self-esteem was associated with lower stages of identity development. When individuals reached the stage of "achieved identity" and had a clear sense of who they were, their self-esteem was higher than that of individuals who were in the identity foreclosure or moratorium stages of identity development. This finding was true for all ethnic groups, although the relationship was stronger for members of minority groups (see Phinney, 1990, for a review of this research).

Influence of Family and Peers

Although parents and family continue to play a central place in the lives of young adults, the importance of the **peer group,** *individuals who share certain characteristics (e.g., background, age, status, class) and interact on generally equal terms,* increases considerably during adolescence. The importance of peers is also discussed in Chapter 8 in relation to family structure; however, here we will focus on the social relationships and social influence between peers. Adolescents look to their parents and other adults as models for adult roles and behavior. They look to their peers for opinions, lifestyles, and experiences that are different from those to which they have been exposed through their families. However, adolescents in different cultures seem to perceive their social networks quite differently. A comparison of adolescents in Zimbabwe and the United States showed that parents and friends have different functions in the two cultures (Harrison, Stewart, Myambo, & Teveraishe, 1995). In Zimbabwe, adolescents considered adults (including extended family and teachers) both as mentors and disciplinarians, whereas American youths perceived their relatives as primarily providers of emotional support. Second, Zimbabwean young people felt closer to their siblings, relatives, teachers, and fathers than did Americans, who felt closer to their friends. Finally, African adolescents experienced more conflict with their teachers and best friends, whereas American adolescents struggled more with their mothers, fathers, and relatives.

Findings such as these indicate that both parents and peers have a strong influence on adolescents' prosocial as well as antisocial behavior, although this influence may vary from culture to culture. For example, the strong orientation toward family among traditional Puerto Rican male adolescents appears to lower their likelihood of engaging in interpersonal violence and illicit drug use (Sommers, Fagan, & Basin, 1993). In contrast, young men who have acculturated to the majority culture in the United States are more likely to show violent behavior.

There is also some evidence that parental attitudes are related to adolescents' choice of peers. In their study of European-American adolescents, Durbin and her colleagues (1993) found that adolescents with authoritative parents tended to choose peer groups that conformed to the norms their parents valued. For example, these young people gravitated either to groups known as "brains" (the smart students), "populars" (socially active students), or "jocks" (student athletes), depending on parental values. Adolescents from households in which parents were not demanding and less attentive were more likely to engage with peers who did not endorse adult values (e.g., "druggies" or "partiers"). Smith and Blinn Pike (1994) also observed a relation between social contact and the self-image and attitudes of Jamaican adolescents. Adolescents had stronger overall family relationships, were better adjusted, and had more positive career goals when they chose adults as their socializing partners compared with adolescents who socialized primarily with their peers.

Parents' attitudes toward drugs and their own use of drugs and alcohol as well as parent-child communication were among the strongest predictors for the use of tobacco, alcohol, and other drugs among Spanish adolescents. Recio Adrados (1995) argues that parents and friends act as role models and that their use of and attitudes toward drugs and their relationships with the adolescents predicted drug use by adolescents.

On the other hand, peer group influence does not always facilitate delinquent behavior. Berndt and Zook (1993) have proposed that whereas antagonistic friendships frequently foster antisocial behavior, friendships characterized by closeness and prosocial behavior tend to facilitate social adjustment. In particular, peer groups provide social support in achieving social competence. For example, one study demonstrated that Costa Rican peer groups emphasize the generally cooperative and collectivist social attitudes necessary for functioning in the larger society (DeRosier & Kupersmidt, 1991). In contrast, American adolescents often stress the importance of having one "best" friend among peers, reflecting the cultural importance of individuality.

Clearly, young people's cultural definitions of acceptable and unacceptable relationships may sometimes lead to difficulties. Roberts (1994) describes the dilemma African-American men experience when relating to each other. The dominant Euro-American culture defines male styles of relating to each other, disregarding the cultural context of relationships experienced by African-American men. The white American relationship between men is typically highly competitive and characterized by power and control and a lack of emotion, trust, and connectedness. In contrast, the African-American mode of relating emphasizes interconnectedness, caring, and the importance of community over individual needs. Roberts asserts that African-American men must try to integrate two models of relationships that at times are quite incompatible. As a result, their relationships with male (and female) peers are often difficult and fail to provide much-needed social support. Roberts states, "It would seem that the statement 'like a brother' reflects a common expectation among Black men that their relationships with other men reflect the trust, caring, openness, and honesty associated with one's brother. Unfortunately, the majority of the evidence suggests that Black men are not getting (or giving) what they desire and expect in relating to each other" (pp. 387–388).

Cultural Influences

Arnett (1992) suggests a theoretical framework that is helpful in understanding why adolescent behavior is judged so differently in different cultures. He suggests that the socialization of adolescents is largely influenced by factors other than family and peers within the microsystem. The larger cultural influences include school, community, legal system, cultural beliefs, and the media (meso-, exo-, and macrosystems). According to Arnett, some cultures are characterized by **broad socialization** in which *independence and free self-expression are more highly valued than conformity*. Cultures such as these have no commonly accepted belief systems that judge right and wrong behavior, and deviations from cultural expectations are not severely punished. In these cultures, the range of behavior that falls within the norm is much greater than in so-called **narrow socialization** cultures. The latter clearly *prescribe an ideology that strictly sets forth the basis for right and wrong behavior*. These cultures value conformity and adherence to the standards of the community rather than autonomy and severely punish deviations from community norms.

Arnett's framework is useful in explaining why behaviors considered delinquent in one society are merely frowned on or even acceptable in others. For example, drinking is unacceptable for adolescents in many kibbutzim in Israel, with the exception of some Jewish festivities, during which moderate alcohol consumption is allowed (Kaffman, 1993). In contrast, the attitude toward alcohol consumption by adolescents in Jamaica is casual, and few legal restrictions apply. In Jamaica, adolescent drinking is not a sign of delinquent behavior (Smith & Blinn Pike, 1994). Similarly, compared to the United States, adolescents in Spain are able to consume more alcohol per week before they are categorized as "drinkers" (Recio Adrados, 1995). Among European countries, the prevalence of weekly drinking varies considerably. For example, adolescents in Greece and Italy drink about twice as much alcohol per week as their counterparts in Ireland (van Reek, Adriaanse, & Knibbe, 1994). Possible explanations for these variations probably can be found in the cultural differences in beliefs related to alcohol consumption and adult drinking patterns.

An additional factor that needs to be taken into account when defining adolescent social behavior is the status of a given group within the larger culture and this group's attitude toward the majority culture. Gotowiec and Beiser (1993) found a much higher rate of school failure, substance abuse, and suicidal behavior among aboriginal Canadian adolescents than among majority culture adolescents. Similarly, drug consumption patterns of Australian aboriginal peoples differs significantly from that of urban Australians, who represent the majority culture (Fleming, Watson, McDonald, & Alexander, 1991).

Calabrese and Noboa (1995) closely examined Mexican-American gang culture. They report that Mexican-American adolescents may decide to join a gang as a way of retaining their culture of origin and of resisting the majority values found in American public schools. In this case, violence must be interpreted from the standpoint of the minority culture, since majority views are rejected (Harris, 1994). Another example of differential perception of delinquent behavior is the street-fighting code of a minority youth culture in Mexico (*cholo*). The mass media in Mexico choose to portray *cholo* youth as uncontrolled, violent, and destructive. In contrast, Cummings (1994) describes a complex system of *cholo* street-fighting rules based on fairness and honor. This social structure contains rules about who can fight with whom about which matters and under which circumstances. For example, fights only take place when the groups involved are perceived as equal in strength or number; women may intervene on men's behalf, but men never interfere with women's fights.

Regardless of the specific parameters of their ecological systems, young people are faced with the difficult developmental task of identifying and establishing their place in the adult world. For some, this process may progress

BOX 7.3

WHAT ARE ADOLESCENTS CONCERNED ABOUT?

The difficult psychological task of defining one's identity is frequently accompanied by many concerns and problems. Studies reveal that there are many concerns that are shared by adolescents and adults around the world. Some of these include questions such as "What will my life look like in five years?" "What kind of person will I be then?" "Will I ever get along again with my parents?"

Gibson and others (1991) examined seventeen nations in Europe, North America, and Asia and found adolescents' primary areas of concern were family, education, and self-concept. Young people in Singapore reported that their worries revolve around succeeding in school, getting a high-status job, and general concern about the future (Isralowitz et al., 1990). Turkish adolescents are concerned about their personal future, relations with others, and their identity. However, they also think about local and universal issues and drug use (Sahin & Sahin, 1995).

Nurmi (1991) provides an extensive review of studies on adolescents' future concerns. This review includes thirty studies conducted between 1959 and 1989 in fourteen different countries. He concludes that there are three main domains of concern shared by adolescents in different cultures: (1) major normative life tasks (e.g., having a career and establishing a family), (2) nonnormative life events related to parents (e.g., death or divorce of parents), and (3) global events (e.g., nuclear war). In spite of these similarities, Nurmi also points out that adolescents from traditional cultures seemed to be more concerned about issues relating to family, whereas those in urban cultures worried more about future education and career.

more smoothly; for others, it may be characterized by inner conflict and turmoil. Nonetheless, young people across cultures share general concerns about the world, their lives, and their future, as described in Box 7.3.

◇ ADULTHOOD AND AGING

While achieving a healthy adult identity is one of the most challenging life tasks, Erikson asserts that psychosocial development does not end with this task. The next challenge (or crisis) faced by adults involves finding intimacy and requires the individual to integrate his own identity with the identity of a long-term intimate partner. (The cultural aspects of this particular stage of development are discussed in detail in Chapter 8.)

Developmental Tasks in Middle and Later Adulthood

The two remaining psychosocial crises or challenges occur in middle and late adulthood and focus on *generativity versus stagnation* and *integrity versus despair* (see Table 2.1 in Chapter 2). The former refers to the *generation of something lasting that represents oneself.* A successful resolution of this developmental issue leads to a sense of accomplishment and achievement. Such accomplishments can be expressed in material wealth, artistic or intellectual creations, raising children, or having achieved status in the community. This developmental phase clearly influences individuals' attitudes and behavior in social and work-related situations.

Integrity versus despair reflects older adults' attempts to *integrate previous identity resolutions and make sense of life as a whole.* Successful resolution of this final stage is characterized by an acceptance of oneself and one's accomplishments and failures. Unsuccessful resolution, on the other hand, leads to bitterness, resentment, and in extreme cases, may be accompanied by withdrawal from the social environment.

Work and Leisure in Middle Adulthood

Cultural beliefs and values influence how individuals come to judge their efforts and accomplishments. Hofstede's (1980) initial examination of more than forty countries revealed significant differences in how people in these countries viewed and interpreted work and approached their social relationships at work. In particular, cultures differed on the following four work-related values: power distance, uncertainty avoidance, individualism/collectivism, and masculinity/femininity.

Cultures low on **power distance** put *less emphasis on organizational hierarchy and status between people.* In some cultures, it may be acceptable for a president of a company and a warehouse worker to socialize outside of work. Examples of countries low in power distance are Denmark, Israel, and Austria. Countries high in power distance are Mexico, Venezuela, and India.

The workplace in cultures low in **uncertainty avoidance** tend to *have few rules, policies, and codes that guide workers' communication and interpersonal relations.* In these cultures, a worker's complaints may be handled by different people in a relatively informal way, rather than by an appointed person according to specific procedures. Cultures low in uncertainty avoidance are Singapore, Denmark, and Sweden. Countries with the highest uncertainty avoidance are Greece, Portugal, Belgium, and Japan.

Collectivism, according to Hofstede, refers to the *degree to which a culture facilitates conformity, compliance, and the striving for harmony in the workplace.* Peru, Pakistan, Colombia, and Venezuela score high on collectivism, whereas the United States, Australia, Great Britain, and Canada tend to foster individualistic work values.

Finally, work environments in **"feminine cultures"** *promote gender equality, interpersonal contact, and group decision making.* This dimension can best be described as "working to live" versus "living to work." Scandinavian countries rate the highest in "femininity," whereas Japan, Austria, Italy, and Switzerland tend to promote "masculine" values.

More recently, Furnham, Kirkcaldy, and Lynn (1994) studied forty-one nations with regard to seven work-related beliefs. Their results showed that people in North and South America scored highest on work ethic (commitment to work), mastery (need to master problems), savings (importance of saving money), and conformity (identification with the organization and its success). Asian and Eastern countries scored highest on competitiveness (motive to be better than others) and money beliefs (importance of money). In addition, European countries scored lower than non-European countries on all seven dimensions, including achievement (need for excellence).

These beliefs about the work environment are also related to the non-work environment. Studies of leisure activities show that these are both similar and different across cultures. Beatty, Jeon, Albaum, and Murphy (1994) questioned adults in the United States, France, Denmark, and New Zealand about their participation in recreational activities. Findings revealed three consistent clusters: *aesthetic-intellectual* (e.g., reading for pleasure, attending the opera, ballet, or dancing), *sports-action* (e.g., attending sports events or individual sports participation), and *social-entertainment* (e.g., going to the movies, having drinks, and enjoying entertainment). Two additional dimensions that were also examined did not replicate across cultures: *outdoor-nature* (e.g., walking for pleasure or bicycling) and *passive-in-home* (e.g., watching TV and playing sedentary games). The United States and New Zealand were most similar in their leisure activity preferences, with both scoring higher than their European counterparts on the sports-action and social-entertainment dimensions.

Among Chinese adults (Hu, 1990) the first choice for a hobby is reading, followed by social and intellectual activities. Physical exercise is third, tied with other productive activities such as knitting or crafts. One could speculate that leisure activities, defined as the antithesis of work (see Beatty et al., 1994), provide an environment or context that fulfills needs not met in the workplace. Therefore, one could possibly draw conclusions from predominant work values about the preferences for leisure activities. For example, individuals in cultures that emphasize collectivist work environments may choose to spend their leisure time in solitary activities, as is the case in China. On the other hand, people in individualistic societies such as New Zealand, Canada, and the United States, where people work independently and often autonomously, may prefer leisure activities that are social and cooperative.

Social Support and Well-Being in Later Adulthood

The relationship between well-being and social support in later adulthood appears to be largely universal. Comparisons of such diverse cultures as those of North America and India show a remarkable similarity in patterns of social support from spouses, relatives, adult children, and friends and the influence on well-being (Ventrakaman, 1995). At the same time, cultural differences can be found in the expectations or norms regarding social relationships maintained by elderly persons.

Normative expectations that children care for their elderly parents in Thailand result in the common arrangement that at least one adult child lives in the same household or at least very close by, thereby providing a minimum level of social support (Knodel et al., 1995). Even if the caregiving is perceived as demanding, a deep sense of family obligation and emotional bond maintains this system of social connection in old age (Caffrey, 1992).

However, cultural change may affect the social support system of some elderly. For example, shifts in familial positions in Taiwan have recently produced situations in which the daughter-in-law gains more importance in some families than the formerly powerful mother-in-law. With decreased responsibilities, older women have begun to experience feelings of uselessness and reduced social support. This change in social relationships has been related to an increase in suicide risk among the elderly in Taiwan (Hu, 1995).

It is not merely the presence of a social support system that is relevant to well-being. Reciprocal relationships, in which individuals both receive and provide support, are related to greater life satisfaction. Such relationships seem to be more prevalent in France than in North America (Antonucci, 1990). For example, the elderly in France perceive their social relationships as more reciprocal than both Caucasians and African-Americans in the United States.

◇ SUMMARY

While virtually all social relationships and roles change over the lifespan, some aspects of them are more salient at different ages. The types of relationships children develop with their primary caretakers early in life set the stage for many social relationships to come. Yet, the attachment patterns of infants are seemingly influenced by caretaking practices and general conditions under which children grow up. As children learn to communicate, they begin to form more social relationships; these are initially built and later maintained through play. Social relationships require basic skills, such as conflict resolution and cooperation, which involve a general understanding of moral principles. Kohlberg's theory of moral development addresses some important aspects of morality, namely the understanding of normative principles of justice. However, Gilligan has demonstrated that individuals may also base their moral decisions on nurturance and caring. Though they represent interdependent elements of moral reasoning, the salience of either of these moral orientations may vary from culture to culture.

Adolescents face the difficult task of defining an adult identity for themselves. This process, which Erikson calls identity formation, has many implications for social relationships, roles, and behavior. In exploring their identities, adolescents redefine relationships with parents and peers and negotiate their role in their community and the larger society.

Middle adulthood is dominated by concerns of productivity, which manifest differently depending on values and expectations. Finally, social support and satisfying social relationships facilitate well-being and peace of mind in older adulthood.

◇ THINGS TO DO AND THINK ABOUT

1. Play, games, and peer culture are important elements of the developmental niche during childhood. Make a list of some of the games you played when you were between about four to seven years of age. Which underlying values, beliefs, skills, or norms did these games involve? How would the rules or the way in which these games were played change if they were played today in cultures with different values, beliefs, and norms (e.g., among Chinese or !Kung children)?

2. Consider Corsaro and Eder's (1990) discussion of peer culture in this chapter. Which of the four themes of childhood peer culture did your childhood games address? Given the importance of play and games for social development in childhood, the advent of computers raises some interesting psychological issues. In industrialized countries, children spend more and more time interacting with computers or other electronic media. Which aspects of peer culture are affected by such technological trends? Which aspects of social development may be affected? What are some potential benefits of such technological changes?

3. Do you perform better under pressure? Some people do and others do not. In this chapter, we discussed the issue of competition versus cooperation. Think about the advantages and disadvantages of growing up in a competitive educational setting in contrast to a cooperative one. In which do you think you would learn more? Are there limits to healthy competition? When does competition become stressful?

4. If you have children under age ten in your family or neighborhood, you can use the pictures and story in Box 7.2 to assess their level of distributive justice reasoning. What did you discover about the ages at which the different levels of reasoning occur? Were there gender differences?

◇ FURTHER READINGS

Elliott M. Avedon and Brian Sutton-Smith. (1979). *The Study of Games.* Huntington, NY: Krieger.

> Although not a recent publication, this book represents a collection of diverse perspectives on the universal phenomenon of games and play. The book includes readings from fields such as anthropology, history, sociology, folklore, psychology, education, and business. Each chapter is followed by a list of selected references. The three sections are (1) history and origins of games (e.g., historical, anthropological, and folklore sources), (2) uses of games (e.g., recreation, military, education, diagnosis and treatment), and (3) structure and function of games.

Cheryl Bentsen. (1989). *Maasai Days.* New York: Anchor Books.

> The author provides a close-up look at this traditional African culture. This book is not so much a scholarly account but an informative and lively view of Maasai everyday life. Among other things, the reader learns about the concerns of two young boys torn between traditional and modern ways, young adult women and their social network, and young men who take great pride in their role as warriors.

CHAPTER EIGHT

THE FAMILY IN
CULTURAL CONTEXT

The sun is just beginning to rise in Boslanti, along the Saramacca River in central Suriname, the smallest country in South America. Sindy Sowidagkijm, twenty-four, and her husband, David, twenty-six, surrounded by a midwife, and several female relatives, including two grandmothers, are nearing the birth of their third child. The two older children, on the other side of the small wooden house, are lulled to sleep by the rhythmic sound of light rain on the corrugated-iron roof. Suddenly, a baby's cry fills the room, and little Jacob makes his arrival known to all. Sindy, exhausted but happy, will breast-feed her newborn and take a deserved rest. David will dream of the day that his new son will join him and his uncles on the family fishing boat. The others will proudly spread the word about the newest citizen in Boslanti.

◇ ◇ ◇

At Mt. Sinai Hospital, in downtown New York City, Walter and Patricia Mezzanotti have just entered the brightly-lit delivery room on the eighth floor. At thirty-eight, this is Patricia's first pregnancy and it has been unusually difficult. She is lightly sedated with an intravenous needle pumping a labor-inducing drug into her arm. Two hours later, following an emergency Cesarean section performed by two doctors and two nurses, she is sleeping quietly in the recovery room awaiting the time she will see her new son for the first time. Just down the hall, relaxing in a rocking chair in a birthing room and talking with her husband, five-year-old daughter, other family members, and two close friends is Anne Kane. In a half hour, she will give birth to a daughter in a quiet homelike atmosphere and begin the bonding process by immediately holding and feeding her newborn.

◇ ◇ ◇

◇ CULTURAL VARIATIONS
IN THE FAMILY LIFE CYCLE

In the words of William Kenkel (1985), *"Families have a beginning, they grow in numbers, their membership next declines, and eventually the original family exists no longer.* The individual is born, grows, enters a period of decline, and inevitably passes from the scene. The striking parallel between the life pattern of a normal individual and the history of a typical family gave rise to the concept **family life cycle**" (p. 375). Although not a literal analogy, this concept provides a framework that allows us to consider the shifting attributes that affect individual behaviors and interactions within the family, community, and cultural context. As we make our way through this chapter, we shall be looking at the family life cycle in terms of the developmental stages used in previous chapters and relating these to real-life examples of families living in a wide variety of ecological settings throughout the world. We begin with the selection of a mate and the process of marriage.

Mate Selection

Buss (1994b) begins his study of mate preferences in thirty-seven cultures with a statement that cannot be disputed: "Every person is alive because of a successful mating. People in the past who failed to mate are not our ancestors" (p. 197). The important questions are "How do we select a marriage partner?" and "What characteristics do we consider important?"

In an effort to answer these questions, Buss (with the help of fifty other researchers) conducted an extensive study of more than ten thousand individuals living in thirty-seven cultures. The approach involved asking subjects to indicate how important each of eighteen characteristics was in selecting a mate and then to rank thirteen of these in terms of their desirability. Findings revealed that, across cultures, men and women looked for mates who were kind and understanding, intelligent, had an exciting personality, and were healthy.

Buss indicated that he and his team of researchers were surprised by some of the results, particularly cultural variations concerning the most variable characteristic—chastity or the lack of previous sexual experience. For example, they expected that men throughout the world would highly value this quality more than would women. It would be surprising if cultures did not vary in the value placed on chastity, since other sources on sexuality usually note cross-cultural variation in practices, values, and expectations (Hatfield & Ropson, 1996; Hatfield & Specher, 1996; Wallen, 1989). Such variation was indeed shown in Buss's study. While chastity was considered irrelevant or unimportant in a prospective mate by both men and women in the Netherlands, Sweden, and Norway, it was viewed as indispensable in

China and scored very highly by those from India, Taiwan, and Iran. Among those who viewed chastity as only moderately desirable were those living in Colombia, Estonia, Japan, Nigeria, Poland, South Africa, and Zambia. Yet, in an overwhelming majority of countries (two-thirds), chastity was desired in a marriage partner more by men than by women. (See Figure 8.1.)

Other categories showing large cultural differences in response were: *"good housekeeper* (highly valued in Estonia and China, little valued in Western Europe and North America); *refinement/neatness* (highly valued in Nigeria and Iran, less valued in Great Britain, Ireland, and Australia); and *religious* (highly valued in Iran, moderately valued in India, little valued in Western Europe and North America)" (Buss, 1994, p. 199). The author cautions that although these differences are important, there is undoubtedly much variability across individuals within these cultures. This once again reinforces our point that there are often greater differences within cultures than between or among cultures.

Looking more specifically at what each of the genders wanted in a mate, Buss (1994) found some interesting differences. As for women: "From the Zulu tribe in South Africa to coastal dwelling Australians to city-dwelling Brazilians, women place a premium on good earning capacity, financial prospects, ambition, industriousness, and social status more than men—characteristics that all provide resources" (p. 199). Men were found to prefer women who are younger than they are—how much younger depends on

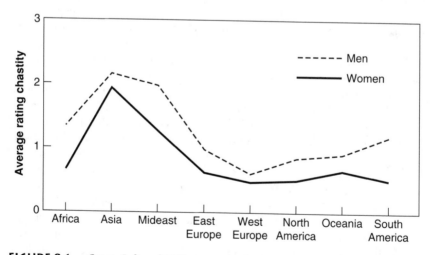

FIGURE 8.1   Cross-Cultural Differences in the Importance of Chastity

Source: From *Love and Sex* (p. 124) by E. Hatfield and R. L. Rapson, 1996, Boston: Allyn & Bacon, p. 124. Copyright © 1996 by Allyn & Bacon Publishing Co. Reprinted by permission.

the culture. For example, "In cultures that permit men to acquire multiple wives, such as Zambia and Nigeria, men prefer brides who are much younger than they are—by as many as 7 or 8 years" (p. 200). In cultures where only one wife is permitted (e.g., Germany, Spain, and France), the preference was for brides only slightly younger. In all cultures, women had a preference for older men, "because men mature somewhat later than women and because older men often have access to more resources than younger men" (p. 200). Finally, "in *all* known cultures worldwide, from the inner-continental tribal societies of Africa and South America to the big cities of Madrid, London, and Paris, men place a premium on the physical appearance of a potential mate" (p. 200). According to Buss, there is a good reason for men to favor youthfulness and physical appearance, even though they may not be fully aware that "these qualities provide the best signals . . . that the woman is fertile and has good reproductive capacity" (p. 200).

Do men and women actually act on these preferences? Perhaps we'll get some answers when we look at the next topic—marriage.

Marriage

Anthropologists have demonstrated that marriage takes many forms in cultures around the world. These include **monogamy** in which *one man is married to one woman,* **polygyny** in which *one man is married to several women,* **polyandry** in which *one woman is married to several men,* and **group marriage** in which *several women are married to several men.* You may be surprised to learn that the most "favored" form of marriage across societies is polygyny. However, Kenkel (1985) points out that "if we were to judge solely on the basis of a preponderance of a given marriage form, then few, if any, societies could be classified as polygynous. . . . No society . . . could arrange for all its males to have plural wives unless . . . the sex ratio could somehow be upset" (Kenkel, p. 22). In other words, for each man married to two women, there would have to be a man who was not married at all. Therefore, only those cultures in which more than one wife is preferred are typically considered to be polygynous. Using this criterion, G. P. Murdock (1967), the pioneering anthropologist, in a study of a large sample of the world's societies, classified 721 as polygynous, 137 as monogamous, and only 4 as polyandrous. Kenkel (1985) states that while "monogamy is actually the preferred form in a relatively small number of societies . . . it [is] . . . the only form of marriage that is permitted and recognized in every society throughout the world, although it is not always the form of marriage that receives highest approval. . . . The great bulk of the world's married population, by lot or by intent, is monogamously wed" (p. 23).

As we have just seen in the previous section, how and why individuals are attracted to each other varies significantly across cultures. Another distinction might be referred to as the "Eastern versus Western ideal." In many Western cultures, perhaps best represented by the United States, marriage is often viewed as the culmination of romantic love. The belief is that each of us has an "ideal" mate that we are destined to meet, fall in love with, marry, and live with "happily ever after." One of the authors (Gardiner) recalls a student telling him how her parents, living in Yugoslavia, met and married. One day, her father climbed a hill next to his village and watched a young woman washing clothes in the river below. He returned the next day and watched her again. On the third day, he walked down to the river, told her he had been watching her for three days and had fallen in love with her and wanted to marry her. She said "yes." They were now celebrating their twenty-fifth wedding anniversary! However, there are other people who find "true love" several times and have the marriage certificates to prove it.

The "Eastern ideal" continues to characterize many of the arranged marriages in Asia, Africa, and some other parts of the world. This ideal is based on the premise that each person has several possible mates with whom they could develop a successful marriage. Frequently, India being one example, families will discuss a possible future liaison between their infant children. Sometimes, the children are aware of this arrangement; sometimes, they are not. They are expected to marry (or bring shame and embarrassment to their families); if they are lucky, they may one day fall in love with each other. A female Indian graduate student, speaking in one of the author's (Gardiner) cross-cultural courses, related that she was returning home to Bombay to get married. When asked what her future husband did, she replied, "I don't know because I've never met him." The liberated young American women in class told her that she shouldn't marry someone she didn't know. Her reply, which makes an interesting point, was that she trusted her parents to make a wise decision regarding a future husband because they knew her and him and his family. In the meantime, she could concentrate on her studies while they (the American women) would have to search for their own husbands, go through the trials and errors of dating, and hope that in the end it would all work out.

Many of those who live in collectivist cultures view marriage as the coming together or blending of two families. For example, in northern Kenya, the creation of a new house is a significant part of the marriage ceremony. Once the wedding date is established, based on lunar calculations, the groom's family literally disassembles the new house, moves it to the bride's village, and rebuilds it. Prior to the wedding ceremony, the bride is taken through a rite of passage during which she is initiated into womanhood by the village's female elders and is taught what to expect from married life. Among the Mande, another African group, girls between ages twelve and eighteen attend clitoridectomy schools, where they have their clitorides removed and are formally taught how to be wives. They learn secret languages and codes that allow them to communicate with other married women. In today's Africa, wedding customs are undergoing change and reflect a mixture of the traditional as well as the modern (Hudgins & Williams-Snyder, 1995).

The same might be said of contemporary Japan, where love marriages have increasingly replaced the earlier practice of arranged marriages. Whichever practice is followed, certain traditional customs remain. For example, according to Fukada (1991), a *yuinou,* or ceremonial betrothal gift (often in the form of money), is first presented by the bridegroom-to-be, through a go-between, to the bride-to-be's household. In anthropological terms this represents the bride price. The bride's parents are then expected to spend several times the value of the *yuinou* on a new home for the couple. Most wedding ceremonies in Japan are performed according to Shinto customs, followed by the drinking of sake (rice wine) as confirmation of the marriage and later by a celebration party.

In Thailand, couples tend to marry at later ages (late twenties to early thirties) as they continue their education and establish careers. According to Gardiner and Gardiner (1991), "While young people frequently reject arranged marriages in favor of making their own choices, they still observe the traditional ceremonies associated with marriage, including the morning blessing and chanting by monks, the pouring of lustral water, and a large evening reception for friends and relatives" (p. 180).

Harry and Ormsin Gardiner's Thai wedding ceremony. (Courtesy of the authors)

◇ THE BIRTH PROCESS ACROSS CULTURES

As the vignettes that opened this chapter illustrate, although newborns arrive every day in cultures around the world, the birth experience depends very much on cultural traditions and is deeply embedded within an ecological setting influenced by family, community, and culture.

In some societies, having a baby is just another normal event in one's life and takes little preparation. This is illustrated in the following example taken from the !Kung in the Kalahari Desert of Africa: "The first labor pains came at night and stayed . . . until dawn. That morning, everyone went gathering. Mother and I stayed behind. We sat together for a while, then I went and played with the other children. Later, I came back and ate the nuts she had cracked for me. She got up and started to get ready. . . . We walked a short way, then she sat down by the base of a large nehn tree, leaned back against it, and little Kumsa was born" (Shostak, 1981, pp. 53–54). Similarly, in rural Thailand, pregnancy does not significantly change a woman's behavior, and she "generally carries on with her household chores until the time of birth—even, in some cases, up to the last few minutes before delivery. Rural children are usually born at home with the mother resting on a mat or mattress on the floor assisted by a non-medically trained midwife and older relatives or neighbors" (Gardiner and Gardiner, 1991, p. 183). A few hours later, the new mother is often up and participating in family activities.

In many parts of North America, including the United States, fathers-to-be are typically present during labor and encouraged to actively participate in the delivery of their child, whether it is at home or in a hospital. Not so in some parts of the former Soviet Union or in East Africa, where an expectant Ngoni mother is assisted by other women while husbands and other men are completely excluded.

Clearly, not every culture approaches childbirth in the same way. In the next section, we shall look at the birth process in more detail and consider some of its variations across cultures.

The Ecology of Birth

For a long time, what we knew about childbirth practices came from a Western, largely American, perspective that viewed the procedure as a medical event. Interestingly, this was not always the case. In fact, according to Wertz and Wertz (1979), childbirth in Canada and the United States, like a majority of other countries, was handled exclusively by women until the middle of the nineteenth century, when physicians, almost all of whom were men, began delivering babies and made it a medical rather than a social event.

In the original edition of her now classic cross-cultural investigation of childbirth in four cultures, Brigitte Jordan (1978) anticipated the approach we take here when she noted that "we have paid little attention to the social-interactional and socio-ecological aspects of birth [which address] . . . what is biological and what is social and cultural in the process of childbirth" (Preface). In the Preface to the fourth edition of this book, Jordan (1993) states that "an anthropology of birth must focus on the study of birthing *systems* and not the comparison of individual and isolated practices. We know that birth is everywhere a socially marked crisis event that is consensually shaped and socially patterned [consisting of] . . . practices that make sense from the inside out, though not necessarily from the outside in" (pp. xi–xii).

In a section of her book titled "The Ecology of Birth," Jordan discusses the particular locations in which babies are born and how these reflect culture-specific patterns (or ecological settings, as we would view them) within which individuals' lives are forever entwined. She also comments on the cultural implications of these specific arrangements.

Yucatan

Of the four cultures studied by Jordan (1993), the Yucatan imposes the least changes in the expectant mother's surroundings, maintaining its familiar and reassuring qualities by encouraging the Mayan woman to lie in the same hammock in which she sleeps each night "whose strengths and tautness she knows to exploit for maximum support and comfort [thereby providing] . . . the kind of security that marks the event as a normal part of family life" (p. 68).

In Yucatan, there is a clear expectation that the father-to-be will be present during labor and birth, not only to take an active role, but also in order to observe "how a woman suffers."

Frequently, if a child is stillborn, it is blamed on an absent father. In addition, the pregnant woman's mother should be present, often in the company of others from the family microsystem, including sisters, sisters-in-law, mothers-in-law, godmothers, and sometimes neighbors and close friends. According to Jordan (1978), all of these people make a contribution to a successful birth, and the intensity of their emotional and physical involvement is "mirrored in the strain on their faces and in the signs of fatigue that become evident in them as well as in the mother" (p. 38).

Immediately following birth, it is believed that the mother and her child are susceptible to the influence of evil spirits from the bush and must remain inside the house for one week before returning to normal activity. An infant girl will have her ears pierced within the first hour after birth and sometime within the next three days will receive her first earrings, often a family heirloom.

A Mayan woman, lying in her hammock, surrounded by her husband and a midwife, gives birth. (From *Birth in Four Cultures,* 4th ed., by B. Jordan, 1993, Prospect Heights, IL: Waveland Press, Inc. Reprinted by permission of Waveland Press, Inc.)

Nearly all newborns are breast-fed, with nursing beginning a few minutes after birth and continuing whenever the infant appears hungry or anxious.

Holland and Sweden

In Holland, like Yucatan, women generally give birth at home, assisted by a midwife or physician, and the country continues to maintain one of the lowest infant mortality rates in the world (U.S. Bureau of the Census, 1992). In Sweden, often cited as the country with the lowest infant mortality, almost all babies are delivered in hospitals with the help of highly trained midwives. According to Jordan, what these two countries have in common is a program of government-sponsored prenatal care for every woman as well as availability of abortion on demand, with the result that "for all practical purposes, all pregnancies are wanted pregnancies and all babies are wanted babies" (p. 46).

In both Holland and Sweden, the mother-to-be is usually assisted by a midwife and her assistant and sometimes by a husband, male or female friend, or relative, who is there to provide help and emotional support. According to Jordan (1978), Dutch and Swedish midwives do not view the woman as a patient to be delivered but as an individual capable of giving birth on her own. Their role is to give encouragement, be prepared for complications, and take care of cutting the umbilical cord.

United States

In the United States, ranking twenty-first in the world in infant mortality, the majority of births (approximately 98 percent) continue to be in hospital settings under the control of medical specialists (Declercq, 1993). However, unlike the three countries mentioned above, there is a wider range of options available. For example, while some families prefer to have their babies delivered at home with the assistance of a midwife, increasing numbers, like the Kane family in our opening vignette, are taking advantage of birthing rooms located in hospitals, where technology is available but a home atmosphere is provided.

In this regard, an experimental project cited by Jordan is of historical (and perhaps contemporary) interest. Over a period of three years during the early 1970s, two nurse-midwives conducted the majority of normal deliveries in a California hospital. During this period, there was a dramatic drop in the number of stillbirths, fetal deaths, premature births, and neonatal deaths. When physicians once again took charge, all of these types of incidents increased, with the prematurity rate going up nearly 50 percent and neonatal mortality more than tripling (Levy et al., 1971). Jordan concludes that not only is the birth experience significantly influenced by who is allowed to be present during birth but so is the outcome of the birth process itself.

Discussing the consequences of a culture's choice of birth setting (home, hospital, bush, or elsewhere), Jordan (1993) makes an intriguing comment when she notes that when babies are delivered in hospitals, "responsibility and credit are clearly the physician's . . . visible in the handshake and 'thank you' [exchanged] . . . after the birth. . . . Typically, nobody thanks the woman [who] . . . has delivered rather than given birth" (p. 71). However, when babies are delivered at home, birth arrangements are the choice of the expectant mother and her family—"Their choice, their problem, their task, and . . . finally . . . their achievement" (p. 71). These may be subtle differences in language but they represent significant differences in cultural views and belief systems that form a crucial part of one's experiences within different developmental niches and ecological surroundings.

Writing nearly twenty years ago, Jordan (1978) concluded her original birth study with the following statement: "What we need to keep in mind here is that birthing systems themselves are part of a larger cultural system . . . within an economic and political structure, via the socialization of birth participants" (p. 73). This point is even more relevant today, especially in light of our recurring themes, which focus on the cultural context in which development takes place.

In a sense, if you know a society's approach to childbirth, you will understand a great deal about the values and beliefs that are at the heart of its ecocultural system, how it socializes its members, and how it conducts its interpersonal relationships.

◇ THE TRANSITION TO PARENTHOOD

Kenkel (1985) puts the transition to parenthood in perspective when he states that "one of the significant features with regard to the parent role is a general lack of preparation for it. . . . Related to [this] . . . is the fact that the transition . . . is abrupt [and] . . . is largely irrevocable" (pp. 455–456).

Becoming a parent results in major life changes that affect not only the parents and their infant but also many others within the ecological setting in which this event occurs. For example, Heinicke (1995) writes that within a family system "the personality characteristics of the parents as well as their relationship support systems (partner and extended family) to a significant extent define future parenting transactions with their child" (p. 277). We might ask "What about other niche influences such as the social and physical environment and customs of child care?" These surely play an equally important role and are worthy of future research on the part of those interested in cross-cultural human development.

In this regard, Belsky (1985) hypothesizes that "supportive developmental experiences give rise to a mature healthy personality, that is then capable of providing sensitive parental care which fosters optimal child development" (p. 86). This again points to the importance of the ecological setting and the transmission from one generation to another of successful parental belief systems learned within a healthy family environment. In fact, Vondra and Belsky (1993), in a recent study of the developmental origins of parenting, state that "by assuming an ecological perspective . . . and by adopting a longitudinal design, research has begun to provide a more adequate test of developmental and clinical theory on the origins of parenting" (p. 25).

◇ INFANCY AND CHILDHOOD

According to the National Center for Health Statistics (1994), each day throughout the world, approximately 750,000 individuals become new parents. Contrary to what many of these parents may think, a newborn is not always the pretty, smiling, curly-haired cherub they have imagined or seen in pictures or television commercials. Rather, a newborn is frequently an unattractive little creature—sometimes very small (or very big), often bald, toothless, hungry, and complaining—that has come to live with the new family for many years. During the first few days and weeks, most new couples wonder if they are capable of nurturing this new person and attending to its needs. Fortunately, the majority of parents are capable and, with later additions to the family, often get even better at it.

On arrival, most **newborns** (the *term applied to babies from birth through the first two weeks*, after which the term *infant* is used) are well equipped to deal with their new environment. For the most part, their senses work well, and they have a large repertoire of reflexes to help them adjust to the world beyond the womb. So effective are these reflexes, and so resilient are newborns, that following the devastating earthquake in Mexico City in September of 1985, babies were found alive in the ruins of one hospital nursery six days later.

In the initial days and months following birth, parents devote much attention and concern to satisfying their child's basic needs for sleep, hunger, and elimination (see Chapter 2). As Bornstein (1995) aptly observes, "Infants forever alter the sleeping, eating, and working habits of their parents; they change who parents are and how parents define themselves. . . . Parenting an infant is a 168-hour-a-week job" (p. 3). As children get older and move into the years of early, middle, and later childhood, development keeps pace. At the center of all this activity, largely determining the nature of the parent-child relationship, are parental belief systems.

Parental Belief Systems

In every culture, parents tend to develop shared ideas about the nature of children, their developmental processes, and the meaning of their behaviors. Strongly influenced by the cultural context, these ideas are entwined with other aspects of life, including time and place, meaning of self, family, and parenthood.

An early contribution to this more sophisticated understanding of parental ideology lies in the pioneering work of Diana Baumrind (1971, 1993), who first described three patterns of common parenting styles: (1) *authoritarian*, emphasizing obedience and strict discipline, associated with children who are either shy or rebellious and have difficulty interacting with others; (2) *democratic or authoritative*, emphasizing direction but allowing for individuality, associated with children who demonstrate self-confidence, independence, and self-control; and (3) *permissive*, allowing a great deal of freedom, often with little discipline, associated with children who are impulsive and immature. While each of these patterns was shown to be correlated with specific child behaviors, Baumrind (1980, 1991) and others (Dornbusch, Ritter, Leiderman, Roberts, & Fraleigh, 1987; Scarr, 1993) have recognized that these findings did not always apply equally well to all cultural and ethnic groups. In a particularly interesting study conducted among Chinese-Americans, Chao (1994) demonstrated that a number of Baumrind's characteristics failed to adequately describe the Chinese approach to childrearing and discipline.

As Harkness and Super (1996) point out in an important contribution to the literature of culture and human development, these cultural under-

standings are organized into categories referred to as **parents' cultural belief systems** and "relate in *systematic ways to action—including . . . styles of talking to children, methods of discipline, or seeking advice from experts.* Ultimately
[these belief systems] . . . exert a powerful influence on the health and development of children, and they are a key component in the development of
parents themselves" (pp. 2–3). Parental beliefs represent one component of
the developmental niche—the psychology of the caretaker.

Developing a philosophy of childrearing is one of the major tasks faced
by new parents (Kenkel, 1985). In a particularly interesting application of
this idea, Richman and others (1988) observed mother-child interactions in
five cultures (three industrial and two agrarian) and reported a number of
prominent differences. Among the more interesting was the finding that
Gusii mothers of Kenya hold their nine- to ten-month-old infants and engage in soothing physical contact more than do middle-class mothers in
Boston, Massachusetts, but, at the same time, look at and talk to them less
often. Why? According to Richman and her colleagues there are several reasons for this behavior, all of which make perfect sense once you understand
the ecology of the cultures involved. For example, among the Gusii (1) infant mortality rates are high, and holding and soothing provide a greater
chance of survival; (2) there is a belief that language is not understood by
children until about the age of two; and (3) the culture teaches that one
should avoid making direct eye contact with others. On the other hand, in
the American culture there is a belief that (1) language learning should begin
early, and (2) placing infants in playpens where they can play by themselves
begins the process of independence so highly valued in American society.

Ever since Sigel (1985) edited one of the first volumes discussing this
concept, interest in parental belief systems as an approach to understanding
cultural similarities and differences has grown rapidly (Goodnow & Collins,
1990; Sigel, McGillicuddy-DeLisi, & Goodnow, 1992). This concept has also
been fostered by the emergence of parallel trends in social anthropology,
psychology, and new interdisciplinary approaches to culture and human development (Harkness & Super, 1996).

Also contributing to this unifying new concept are some of the approaches serving as major themes for this book. For example, the ecological
systems approach of Bronfenbrenner (1989, 1993) provides a dynamic, interactive paradigm of parent-child interactions as they occur within a continually expanding cultural context that shapes the development of effective
parental beliefs and practices. The developmental niche framework proposed
by Super and Harkness (1986) assists in "conceptualizing relationships
among parental belief systems, customs, and practices of childrearing and the
organization of physical and social settings for children's daily lives" (Harkness & Super, 1996, p. 5). The concept of an "ecocultural niche" integrates
ideas from these approaches and connects parental belief systems and

parental behavior with these beliefs and family and community ecology (Gallimore, Weisner, Kaufman, & Bernheimer, 1989). Parents in the ecocultural niche of the family as well as in the developmental niche of individual children play a crucial mediating role between children's experiences and the larger culture in which they live. In the words of Harkness and Super: "The conceptualization of parents in the child or family's niche leads naturally, in turn, to an interest in the cultural construction of experience from the point of view of parents themselves, in particular their cultural belief systems or 'parental ethnotheories' regarding children, families, and parenthood" (1995, p. 228). Finally, the developmental models emerging from the Vygotskian perspective (discussed in detail in Chapter 4) focus on the relationship between individual development and cultural meaning systems as well as between parenting behaviors and symbolic systems (Harkness & Super, 1996; Holland & Valsiner, 1988; Lave & Wenger, 1991; Rogoff, 1990).

After reviewing these and numerous similar studies, we find that the following questions have not been adequately answered by the research literature: "In general, are there relationships between specific parenting beliefs and parenting behaviors?" "Are there universals, as well as variations, in what we might call 'good parenting'?" "Do certain kinds of parenting lead to certain kinds of outcomes for children, both cross-culturally as well as within cultures?" "What form do parental cultural belief systems take in cultures where relatives, other than parents (e.g., uncles, aunts, grandparents, and in-laws) play critically important roles?" We offer these questions in the hope that those who might pursue future studies in these areas will help extend our understanding of human development within the context of culture.

Throughout the remainder of this chapter, we will learn how parents' cultural belief systems influence the manner in which lives develop across cultures, beginning with mothering and fathering behaviors.

Mothering

In their research on mothering, Barnard and Martell (1995) note that cultures consider this behavior extremely important, especially since mothers are the primary day-to-day teachers of culture. The authors also point out that opportunities to view similarities and differences in the mothering role have been limited because mothering generally takes place within the privacy of the family. Although these researchers do not use Bronfenbrenner's ecological systems terminology, their thinking sounds similar. For example, they state that "the role [of mothering] . . . develops in relation to the family system wherein roles of father, siblings, and other extended family members are enacted as well. . . . Each person's role is connected with all others in the family system and because that is true there are always variations within cultures. [For example] . . . as the position of women changes, aspects of the mothering role will be assumed by others in the family or in the society" (p. 3).

According to Harkness and Super (1995), mothering has historically been associated with women, because in most cultures women have provided primary care for children. In this regard, and in light of our discussion of Japanese families in this chapter, it is interesting to consider Barnard and Martell's (1995) analysis of the Japanese words for *woman, mother, man,* and *father:* "The character for woman is a stick figure with a protuberance, resembling a pregnant abdomen, whereas the character for mother resembles the chest with two breasts. The symbol for man, on the other hand, is the rice field illustrating work. The character for father is a stone axe symbolizing power" (p. 4). More accurately, the symbol for man is a combination of two characters, one representing a rice field and the other representing power which symbolizes hard work (Gardiner, 1996). *Parenting* is represented by three characters literally translated as "to stand," "a tree," and "to watch," which, when combined, can be interpreted as "watching over a growing child" (Gardiner, 1996). For a visual representation of these characters, see Figure 8.2.

Barnard and Martell also point out that these characters came from the original Chinese language and represent ethnic and intergenerational thinking about these roles within both these cultures. These character distinctions raise several intriguing questions: "Are mothering, fathering, and parenting

FIGURE 8.2   Japanese Characters Related to Parenting

Source: Drawn by Alan V. Gardiner.

distinct roles?" "Are birthing and nurturing unique characteristics of the mother's role whereas support and family control are assigned to the father's role?" "Is parenting different than mothering and fathering?" Hopefully, with an increased interest in cross-cultural analysis, these and related issues will be answered in the not too distant future.

Fathering

Research on the role of fathers is of relatively recent origin (Biller, 1993; Parke, 1995; Mackey, 1985), and research on cross-cultural comparisons is still comparatively rare (Gardiner, 1994; Lamb, 1987). However, it is promising to note that when fathering is studied, it is being increasingly observed from both the ecological systems and contextual approach (Bronfenbrenner, 1989; Repetti, 1993) as well as the lifespan perspective (Elder, Modell, & Parke, 1993; Parke & Stearns, 1993). In this regard, Parke (1995) stresses "the importance of examining developmental changes in the adult because parents continue to change and develop during adult years" (pp. 27–28). He points out that the age at which an individual becomes a parent can significantly affect the ways in which men and women carry out their paternal and maternal roles and that education, self-identity, and career tasks are related to the demands of being a parent. For example, the average age of marriage in Egypt and the Sudan is twenty-five to thirty-five years for men and twenty to thirty years for women in urban areas, twenty to twenty-five for men and sixteen to eighteen for women in rural areas (Ahmed, 1991). In Nigeria, among the Muslim Hausa, a boy usually enters his first marriage around the age of twenty, often to a girl of thirteen or fourteen who has just reached puberty. For a Yoruba male, marriage typically takes place when the man is in his middle to late twenties and the girl is about sixteen to eighteen years of age (Okafor, 1991). Among the Southeast Asian Hmong, large numbers of whom have migrated to the United States, it is common for men in their twenties to thirties to marry young girls in their early to middle adolescent years. While many of these young people may be adequately prepared, as part of their developmental niche, to assume parental responsibilities at these relatively young ages, others are not and, being recently children themselves, will find married life and childrearing difficult.

One of the leading views of fathering or father involvement has been presented by Lamb, Pleck, Charnov, and Levine (1987) who consider three components to be of crucial importance: interaction, availability, and responsibility. They describe these in the following way: "Interaction refers to the father's direct contact with his child through caregiving and shared activities. Availability is a related concept concerning the child's potential availability for interaction . . . whether or not direct interaction is occurring. Responsibility refers to the role the father takes in ascertaining that the child is taken care of and arranging for resources to be available for the child" (p. 125). In addition, Radin (1993) has recommended that a distinction be made between absolute and relative involvement as well as between a father's participation in child-care activities and in leisure, play, and related activities, since these are likely to be independent and have an effect on the way children and adults view the father's role.

In cross-cultural studies focusing on a variety of cultures (United States, Great Britain, France, Belgium, Israel, Sweden, and Australia), in which quantitative assessments were made comparing mother and father involvement with children of a wide age range (one month to sixteen years), on a large number of measures (basic care, holding, reading, verbal interactions), the overall pattern was the same: mothers spent more time and engaged in more activities with their children than did fathers (Collins & Russell, 1991; Coltrane, 1996; Jackson, 1987; Lamb et al., 1982; Russell & Russell, 1987).

In concluding his review of father-child relationships, Parke (1995) points out that studies of this topic are now "a more fully contextualized issue. Fathers in the context of their social relationships both within and beyond the family are increasingly the appropriate point of entry for understanding the issue of both parental roles and their impact on themselves and others" (p. 56).

This approach and the need for meeting the needs of fathers within an ecological perspective has been effectively presented in the recent work of Meyers (1997). In order to provide maximum benefits for fathers (and mothers), he proposes that parent education programs address issues such as the enhancement of child and marital communication skills, provide social support for parents, increase their involvement in childrearing, and provide authoritative child-care knowledge while acknowledging diversity among parents in terms of their differing social and cultural backgrounds, including parents who are single, adolescent, low-income, or minority.

✧ ADOLESCENCE

According to Holmbeck, Paikoff, and Brooks-Gunn (1995), parenting of adolescents has only recently become a topic of concern in the research literature. In fact, as recently as a decade and a half ago, one author found so little information on family relationships during the adolescent years that it was impossible to write a very lengthy review of the area (Adelson, 1980, 1985). While a significant body of relevant literature, as well as several useful reviews, have since appeared (Collins, 1990; Paikoff & Brooks-Gunn, 1991; Steinberg, 1990), little detailed attention has been given to the study of adolescence in many cultures other than the United States and a few other societies around the world.

The lack of cross-cultural parent-adolescent research from the standpoint of cultural context may be the result of several factors. First, many theories of adolescent development place greater emphasis on biological than on social or cultural factors as primary determinants of psychological characteristics. Second, there is continuing disagreement within the field as to whether or not adolescence represents a universal period of development. While some theorists take the viewpoint that it does, others argue that adolescence may be a developmental stage in some cultural settings but not in others (Whiting, Burbank, & Ratner, 1986).

Among those specifically interested in studying adolescence from the ecological perspective are Garbarino (1985) and Muuss (1988). In the words of Muuss (1988), a strong adherent of this approach: "An ecological model goes far beyond what is presently known, opening up new perspectives and generating new hypotheses that are bound to move developmental research from the clearly defined, easily controllable research laboratory into the ecological field" (p. 300).

The Ecological Systems Approach and Adolescence

From an ecological systems perspective, we will look at the structures that influence the development of adolescents, irrespective of the cultures in which they live. First, various microsystems are involved, including the primary one of the family (parents, siblings, extended family members); the system involving friends, peers, and school; and perhaps other systems made up of neighbors and other social groups. As we learned in earlier chapters, microsystems are continually undergoing change, as are the individuals who move in and out of them. As Muuss (1996) points out, a healthy microsystem is one based on reciprocity, especially in the relationships between parents and adolescents: "If a microsystem is rich in information, it enhances learning and development by providing opportunities in which questions are asked and answered, exploration and experimentation encouraged, and guidance provided [and it] . . . will foster opportunities for success in later life" (p. 324).

Next, there is the mesosystem, which links the adolescent's various microsystems (e.g., family, school, and peers). In many cultures, conflicts exist between the parents' values and peer group values. This lack of agreement can result in family conflict, regardless of culture. White (1993) provides the following quote from a Japanese adolescent (which could just as easily have been made by a North American, European, or Latin American young woman): "When I'm with my best friend I feel safe. Talking to her gives me peace. She never gets angry, or tries to get me to change. And she never embarrasses me in public the way my mother does" (p. 144).

While an adolescent may not actively participate in the next ecological level, the exosystem, much of what goes on there (e.g., at local government meetings, in parents' workplaces, or in the mass media) may indirectly affect her (Muuss, 1996). For example, the school board in Salto, Uruguay, may determine that school enrollment will be down next year and be unable to hire fourteen-year-old Manuel Sacco's mother, Graciela, to teach for them. This will lower the family income and mean that Manuel and his brother and sister will have fewer new clothes and less food and may have to transfer to other schools.

Finally, there is the adolescent's macrosystem. Although of considerable importance, this is probably the least studied of all ecological systems; except for anthropological research, it almost never receives systematic investigation. As Muuss (1996) points out, "Although the macrosystem does not impinge directly on the life of the individual adolescent . . . it contains an overarching societal ground plan for the ecology of human development. [This includes] . . . a core of general cultural, political, social, legal, religious, economic, and educational values and, most important, public policy. As such, a macrosystem may be thought of as a societal blueprint" (p. 330).

These macrosystem values frequently find expression in social customs and what the culture considers fashionable at various times. For example, the macrosystem determines standards of physical attractiveness and what is appropriate and inappropriate behavior for each sex (Muuss, 1996). Physical attractiveness appears to be important to adolescents throughout the world, yet one culture's definition of physically attractive may differ from another's. As we will see in Chapter 9, in many Western countries, especially the United States, the media (television, movies, magazines) portray thinness as the female ideal. In certain African cultures, scarring of the face is considered physically attractive. In China, at one point in its history, binding a woman's feet to keep them small and dainty was a sign of beauty.

Using modern video and computer techniques, Langlois & Roggman (1990) were able to generate a series of composite faces constructed from photographs of "average" men and women and discovered that subjects found these composites more appealing than any of the individual faces. According to Hatfield and Rapson (1996), "The average of many imperfect faces resulted in . . . perfection. . . . Attractive faces are only average" (p. 33). Preference for the average face (or as Hatfield and Rapson have described it, "the appealingly mediocre") has been found in a wide variety of cultural groups, including Indians in eastern Paraguay, several hunting and gathering societies in Africa, and in Russia and Brazil (Gangestad, Thornhill, & Yeo, 1994; Jones & Hill, 1993).

Cross-Cultural Differences in
Adolescent Peer Relationships

The role of **peers**—*individuals of similar age and sometimes the same gender*—is very important in the microsystems and exosystems of some adolescents. There are significant social and cultural differences in the specific influences peers and friends have on adolescents. For example, Muuss (1988) suggests that peer groups play a much greater role in Western societies, where extended education is the norm, than in more traditional societies, where schooling ends in the early adolescent years. In the latter, he points out, orientation becomes vertical in relation of one's elders, rather than horizontal in relation to one's peers. As evidence, he cites an early study by Hsu, Watrous, and Lord (1961) in which second-, third-, and fourth-generation adolescents of Chinese background in Hawaii were compared to a matched group of Chicago adolescents. Findings revealed that the Hawaiian group was more family oriented, less rebellious, and less troubled by adolescence than the Chicago group, which tended to be more oriented toward peers. More recent research suggests that the influence of peers versus parents and family undergoes a significant transformation during the middle to late adolescent years (Grotevant & Cooper, 1985).

Along similar lines, Bronfenbrenner (1967), looked at the role of peer groups in the Soviet Union, his native country, and the United States, his adopted country. He noted that in the United States, a country whose macrosystem consists of pluralistic political and social structures, the distance between peer group and adult values is greater than it is in the Soviet Union, where the values of these two groups tend to cluster around a politically endorsed nucleus. The result, he suggests, is that adolescents in the United States (and in cultures with similar ecological structures) will be more likely to be influenced by peer group pressures. On the other hand, in a now classic comparison of human development in the United States and the Soviet Union, Bronfenbrenner (1970) expresses his concern that the Russians "have gone too far in subjecting the child and his peer group to conformity to a single set of values imposed by the adult society" (p. 165). With the breakup of the Soviet Union and the infusion of democratic ideals into Russian society, it would be interesting to revisit this issue and consider any changes that may have resulted from these events.

Schlegal and Barry (1991), in a well-designed and pioneering interdisciplinary study, looked at a wide range of cultural groups and the role played by the cultural context in adolescent development, particularly the influence of group similarities and differences. This work provides a model for future research on cross-cultural human development. Using data from 186 cultures and 340 variables representing a broad range of adolescent issues,

Schlegel and Barry offer detailed comparisons and contrasts on parent-adolescent relationships, adolescent sexuality, social markers defining transitions from childhood to adolescence and to adulthood, rites of passage, changes in social roles, and a variety of other topics. Throughout their investigation, they attempt to assess adolescent behavior as it occurs across cultures while carefully analyzing which behaviors appear to be culture-specific and which can be considered universal.

One final comment from White (1993) effectively illustrates how parental belief systems affect the way parents perceive the role of peers in the United States and in Japan: "Peer pressure in America is popularly seen as a negative force, rather than, as in Japan, a source of support and socialization for adult roles" (p. 37). With this said, we move to adulthood and aging.

◇ ADULTHOOD AND AGING

Early in this book, we noted that we would be looking at development from a lifespan orientation. There is a good reason for this, as illustrated by parent-child relationships in the years of adulthood and old age. As Zarit and Egge-been (1995) make clear, "Parent-child relationships are a life-span issue. Rather than ceasing when children are launched from the family, these relationships endure with often complex patterns of interaction, support, and exchange that wax and wane around key transitions in the adult years" (p. 119).

If couples have been successful in meeting the challenges of parenthood and have been able to get their own children grown up and on the way to parenthood themselves, they may look forward to the day when they achieve a new status in the life cycle—that of grandparents.

Grandparenthood

Smith (1991) has pointed out that when the first articles focusing on grandparents appeared during the 1930s and 1940s, they tended to portray grandparents in negative terms. During the next two decades, a more balanced view began to emerge (Staples, 1952).

With a few notable exceptions, the majority of grandparent research has been conducted in the United States (Cherlin & Furstenberg, 1986; Kornhaber, 1996). However, more recent studies from a variety of European industrialized societies as well as African nonindustrialized cultures have become available (Smith, 1991; Sangree, 1992). Nevertheless, it is clear that more comparative cross-cultural studies, using the ecological systems approach and other theories, are necessary if we are to describe, explain, and understand both the similarities and differences in grandparenting between and across cultures.

According to Smith (1995) the study of grandparenting is at the same time both easier and more difficult than the study of parenting. It is easier because objective analysis of grandparent-parent-grandchild relationships does not involve as intense emotions as those present in parent-child relationships. It is more difficult because "there are more varieties of grandparent than of parent, and one is studying three generations rather than two. . . . The study of grandparenthood is also challenging, in that the grandparent-parent-grandchild set of relationships confronts us squarely with the processes of socialization, intergenerational transmissions, and change over historical periods" (p. 89).

Due to the high divorce rate in the United States and the increase in single parents, who often have difficulty managing childrearing on their own, increasing numbers of grandparents are actively involved in raising their grandchildren. This adds a new layer of influence to the ecological system, as grandparents represent specific beliefs and values from a different historical period that may be contrary to the values of their children or even their own parents. Recalling the definition of culture (Chapter 1), just as individuals in Thailand or Mexico exhibit cultural differences, so do grandparents and parents represent two distinct cultures, each with their own shared set of values and beliefs.

In a pioneering longitudinal study of contemporary grandparenting, Kornhaber (1996) has noted that a body of research, based on a historical and cross-cultural perspective, is beginning to emerge and helping to clarify the meaning of grandparenthood and its function in various cultural settings. While pointing to the stable and important role grandparents play in modern societies, he also comments that "one of the dangers of 'modernization' most feared by leaders of emerging countries is the possible dismembering of the family and the inevitable loss of the grandparent's honored place in the family and society" (p. 22). Considering what we have said in earlier chapters about a culture's attitudes toward the aging process and the elderly, it should be apparent that these attitudes contribute to determining the status of grandparents. In cultures characterized by large extended families and a reverence for elders (e.g., China, Mexico, and many Asian and African societies), grandparents are likely to live with their families, be part of the social support system, and contribute to an intergenerational ecological setting (Lubben & Becerra, 1987; Thomas, 1994).

Let us now look at some of the interactions among these characteristics and the specific roles played by grandparents in several of the world's cultures.

Japan

Japan, a country continuing to experience modernization, is an interesting example of a culture dealing with the changing role of contemporary grandparents. Traditionally, Japanese grandparents have been respected, honored, and provided with ritualized status through a rite of passage that allows grandmothers to "wear the color red as a badge of her status" (Kornhaber, 1996, p. 22). This once-privileged role is undergoing dramatic change, causing increased concern among some social scientists (Strom et al., 1995; Strom & Strom, 1993). Before World War II, most Japanese lived in an extended family made up of three or more generations and governed by a rigid hierarchical system characterized by filial piety (respect) and strong parental authority. Following the democratization of the country at the end of the war, family life underwent significant changes (e.g., abolishment of the patriarchal family structure and granting of equal legal status to women) (Fukada, 1991).

In an extensive three-generation study, Strom and his colleagues (1995) found that Japanese grandparents believe their status in the family is eroding. While they want to continue to have an influence, social policy has yet to include education for their changing role in society. The authors analyzed responses to a questionnaire identifying strengths and needs of Japanese grandparents as perceived by 239 grandparents, 266 parents, and 274

A Japanese grandfather enjoys an outing with his grandchild. (Bill Gillette/The Gamma Liaison Network)

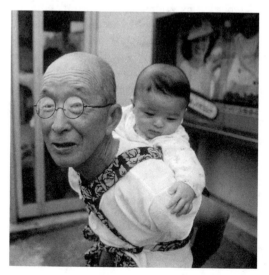

school-age grandchildren from cities and small towns across Japan. Their findings reveal that grandparents report more satisfaction, greater success, and more extensive involvement in teaching than was observed by parents and grandchildren. In addition, grandparents said they felt greater difficulty, more frustration, and less informed to carry out their grandparenting role than was reported by parents and grandchildren. According to the authors, the factors most influencing responses related to grandparent performance were generation, grandchild's gender and age, generations living together, frequency of grandchild care by grandparent, and the amount of time they spent together. The authors proposed the development of education programs to assist grandparents in adapting to their changing roles.

In a study of adolescents coming of age in Japan and the United States, White (1993) noted that grandparents often play a crucial role, particularly when they live near, although not with, the family and are able to provide support for the young person without creating dissension within the family. White quotes one working adolescent who delays going home by stopping at her grandmother's: "My mother asks too many questions. . . . So I go to my grandmother's house whenever I can, and I sometimes even call home to say I'm staying overnight there. She empties her refrigerator to cook wonderful meals for me. I am her favorite. And when I leave, she loads me down with fruit and food and sweets" (p. 68). Another adolescent, who takes care of a disabled grandmother, said, "I give her a massage every afternoon after school. I like to do it because she tells me stories about living in Nagano in the old days, and she really listens to me, and helps me with my problems" (p. 68).

Urbanization and technological advancements have contributed to a steady decrease in the number of Japanese extended families, from about 44 percent in 1955 to approximately 15 percent in 1985. The result is that the number of elderly (*rojin*) living on their own has risen sharply and will continue to rise in the future, presenting serious problems for a nation once known for its extended family structure. Still, according to Fukada (1991), Japan is finding creative ways to make use of its elderly and their skills. One such innovative concept is "silver banks." *Rojin* with superior abilities or knowledge in various fields are matched, through applications, with those needing their expertise and are paid for their services.

China

In the People's Republic of China (mainland China), grandparents have historically played a critical function in family life. According to Tien and Lee (1988), in the decade of the 1980s, about 40 percent of rural families and 24 percent of urban families were made up of three generations. Wolf (1978) notes that it was common for grandmothers to frequently intervene when they felt parents were punishing children too harshly. In commenting on the role of Chinese grandfathers, Wolf states that they are "a source of pennies for sweets, an occasional place for solace when the rest of the childhood world turns against them, and a good place for stories when nothing else is doing" (p. 142).

In an extensive investigation, similar to the one conducted among Japanese grandparents, Falbo (1991) surveyed almost 1,500 Chinese school-children between the ages of six and ten to determine the impact of quality contact on children's behavior. Among her findings, she reports that con-trary to the popular image of grandparents overindulging their grand-children, there appears to have been no negative effect on personality or aca-demic performance. In fact, "contact with educated grandparents was correlated with positive academic achievement. Contact with better educated grandfathers was correlated with . . . a more desirable personality as judged by both mothers and teachers" (p. 372). Her conclusion is that Chinese grandparents have a very positive influence on their grandchildren.

Stevenson, Chen, and Lee (1992) suggest that this influence, and the role grandparents play in families, largely depends on the sex of their own child as well as the sex of their grandchildren. For example, they state that "their son's children are considered to be their 'true' grandchildren . . . the ones for whose socialization they bear an important responsibility and for whom they assume a role as disciplinarian. . . . Grandparents feel no great need to be responsible for the children of their daughter, for their daughter's children are considered the children of their son-in-law. In fact, they are called 'outside' grandchildren, with whom it is permissible to establish a more playful relationship than with the 'true' grandchildren" (p. 23).

United States

According to Tinsley and Parke (1984), about 70 percent of American men and women will one day be grandparents. Women will typically become grandmothers around the age of fifty and men will be grandfathers about two years later. As Smith (1995) states, "Grandparenthood is thus an impor-tant part of the life cycle for most people, both as a personal experience and for its impact on others" (p. 90).

As mentioned earlier, most of the relatively limited research on grand-parenting has been conducted in modern, urban, industrialized societies such as the United States and, to a lesser degree, some of the countries in Western Europe. In one study of American grandparents and their satisfaction with their role, Brubaker (1985) reported that 80 percent were happy in their rela-tionships and a majority found it easier and more enjoyable than parenting.

Several researchers (Cherlin & Furstenberg, 1986; Peterson, 1989) hy-pothesize that the role grandparents play and their interactions within families will change significantly as family structures change and life expectancy increases. For example, four-generation families are becoming more common, with some grandparents becoming great-grandparents. With higher rates of divorce and remarriage, the issue of visitation rights for grandparents is becoming an increasing concern for many.

Another aspect of grandparenting in the United States that is different than that in other countries results from ethnic diversity. According to Lockery (1991), grandparents of Asian-American, African-American, Hispanic-American, and Italian-American backgrounds are more likely to play an active role in the lives of their grandchildren than are those of other ethnicities. In fact, as Barresi and Menon (1990) report, increasing numbers of older African-Americans are becoming actively involved in caregiving among their grandchildren and great-grandchildren. According to Minkler and Roe (1991), approximately 13 percent of African-American children, 3 percent of Hispanic-American children, and 2 percent of European-American children live with their grandparents.

Having active and vital grandparents can provide grandchildren with positive role models for old age, as illustrated by the following quote from a young girl named Patty, who said with great admiration about her grandmother, "She is a dynamo. A speedball. When my mom was in the hospital, she came over and cleaned the house and did the cooking. I helped her; we did it together. We dance, and I get tired before she does. She even chops wood. I hope I am like that. She says I am" (Kornhaber, 1996). (For more about grandparenting in the United States, we recommend the book by Kornhaber in the Further Readings section of this chapter.)

Caring for the Elderly

For generations, respect for those who have reached their later years has been higher in Japan, China, and many other countries than it has in the United States (Ikels, 1989; Yu, 1993). While this may still be true, in the case of the Japanese, the image may be overly idealized (Takada, 1993). As we pointed out earlier in this chapter, fewer elderly Japanese today are living with their children, and more are returning to low-paying jobs in order to support themselves.

Just as Japan is changing, so too is China, another of the world's oldest cultures. In China the elderly were once revered, and the extended family was the primary unit of care for the elderly. While the family is still a central focus, it is facing problems and its role is changing. For example, with increased industrialization, many rural farmers are moving to the cities, leaving their aging relatives behind (Kosberg, 1992). Those families that remain in rural areas often develop a reciprocal arrangement in which a married son provides for his elderly parents and in return receives help from them with child care, housework, and even gardening (Olson, 1994). Those who are elderly and have no children may be eligible to move into one of the country's new homes for the elderly. To do so, one must meet four criteria: (1) have no living children nearby to provide care, (2) not be bedridden or require constant medical care, (3) be willing to enter the home, and (4) qualify for local welfare assistance (Olson, 1994). In addition to the difficulties already mentioned, elder abuse, inadequate housing, and insufficient retirement programs are becoming serious problems.

In Germany, community-based services are also increasing but are unable to meet the growing numbers of elderly, 75 percent of whom need help with daily activities and 10 percent of whom are bedridden (Olson, 1994).

In the United States, and many other countries, as individuals live longer, it is becoming increasingly common that adult children in middle adulthood are required to provide care for aging relatives, particularly parents (Coward, Horne, & Dwyer, 1992) as well as for their own children. Finding themselves caught between the needs of two generations, these individuals are often referred to as the *sandwich generation*. As Olson (1994) has shown, up to 70 percent of this caregiving is currently provided by women, most often adult daughters, wives, and daughters-in-law. In the United States, families provide about 80 percent of all long-term care for the elderly (Kosberg, 1992).

In many countries—notably France, Sweden, Finland, and Israel—health care and social services are considered "rights," not privileges for those who can afford them. This is becoming a particularly difficult problem in France, where in the last couple of decades there has been a drop in the fertility rate accompanied by a corresponding increase in life expectancy. Currently, France has one of the longest life expectancies in the world, with approximately 3.8 million people over the age of seventy-five. This figure is expected to increase to 5.6 million by the year 2020 (Olson, 1994). The French microsystem is not working very well, as less than 10 percent of those sixty-five years or older live with family members and barely 5 percent live in institutions. This means the majority of elderly are living on their own. It is obvious that new ways of providing care are needed, and soon.

While the elderly in most nonindustrialized traditional societies continue to receive respect from younger people and to play a continuing role in their culture, this is not as true in faster-changing, modern, industrialized societies. Considering what has been covered in this section, the ecological systems approach seems to be alive and well and functioning effectively in more traditional cultures. Perhaps it is time to return to this model, consider its many positive characteristics, and possibly adapt and fine-tune it to the evolving cultures of today's contemporary world.

◇ THE CHANGING CONTEXT OF FAMILIES

Before bringing this chapter to a close, we should recognize that the ecological settings of families throughout the world have been changing over the last several decades. This is especially true in the United States. The stereotype of the "all-American family," consisting of two children (a girl and a boy) living in a single-family home in a middle-class neighborhood with the father working and the mother staying at home to provide child care, is no longer the norm—if it ever was.

According to Fuller (1992), only 7 percent of mothers in two-parent homes stay with children while their spouses go to work. Today's families are more likely to consist of single parents, parents who are not married but living together, or gay parents; blended families made up of stepparents and stepchildren; or families in which grandparents are responsible for raising minor-age children. As Fay (1993) has reported, families headed by a married couple declined from 40.3 percent in 1970 to 25.9 percent in 1991, while only 30 percent of adults in 1991 were married with children, down 9 percent from 1977.

In addition to these changing demographics, efforts to understand the ecology of families and the developmental niche of children within them are complicated by the fact that some children are born into an intact family, spend time in a single-parent family following a divorce, move into one of thirty-two different types of blended family environments when the custodial parent remarries, and may even be cared for by grandparents at some point as well (Fuller, 1992).

While the challenges may be great, the need to understand how families throughout the world raise their children and the influence culture has on this process is even greater.

◇ SUMMARY

This chapter opened with a description of the family life cycle and was followed by a discussion of mate selection and marriage rites in a variety of cultures throughout the world stressing the influence of one's ecological setting in determining the important influences on each of these events. In an exploration of the birth process, the focus was on the ecology of birth and similarities and differences in cultural practices, most notably in Yucatan, Holland, Sweden, and the United States. With the transition to parenthood, cultural belief systems begin to play a major role in family decision making as illustrated in mothering and fathering behavior during the years of infancy and childhood. Next, adolescence was viewed from the ecological systems approach and the importance of peer relationships was discussed from a cross-cultural perspective. For many, the years of adulthood frequently consist of the raising of adolescent children (and even adult children) as well as caring for elderly parents. Finally, the transition to becoming a grandparent in Japan, China, and the United States received considerable attention as did the recognition that family ecology is undergoing dramatic change.

◇ THINGS TO DO
AND THINK ABOUT

1. Think about the discussion devoted to cultural variations in grandparenting and try to answer each of the following questions. "What is your image of grandparents?" "If you have several living grandparents, are their styles different?" For example, would you consider their style as *remote* (a symbolic figure, geographically or emotionally distant), *companionate* (affectionate, seen frequently, sharing activities), or *involved* (helping with child care, giving advice, sometimes playing the role of substitute parent)? Talk with someone from another culture and compare your grandparent experiences. (For an interesting discussion of the grandparenting styles mentioned above, see the book by Cherlin and Furstenberg, 1986, cited in the reference section.)

2. In this chapter, we commented on the Japanese characters for *man, woman, mother, father,* and *parenting* and pointed out that the distinctions notable among these characters raised several as yet unanswered questions regarding these roles. Take some time to reflect on the following questions and how you might answer them:
   - Are mothering, fathering, and parenting distinct roles?
   - Are birthing and nurturing unique characteristics of the mother's role?
   - Are support and family control assigned to the father's role?
   - Is parenting different from mothering and fathering?

3. Talk with your parents and grandparents about dating and courtship practices when they were adolescents or young adults. If you don't already know, have them tell you how they first met and what the reactions of their parents were to the announcement that they wanted to marry. After you have done this, find someone from another culture and discuss similarities and differences in dating and marriage customs. Try to view these from your own ecological setting.

◇ FURTHER READINGS

Leonore Loeb Adler. (Ed.). (1991). *Women in Cross-Cultural Perspective*. Westport, CT: Praeger.
> A vivid presentation of traditional and evolving socialization of women and cultural perceptions of their contemporary roles. Seventeen chapters range across the globe from the Arctic to Latin America, Poland to Egypt and the Sudan, Thailand to Australia, India to Samoa. Each chapter contains short historical background sketches followed by chronologically organized information from infancy through school years, marriage, pregnancy and childbirth, adult activities, and aging.

Arthur Kornhaber. (1996). *Contemporary Grandparenting*. Thousand Oaks, CA: Sage.
> The first text of its kind, written by one of the key figures in the grandparenting activist movement. This book brings to life the diversity of today's grandparents in a lively and readable way. "A must read."

Helene Tremblay. (1988). *Families of the World* (Vol. 1). New York: Farrar, Straus & Giroux.
> A wonderfully original ethnography providing profiles of daily life among "typical" families in thirty-six countries throughout the Caribbean, South, Central, and North America. Each profile is six pages in length, consisting of two pages of color photographs of the families and the interior and exterior of their homes, two pages of text describing a typical day, and two pages of country demographics (geography, population, age and ethnic groups, social indicators, educational information, and other details). Written so well you feel you have actually visited these families.

Helene Tremblay. (1990). *Families of the World* (Vol. 2). New York: Farrar, Straus & Giroux.
> An engaging pictorial follow-up to the volume mentioned above, this time focusing on the daily lives of families in twenty-six countries in East Asia, Southeast Asia, and the Pacific. Fascinating reading.

CHAPTER NINE

CULTURE AND HEALTH

Hiroki Hashimoto is fourteen and lives with his family in the northern city of Akita on the island of Honshu. He attends a private school, where one of his British teachers, Alison Perrin, is concerned about Hiroki's obsessive neatness, extreme shyness, and apparent lack of many close friends. Based on her previous experiences with adolescents in her own country and during a teaching appointment in Canada, she feels he may have an obsessive-compulsive neurosis as well as very poorly developed interpersonal skills. She mentions to a Japanese colleague that she is about to recommend that his parents take him to see a child psychologist. Her colleague explains that Hiroki is more likely showing signs of a rather common disorder in Japan known as taijin kyofushu syndrome (TKS) in which an individual is afraid of offending others while engaged in social situations. Loosely translated as "interpersonal anxiety" or simply "fear of people," TKS appears related to two salient behavior patterns in Japanese culture: an almost universal appearance of shyness or modesty and a great concern with cleanliness.

◇ ◇ ◇

The sun has just appeared over the small village near Huascaran, an extinct volcano and the highest peak in the Andes Mountains, in the Peruvian highlands, where Eric Summerville, an Australian physician, works among the runakuna (native Quechua people). He has just been summoned to the thatched-roof home of a family whose young daughter appears to be suffering from susto, a disorder he has observed many times before among Indian tribes in Peru, Colombia, and Bolivia. Susto (Spanish for fright) is frequently the result of a frightening experience, and its symptoms may include excitability, severe anxiety, depression, rapid heartbeat, and often loss of weight. According to cultural beliefs, it can be caused by a variety of circumstances, including contact with strangers, supernatural spirits, or even "bad air" from cemeteries. The village healer has already made the traditional diagnosis by examining a guinea pig's intestines. Dr. Summerville now assists with the usual treatment of rubbing a variety of plants over the girl's skin while the healer performs an animal sacrifice to pacify the Earth, where it is believed the girl's soul is trapped.

◇ ◇ ◇

As individuals, we differ from one another in numerous ways, but in one way we are all alike—our susceptibility to becoming ill. Each of the above vignettes illustrates a unique cultural orientation to the diagnosis and practice of medicine. In both cases, making an accurate diagnosis and planning effective treatment are of chief importance. However, the explanations for the behavior and the etiology (causes) of the symptoms differ. In the case of Hiroki, cultural beliefs about social behavior and expectations within his ecological setting play a major role in his symptoms. In Peru, native beliefs about a variety of frightening circumstances lead to a culturally unique diagnosis and treatment using indigenous methods that are an extension of the developmental niche.

◇ MEDICAL DIAGNOSIS ACROSS CULTURES

Cultural traditions determine, in large part, how individuals look at their physical and mental health. What is considered healthy behavior in one society may be viewed as unhealthy in another. For example, there are many ways in which people deal with stress and tension (e.g., withdrawal, overt expressions of anger, overeating, or not eating at all). Which approach to dealing with problems would one consider healthy and which unhealthy? The answer will vary depending on the culture, developmental niche, and interaction among unique ecocultural systems: the individual (microsystem), who lives and interacts with others in a particular village or neighborhood (mesosystem), and the specific cultural health beliefs and practices that help to shape what goes on within the wider exosystem and macrosystem.

Culture influences attitudes toward health in a variety of ways. A reciprocal process exists in which cultural beliefs, traditions, and progression of knowledge about health shape the views of a particular society, and the views of society, in turn, determine methods and treatments. Frequently, the signs and treatment of an illness are manifested in the beliefs themselves. For example, in remote parts of Sabah and Sarawak in East Malaysia, an individual who exhibits the symptoms of depression would seek the treatment of a village *bomoh* (medicine man) to remove the charms presumably evoked by jealous clans. In contrast, many North Americans view depression as a biological disorder explainable as a chemical imbalance in the brain and usually treated with antidepressants. You can imagine how the nature and treatment of depression in either culture might be perceived by the other.

This gives rise to an important concept in cross-cultural psychology discussed earlier—the distinction between emic and etic factors. As you may recall, **emic** refers to *culture-specific concepts,* whereas **etic** refers to *culture-general concepts* (Berry, Poortinga, Segall, & Dasen, 1992). In this regard, the symptoms characteristic of certain illness in one culture cannot be generalized across cultures. For example, Beardsley and Pedersen (1997) point out that while eating disorders are particularly unique to young women in Western countries, such disorders may not be as common in developing countries, where the food supply is scarce. Each culture's delicate balance of ecological systems and developmental niches make up the emic values to be considered when diagnosing and treating illness.

The emic-etic distinction is germane to another important issue in culture and health—namely, the reliability and validity of diagnostic tests and measurement. Before making a diagnosis, physicians and other health professionals need to consider the medical criteria on which they make their decisions for treatment. Often, doctors trained in Western societies use their familiar inventories and diagnostic criteria to evaluate medical conditions in patients from non-Western societies, with a resulting misdiagnosis. The emic or culture-specific values and beliefs that are part of a particular doctor's ecocultural perspective cannot be readily applied in diagnosing and treating people raised in a culturally different developmental niche. Lonner and Ibrahim (1989) suggest that accurate assessment should take into consideration the beliefs, values, and perceptions of the patient and that doctors should employ culture-specific criteria when diagnosing illnesses.

In an interesting study focusing on illness beliefs, Cook (1994) asked 182 adult Chinese, Indian, and Anglo-Celtic Canadians about their beliefs concerning chronic illness and how they should be treated. He found that each ethnic group viewed the causes and treatment differently, depending on geographical orientation, generation, and age. For example, older first- or second-generation Chinese emphasized a more traditional, spiritual dimension to help explain and treat physical illness, whereas younger Chinese tended to look to biomedical intervention. Once again, an individual's unique developmental niche and place in a specific ecological system help shape attitudes toward health. Failure to recognize this important link may result in misdiagnosis of medical conditions.

When individuals are misdiagnosed, their health generally deteriorates even more. There is little or no relief because treatment is completely ineffective. The chances of this occurring are greatest when physicians and health care professionals from one cultural orientation treat individuals from another. For example, in 1985, more than one hundred Cuban refugees were initially rejected from applying for U.S. citizenship because a medical review board composed entirely of American psychiatrists diagnosed them as having antisocial personality disorder. However, this diagnosis was overturned after an official appeal was made to a second medical board composed of physicians and psychiatrists from several different countries. Many of the psychiatrists serving on the initial screening board subsequently admitted not being aware of crucial ethnic and cultural differences when they made their original diagnosis (Boxer & Garvey, 1985).

Beardsley (1994) has outlined several reasons for misdiagnoses. A first reason is the use of clinical manuals (e.g., the *Diagnostic and Statistical Manual– Fourth Edition, DSM-IV*) in societies significantly different from the ones for which they were originally intended. For example, while Chinese and American psychiatrists largely agree on some clinical evaluations such as schizophrenia, they disagree on others, including depression and anxiety disorders.

A second reason for misidentifying a health problem frequently centers on the difference in definition between disease and illness behavior. According to Beardsley, **disease** is a *biological process,* whereas **illness behavior** is a *psychological experience and the social expression of disease* (p. 281). She goes on to point out that "cultural variables interact with biological processes, and as a result, there is overlap between culture-specific (emic) and culture-general (etic) features of a disease" (p. 281). A similar point has been made by Brislin (1993).

Finally, the use of culturally biased instruments and tests may contribute to misdiagnosis. For example, standardized intelligence tests, such as the Stanford-Binet and the Wechsler Intelligence Scale for Children (WISC), as well as personality inventories such as the Minnesota Multiphasic Personality Inventory (MMPI), were developed for use with specific American populations and even when carefully translated are not always appropriate for use in other cultures. Consequently, use of these instruments may result in a patient or client receiving ineffective treatment. For example, one of the authors (Gardiner) once had a Chinese student come to his office in tears because she had been given the results of her MMPI and the computerized analysis indicated she "demonstrates bizarre behavior and should be institutionalized and treated immediately." Knowing the cultural specificity of certain items on this test used to assess "psychopathological tendencies," he was able to calm her down by showing her how the answers she gave, while reasonable and healthy for her particular culture, were considered inappropriate and unhealthy when given by someone born and raised in the American culture. He strongly recommended that the personnel in the college counseling office, none of whom had had cross-cultural training, not use this instrument as a measure of anything with international students. As Brislin (1990) aptly states, "It is decidedly a creation of the 'Western' view of etiology and psychiatric classification (and is, therefore, culture-bound); its original normative samples came from small, rural parts of Minnesota (in the United States); and there is little or no 'theory' guiding its cross-cultural use" (p. 69). Nevertheless, the MMPI is available in more than one hundred languages and, since the incident mentioned above, has undergone revision and is seen by some as worthy of cross-cultural attention (Butcher, 1990, 1995; Butcher et al., 1990). However, we still agree with Brislin who argues for caution if employing this instrument because "its misuse can lead to terrible errors and tragic consequences" (1990, p. 70).

The World Health Organization (WHO) has as its goal the promotion of health and prevention of misdiagnoses as well as the provision of medical services to countries throughout the world. One of WHO's major efforts is the Mental Health Program, which is aimed at protecting and promoting mental health. According to Sartorius (1994), this program consists of four parts: "(1) Mental Health programme formulation and evaluation, (2) psychosocial and behavioural factors affecting health and development, (3) organization of services for the prevention and treatment of mental and neurological illnesses, and (4) biomedical research on mental functioning in health and disease" (p. 262). Developing guidelines for improving mental health care and training mental health professionals are also integral parts of this program. As a result of these and other efforts, health care professionals are becoming more culturally sensitive (see Box 9.1).

BOX 9.1

 ### TRAINING HEALTH CARE PROFESSIONALS TO BE CULTURALLY SENSITIVE

In the United States, emergency rooms are treating increasing numbers of individuals from ethnically and culturally diverse backgrounds. For example, in 1992, more than a million legal immigrants and refugees entered the United States, many speaking little or no English. In an article in *U.S. News and World Report* (February 1993), Goode speaks to the importance of physicians becoming more sensitive to cultural diversity. Today, hospital staff are taking steps to ensure greater awareness and better understanding of cultural differences. Failure to do this will only increase the possibility of misdiagnosis, as in the case of a Mexican peasant woman who invented her symptoms because she was too embarrassed to describe her real problem (rectal fistula). Needless to say, such misunderstanding not only jeopardizes patients' health but also opens up the possibility of a lawsuit. Thus, many physicians are taking courses in multiculturalism and are enlisting the help of relatives or friends of patients when making daily rounds. In New York, a Chinatown outreach team from St. Vincent's Hospital is learning about the use of herbal remedies to treat ailments of the elderly. Also folk healers are recruited at University Hospital in Minneapolis to help serve the large community of Laotian Hmong refugees.

Success in these efforts requires an understanding of human development from a cross-cultural perspective. The focus of this chapter, therefore, will be to investigate how health is mediated by cultural factors across the lifespan.

◇ INFANCY AND CHILDHOOD

Professionals in today's health care delivery systems see infant care as one of their major challenges. Technological advances allow premature and extremely low-birth-weight babies that would not have survived a decade ago to live and grow into healthy children and adults. But the process is not always easy, and success or failure frequently depends on cultural factors.

Problem Births: Premature and Low-Birth-Weight Infants

What are premature and low-birth-weight infants? Most health care workers consider an infant **premature** if it is *born at less than thirty-eight weeks* and classify it as **low-birth-weight** when it *weighs less than five and a half pounds.* However, in some countries, a baby over five pounds might be seen as healthy and quite large, depending on the size of the mother. In recent years, research has shown that premature infants gain weight faster and show fewer respiratory problems when physically stimulated by rocking, massage, snuggling, and, in some cases, listening to recordings of simulated heartbeats (Rosenthal, 1992; Thoman, 1993; Field, 1992).

This level of infant care is expensive and not affordable by everyone. In many European countries (e.g., Norway and Sweden, where socialized medicine is practiced), health care is free, and medical treatment for premature infants is readily available. In China, infant care is a top priority, and the government offers quality medical care for premature infants at no cost and even conducts weekly or monthly health screenings when children enter the nation's preschools. But what about those who live in countries where care for premature infants is not always free (e.g., the United States)? Those families with insurance or sufficient funds to pay can get the necessary care and attention. For those who cannot pay, at least one of two situations may occur: either parents do not take their infants to health care professionals and the infants die or have more serious problems later, or parents take them for treatment and are then burdened with excessively high, unpayable medical expenses.

The causes of prematurity are numerous and vary from country to country. One chief contributing factor appears to be population growth. According to Davidson (1994), over the next forty years we will experience the greatest population increase in history. Obviously, this will have significant ramifications for the health of individuals everywhere and may, in part, contribute to the occurrence of more premature births.

Sudden Infant Death Syndrome (SIDS)

In addition to the problem of premature and low-birth-weight babies, **sudden infant death syndrome (SIDS)** is another public health concern. In the United States, SIDS is the second leading cause of infant mortality, after complications from birth defects (USDHHS, 1992). In SIDS, for reasons still not clearly understood, *newborns who test normal on post-delivery neurological and respiratory tests and appear healthy for much of the first year of life, suddenly stop breathing and die.* While several medical explanations have been offered, data from an international investigation of SIDS cases in the United States, Australia, the Netherlands, and New Zealand suggest that SIDS may be a result of infants sleeping on their stomachs (AAP Task Force, 1991).

The fear of suffocating infants is not new and has existed for centuries. In the Middle Ages, infants were sometimes asphyxiated when their mothers, sleeping in the same bed, rolled over on them in the middle of the night. This happened so frequently that local church authorities wrote a decree forbidding parents to sleep next to their newborns (Nakajima & Mayor, 1996). Since then, health officials in many Western countries have attempted to discourage the practice of mothers and infants sleeping in the same bed because it is believed to increase the chances of the infant dying from SIDS. However, cross-cultural research conducted in Japan, where cosleeping is common, has shown this not to be the case. In fact, fewer babies die from SIDS in Japan and Sweden each year than almost anywhere in the world (Hoffman & Hillman, 1992). Nakajima and Mayor (1996) report research carried out in sleep laboratories in California that shows that infants who slept with their mothers, rather than in separate bedrooms, doubled their chance of being breast-fed, which provides nutrition and promotes healthy attachment (see Chapter 2). In addition, infants who slept with their mothers showed less distress and cried less often during the day.

This raises an important question: "How is the parent-infant relationship affected by the health of the infant?" Generalizations about parents' reactions to a premature baby are difficult to make. However, for most parents it is a time of intense confusion. On the one hand, they are happy with the birth of their newborn, but at the same time, they are worried and concerned about the possibility their infant might die from a variety of complications. In the next section, we shall consider the role culture plays in caring for premature babies or children with health problems.

Breast-feeding young infants is commonly practiced throughout the world. (Jim Whitmer/Stock Boston)

Parental Beliefs About Caring for Infants and Children

Most parents are interested in knowing the long-term consequences of their child's medical condition. Findings from a landmark longitudinal study conducted by Werner and her colleagues (1989) provide important information on this topic. Beginning in the 1950s, more than 650 infants born on the Hawaiian island of Kauai were monitored for cognitive and emotional development throughout childhood and adulthood. While most were born without complications and were raised in supportive homes, a substantial number experienced a variety of difficulties, including some perinatal stress and prematurity. The researchers reported that infants raised in supportive and nurturing homes showed more competence than those who were not reared in such environments. Not surprisingly, they also found that premature and low-birth-weight infants developed significantly more slowly when their prenatal problems were combined with impoverished living conditions, dysfunctional family situations, and inadequate parenting. The premature infants who made the greatest progress tended to grow up in families with a great deal of physical stimulation, interaction with other family members, and supportive caregiving.

In a more recent study, Beckwith, Rodning, and Cohen (1992) lent additional support to the importance of providing premature infants with warm and caring home environments. They reported that children born premature but raised in responsive environments had a number of advantages over those not raised in some homes, including improved self-esteem, higher measures of intelligence, and fewer behavioral problems.

The health of children is one of the world's most important concerns, since the survival of any society rests to some extent on the health of its children. How healthy are the world's children? In a United Nations report on the state of children's health, Grant (1993) estimated that the largest proportion of child deaths are caused by pneumonia, diarrhea, tetanus, and tuberculosis. Most of these illnesses occur in countries with the fewest resources to deal with them and could be prevented if a variety of antibiotics and vaccines were available.

On a more positive note, over the past one hundred years, we have witnessed a significant reduction in such often fatal communicable childhood illnesses as measles, smallpox, and scarlet fever. Many international health organizations dedicated to developing and maintaining programs that promote children's health, such as UNESCO and WHO, have been successful in increasing the awareness of children's health issues, including those of street children (see Box 9.2).

✧ ADOLESCENCE

Writing about the hurried child, Elkind (1984, 1988) characterizes American youth as growing up too fast too soon and states that "like Superman, Superkid has spectacular powers and precocious competence even as an infant. This allows us to think that we can hurry the little powerhouse with impunity" (p. xii).

The pressure to grow up affects most children at some point, but each culture has its own beliefs about when this is supposed to occur. In some societies, the process is gradual, whereas in others it is abrupt. No matter how smooth the transition might be, it brings with it challenges, possibilities, and health concerns.

Adolescence, *the time between childhood and adulthood,* was initially called a period of "storm and stress" by the "father" of modern adolescent psychology, G. Stanley Hall (1904), who described the frequent mood swings

BOX 9.2

STREET CHILDREN
AND ISSUES OF HEALTH

With advances in satellite communication, we are able to witness firsthand the devastating effects of war and poverty on the lives of children in many of the world's countries. Aptekar (1994) and others (Lusk, 1992; Cosgrove, 1990; Visano, 1990) have spent more than a decade investigating street children in the developing world. Often, being victims of physical or sexual abuse and neglect, children in many cultures take to the streets in hopes of finding safety. In fact, for some children, life on the street is healthier than life at home (Connolloy, 1990). Aptekar (1988) believes that in some cases, street children have better physical and mental health than siblings living at home. It is estimated that there are between 40 and 50 million street children in Latin America alone (Aptekar, 1994; Ortiz & Poertner, 1992). For some children, life on the street is the only life they have ever known, since they were born on the streets from parents who were street children themselves (Aptekar, 1994). However, street children are more often victims of extraordinary poverty and rely on begging for a living (Ojanuga, 1990). Out of sheer desperation, many of these children resort to child pornography and prostitution to support themselves. Gang violence, theft and robbery, alcohol and drug abuse, and extortion and racketeering are common experiences for many of these children. As the number of street children rises throughout the world, health authorities have become increasingly involved in efforts to reduce the growing incidence of runaway children and the health risks to which they are exposed.

In a review of the literature on street children, Aptekar (1994) cites a comparative study carried out by Veale (1992) involving street children in Ireland during the mid-nineteenth century and those currently living on the streets in Sudan. In both countries, civil unrest was the reason children chose life on the street. Violence from warring factions and political instability were responsible for the large number of street children in South Africa (Swart, 1988). Aptekar points out that other countries, such as Tanzania, have not experienced civil unrest, and consequently have fewer street children. What becomes of these children is still a subject of much debate. Aptekar believes that further cross-cultural research is needed to build a model to predict which combination of physical, economic, sociocultural, and psychological factors will most likely lead to a child choosing life on the street and what potential health risks are involved for themselves and others.

and conflict thought to characterize the period. Many of these early ideas have been refuted by more recent researchers (Feldman & Elliott, 1990; Medicus, 1992). Today, most lifespan psychologists view adolescence as a continuous process rather than a fixed stage in the life cycle (Muuss, 1996).

Adolescence is nevertheless a complex concept and is shaped by socio-cultural beliefs and historical events. For example, in the years just before the turn of the century in the United States, the concept of adolescence did not exist. Young persons were simply expected to take on adult responsibilities and contribute to the welfare of the family as soon as they were physically able to do so. Over time, however, this idea changed, and societies (especially those in the West) became more accepting of adolescence as a distinct stage in adult preparation. In recent years, the period of adolescence has shown signs of expanding so that children enter it earlier and stay in it longer, in some cases well into their early to mid-twenties. For many, biological changes during the adolescent years can be enormously stressful. (For a review of adolescent physical development, see Chapter 3.) For example, hormonal changes associated with puberty are frequently accompanied by fluctuations in social and emotional development. For many adolescents, these changes produce only minimal health risks although, for others they can contribute to serious health problems, including eating disorders or alcohol and drug addiction.

Eating Disorders

Over the years, the topic of adolescent health has taken on new dimensions in cross-cultural human development. Because of the impact childhood illnesses can have on adult development (e.g., obesity and diabetes), international health organizations and relief agencies have devoted increasing attention to the identification of physical and mental illnesses among the world's adolescents. Today, a growing health concern among many professionals is the dramatic rise in the incidence of eating disorders, especially in highly industrialized societies.

While in some societies stoutness is associated with good health and prosperity, in others it is not. For example, in parts of Southeast Asia, a plump waistline suggests abundance, wealth, and good fortune. It has been reported that young women of the nomadic Moors of Mauritania or the An-nang of Nigeria are force fed because large women are considered the most desirous (Brink, 1989; Cassidy, 1991). On the other hand, in North America, being slim and fit is important, whereas being overweight can be embarrassing. An obsession with being thin appears to be especially common among young women (Jackson, 1992).

A particularly interesting example of the desire for thinness in American society is the recent celebration of the one-hundredth birthday of the Statue of Liberty. A new $50 coin was issued with a likeness designed to resemble the original, with one exception: Lady Liberty's figure on the new coin had been "slimmed down" to more closely represent the culturally popular Western ideal of feminine thinness (Nichter & Nichter, 1991).

Research, as well as everyday experience, has demonstrated that adolescent girls are more likely to be dissatisfied with their physical appearance, particularly their weight, than are adolescent boys and are therefore more likely to go on diets (Pipher, 1995). While dieting alone does not produce a health risk, excessive dieting can lead to a number of serious disorders, including anorexia nervosa and bulimia.

Cultural Variations in Anorexia and Bulimia

Anorexia nervosa is *an eating disorder,* found primarily among young adolescent girls, *characterized by loss of appetite and extreme loss of weight.* In severe cases, hospitalization becomes necessary, menstruation may stop, and an individual may lose fifteen to twenty-five percent or more total body weight (Slaby & Dwenger, 1993; Thompson, 1992). It is estimated that between 5 and 15 percent of anorexic girls die of this disorder each year (Fisher & Brone, 1991; Hsu, 1986). By contrast, adolescents suffering from **bulimia,** again typically young women, *eat extremely large amounts of food, then purge it all by means of self-induced vomiting.* The aim is not to lose or gain weight but to maintain a specific weight. This practice dates to the Roman Empire, when guests of the emperor were invited to the coliseum to celebrate an auspicious occasion by stuffing themselves with food and wine, followed by a trip to the "vomitorium" where they would ceremonially throw it all up. This was thought to relieve gas and stuffiness as well as cleanse the body from the inside out.

Both of these eating disorders can have serious adverse effects on one's personal health. But just how common are these disorders in countries throughout the world? Among the small number of cross-cultural studies looking at this problem, findings reveal fewer eating disorders and less dissatisfaction with body image among samples in Japan (Iwawaki & Kerner, 1974), Australia (Tiggemann & Rothblum, 1988), and Spain (Raich et al., 1992). There also is evidence showing a relationship between acculturation into some Western societies (e.g., the United States and Great Britain) and increases in negative body image as well as a preference for a thin figure (Furnham & Alibhai, 1983; Mumford, Whitehouse, & Choudry, 1992; Nasser, 1986). Unfortunately, the number of studies focusing on these disorders in developing countries remains small. Future research might well look at this and its possible relationship to ecological settings and the concept of the developmental niche.

In a recent cross-cultural study, Mukai and McCloskey (1996) investigated attitudes toward eating among 108 Japanese and American schoolgirls between eight and eleven years of age. Administering a children's version of an eating disorder test (ChEAT-26) and a revised form of the Demographic and Dieting Questionnaire (Maloney et al., 1989), the authors report that nearly half of the girls in both Japan and the United States wished they were thinner and about a third indicated they had attempted to lose weight. In both countries, the dieting practices of friends had a significant influence on eating attitudes.

In another study (Furnham & Alibhai, 1983), comparisons were made among three groups of subjects: Caucasian women residing in Great Britain, Asian women living in Kenya, and Asian women living in Great Britain who had once resided in Kenya. In all cases, subjects rated drawings of women depicting body types ranging from anorexic to obese. Findings showed that the drawings of thin women were rated more positively and drawings of heavier women more negatively by the Asian immigrant and Caucasian women than they were by those Asian women who lived in Kenya. Our interpretation of these results suggests that these women were responding to these drawings on the basis of their developmental niche and the cultural beliefs that helped to define it.

Indran (1995) administered the EAT questionnaire to 140 Form Five women students (equivalent to approximately grade eleven or twelve in the United States) at a secondary school in the suburbs surrounding Kuala Lumpur, Malaysia. The findings, once again, support the interaction of our recurring themes, ecological systems theory and developmental niche, revealing that culture and family attitudes play a pivotal role in the Malaysian girls' eating habits. Interestingly, Malaysian girls paid less attention to being thin (than did Western girls) and paid greater attention to working hard to please their parents through academic success.

Finally, Cogan, Bhalla, Sefa-Dedeh, and Rothblum (1996) conducted a more recent study of perceptions of obesity and thinness using 349 Ghanaian undergraduate students at the University of Ghana and 219 American undergraduates at the University of Vermont. All subjects completed a questionnaire containing demographic information and six measures of perceptions of obesity and thinness, including an eating disorders inventory. As hypothesized, compared to U.S. students, Ghanaian men and women rated a larger body size as the ideal. In addition, more Ghanaian than American students tended to select from a wider range of body sizes as "acceptable figures." For example, American subjects tended to have a narrower definition of the ideal figure and also tended to identify with figures smaller than they were and, in some cases, two sizes smaller than Ghanaian students, reflecting a thinner ideal. This was more true for females than for males. When weight preference was considered, both Ghanaian men and women agreed that heavier was best and idealized heavier-set body builds. For the U.S. sample, men tended to prefer somewhat heavier models than did women. Furthermore, Americans associated thinness with such positive attributes as extroversion, attractiveness, self-discipline, and self-confidence. Many American women also associated thinness with happiness. This was not the case for any of the Ghanaian students. Finally, American women reported more incidents of eating disorders than did American men or Ghanaian men or women.

These findings, along with others already mentioned, reflect a cultural orientation in which young American women place a higher value on being thin and have a higher occurrence of eating disorders than young women in developing countries. Tiggemann and Rothblum (1988) provide further evidence in a comparison of Australian and American students' perceptions of thinness and obesity. They found that while students in both countries were concerned about weight, the U.S. sample reported significantly more concern. For example, dieting was more common among American students, who also reported being more self-conscious about their bodies than were Australian students.

A final example is a study by Banks (1992) that looks at anorexia nervosa and its possible relationship to religious and cultural contexts. Banks cites the cases of two anorectic women as evidence that for some, self-starvation may be interwoven with religious idioms and symbols about the body, food, and self. In an exhaustive review of the literature, she notes an interesting link between anorexia nervosa and **asceticism,** or the *practice of self-denial,* and hypothesizes that asceticism may be subjectively expressed through religious concepts about the body and food. She encourages further cross-cultural research examining the relationship between religion and other rituals of fasting and vomiting.

Taken as a group, these studies are important because they indicate that negative perceptions of body image and incidences of eating disorders tend to occur more often in Western societies in which thinness is viewed as a cultural ideal that young women feel they need to achieve.

Culture and Sexually Transmitted Diseases (STDs)

As adolescents become sexually active, they are more likely to acquire sexually transmitted diseases (STDs) than is any other age group (Quadrel, Fishoff, & Davis, 1993).

One sexually transmitted disease in particular, AIDS and HIV, has become a critically important international health issue. Since 1981, when

AIDS was first diagnosed in Los Angeles, people with HIV have been found in more than 169 countries (Cotran, Kumar, & Robbins, 1994). **AIDS** is *a virus that attacks the body's immune system,* leaving an individual weak and susceptible to infections that generally prove fatal. With an increasing number of adolescents becoming sexually active at younger ages and large numbers engaging in unsafe practices, there is serious concern that many have become infected with the HIV virus and will die of AIDS when they reach the third decade of their lives (Centers for Disease Control, 1992).

Discussion of HIV and the AIDS epidemic should be made within the context of culture and how it influences the interpretation, diagnosis, and treatment of the disease. In an unusually persuasive article on the relationship between culture and the media's influence on HIV and AIDS in Asia, Wolffers (1997) stresses that culture is not a passive entity but rather a dynamic process within which members of a society are continuously acting on their needs and interpreting what they see and experience. One of the major sources of cultural influence throughout the world is the media. In Southeast Asia, the media has devoted considerable time and energy to informing and educating the public about the causes and transmission of HIV. However, as Wolffers points out, many local newspapers have a policy of not printing information about HIV and its relationship to sexual behavior, because this sometimes conflicts with religious and cultural beliefs. Instead, in an effort to combat the illegal use and trafficking of drugs, emphasis is often placed on the occurrence of HIV and AIDS among drug users and their use of dirty needles. The concern, as Wolffers points out, is that under these circumstances many people, particularly those who are young, uneducated, and living at the poverty level, will not be adequately informed about the potential sources of contracting the virus and that this ignorance will substantially contribute to the increasingly large number of AIDS cases throughout the world.

Culture and Adolescent Drug Use

Misuse of drugs and alcohol has also become a global health concern. In North America, young people are experimenting with alcohol and drugs at increasingly younger ages. One national survey reported that nine out of ten high school seniors had consumed alcohol on occasion and many had experimented with illegal drugs at least once (Johnston et al., 1992). Drugs most often abused are alcohol, tobacco, and marijuana (U.S. Bureau of the Census, 1992). Health problems associated with such abuse include chemical dependency, diabetes, cirrhosis of the liver, kidney failure, cardiac and lung complications, fetal anomalies, injuries from accidents, and homicide. In addition, adolescents who use drugs and alcohol regularly are likely to engage in unprotected sex, thereby increasing the chance of contracting HIV (Jemmot & Jemmot, 1993).

In a longitudinal study involving male adolescents who consumed alcohol regularly in France, Weill and Le Bourhis (1994) identified several psychological correlates predictive of future drinking. They found the heaviest drinkers were those who possessed negative, self-defeating attitudes, whereas those who were positive and enthusiastic and exhibited more religiosity consumed less alcohol and were more aware of the health dangers associated with drinking.

In the United States, drug use is highest among minority populations living in the inner city or on Indian reservations (Beauvais, Oetting, Wolf, & Edwards, 1989; Swaim et al., 1993). However, according to some authorities, the strongest factor in predicting drug use among adolescents is the type of friends they associate with (Oetting & Beauvais, 1986, 1987).

Swaim and colleagues (1993) investigated the nature and extent of drug use among eleven- and twelve-year-olds on American Indian reservations using the peer cluster theory—dyads of best friends who support and encourage each other in the use of alcohol and drugs. Over four hundred northern Plains and Southwest American Indians from two reservations were given a survey consisting of several different scales, including a Religious Identification and Peer Drug Association Scale. Data were compared to findings reported in an earlier study by Oetting and Beauvais (1987) among Anglo adolescents. With rare exception, most variables correlated higher among Anglos than among American Indians. For example, there were more peer clusters formed among Anglo adolescents than among American Indian adolescents. Swaim and colleagues (1993) conclude, "Association with drug-using peers does not appear to play as central a role in the substance use of Indian youths as it does among Anglos" (p. 640). According to the authors, the extended family system common in American Indian culture may account for the difference in the use of peer clusters. On the reservation, young people live together, often in crowded facilities, with same-age siblings, aunts, uncles, and cousins that may be regarded as "peers" or "friends" and perform the same role as peer clusters in Anglo adolescents.

These and other health concerns not only directly affect the lives of adolescents but also have relevance for the health of adults.

◇ EARLY AND MIDDLE ADULTHOOD

The transition from adolescence to adulthood is more gradual than that from childhood to adolescence. Exactly when an individual becomes an adult is not always clear and there is likely to be just as much variation within cultures as there is among cultures.

Transition to Maturity

The manner in which individuals move from adolescence into adulthood is determined largely by their culture—its ecological setting and developmental niche. Each culture has its own way of recognizing this change in status, and its unique rituals can encourage an easy, healthy transition or can cause stress that may produce unhealthy changes or responses.

In a cross-cultural study involving New Zealand–born Chinese high school students, New Zealand–born Maori young adults, and Filipino university students, Siegert and Chung (1995) noted the frequency of four illness clusters: general illnesses, sleep disturbance, anxiety and dysphoria, and severe depression. While the primary goal was to further validate the cross-cultural use of the General Health Questionnaire (Goldberg, 1972), findings indicated that students in all three groups reported experiencing all clusters of illness to about the same extent. At times, these illnesses produced significant emotional distress, frequently affecting scholastic achievement and the quality of relationships with others and thereby adversely affecting students' overall general health.

In another study, Essau and Trommsdorff (1996) administered the Ways of Coping Checklist (WOCC), a problem-focused scale, and an emotion-focused scale to determine how university students coped with emotional problems, some of which were caused by stress, and how these problems contributed to overall feelings of being healthy or unhealthy. Subjects surveyed were from Malaysia, Germany, Canada, and the United States. The researchers hypothesized that Malaysian students, living in a collective culture, would score higher on emotion-focused coping and lower on problem-focused coping than North American and German students from highly individual cultures. Results showed that Malaysian students coped with emotional problems by keeping to themselves, fearing to bother family members or friends with their problems. In this culture, it is more important to put group members ahead of individual concerns. In this culture there is a strong devotion to Islam, a religion that stresses the importance of submitting all matters to God. On the other hand, North American and German students tended to focus on the problems and seek help from friends as a way of reducing stress.

In a comparative study of 300 Italian and 250 Dutch university students, Zammuner and Fischer (1996) presented subjects with several vignettes that provoked stress and severe emotional reactions. While both groups exhibited some signs of physical distress, there were differences in the expression of emotion. For example, Dutch students tended to display more anxiety and surprise than Italian students, who were more annoyed and angered by situations perceived as flirtatious. Women in both groups were more open in expressing their emotions, particularly when responding to vignettes about personal relationships.

Acculturation and Adaptation

The challenge of living, studying, or working in another culture, a common experience for an increasing number of today's young adults, brings with it stresses that have both physical and psychological consequences for health. These stresses and their relation to the process of acculturation have received a great deal of attention in cross-cultural psychology (Berry, 1994, 1996).

Cross (1995), in an extension of an earlier cross-national longitudinal project (Cross, 1990), focused on adaptation strategies employed by East Asian and American graduate students at the University of Michigan. Students in the study came from South Korea, the People's Republic of China (PRC), and Japan. During their first year of graduate school, the students completed a questionnaire measuring coping styles, social support, and psychological well-being. As predicted, East Asian students placed more emphasis on the importance of community and interdependence when dealing with matters of adaptation than did American students. On the other hand, American students exercised strong self-reliance and independence. When adapting to new surroundings, Americans considered expressing oneself and being an autonomous thinker as important cognitive skills. Those East Asian students who on occasion placed more emphasis on independence also used more direct coping strategies when addressing problems related to stress and school. These strategies were closely related to reduced levels of perceived stress. That is, students of both cultures who were willing to take direct action when confronted with problems of adaptation were less distressed and healthier.

In 1995, Altrocchi and Altrocchi examined the psychological acculturation of traditional Cook Islanders living off the coast of New Zealand. They compared those who had migrated to New Zealand with those born in New Zealand. Subjects responded to the "I am" inventory, developed by Triandis, McCusker, and Hui (1990) and a questionnaire on childrearing customs (James, 1991). As expected, despite being heavily influenced by Western ideas, families who migrated to New Zealand tended to reaffirm their cultural heritage and childrearing beliefs by emphasizing the importance of family cohesiveness and respect for elders. This was viewed as a healthy approach in adapting to a new culture, since it tended to reduce stress and strengthen identification. Families that dropped important cultural traditions in favor of the new cosmopolitan culture experienced more distress and displayed more confusion over identity than those who held on to their "roots." In addition, this study points out the importance of finding a healthy balance between maintaining one's cultural traditions and adapting to the new culture. For example, those Cook Islanders who had migrated to New Zealand and were heavily involved in Cook Island activities had developed a stronger sense of belongingness than those who had not become so involved. These individuals were able to successfully adapt to a new ecological setting and find a comfortable niche within the new society.

In a recent investigation of psychological acculturation and stress, Liebkind (1996) studied the problems encountered by Vietnamese refugees and their parents. The sample included 159 young male and female refugees (average age eighteen), who were born between 1969 and 1976 and had arrived in Finland between 1979 and 1989, and their parents and caregivers. Acculturative stress was assessed by the Vietnamese Depression Scale (VDS) developed by Kinzie and others (1982) and the Hopkins Symptom Check List (HSCL-25) of Mollica and others (1987).

In this study, gender and generation were the strongest predictors of acculturation attitudes and degree of acculturation. As expected, due partly to a need to fit in with their Finnish friends at school, the younger generation exhibited more resistance toward maintaining the customs of their own culture than did the older generation. In other words, adults were less acculturated than were the young people. In addition, men in both generations displayed more positive attitudes toward acculturation than did women. In fact, adult women were the least acculturated group, particularly when it came to dealing with their children's autonomy and freedom of choice. This is consistent with an earlier study by Berry (1990) which indicated that adult females were the most distressed over acculturation. In short, the more they opposed Western ways for their children, the more adult women exhibited anxiety symptoms, including fluctuations in mood swings and depression, which in turn affected their overall health.

Adult Taiwanese, adjusting to life in the United States, experienced similar patterns of acculturation. Ying and Liese (1994) recruited individuals at a seminar sponsored by the Taiwan Ministry of Education designed to prepare them for their overseas study. The sample consisted of eighty-one women and ninety-one men approximately twenty-five years of age. More than half of the participants were single and came from middle- to upper-middle-class backgrounds. As part of a follow-up to a study that had begun in 1988 (Ying & Liese, 1990), a questionnaire was sent to participants prior to departure and completed two to three months after arrival in the United States. Items on the questionnaire (CPI) measure personality and require a "true" or "false" response. Three additional scales assessing such areas as homesickness, physical complaints associated with stress, levels of control, loneliness, social support, relationship problems, and perceptions of Americans' hospitality were also included in the study. Results indicated that younger individuals adjusted better than those who were older. However, contrary to the findings of Liebkind (1996), no sex differences were found. One possible explanation may be the large number of single participants in the 1994 study.

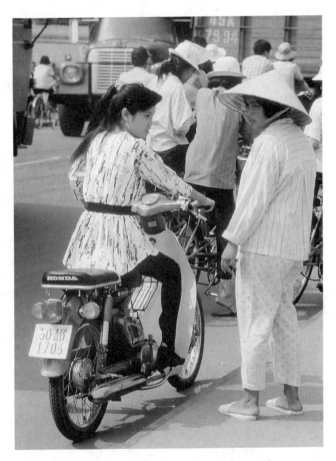

Intergenerational differences within cultures often can be quite striking. (Wolfgang Kaehler)

It appears that those adults who took greater risks and became more actively involved during their studies were healthier and better adjusted. They experienced fewer physical difficulties than those who practiced traditional Chinese customs and declined involvement in day-to-day activities on campus. Chinese adults who formed relationships with Americans also reported feeling healthier and better adjusted than those who restricted their friendships to other Chinese individuals. Poorer adjustment was also related to a sense of control; individuals felt more secure when they made decisions on their own, apart from family interference. Conversely, a decline in perceived control was associated with feelings of pressure to comply with family directives to strictly adhere to Chinese traditions.

Perhaps the most important finding from this study is that those who prepare well for an overseas experience have less stress, enjoy themselves more, and are generally healthier.

Other Health Issues

In addition to the effects of stress, other health issues concern adults. Among these are depression and schizophrenia. While it is not our intention to provide a comprehensive analysis of psychopathology in adulthood, we will examine some of the different approaches to viewing these illnesses from a cross-cultural perspective.

Depression

As already noted, every culture has its own beliefs regarding the causes and treatment of illness and stress. This is true for depression as well, and once again, there is often more variation in interpretation within cultures than among cultures. For example, in the United States, individuals react in many different ways when hearing that someone is experiencing depression. Responses may range from "There's nothing to worry about, he's just a little moody these days. He'll soon be fine" to "She's had a long history of serious depression, just like her mother and father. It seems to run in the family." Because the term tends to be used so freely in everyday conversation and in the media, it is sometimes difficult to recognize the symptoms of depression.

Depression is *a serious psychological disorder* involving periods of sadness and other negative feelings, such as hopelessness, despair, sleep disturbance, and loss of energy. Cultural variations in beliefs about depression and other illnesses have important implications for the health status of individuals worldwide. Health authorities have become increasingly alarmed by the growing number of reported cases of depression among adults. It is estimated that at least 100 million people around the world experience the symptoms of depression each year (Douki & Tabbane, 1996). This figure is expected to rise as people live longer and more people are exposed to chronic stress. It is also feared that the sudden exodus of families migrating to new countries and abandoning native customs and traditions, as well as the breakup of the extended family, will result in increased incidences of depression in younger people. Some experts worry that this will lead to greater consumption of alcohol and the abuse of drugs, which will only intensify the depression (Sartorius, 1993). Obviously, the magnitude of this problem presents enormous public health concerns.

Since depression has varying emotional, physical, and behavioral symptoms, it is common for many cases to go undetected. For this and other reasons, diagnosing and treating depression among young adults continue to be a major problem for health care professionals in a number of cultures. In Western countries, depression is described in terms of being sad, disconnected, and withdrawn. Sometimes, these are accompanied by somatic complaints, such as headaches, stomach cramps, or nausea. However, in parts of India and South Africa, depression is described in quasi-spiritual or metaphysical terms—"suffering of the spirit" (Douki & Tabbane, 1996). Recent findings suggest that depression in some developing countries is gradually beginning to mimic depressive symptoms seen in the West. For example, an epidemiological study done among adults in Tunisia revealed that out of the five thousand patients sampled, most registered the same complaints concerning depression as their Western counterparts. Rapid socioeconomic development and mass urbanization were two of the reasons given to explain the depressive symptoms of young Tunisians (Douki & Tabbane, 1996). Thus, it appears that while there are certain culture-specific characteristics associated with depression, there also are a number of universal features.

In 1983, the World Health Organization (WHO) conducted a cross-national study of patients in Canada, Japan, Switzerland, and the Islamic Republic of Iran. Findings revealed a cluster of core depressive symptoms, including long periods of sadness, lack of energy and affect, inability to concentrate, feelings of inadequacy, and loss of self-esteem. As Douki & Tabbane (1996) indicate, while the frequency and extent of reported depressive cases may vary among cultures, depression is a major universal problem that usually requires treatment.

In China, depressive episodes and stress-related disorders among adults are often accompanied by somatization (Kleinman, 1982). This has also been reported in parts of Latin America, Asia, and Africa (Tseng & Hsu, 1980). Somatization refers to physical ailments resulting from stress or emotional distress. One explanation may be that in many collectivistic societies individuals are discouraged from voicing their psychological complaints in the company of friends or extended family members. Furthermore, depression is viewed as a minor, transient illness not requiring immediate family intervention. Consequently, an individual who experiences a depressive episode is often forced to use somatization to signal distress and thereby gain attention. As Draguns (1990) states, in the case of depression, "somatization serves as a culturally sanctioned cry for help" (p. 311). Thus, the nature and treatment of depression, like many other illnesses, reflects the interaction among ecocultural systems, historical and sociocultural factors, and developmental niche.

Today, depression is often referred to as the "common cold" of psychological disorders, and Prozac (used to treat depression) is one of the most widely prescribed drugs in the world. It is customary to think of depression as occurring primarily in developed countries, often as a result of living and working in a highly industrialized and hurried society. However, as Draguns (1994) points out, "Depression is not the exclusive property of Judeo-Christian cultures" (p. 168). In fact, depression is probably experienced to some degree in most, if not all, of the world's cultures. Even so, health care professionals have yet to agree on a set of depression symptoms that can be universally applied, and it is unlikely that they ever will because of the role played by cultural variables. Draguns (1994) affirms this: "The cross-cultural study of depression has not yet progressed to the point of being able to pinpoint the worldwide invariant manifestations of depression" (p. 168).

Schizophrenia

During the last two hundred years, schizophrenia has been one of the most frequently studied psychopathic disorders. **Schizophrenia** refers to *a group of severe psychological disorders characterized by disturbances in thought, perception, and affect or emotion.* In recent years, increasing attention has been given to the study of cultural variations in schizophrenia. For example, beginning in 1973, the World Health Organization has been conducting a series of studies in China, Taiwan, Colombia, Czechoslovakia, Denmark, India, Nigeria, the former Soviet Union, the United Kingdom, and the United States. The goal of these investigations has been to determine the extent of schizophrenia and the sociocultural and historical factors surrounding it. Findings have pointed to the identification of several core symptoms, including restricted affect, thinking aloud, lack of insight, poor rapport, incoherent speech, and widespread bizarre delusions (Draguns, 1994). In addition, three symptoms were identified that although exotic or unusual, would not be considered symptoms of schizophrenia: waking early, depressed facial features, and expressions of extreme elation (Draguns, 1990). Subsequent research conducted by WHO (1979) and Sartorius, Jablensky, Korten, and Ernberg (1986) reports a greater likelihood of these symptoms occurring in Colombia, India, and Nigeria than in the other six industrialized countries mentioned earlier. One explanation may lie in the finding that schizophrenia is inversely proportionate to educational and occupational level (Dohrenwend & Dohrenwend, 1969). In fact, according to Draguns (1994), poorer and less educated patients in developing countries (e.g., India and Nigeria) recovered most quickly from this illness.

In the last ten years, WHO has continued to conduct cross-cultural research on more than three thousand schizophrenic patients in over twenty countries. Results indicate that schizophrenia occurs in nearly all cultures and that the prognosis is better in developing countries than it is in highly industrialized developed countries. Apparently, the support and encouragement provided by extended family members help reduce some of the symptoms associated with schizophrenia (Jablensky et al., 1992; Lin & Kleinman, 1988).

Day and his colleagues (1987) investigated the nature and prevalence of schizophrenia in nine countries in Asia, Europe, and South and North America. Contrary to the medical model often used to explain schizophrenia in the West, most of the these schizophrenias were associated with stressful events not initiated by the patients themselves but caused by external forces (e.g., charms or evil spirits).

Schizophrenia has been studied in India, where Katz and his colleagues (1988) found the symptoms to be similar to those reported by schizophrenics in Western countries and to include hallucinations, delusions, and withdrawal. The separation of the schizophrenic from others and the disruption of the cohesive family system is the most mysterious aspect of this illness to the normal population. It is not the disease itself that is puzzling but rather the inclination toward self-indulgence and egocentrism. The nature of the disease threatens collectivist values and clashes with ecological orientation and developmental niche.

◇ LATER ADULTHOOD

When we think of aging, we frequently have mixed reactions. On the one hand, we think of a group of elderly people enjoying their "golden years" by visiting grandchildren, traveling, and perhaps volunteering. On the other hand, we sometimes perceive the elderly as frail, weak, dependent, and in need of extensive medical care. Certainly, among many North Americans, this can be a disturbing and confusing time.

Disease and Premature Aging

Senescence, or *the process of biological aging,* and the health issues surrounding it have been the topic of much research and debate. Elderly persons experiencing the normal signs of aging often complain of reduced energy, vision and hearing loss, dried and wrinkled skin, brittle bones, slower reaction time, diminished motor skills, and sometimes a loss of memory. These complaints, some subtle and others less so, are common in most cultures and are often legitimate. But what about those who age before their time?

Following research conducted on a rare and cruel disease known as Werner's syndrome, scientists at the University of Washington have recently put forth some ideas regarding the aging process. People suffering from this disorder experience all the signs of normal aging, but they do so beginning in their mid-twenties and usually die before they reach their fiftieth birthday. They gray prematurely and develop wrinkled skin, first on the face, then on their hands, legs, and feet. They catch frequent colds, which frequently lead to pneumonia, and develop cancer, kidney and heart trouble, and osteoporosis. In addition, they show some of the same symptoms seen in Alzheimer's patients (e.g., problems in concentration, remembering, and decision making). In April 1996, scientists released findings that could be a major breakthrough in explaining why we age. They identified the Werner's gene, the first gene known to cause human aging. Although optimistically cautious, scientists at the National Institute on Aging are calling this discovery remarkable.

With more accurate identification and treatment of illnesses, as well as rapid advancements in technology, many cultures are experiencing lower mortality rates and longer life expectations. However, the longer people live, the greater the chance of encountering a major physical or psychological problem. Throughout the world, many elderly die each year from heart disease, cancer, or stroke, and arthritis, osteoporosis, and injuries resulting from falls and other accidents require extended hospitalization or nursing home and hospice care for elderly sufferers.

Cultural Views on Dementia and Alzheimer's Disease

What is the relationship between age and psychological decline? How do a culture's ecocultural system and an individual's developmental niche contribute to the aging process? As just noted, in many industrialized nations people are living longer but at a cost to society. As the average lifespan has expanded, we have seen dramatic increases in cases of **dementia,** especially Alzheimer's disease (Davies, 1988). In the United States persons diagnosed with Alzheimer's represent about 10 percent of the population over the age of sixty-five and as much as 50 percent of those over eighty-five and older (Skoog, Nilsson, Palmertz, Andreasson, & Svanborg, 1993).

In the early stages, Alzheimer's disease resembles normal aging. There is periodic memory loss, frequent agitation, problems speaking, and difficulty concentrating for long periods of time. However, as the disease worsens, the signs become more apparent. In the later stages, individuals forget how to perform the most basic tasks, such as changing clothes, eating, and going to the bathroom. They become completely dependent, require twenty-four-hour supervision, and are unable to recognize family members and medical personnel.

One of the factors that compounds the tragedy of Alzheimer's disease is our lack of understanding regarding its causes and diagnosis. Currently, the only reliable way of determining whether a person has Alzheimer's is after death when an autopsy is performed. Analyses from some autopsies have shown a cluster of plaques and neuron tangles located near the hippocampus; these have been associated with rapid destruction of healthy brain tissue (Cai, Golde, & Younkin, 1993). This is a crippling disease that touches many people, including Ronald Reagan, former president of the United States.

Cultural Beliefs About Caring for the Elderly

How do caregivers in different cultures respond to an elderly person suffering from Alzheimer's or similar diseases of aging? How do cultural beliefs about family values and relationships influence the course of these diseases?

Regardless of where it strikes, the devastating effects of Alzheimer's disease affect many people. For example, caring for a loved one with Alzheimer's can be very stressful. This is evident in Strong's (1984) study of caregiver support for Alzheimer's disease patients in which she compared American Indian and Caucasian caregivers and found that both groups felt equally frustrated, angry, guilty, anxious, and helpless. The gradual deterioration of the patient left caregivers in both groups searching for answers. American Indian caregivers were much more communal and interdependent and employed more supportive, although passive, strategies in coping with the stress. For instance, common comments were "We just have to get used to this. There's nothing you can do about it but try and make them comfortable." Caucasian caregivers, on the other hand, initially tried to handle the situation by themselves, rarely turning to others for help and support.

The difference in the way the two groups responded to the stress of caregiving reflects their culture's ecocultural system and their own developmental niche. Strong (1984) reports the perspective of an American Indian caregiver: "The white man . . . is torn between two ideals; on the one hand he believes in freedom, in minding his own business, and in the right of people to make up their own minds; but on the other hand, he believes that he should be his brother's keeper" (p. 29). In Indian society, taking care of family members is the chief responsibility of each person, and nobody is exempt.

In another study, Cox (1993) conducted personal interviews with eighty-six Hispanic caregivers in New York to examine the ways in which cultural values and norms influence behavior. Her findings concur with those of Strong's (1984), suggesting that family cohesiveness plays a significant role in caregivers' behavior. As with American Indian caregivers, Hispanics appeared to passively accept the stresses of caregiving and believe it is part of their heritage to take care of the afflicted member. At no point did caregivers in either study consider admitting their relative to a nursing home or hospice.

In 1991, Meng conducted a survey in China and reported that 96 percent of elderly persons reside with family members and are cared for until they die. Strong family interdependence and cohesiveness were shown to have a positive impact on the physical and mental health of weak and frail elderly parents living at home. At no point in caring for their aging parents did caregivers consider the possibility of sending them to a medical facility or nursing home. To do so would have brought immediate disapproval and shame from the community. These findings are consistent with those obtained by Frazier and Glascock (1994) in their work with the frail elderly living in a kibbutz community in Israel. Kalu and Kalu (1993) found that frail elderly parents in Nigeria responded somewhat differently. Those who were plagued by physical and mental infirmities retrieved their umbilical cords, buried at birth in their native village. This act is believed to help slow down the aging process. The event is a festive, colorful celebration attended by family members and friends, who surround their loved one with love and support.

As we learn more about the genetic and environmental foundations of Alzheimer's and other diseases common among the elderly, along with methods of treatment from different parts of the world, we can anticipate that cures will be found in the future. In the meantime, efforts to discover why a person's brain at some point in the lifespan begins to self-destruct continue.

◇ SUMMARY

When we think about health and related issues, we usually don't consider the many ways these might be affected by culture. How do cultural beliefs influence one's well-being and ill health? This chapter explores cultural differences in health care and beliefs that influence development across the lifespan. We began with an overview of how a variety of standardized tests and diagnostic techniques often are incapable of detecting medical problems in cultures other than those for which they were originally designed.

Health problems, at birth and shortly afterward (e.g., preterm and low-birth-weight infants), can cause considerable concern for parents in many cultures. Variations in parental cultural beliefs, discussed extensively in previous chapters, play a major role in the way cultures care for problem birth infants.

Health issues during adolescence focus on the adolescent's search for the perfect body and physical appearance. Cultural variations in the occurrence and treatment of eating disorders such as anorexia and bulimia were examined in depth. Attention was also given to a discussion of sexually transmitted diseases (STDs), including AIDS.

In early adulthood, pressures to achieve and to form interpersonal relationships with one's peers are frequently accompanied by the stress of adaptation and acculturation; these stressors produce a variety of medical problems. The ability to maintain a healthy lifestyle grows increasingly difficult for families that migrate to different countries. Similar difficulties exist for students who pursue formal education in other countries. Several cross-cultural studies involving the resettlement of young adults were examined.

Middle adulthood is sometimes referred to as the "sandwich generation" during which parents attempt to balance their own needs with the physical and emotional needs of their aging parents and growing children. This period can present unique challenges and also produce medical problems, including depression and schizophrenia. Cross-cultural research indicates that each culture approaches and treats these illnesses differently, depending on the ecocultural system and developmental niche.

The last stage in the lifespan, later adulthood, is often viewed as the "golden years," with opportunities for retirement and travel. However, this stage is also characterized by health problems. In the closing section, a cross-cultural comparison of the status of the elderly was addressed, along with cultural practices for nurturing those afflicted with dementia and Alzheimer's disease.

◇ THINGS TO DO AND THINK ABOUT

1. In the opening pages of this chapter, a serious point was made regarding how cultural bias can influence the evaluation and treatment of medical conditions. If possible, visit a local hospital or clinic and interview a physician or clinical expert from a country different than your own and ask the following questions:
   - What diagnostic instruments would you typically use to assess intelligence, somatization, and depression?
   - What specific treatment plans might be used in treating these illnesses?
   - What explanations would likely be offered to account for these illnesses?
   - What would be the prognosis of a full or partial recovery?

2. In many Western countries, it is considered desirable to be thin, particularly for young women. In this chapter, we discussed the prevalence of eating disorders and reviewed cross-cultural studies showing how different societies cope with anorexia nervosa and bulimia. Using the examples presented in this chapter, record your perceptions of body image and the experiences you have had with eating disorders. Include some examples from the media to show how U.S. culture has affected your ideas.

3. In the section on adolescence, the topics of STDs and AIDS were presented. With the alarming rate of new cases each year, it is likely that you may know someone with HIV or AIDS. If possible, spend part of this year volunteering at an organization that serves those with AIDS. Keep a journal of your experiences. If you like, share these experiences with others. Hopefully, you will gain increased awareness of this serious problem.

4. Becoming acculturated to a new society can be extremely stressful. Interview one or two international students on your campus and ask them what they found most difficult in their adjustment. In their opinion, are host students receptive to internationals? Are they invited to special campus activities? If you have had the opportunity to study abroad, compare your experience with theirs. Be specific and highlight sensitive issues.

◇ FURTHER READINGS

Boston Women's Health Book Collective. (1992). *The New Our Bodies, Ourselves.* New York: Simon & Schuster.

>This highly enjoyable and easy-to-read paperback addresses a wide range of women's health concerns in the 1990s. Topics covered include STDs and AIDS, chronic fatigue syndrome, sexual myths, menopause, breast reconstruction after mastectomy, and depression. A great book for either casual reading or for sparking open classroom discussion.

Theresa Huntley. (1991). *Helping Children Grieve.* Minneapolis: Augsburg Fortress Press.

>This book is written for parents and nonparents alike and offers a developmental approach for helping children cope with either their own impending death or the death of someone close to them. An excellent book for young and old.

Nancy Mace and Peter Rabins. (1981). *The 36-Hour Day*. Baltimore, MD: Johns Hopkins University Press.

This book addresses issues of Alzheimer's disease and provides a guide for families dealing with it. A comprehensive and insightful analysis of family life around Alzheimer's disease and helpful suggestions about placing loved ones in a hospice or nursing home.

CHAPTER TEN

LOOKING TO
THE FUTURE

Phyllidia Ramirez is eleven and lives with her mother, Nina, in a village high in the mountains in the middle of Nicaragua's Central Highlands. Like many Nicaraguan women, Nina has lived a large part of her life as a single mother. Her husband, Luis, was a migrant laborer who left home each year for several months to harvest cotton in the lowlands of the Pacific region. The long absences caused serious disruptions, and he abandoned the family when Phyllidia was five years old. Nina and Phyllidia both work part time harvesting coffee. Although schools in the area are underfunded and inadequate, family and kinship are important and through compadrazgo—*a system of "coparenthood" that links parents, children, and godparents—Phyllidia is learning Spanish and weaving skills from her godmother, Maria.*

◇ ◇ ◇

Montreal, the largest city in the province of Quebec, differs greatly from the rest of Canada due to the prominence of its French culture and language as well as the fact that most of its inhabitants belong to the Roman Catholic Church. It is here that Michel Lamoureux, thirteen years old, lives with his mother Sylvie, father Jacques, brother Pierre, and sister Lise. His parents are well-to-do and are able to send their children to private Catholic schools and provide private lessons in foreign language, golf, and tennis. They set high standards for their children and, because their careers frequently keep them away from home, give Michel, the oldest child, a great deal of responsibility for the care of his younger brother and sister.

◇ ◇ ◇

Our exploration of lives across cultures is nearly over. Before our journey comes to an end, we would like to briefly revisit our major themes, reconsider some of the theories we have discussed, and offer suggestions for modifying these to meet the needs of a rapidly changing world. A few simple revisions in specific theoretical positions might help make these theories more useful and appropriate for the study of lives across cultures. Finally, as we come to the end of our journey, we would like to gaze into our crystal ball and speculate as to where the young field of cross-cultural human development might be heading and make some recommendations for future research as we prepare to enter the twenty-first century.

◇ LOOKING BACK: A REVIEW OF MAJOR THEMES AND THEORIES

We begin with a review of the major themes and theories introduced in the opening chapter and addressed throughout subsequent chapters. These include the ecological systems approach, developmental niche, and cross-cultural perspective, along with the work of Piaget, Vygotsky, Erikson, Kohlberg, Gilligan, and others.

Our purpose in doing this is to take one last look at the ideas we have scattered throughout chapters and pull them together into a final statement stressing the importance of viewing human development from a cross-cultural perspective and within a cultural context.

Ecological Systems Approach

As you will recall, the ecological systems approach of Bronfenbrenner (1989) focuses on the reciprocal relationships between and among children, their parents, and other family members and their connection with larger social and cultural traditions as well as the interaction among biological, sociocultural, and psychological factors in human development. Throughout the pages of this book, we have seen, through the use of opening vignettes, how the lives of individuals are deeply embedded in distinctly different ecocultural systems reflecting long-held and well-established patterns of thought and behavior governed by the interaction of micro-, meso-, exo-, and macrosystems (see Figure 1.1 in Chapter 1).

In terms of the microsystem (the cultural setting in which adult-child interactions take place at home or at school), we can see that the young lives of Phyllidia in Nicaragua and Michel in Canada have been influenced in a variety of ways by their cultural surroundings.

At the same time, parts of each of their microsystems have been in contact with a second, larger circle of influence, the mesosystem, consisting of a number of overlapping social settings that have also helped to shape the individual development of Phyllidia and Michel. For example, Michel's private tutorial sessions are a routine activity among the upper-middle-class families in the educational community in Montreal.

Beyond this is the exosystem, consisting of community institutions that individuals experience indirectly. In Michel's case, his private school curriculum reflects the content and skill areas believed to be important in attaining competency, even though he was not directly involved in setting curricula.

Finally, there is the macrosystem made up of the prominent cultural values and attitudes that influence a person's maturation. In Michel's case, beliefs about God and religion provide the foundation for worship and daily living. In Phyllidia's single-parent household, her part-time job and close contact with extended family reflect the values of the macrosystem found in most Nicaraguan villages.

The work of harvesting coffee is regularly performed by Nicaraguan women and girls. (Larry Luxner/DDB Stock Photo)

As we saw in earlier chapters, sometimes several macrosystems operate within a single culture. In Malaysia and Singapore, for example, one macrosystem consists of a rapidly emerging group of young middle-class wage earners who are moving out of their parents' homes in an effort to achieve personal success and financial independence. Another represents the more traditional extended family system in which parents and grandparents serve as principal caregivers for children, even those well into their adult years.

Since one of the major goals of cross-cultural research is to be aware of the varying influences of culture on behavior, by looking at how children interact within their culture's unique ecological system and gradually carve out a developmental niche, we hopefully have laid the foundation for a better understanding of how these forces shape and change development across the cultures we have considered as well as those the reader may come into contact with in the future.

Developmental Niche

The concept of a developmental niche emerged from cross-cultural research conducted in Kenya (Super & Harkness, 1994) and has contributed greatly to our understanding of the ways in which different components of a culture work together as a system and how parents and children behave within normal everyday settings.

The term *niche* originally was used in biological ecology and refers to the manner in which an animal or species adapts to its physical surroundings (e.g., our example of the pigeon and robin in the city park in Chapter 1). Super and Harkness (1994) set forth three components that they propose make up a specific child's developmental niche. These consist of one's everyday physical and social settings, child-care and childrearing customs, and the unique psychology of one's caretakers. Of particular interest to cross-cultural researchers is the influence a developmental niche may have on the development of a variety of lifelong behaviors. For example, as we have seen in earlier chapters, there is a significant body of findings that lend support to the notion that the cultural experience of childhood plays a critically important role in continuing to shape the thoughts, feelings, and behavior of individuals throughout their lives.

Applying the concept of a developmental niche to the vignettes at the opening of this chapter, we can see how Nina's experience as a single mother affects her daughter Phyllidia's views of work and family relationships. Similarly, Michel's parents' expectations regarding his responsibilities toward caring for his younger brother and sister help shape Michel's values and attitudes. Each of these vignettes presents the child's unique developmental niche and how it operates within the larger ecological system (see Figure 2.1 in Chapter 2). Over the lifespan, Phyllidia and Michel will each continue to react and respond to thousands of cultural messages that will eventually become internalized and help them understand their world and themselves.

Taken together, the ecological systems approach and the developmental niche provide a method for examining the social context of any group of people and explaining the similarities and differences in behavior from a cross-cultural and developmental perspective.

Vygotsky's Cultural-Historical Theory

As we discussed in Chapter 4, Vygotsky offers a contextualist's approach to the study of cognitive development. While most mainstream Western developmental theories have traditionally viewed individuals as separate from their physical and social environments, Vygotsky proposed a socio-cultural-historical theory. He believed that human development occurs over time within the context of culture. His influential mentor and friend, Alexandria Luria (1981), captured the essence of Vygotsky's theory best when he stated, "In order to explain the highly complex forms of human consciousness one must go beyond the human organism. One must seek the origins of conscious activity . . . in the external processes of social life, in the social and historical forms of human existence" (p. 25). Consider the disparity between the highly individualistic perspective that characterizes the majority of Western psychological research and the historical and socio-cultural-contextualist approach suggested by Vygotsky.

As Kagitcibasi (1996) has cogently observed, "This important body of thinking and research has brought in a corrective to traditional work in mainstream developmental psychology that was oblivious of culture. It has also helped to create a recognition of the 'indigenous' cognitive competence of people (children and adults alike) who were too readily labeled as lacking in competence because they did not perform well on standard psychometric tests . . . or school-related activities. Finally, it has contributed to a better understanding of the interactive nature of the learning process" (pp. 39–40).

You may recall from our discussion in Chapter 4 that Vygotsky theorized a zone of proximal development, or the distance between a child's present level of functioning and her or his overall potential when guided by an adult or capable peer (e.g., the amount of assistance an individual needs from others in contrast to how much he can do without help). Vygotsky viewed the zone of proximal development as a dyadic process involving an adult and a child in which the adult nurtures the cultivation of a child's mental abilities by adjusting behavior (or providing guided participation) to fit the child's cognitive level as he moves successfully through the zone. From the perspective of Vygotsky, learning ultimately occurs when a child and a more competent adult arrive at a shared understanding on how to attain mutual goals.

According to Vygotsky, individuals develop as a result of their participation in collaborative activities with more skilled individuals. It is social interaction and cultural context that provide the foundation for the development of mental abilities. Since development is a product of social interaction, Vygotsky reasoned that by changing the nature and the conditions of social interaction, one can bring about change that allows children to increasingly adjust to new and different social contexts so that they eventually require less assistance from adults.

If we apply Vygotsky's zone of proximal development to this chapter's opening vignettes, we see that the guided instruction provided by Phyllidia's godmother in the teaching and learning of weaving, reflects both the family's ecological surroundings as well as her developmental niche. As Maria, the godmother, mentors Phyllidia's apprenticeship, she will move through the zone and increase her weaving skills. Her contributions to the family's collection of woven blankets and other objects strengthen her creativity while promoting family cohesiveness, cultural identification, and interdependency.

In the case of Michel, he is being carefully trained by his golf coach to develop good putting skills. In the early stages, Michel needed lots of advice to master the basics of good form and practice drills. As Michel has improved and moved through the zone, demonstrating increased competency, his coach gradually removes the amount of assistance offered until Michel can proceed without further help. In both of these situations, it is likely that elements of the ecological context—such as climate, types of terrain, urban or rural setting, population density, health care, and other factors—will be intertwined within a variety of social contexts. In short, culture is, to a large extent, a group's response to its physical ecology, ancestral heritage, and developmental niche.

Vygotsky's theory does have its problems, however, especially in its inability to transfer learning from one task to another unless, as Berry and his colleagues (1992) point out, similarities exist in the specifics. On the other hand, several researchers (Carraher, Schliemann, & Carraher, 1988; Nunes, Schliemann, & Carraher, 1993) report successful transfer of everyday mathematical skills and formal reasoning practices.

We believe that Vygotsky's theory is certain to receive increased attention from cross-cultural developmental researchers as we move into the next century. This has surely been the case during the latter part of this century with the theorist we look at next—Jean Piaget.

Piaget's Cognitive Developmental Theory

At the core of Piaget's theory of cognitive development are schemes—the building blocks of cognition, consisting of patterns of thought used to organize ideas and objects in the environment. Common to infants' experience are schemes for sucking their mothers' breast, grasping and holding objects, listening, and babbling. With growth and maturation, children become more experienced at manipulating objects, and increasingly more complex schemes develop to assist them in adapting to their environments. Continually confronted with new ideas and information, children strive to achieve a balance between assimilation (fitting new information into existing schemes) and accommodation (adjusting existing schemes to fit new information).

According to Piaget, cognitive development passes through four stages, each building on its predecessor. These stages (described in detail in Chapter 4) begin with the sensorimotor stage (birth to two years), when a child's behavior moves from a reliance on reflexes to increased use of sensory and motor abilities and an understanding of object permanence (recognition that objects continue to exist even when they cannot be seen). This is followed by the preoperational stage (two to seven years), when preschool children demonstrate their increasingly sophisticated ability to think and use language in symbolic ways, although their reasoning tends to be mainly subjective and intuitive.

With movement into the concrete operational stage (seven to eleven years), school-age children begin to think more like adults, even though their understanding of the world around them tends to be simplistic or concrete. During this period, children generally achieve conservation (the ability to recognize that properties of objects—such as number or amount—remain the same in spite of rearrangement or superficial modification in their appearance). For example, a child realizes that an older sister does not have more food because her sandwich is cut into quarters (four pieces) and his is cut into halves (two pieces).

In the fourth and final stage of formal operations (eleven years and older), adolescents and adults develop the ability to deal with hypothetical problems and abstract thinking.

When initially presenting his theory, Piaget stated that cognitive changes occurring during each of these stages were universal. However, cross-cultural findings suggested this might not be completely accurate—that is, although the same sequence of stages may occur in nearly all cultures, the age at which they are achieved may vary considerably across cultures. Piaget, to his credit, revised his position on the universality of his theory, especially with regard to the concrete and formal operational stages (Rogoff & Chavajay, 1995).

In applying Piaget's theory to our opening vignettes, it is clear that eleven-year-old Phyllidia's ability to recreate her godmother's weaving skills requires that she has the ability to distinguish between types and amounts of materials used, to be able to use symbols creatively, and to infer cause-and-effect relationships—all characteristics of concrete operational thinking. On the other hand, Michel's ability to hold the golf club properly and to speculate what will happen if the ball is driven three hundred yards or more requires that he be able to make use of hypotheses and form abstractions regarding golf skills. When he is able to do this, he displays some of the characteristics associated with formal operational thinking.

While each of these vignettes describes life in different cultures, the unique ecological settings, specific developmental niche, and distinctive social interactions experienced by Michel and Phyllidia strongly influence the nature and timing of the development of their cognitive abilities.

Kohlberg's Theory of Moral Development and Gilligan's Critique

According to Kohlberg (1981), morality is based on a belief in general principles of justice. He proposes that moral development consists of six levels ranging from an immature obedience and punishment orientation to an advanced application of universal ethical principles (see Chapter 7 for a detailed description).

The original research was based on responses to a number of hypothetical moral dilemmas by undergraduate males at Harvard University. These moral dilemmas (stories involving conflicts between an individual's desires or needs and the rules of society) focused on moral issues Kohlberg viewed as universal (e.g., stealing, keeping promises, breaking rules, and so on).

Gilligan (1982) severely criticized Kohlberg for his definition of mature morality as an orientation toward abstract norms of justice. Her own research showed that women reason about the same moral dilemmas "in a different voice." She suggested that moral reasoning among women is more likely defined by a caring attitude and the maintenance of a network of relationships rather than by rules and abstract principles of justice. However, Gilligan did not take the next logical step and formulate an alternative developmental model that would integrate both orientations (caring and justice) into an understanding of moral development.

From a cross-cultural perspective, Kohlberg's model is clearly limited in its research application. Based on Gilligan's critique that the justice orientation is not the only way of viewing morality, we wonder how many other moral orientations may be present in other cultures. For example, in Japan an individual frequently makes moral decisions based on a strict code of honor in which behavior is seen as right because it is the honorable thing to do. A common example involves the resignation of a company's president when someone in the organization behaves badly or commits an immoral act (e.g., overbilling), even though the president had no direct knowledge of, or connection to, the misbehavior. Moral reasoning such as this fits neither the justice nor the caring orientation and suggests that there are significant opportunities for more research in the area of moral development.

In this regard, a rarely cited model of moral development has been put forth by Haan, Aerts, and Cooper (1985). She and her colleagues propose that development of moral reasoning is not determined by general orientations such as caring or justice but is the result of understanding the interdependence of self and others that occurs in social interactions. In her model, the most mature moral reasoner attempts to make a moral decision that balances her needs, desires, strengths, and weaknesses with those of others affected by a particular moral issue. In this view, moral reasoning would take on different forms in different cultures simply because of wide variations in what is considered a need, desire, strength, or weakness.

The potential usefulness of Haan and others' model for the study of moral development across cultures as well as its relevance to the major themes expressed throughout this book permit us to study moral reasoning within the context of culture-specific interactions and culture-specific moral issues, resulting in an emic approach to moral development. For example, in a highly individualistic culture such as the United States, most individuals accept as fair the notion that those of greater ability receive higher pay. However, in a collective setting, like the one found in a kibbutz, it may be equally fair that individuals get paid according to their needs, not what they actually earn by their own work. While both concepts of what is fair or right are valid in each culture, they can only be reasonably evaluated within the appropriate context.

Applying these concepts of moral development to our opening vignettes suggests that Michel's view of what is right or wrong is strongly influenced by the religious values taught as part of his Roman Catholic faith, a centerpiece of the Quebec culture in which he lives. Although the majority of Nicaraguans during the early 1990s were nominally Roman Catholic, according to Merrill (1994), the church "touches the lives of most Nicaraguans only sporadically at best" (p. 84). Like most living in rural villages far from an organized church, Phyllidia has likely been taught the basics of moral behavior as defined by her parents and community—for example, being nice to others, saying only good things, not stealing, and "having a strong belief in divine power over human affairs . . . reflected in the use of phrases such as 'God willing' or 'if it is God's desire' in discussions of future events" (Merrill, 1994, p. 85).

Erikson's Theory of
Psychosocial Development

We can think of Erikson's theory as analogous to a book with eight chapters. Like chapters in a "Book of Life," Erikson's developmental stages follow one another. Sometimes an issue introduced in one chapter is carried over into the next and may not be fully resolved until much later in the book. In order to understand the story completely and make sense of the plot, the reader must read the eight chapters in chronological order. As infants and children pass through the first four stages of Erikson's theory, they are confronted by a series of psychosocial crises (turning points with two possible resolutions, one positive and one negative) requiring successful resolution if healthy development is to take place at a later stage. These crises center on trust versus mistrust, autonomy versus shame and doubt, initiative versus guilt, and industry versus inferiority. The adolescent and young adult encounter the issue of identity versus role confusion, or identity diffusion. The mature adult first faces the challenge of intimacy versus isolation, followed by generativity versus stagnation or self-absorption. Finally, the older adult needs to resolve issues related to integrity versus despair. Erikson views these crises as a natural development common to everyone, regardless of their culture, through which we come to understand ourselves and our relationships with others. However, as with other stage theories, Erikson's approach is subject to the criticism that stages may vary from one culture to another in the time of occurrence, duration, and content.

Considering what we know about the subjects in our opening vignettes, we might hypothesize that Phyllidia and Michel have both been raised in warm and caring family environments in which they developed the trust that allowed them to explore their surroundings and establish positive social relationships with family members. With supportive parents, they gradually developed control over their behavior, realizing that their intentions could be acted out through imitation of those around them. Michel, guided by his teachers in school, influenced by his golfing instructor in private lessons, and encouraged by his parents to take responsibility for his younger siblings, has developed a strong sense of industry and is on the verge of establishing a strong personal identity. Phyllidia, working part time alongside her mother harvesting coffee as well as learning her culture's weaving skills from her godmother, feels an equally strong sense of industry and, in the life of her village, is on the verge of womanhood and preparing to assume an adult identity.

While Erikson's theory works well as a general framework within which some specific lifespan changes can be described and interpreted, it is less useful as a model for cross-cultural experimentation. An approach that may be more useful in accounting for the cultural context of lifespan development has been offered by Cantor and her associates (Cantor & Kihlstrom, 1985; Cantor, Norem, Niedenthal, Langston, & Brower, 1987).

Using the concept of "life-tasks" (the underlying goals that guide an individual's life or everyday behavior at a given time), Cantor and others (1987) studied a group of undergraduate students in the United States by having them keep records detailing their daily activities. While recording their activities, they also answered questions about the people they were with and their feelings about the activities. Findings revealed that students shared several "life-tasks," the two most important being "making friends" and "getting good grades." One advantage of using an approach like Cantor's in cross-cultural research is that it relies on self-generated "themes" based on people's culture-specific experience. This makes for a more emic approach than imposing a set of preformulated "themes" on individuals, as is the case with universalist theories such as Erikson's.

We are encouraged by the development of new approaches like this and encourage others to consider using them in formulating their cross-cultural human development research efforts.

◇ INTERPRETING THEORY IN AND OUT OF CULTURAL CONTEXT

As our earlier discussion has made clear, attempts to employ theoretical concepts or interpretations developed in one cultural setting to situations found in another may not always be appropriate and can lead to much misunderstanding of cultural behavior. This is illustrated in the experience one of us (Mutter) had while teaching in Malaysia. Box 10.1 provides a good example of what can happen when we interpret theory outside cultural context.

As an extended example, let us consider what might happen if we applied Erikson's theory of psychosocial development. As we noted earlier, infants as young as one year old begin to express their autonomy through the use of a few simple words or by exploring their environment (and frequently hiding in boxes or closets, getting too close to the monkey cage at the zoo, or deliberately jumping in a mud puddle). During early childhood, they struggle to achieve a sense of competence and industriousness by expanding their social development within peer and play settings and by learning to handle the tools of their society. At this age, the "tool world" consists of paper, paste, crayons, paints, and scissors (Gander & Gardiner, 1981). Independence becomes a prerequisite for establishing identity in adolescence, and the identity crisis has to be resolved before a young adult can enjoy true intimacy.

According to Erikson's perspective, a healthy individual is one who becomes increasingly independent. In North America, personnel managers often seek "self-starters" who exercise large degrees of autonomy and independence developed and nurtured over years of individual practice and private self-reflection. However, this is not the practice in many Pacific Rim cultures, such as Malaysia, which tend to promote strong collectivistic values.

BOX 10.1

 MALAYSIA ISN'T
LIKE HOME

While serving as a Peace Corps volunteer in Malaysia, I (Mutter) taught a variety of undergraduate psychology courses in the Department of Anthropology and Sociology at the University Kebangsaan Malaysia (National University of Malaysia). Among the courses taught were Theories of Personality and Lifespan Development. These were primarily survey courses that introduced students to a variety of traditional mainstream psychological theories. During this experience I quickly realized that applying theories heavily grounded in Western philosophy to the Malaysian culture made little sense to the students I was teaching. For example, in presenting Erikson's theory of psychosocial development, it is clear that successful advancement through the eight stages (crises) results in the individual becoming increasingly autonomous, independent, industrious, and self-initiating. These are prerequisites to resolving the identity versus role confusion crisis in adolescence. Successful resolution of the next stage, intimacy versus isolation, is contingent on first achieving identity. However, Erikson's progression of stages embraces the values of "rugged individualism" and does not apply to Malaysia's traditional cultural infrastructure, which tends to be heavily collectivistic in orientation. In Malaysia, the belief is that you can only know who you are when you have experienced intimacy. The values associated with the West (e.g., autonomy, independence, industriousness, and self-initiative) are replaced in Asia by interdependence, self-sacrifice, and loyalty to family and group members.

Maslow's theory of self-actualization (development of one's potential) is another example of interpreting theory out of cultural context. According to this theory, individuals are motivated to first satisfy basic biological needs, followed by needs related to safety, belongingness, and self-esteem. Only then are they ready to try to achieve their full potential—self-actualization. This theory, too, is grounded in traditional Western philosophy, in which the emphasis is on attaining individual goals that lead to self-actualization. These values conflict strongly with Malaysia's emphasis on group harmony and interdependency. One does not strive for "self-actualization" but rather for family identification.

These examples clearly illustrate how theories, applied out of cultural context, will be meaningless. This does not mean that such theories should not be presented in non-Western cultures. It simply means that when we discuss them we need to do so cautiously, with sensitivity and consideration for the culture we are in.

BOX 10.1 CONTINUED

In addition to learning the value of examining theory within a particular cultural context, my experience of teaching in Malaysia also taught me the importance of achieving cultural interdependence. In a model of cultural identity presented later in this chapter, Gardiner, Mutter, and Kosmitzki (1997) show how individuals advance through three levels: dependence, independence, and interdependence. Cultural dependence refers to establishing an understanding and appreciation of one's own cultural heritage. Following this, individuals move to the level of independence, where the emphasis lies on extending beyond their own cultural boundaries and experiencing life in another culture. On returning home, individuals share their knowledge and experience with family and friends, thereby fostering greater interdependency.

I grew up in the midwestern part of the United States, where many of the values in my family centered around independence, initiative, and perseverance. This provided me with a strong sense of family pride (cultural dependence). Many years of formal education deepened sensitivity to the American way of life. When I joined the Peace Corps, I ventured out of my immediate cultural experience and entered the level of independence. As shown above, it was during this period that I learned the importance of examining developmental models and theories in the context in which they were created. After returning home, I entered the level of interdependency, where the sharing of insights gained from my cross-cultural experience helped to enrich the current undergraduate and graduate curriculum in cross-cultural human development at Saint Mary's University, where I now teach.

For example, in Malaysia, privacy, as many understand and practice it in Western societies, is nearly nonexistent. Children are raised to be reliant on parents, grandparents, and older siblings. In this society, intimacy needs to occur before one can be successful in achieving an identity. Anyone who attempts to compare and contrast the development of children and adolescents in Malaysia with any Western country, according to Erikson's theory, needs to be aware of these differences before interpreting findings, or the results will be totally inaccurate.

Misinterpretation of theories outside cultural context relates to the emic-etic distinction. As Poortinga (1997) aptly states, "Behavior is *emic*, or culture-specific, to the extent it can only be understood within the cultural context within which it occurs; it is *etic*, or universal, in as much as it is common to human beings independent of their culture" (p. 352). It follows that when a researcher or observer of behavior assumes that his own emic-etic distinction is true for all cultures, he is operating from an ethnocentric point of view and that cultural misunderstanding will result. For example, in the case of Erikson's theory, the development of autonomy and independence (the emic) "fits" well with Western cultural values. However, when we assume that independence is the goal of all (or even many) cultures, we are dealing with an "imposed etic" (Berry, 1994; Berry et al., 1992). The approach we have taken throughout this book—namely, viewing human development within cultural context by using the ecological systems approach and the concept of the developmental niche—keeps one aware of the need to avoid ethnocentric thinking and to be alert to and accepting of the richness of cultural variation.

The study of cross-cultural human development will be more effective and of greater practical value in the decades ahead if we refine and modify existing theories, discover new ways to apply them, and begin to utilize some of the more contemporary but underused theories we have just reviewed.

As we saw in Box 10.1, venturing out of one's native culture to experience a different culture creates an awareness of the importance of interpreting theories in versus out of context. By taking advantage of such opportunities, individuals generally increase their cultural awareness and sensitivity and frequently modify their cultural identities. In the next section, we briefly consider a model that attempts to explain the development of multicultural awareness and the concept of cultural identity, both of which are rooted in the ecological systems of the culture and become part of an individual's unique developmental niche.

◇ MULTICULTURAL AWARENESS AND CULTURAL IDENTITY

In a series of research papers, Gardiner and Mutter (1992a, b; 1993; 1994) have proposed a model for developing multicultural awareness and identity. This model has recently been refined and expanded to include supporting data on identity formation among monocultural and bicultural German and American subjects (Gardiner, Mutter, & Kosmitzki, 1997).

At the center of this model is the concept of **cultural identity,** defined as *an individual's awareness and appreciation of his or her heritage and values and the affective importance that he places on psychological membership in a particular cultural group.* As with the many behaviors we have discussed previously, cultural identity clearly emerges from the ecological setting in which one is raised and is strongly influenced through socialization and the acceptance of parental and cultural beliefs.

Children and adults find pride and identity in their ethnic heritage and traditions. (Photo Researchers)

Closely related to identity are the concepts of attitude and experience, as well as an understanding of the impact these have on one's behavior. **Attitude** is defined as *a way of thinking, believing, or feeling;* a way of viewing the world, other people, and oneself. Those individuals who have developed cross-cultural awareness and sensitivity are characterized by an attitude of openness and willingness to explore a diversity of cultures and consider alternative ways of behaving. **Experience** refers to *actions, events, or circumstances that characterize one's life.*

We hypothesize that cross-cultural experiences, combined with positive attitudes, will lead to a reaffirmation of one's native cultural identity (see Kosmitzki, 1995). Cross-cultural experiences, activities, or events that involve contact with another culture may occur in at least two ways: (1) visiting another culture and experiencing it directly; or (2) experiencing it indirectly, from a distance (in the comfort of one's home, classroom, theater, or other setting).

Just visiting another country does not guarantee that the individual has had a meaningful cross-cultural experience. Many individuals travel abroad but learn little from the experience because they stay in comfortable hotels, eat familiar (often fast) foods rather than native dishes, speak their own language without attempting to converse in the local language, and sit in hotel rooms watching reruns of favorite television shows instead of participating in local events. Such individuals may have had cross-cultural "experiences" but did not have a cross-cultural "attitude" that would have allowed them to benefit from the experiences by moving out of their developmental niche and into another level of Bronfenbrenner's ecological model (Gardiner & Mutter, 1992b).

On the other hand, there are individuals who accumulate a rich repertoire of cross-cultural experiences without ever leaving their own culture. They may host a foreign student, study a foreign language simply for the enjoyment it brings, attend cultural events, or watch foreign films or television programs. They have both the cross-cultural "attitude" as well as the "experience." When presented with a cross-cultural opportunity, we hypothesize that an individual makes a conscious decision to behave in one of three ways: resistance to change, tolerance of differences, or acceptance of change. Figure 10.1 presents these behaviors and their outcomes.

The first, more negative reaction is one of active resistance to change. Most people attempt to maintain a fairly high degree of consistency between and among their various attitudes, feelings, and behaviors. Failure to do so produces a state of tension or discomfort, often leading to an attitude of ethnocentrism in which one's own culture is viewed as superior to others. This sometimes results in a stagnation of ideas and promotes what might be referred to as **border consciousness,** or an *inability to allow oneself to see beyond*

Behavior	Outcome
a. Resistance to change ⟶	• Ethnocentrism • Stagnation of ideas • "Border consciousness"
b. Tolerance of differences ⟶	• Compliance to existing social and legal practices
Remaining in one's "comfort zone"	• Maintaining the status quo
c. Acceptance of change ⟶	• Critical and creative thinking • Personal growth • Cross-cultural sensitivity
Stepping outside one's "comfort zone"	• Engaging in new experiences

FIGURE 10.1   Reactions to Cross-Cultural Experiences

Source: Adapted from "An Approach to Integrating Teaching and Formal Learning in a Multicultural Context" by H. W. Gardiner and J. D. Mutter, 1993. Paper presented at the twenty-second annual meeting of the Society for Cross-Cultural Research, Sante Fe, NM.

a limited perspective because it is safer, less threatening, and more comfortable. It follows that individuals are then less likely to look for, or take advantage of, experiences that are new and stimulating.

A second, or intermediate, reaction is a tolerance of cultural differences in which one complies with existing social practices and/or legal regulations out of fear for social or legal reprisal or punishment. While cultural differences are tolerated, there is no genuine conviction or effort to change one's attitudes. In short, one maintains the status quo.

The third, more positive reaction involves active acceptance of change, with the individual beginning to think critically about possibilities and making choices among them, resulting in new learning and understanding. In a sense, it becomes necessary for a person to leave the comfort zone with which he has become familiar and show a willingness to take risks (e.g., trying a new food, talking with someone from another culture, attending a religious service with which one is not familiar). We suggest that only by adopting such an attitude is one able to take full advantage of cross-cultural opportunities and thereby gain new insight or awareness from them (Mutter & Gardiner, 1992).

In his book, *The 7 Habits of Highly Effective People,* Stephen Covey (1990), in discussing how positive attitudes can be used to enhance interpersonal effectiveness, identifies three concepts positioned along a continuum: dependence, independence, and interdependence. Using these concepts as a starting point, we have proposed a cyclical model of cultural identity formation that can apply to persons moving between their individualist or collectivist native culture and an individualist or collectivist host culture (see Figure 10.2).

FIGURE 10.2   A Cyclical Model of Cultural Identity

Source: Adapted from "Measuring Multicultural Awareness and Identity: A Revised Model" by H. W. Gardiner and J. D. Mutter, 1994. Paper presented at the twenty-third annual meeting of the Society for Cross-Cultural Research, Sante Fe, NM.

In our model, an individual moves from **cultural dependence,** where *an understanding and appreciation for one's own culture have been formed as part of his or her unique developmental niche,* to **cultural independence,** where she *steps outside the ecological setting of her culture to engage in new cross-cultural experiences,* to **multicultural interdependence,** where she *shares with her native culture new ways and experiences of viewing the world* and by so doing influences the ecological settings that make up the native culture.

This model shares some similarities with the typology for expanding ethnic identification found in the work of Banks (1988). Similarities include an experiential rather than theoretical perspective and a strong component of cultural awareness and understanding. For example, our concept of cultural dependence is analogous to Banks's ethnic identity clarification in which individuals develop a strong appreciation for themselves and their own cultural heritage. In addition, our concept of cultural independence is comparable to Banks's globalism and global competency, in which individuals venture out on their own to experience life in different cultures.

At the same time, there are significant differences between the two models. Banks's model consists of a hierarchical pattern and an emphasis on discontinuous behavior, whereas our model has a cyclical pattern and focuses on continuous behavior. Most important, perhaps, is that whereas Banks's approach ends with individuals experiencing a new culture, but not going beyond that experience, our approach takes individuals beyond independence (immersion in a cross-cultural experience) to multicultural interdependence (returning to their respective cultures to share their experiences with others). In short, while Banks's model allows individuals to become independent as a result of their cross-cultural experiences, his approach stresses traditional Western individualistic cultural values because it does not facilitate a sense of collectiveness and sharing of experiences with the original culture (one of the major goals of our model). We believe that one of the major benefits of experiencing multicultural interdependence is the positive change that takes place in people's attitudes about how they view themselves and others.

Empirical support for this model comes from data obtained in a study conducted by Kosmitzki (1996) in which she found that individuals who actually experience intercultural contact for an extended period of time reaffirm their original identity. This "reaffirmation" is revealed in the way they perceive themselves in relation to their native and nonnative cultural groups and their general perceptions of these groups. In other words, in terms of this model, while involved in an intercultural experience, people maintain their cultural dependence, which provides a secure basis for identity from which the nonnative culture can be explored.

Kosmitzki's findings (1996) showed that bicultural individuals who are in direct contact with a nonnative cultural group saw themselves as more similar to their native cultural group than did monocultural individuals (see

Table 10.1). In contrast, biculturals did not see themselves as more similar to the outgroup. German and American bicultural raters evaluated their native cultural group more positively than did the respective monocultural groups. Interestingly, both bicultural groups also evaluated their outgroups more favorably than their monocultural counterparts. In general, these findings lend strong empirical support to the thesis set forth in our multicultural awareness model—namely, that cultural contact increases both appreciation for one's native culture as well as positive regard for the host culture. Furthermore, biculturals saw the two cultures as less similar to each other. This result suggests that biculturals focus more on characteristics that distinguish their group from members of the host culture.

Overall, these comparisons suggest that individuals who are directly involved in intercultural experiences (cultural independence) seem to "reaffirm" their native cultural identity (cultural dependence). They tend to see themselves as more distinctive members of their native culture, develop a greater appreciation for the characteristics of their native culture, and are more aware of the characteristics that make their culture unique and that distinguish it from the host culture, especially when sharing their cross-cultural experiences with others (cultural interdependence).

TABLE 10.1   Perceived Similarity of Self and Cultural Groups

	BICULTURALS		MONOCULTURALS	
	Germans	*Americans*	*Germans*	*Americans*
Perceived Similarity of Self and Culture				
Native culture	.30	.24	.15	.14
Nonnative culture	.16	.23	.21	.25
Evaluation of Culture and Perceived Similarity of Self and Culture				
Native culture	.35	.37	.20	.29
Nonnative culture	.28	.22	.22	.08
Perceived Similarity Between Cultural Groups				
Native/Nonnative culture	−.02	−.04	.32	.22

Note: All correlations are based on a r-to-z-to-r transformation. The numbers reported here represent mean scores of indexes that are correlation coefficients. Since the figures in this table are aggregated correlations across all members of the sample, significance levels are not reported.

These results show that individuals who leave one ecological setting and the comfort of their long-held developmental niche to engage in cross-cultural experiences in another very different ecological setting have a qualitatively different sense of cultural identity than those who lack this experience. In particular, individuals form an appreciation for and an acceptance of themselves as members of their native culture and, in the process, achieve what we refer to as cultural dependence.

As stated earlier, one of the functions of cultural dependence is to form a "secure" cultural identity, which then enables individuals to seek intercultural experiences and contact (cultural independence) without experiencing a threat to identity. In fact, bicultural individuals showed more positive regard for the nonnative culture than did individuals who had no direct cross-cultural experience and a different sense of cultural identity. Findings reveal that individuals who had explored their native culture had greater appreciation for its attributes (cultural independence) and demonstrated a more positive attitude.

Although not directly measured as a part of this study, the bicultural German and American subjects cited above appear to illustrate the emergence of the next step of cultural interdependence. For example, the empirical evidence obtained by Kosmitzki (1996) suggests that these bicultural individuals have successfully passed through the stages of cultural dependence and independence and as a result have strengthened their cultural identity and increased their intercultural awareness. According to the model they are now ready to share their experiences with others, thereby achieving multicultural interdependence. This is an area we plan to explore further.

Clearly, this model has widespread practical applications for the growing area of cross-cultural human development. For example, we are currently engaged in efforts to extend this model to the study of cultural identity among those from a wider distribution of ecological settings and developmental experiences, including (1) international students studying in a variety of cultural settings; (2) Native Americans, many of whom have traditionally grown up experiencing biculturalism as an integral part of their ecological system; (3) individuals engaged in cross-cultural marriage and childrearing, who need to combine and blend their diverse parental belief systems, ecological experiences, and understanding of cultures in order to raise children to have an appreciation for their bicultural identities; and (4) expatriates living and working in other countries.

◇ SOME FINAL THOUGHTS

Traditionally, the literature in mainstream developmental psychology has emphasized a Western European and North American orientation. For too long, the assumption has been that research findings applied equally to everyone.

Although we have seen a steady increase in developmental studies in recent years, much of this research still focuses on childhood and adolescence within a Western context (Gardiner, 1994). By comparison, relatively few studies have addressed cultural variations in adulthood and old age, and even fewer have examined the end of the lifespan in non-Western societies.

By placing culture at the center of human development, we gain a better appreciation for the enormous influence culture has on our physical, cognitive, social, and emotional development. In the process, we may also find solutions for some of our most pressing global concerns. More than a decade and a half ago, Heron and Kroeger (1981) stated that "any serious and systematic attempt to study human behavior and experience must, in the very nature of things, be both developmental in depth and cross-cultural in breadth" (p. 1). Not long ago, a similar concern was expressed by Valsiner and Lawrence (1997), who make the point that "to understand how development occurs throughout life it is necessary to locate developing individuals within their specific cultures" (p. 71).

As we move into the next century, we predict there will be an increasing interest in viewing human development within an ecological and cross-cultural developmental perspective. Several recent efforts are at the forefront of this movement. One is the previously mentioned work of Kagitcibasi (1996), which looks at family and human development from the perspective of what were once called "Third World countries" but that Kagitcibasi more accurately calls the "Majority World"—"countries that do not participate fully in the benefits and problems of the industrial and postindustrial West" (p. ix). Her perspective is similar to ours, in that she takes a contextual-developmental-functional approach to human development, with the added goal of applying her findings to social policy issues in her native Turkey, most notably in the "Turkish Early Enrichment Project." In doing this, she moves from a position of theory to one of application, focusing on the fields of early childhood care and education. These are areas of induced change in which cross-cultural findings on human development can be used to develop intervention strategies and policy positions relevant to children and families within varying cultural contexts.

Another example of the type of research we hope to see more of in the future is an extensive study by Mishra, Sinha, and Berry (1996) examining the psychological adaptation of tribal groups in India. Three groups (the Asur, Oraon, and Birhar), differing in settlement and occupation patterns, were compared in terms of cultural lifestyles, patterns of child socialization, cognitive behavior, and acculturation attitudes and experiences. Similar to Kagitcibasi, the authors focus on the application of their findings, this time to problems of acculturative stress. In the decades ahead, we predict there will be more studies that stress the practical application of findings to real-world problems. We only wish there were more such examples at the present time.

In a recent review of cultural influences on child development, Super and Harkness (1997) have presented theoretical principles and research evidence in support of three specific approaches that, while varying in focus, emphasize "the structured, dynamic and integrative nature of the environment." These approaches include their developmental niche concept (Harkness & Super, 1992; Super & Harkness, 1986), which we have referred to extensively throughout this book, Worthman's proposed theory of developmental microniche (1994, 1995; Worthman, Stallings, & Jenkins, 1993), and Weisner's work on the ecocultural niche (Gallimore, Goldenberg, & Weisner, 1993; Weisner, in press; Weisner, Matheson, & Bernheimer, 1996).

Following a comprehensive review of contemporary evidence, they point to three recurring themes they believe "will continue to occupy a central place in the work that lies ahead: how best to conceptualize variability within and across cultural settings, to characterize activities of the child's mind, and to improve methodological rigor in research in culture and development" (Super & Harkness, 1977, p. 30).

In stressing the need for conducting more comparative studies and the benefits they can provide, Super and Harkness (1977) state, "Comparative studies remind us that even in our own cultures we too often assume we know—or we overlook entirely—what kinds of settings, customs, and ideas characterize our children's lives. In this sense we cannot understand the development of our own children until we can understand the children of others" (p. 31).

In concluding an earlier review of child development studies, Gardiner (1994) made the following comment: "Cross-cultural study of development frequently resembles a confused mosaic of often contradictory findings. Yet therein lies the promise and excitement of future endeavors. . . . Much more needs to be done, and as the cross-cultural perspective reveals, discovery of similarities and dissimilarities in human behavior will make our understanding both easier and more difficult" (p. 72). This was true then, and it is true now.

Ahead of us lie tremendous challenges and opportunities. Speculating about where our cross-cultural journey will take us next is difficult. Wherever we go, it is certain to be an interesting and exciting adventure. Perhaps some of you will be the pioneer theorists and researchers who take us to the next point on this journey. We eagerly look forward to that day.

REFERENCES

Abbott, S. (1992). Holding on and pushing away: Comparative perspectives on an Eastern Kentucky child-rearing practice. *Ethos, 20,* 33–65.

Abbott, S. (1997). *"You give 'em lots of love and use the flat of your hand": Patterns of child rearing in the mountains.* Paper presented at the twenty-sixth annual meeting of the Society for Cross-Cultural Research, San Antonio, TX.

Abel, E., & Sokol, R. (1987). Incidence of fetal alcohol syndrome and economic impact of FAS-related anomalies. *Drug and Alcohol Dependency, 19,* 51–70.

Adelson, J. (1985). Observations on research in adolescence. *Genetic, Social, and General Psychology Monographs, 111,* 249–254.

Adelson, J. (Ed.). (1980). *Handbook of adolescent psychology.* New York: Wiley.

Ahmed, R. A. (1991). Women in Egypt and the Sudan. In L. L. Adler (Ed.), *Women in cross-cultural perspective* (pp. 107–133). Westport, CT: Praeger.

Ainsworth, M. D. S. (1967). *Infancy in Uganda: Infant care and the growth of love.* Baltimore: Johns Hopkins University Press.

Ainsworth, M. D. S. (1982). Attachment: Retrospect and prospect. In C. M. Parks & J. Stevenson-Hinde (Eds.), *The place of attachment in human behavior* (pp. 3–30). New York: Basic Books.

Ainsworth, M. D. S., & Wittig, B. A. (1969). Attachment and exploratory behavior of one-year-olds in a strange situation. In B. M. Foss (Ed.), *Determinants of infant behavior IV* (pp. 111–136). London: Methuen.

Altrocchi, J., & Altrocchi, L. (1995). Polyfaceted psychological acculturation in Cook Islanders. *Journal of Cross-Cultural Psychology, 26*(3), 426–440.

American Academy of Pediatrics (AAP) Task Force on Infant Positioning and SIDS. (1992). Positioning and SIDS. *Pediatrics, 89*(6), 1120–1126.

American Psychological Association (APA). (1994). *Diagnostic and statistical manual of mental disorders* (4th ed.). Washington, DC: American Psychiatric Press.

Anderson, J. L., Crawford, C. B., Nadeau, J., & Lindberg, T. (1989). Was the Duchess of Windsor right? A cross-cultural review of the socioecology of ideals of female body shape. *Ethology and Sociobiology, 13,* 197–227.

Annett, M. (1985). *Left, right, hand, and brain: The right shift theory.* Hillsdale, NJ: Erlbaum.

Aptekar, L. (1988). Colombian street children: Their mental health and how they can be served. *International Journal of Mental Health, 17,* 81–104.

Aptekar, L. (1989). Colombian street children: *Gamines* and *chupagruesos. Adolescence, 24,* 783–794.

Aptekar, L. (1994). Street children in the developing world: A review of their condition. *Cross-Cultural Research, 28*(3), 195–224.

Armstrong, S. (1991, February). Female circumcision: Fighting a cruel tradition. *New Scientist*, 42–47.

Arnett, J. (1992a). Reckless behavior in adolescence: A developmental perspective. *Developmental Review, 12*, 339–373.

Arnett, J. (1992b). Socialization and adolescent reckless behavior: A reply to Jessor. *Developmental Review, 12*, 391–409.

Ashmore, R. D. (1990). Sex, gender, and the individual. In L. Pervin (Ed.), *Handbook of personality: Theory and research* (pp. 486–526). New York: Guilford Press.

Atkinson, D., Morten, G., & Sue, D. (1983). *Counseling American minorities*. Dubuque, IA: Brown.

Austin, J. K., Champion, V. L., & Tzeng, O. C. S. (1989). Cross-cultural relationships between self-concept and body image in high-school-age boys. *Archives of Psychiatric Nursing, 3*, 234–240.

Avedon, E. M., & Sutton-Smith, B. (1971). *The study of games*. New York: Wiley.

Baca Zinn, M., & Eitzen, D. S. (1993). *Diversity in families* (3rd ed.). New York: HarperCollins.

Baltes, P. B. (1987). Theoretical propositions of life-span developmental psychology: On the dynamics between growth and decline. *Developmental Psychology, 23*, 611–626.

Baltes, P. B. (1993). The aging mind: Potential and limits. *Gerontologist, 33*, 580–594.

Banks, E. (1988). Temperament and individuality: A study of Malay children. *American Journal of Orthopsychiatry, 59*, 390–397.

Banks, J. A. (1989). *Multicultural education: Theory and practice* (2nd ed.). Boston: Allyn & Bacon.

Barnard, K. E., & Martell, L. K. (1995). Mothering. In M. H. Bornstein (Ed.), *Handbook of parenting* (Vol. 3, pp. 3–26). Mahwah, NJ: Erlbaum.

Barresi, C. M., & Menon, G. (1990). Diversity in black family caregiving. In Z. Harel, E. A. McKinney, & M. Williams (Eds.), *Black aged: Understanding diversity and service needs*. Newbury Park, CA: Sage.

Barrett, D. E., Radke-Yarrow, M., & Klein, R. E. (1982). Chronic malnutrition and child behavior: Effects of early caloric supplementation on social and emotional functioning at school age. *Developmental Psychology, 18*, 541–556.

Basseches, M. (1984). *Dialectical thinking and adult development*. Norwood, NJ: Ablex.

Basseches, M. (1989). Dialectical thinking as an organized whole: Comments on Irwin and Kramer. In M. L. Commons, J. D. Sinnott, F. A. Richards, & C. Armon (Eds.), *Adult development: Vol. 1. Comparisons and applications of developmental models*. New York: Praeger.

Bates, E. (1976). *Language and context: The acquisition of pragmatics*. New York: Academic Press.

Baumrind, D. (1971). Current patterns of parental authority. *Developmental Psychology Monographs, 1,* 1–103.

Baumrind, D. (1980). New directions in socialization research. *American Psychologist, 35,* 639–652.

Baumrind, D. (1991). To nurture nature. *Behavioral and Brain Sciences, 14,* 386.

Baumrind, D. (1993). The average expectable environment is not good enough: A response to Scarr. *Child Development, 64,* 1299–1317.

Beardsley, L. M. (1994). Medical diagnosis and treatment across cultures. In W. J. Lonner & R. Malpass (Eds.), *Psychology and culture.* Boston: Allyn & Bacon.

Beck, A. T. (1976). *Cognitive therapy and the emotional disorders.* New York: New American Library.

Beck, C. J. (1995). *Now Zen.* San Francisco: HarperCollins.

Beckwith, L., Rodning, C., & Cohen, S. (1992). Preterm children at early adolescence, and continuity and discontinuity in maternal responsiveness from infancy. *Child Development, 63,* 1198–1208.

Behrman, R. E. (1985). Preventing low birth weight: A pediatric perspective. *Journal of Pediatrics, 107*(6), 842–854.

Beidelman, T. O. (1971). *The Kagura: A matrilineal people of East Africa.* New York: Holt, Rinehart & Winston.

Beilin, H. (1994). Jean Piaget's enduring contribution to developmental psychology. In R. D. Parke, P. A. Ornstein, J. J. Rieser, & C. Zahn-Waxler (Eds.), *A Century of Developmental Psychology.* Washington, DC: American Psychological Association.

Belsky, J. (1985). Exploring individual differences in marital change across the transition to parenthood: The role of violated expectations. *Journal of Marriage and the Family, 47,* 1037–1044.

Bennett, D. A., & Knopman, D. S. (1994). Alzheimer's disease: A comprehensive approach to patient management. *Geriatrics, 49*(8), 20–26.

Berk, L. E. (1992). Children's private speech: An overview of theory and the status of research. In R. M. Diaz & L. E. Berk (Eds.), *Private speech: From social interaction to self-regulation* (pp. 17–53). Hillsdale, NJ: Erlbaum.

Berk, L. E. (1994). *Child development* (3rd ed.). Needham Heights, MA: Allyn & Bacon.

Berman, A. L., & Jobes, D. A. (1991). *Adolescent suicide: Assessment and intervention.* Washington, DC: American Psychological Association.

Berndt, T. J., & Zook, J. M. (1993). Effects of friendship on adolescent development. *Bulletin of the Hong Kong Psychological Society, 30/31,* 15–34.

Bernstein, B. (1971). *Class, codes and control* (Vol. 1). London: Routledge & Kegan Paul.

Berry, J. W. (1969). On cross-cultural comparability. *International Journal of Psychology, 4,* 119–128.

Berry, J. W. (1976). *Human ecology and cognitive style.* Beverly Hills, CA: Sage.

Berry, J. W. (1979). A cultural ecology of social behavior. In L. Berkowitz (Ed.), *Advances in experimental social psychology* (Vol. 12, pp. 177–207). New York: Academic Press.

Berry, J. W. (1983). The sociogenesis of social sciences: An analysis of the cultural relativity of social psychology. In B. Bain (Ed.), *The sociogenesis of language and human conduct*. New York: Plenum.

Berry, J. W. (1990). The psychology of acculturation. In J. J. Berman (Ed.), *Nebraska symposium on motivation 1989* (pp. 201–234). Lincoln: University of Nebraska Press.

Berry, J. W. (1992). *On the unity of the field: Variations and communalities in understanding human behavior in cultural context.* Paper presented at the twenty-third congress of the International Association of Applied Psychology, Madrid.

Berry, J. W., & Dasen, P. (Eds.). (1974). *Culture and cognition.* London: Methuen.

Berry, J. W., Dasen, P. R., & Saraswathi, T. S. (Eds.). (1997). *Handbook of cross-cultural psychology: Vol. 2. Basic processes and human development* (2nd ed.). Needham Heights, MA: Allyn & Bacon.

Berry, J. W., Poortinga, Y. H., & Pandey, J. (Eds.). (1997). *Handbook of cross-cultural psychology: Vol. 1. Theory and method* (2nd ed.). Needham Heights, MA: Allyn & Bacon.

Berry, J. W., Poortinga, Y. H., Segall, M. H., & Dasen, P. R. (1992). *Cross-cultural psychology.* Cambridge, England: Cambridge University Press.

Berry, J. W., Segall, M. H., & Kagitcibasi, C. (Eds.). (1997). *Handbook of cross-cultural psychology: Vol. 3. Social behavior and applications* (2nd ed.). Needham Heights, MA: Allyn & Bacon.

Bersoff, D. M., & Miller, J. (1993). Culture, context, and the development of moral accountability judgments. *Developmental Psychology, 29,* 669–676.

Bertrand, J. T., Ward, V., & Pauc, F. (1992). Sexual practices among the Quiche-speaking Mayan population of Guatemala. *International Quarterly of Community Health Education, 12,* 265–282.

Best, D. L., House, A. S., Barnard, A. E., & Spicker, B. S. (1994). Parent-child interactions in France, Germany, and Italy: The effects of gender and culture. *Journal of Cross-Cultural Psychology, 25,* 181–193.

Best, D. L., & Ruther, N. M. (1994). Cross-cultural themes in developmental psychology: An examination of texts, handbooks, and reviews. *Journal of Cross-Cultural Psychology, 25*(1), 54–77.

Biller, H. B. (1993). *Fathers and families.* Westport, CT: Auburn House.

Birren, J. E., & Schaie, K. W. (Eds.). (1995). *Handbook of psychology and aging.* San Diego, CA: Academic Press.

Bjorkqvist, K., & Niemela, P. (1992). *Of mice and women: Aspects of female aggression.* San Diego, CA: Academic Press.

Blau, F. D., & Ferber, M. A. (1986). *The economics of women, men, and work.* Englewood Cliffs, NJ: Prentice Hall.

Blieszner, R. (1988). Individual development and intimate relationships in middle and late adulthood. In R. M. Milardo (Ed.), *Families and social networks* (pp. 147–167). Newbury Park, CA: Sage.

Block, J. (1983). Differential premises arising from differential socialization of the sexes: Some conjectures. *Child Development, 54,* 1335–1354.

Bochner, S. (1994). Cross-cultural differences in the self-concept. A test of Hofstede's individualism/collectivism distinction. *Journal of Cross-Cultural Psychology, 25,* 273–283.

Bogg, R. A., & Hughes, J. (1973). Correlates of marijuana usage at a Canadian technological institute. *International Journal of the Addictions, 8,* 489–504.

Bolton, R. (1994). Sex, science, and social responsibility: Cross-cultural research on same-sex eroticism and sexual intolerance. *Cross-Cultural Research, 28,* 134–190.

Bongaarts, J. (1994, March). Can the growing human population feed itself? *Scientific American,* 36–42.

Bornstein, M. H. (1992). Perceptual development in infancy, childhood, and old age. In M. H. Bornstein & M. E. Lamb (Eds.), *Developmental psychology: An advanced textbook* (3rd ed.). Hillsdale, NJ: Erlbaum.

Bornstein, M. H. (1995). Parenting infants. In M. H. Bornstein (Ed.), *Handbook of parenting* (Vol. 1, pp. 3–39). Mahwah, NJ: Erlbaum.

Bornstein, M. H., Tal, J., Rahn, C., Galperin, C. Z., Pecheux, M.-G, Lamour, M., Azuma, H., Toda, S., Ogino, M., & Tamis-LeMonda, C. S. (1992). Functional analysis of the contents of maternal speech to infants of five and thirteen months in four cultures: Argentina, France, Japan, and the United States. *Developmental Psychology, 28,* 593–603.

Bornstein, M. H., Tal, J., & Tamis-LeMonda, C. S. (1991). Parenting in cross-cultural perspective: The United States, France, and Japan. In M. H. Bornstein (Ed.), *Cultural approaches to parenting* (pp. 69–90). Hillsdale, NJ: Erlbaum.

Bornstein, M. H., & Tamis-LeMonda, C. S. (1989). Maternal responsiveness and cognitive development in children. In M. H. Bornstein (Ed.), *Maternal responsiveness: Characteristics and consequences* (pp. 49–61). San Francisco: Jossey-Bass.

Bornstein, M. H., Toda, S., Azuma, H., Tamis-LeMonda, C. S., & Ogino, M. (1990). Mother and infant activity and interaction in Japan and the United States: II. A comparative microanalysis of naturalistic exchanges focused on the organization of infant attention. *International Journal of Behavioral Development, 13,* 289–308.

Bouchard, T. J., Lykken, D. T., McGue, M., Segal, N. L., & Tellegen, A. (1990). Sources of human psychological differences: The Minnesota study of twins reared apart. *Science, 250,* 223–228.

Bourguignon, E. (1979). *Psychological anthropology: An introduction to human nature and cultural differences.* New York: Holt, Rinehart & Winston.

Bowlby, J. (1989). *Secure and insecure attachment.* New York: Basic Books.

Boxer, P. A., & Garvey, J. T. (1985). Psychiatric diagnoses of Cuban refugees in the United States: Findings of medical review boards. *American Journal of Psychiatry, 1421,* 86–89.

Bradley, R. H. (1995). Environment and parenting. In M. Bornstein (Ed.), *Handbook of parenting* (Vol. 2, pp. 235–261). Hillsdale, NJ: Erlbaum.

Brink, P. J. (1989). The fattening room among the Annang of Nigeria. *Medical Anthropology, 12,* 131–143.

Brislin, R. (1993). *Understanding culture's influence on behavior.* New York: Harcourt Brace Jovanovich.

Brislin, R. (Ed.). (1990). *Applied cross-cultural psychology.* Newbury Park, CA: Sage.

Brislin, R., & Yoshida, T. (Eds.). (1994). *Improving intercultural interactions: Modules for cross-cultural training programs.* Thousand Oaks, CA: Sage.

Bronfenbrenner, U. (1967). Response to pressure from peers versus adults among Soviet and American school children. *International Journal of Psychology, 2,* 199–207.

Bronfenbrenner, U. (1970). *Two Worlds of Childhood: U.S. and U.S.S.R.* New York: Russell Sage Foundation.

Bronfenbrenner, U. (1975). Reality and research in the ecology of human development. *Proceedings of the American Philosophical Society, 119,* 439–469.

Bronfenbrenner, U. (1977). Toward an experimental ecology of human development. *American Psychologist, 32,* 513–531.

Bronfenbrenner, U. (1979). *The ecology of human development: Experiments by nature and design.* Cambridge, MA: Harvard University Press.

Bronfenbrenner, U. (1986a). Ecological systems theory. In R. Vasta (Ed.), *Annals of Child Development* (Vol. 6, pp. 187–251). Greenwich, CT: JAI Press.

Bronfenbrenner, U. (1986b). Ecology of the family as a context for human development: Research perspectives. *Developmental Psychology, 22,* 723–742.

Bronfenbrenner, U. (1989). Ecological systems theory. In R. Vasta (Ed.), *Six theories of child development* (Vol. 6, pp. 187–250). Greenwich, CT: JAI Press.

Bronfenbrenner, U. (1990). Who cares for children? *Research and Clinical Center for Child Development, 12,* 27–40.

Bronfennbrenner, U. (1993). The ecology of cognitive development: Research models and fugitive findings. In R. H. Wozniak & K. W. Fischer (Eds.), *Development in context: Acting and thinking in specific environments* (pp. 3–44). Hillsdale, NJ: Erlbaum.

Brook, J. S., Lukoff, I. F., & Whiteman, M. (1977). Correlates of marijuana use as related to age, sex, and ethnicity. *Yale Journal of Biological Medicine, 50,* 383–390.

Brown, S. S. (1985). Can low birth weight be prevented? *Family Planning Perspectives, 17*(3), 112–118.

Brubaker, T. H. (1985). *Later life families.* Newbury Park, CA: Sage.

Burbank, V. K. (1988). *Aboriginal adolescence: Maidenhood in an Australian community.* New Brunswick, NJ: Rutgers University Press.

Buss, A. H., & Plomin, R. (1984). *Temperament: Early developing personality traits.* Hillsdale, NJ: Erlbaum.

Buss, D. M. (1988). The evolution of human intrasexual competition: Tactics of mate attraction. *Journal of Personality and Social Psychology, 54,* 616–628.

Buss, D. M. (1994a). *The evolution of desire: Strategies of human mating.* New York: Basic Books.

Buss, D. M. (1994b). Mate preferences in 37 cultures. In W. J. Lonner & R. Malpass (Eds.), *Psychology and culture* (pp. 197–201). Boston: Allyn & Bacon.

Butcher, J. N. (1990). *MMPI-2 in psychological treatment.* New York: Oxford University Press.

Butcher, J. N. (Ed.). (1995). *Clinical personality assessment: Practical approaches.* New York: Oxford University Press.

Butcher, J. N., et al. (Eds.). (1990). *Development and use of the MMPI-2 content scales.* Minneapolis: University of Minnesota Press.

Byrnes, J. P. (1988). Formal operations: A systematic reformulation. *Developmental Review, 8,* 66–87.

Cai, X., Golde, T. E., & Younkin, S. C. (1993). Release of excess amyloid B protein from a mutant amyloid B protein precursor. *Science, 259,* 514–516.

Calabrese, R. L., & Noboa, J. (1995). The choice for gang membership by Mexican-American adolescents. *High School Journal, 78,* 226–235.

Campos, J. J., & Stenberg, C. R. (1981). Perception, appraisal, and emotion: The onset of social referencing. In M. E. Lamb & L. R. Sherrod (Eds.), *Infant social cognition: Empirical and social considerations.* Hillsdale, NJ: Erlbaum.

Camras, L. A., & Sachs, V. B. (1991). Social referencing and caretaker expressive behavior in a day care setting. *Infant Behavior and Development, 14,* 27–36.

Cantor, N., & Kihlstrom J. F. (1985). Social intelligence: The cognitive basis of personality. In P. Shaver (Ed.), *Self, situations, and social behavior* (pp. 15–34). Beverly Hills, CA: Sage.

Cantor, N., Norem, J. K., Niedenthal, P. M., Langston, C. A., & Brower, A. M. (1987). Life tasks, self-concept ideals, and cognitive strategies in a life transition. *Journal of Personality and Social Psychology, 53,* 1178–1191.

Carey, W. B. (1970). A simplified method for measuring infant temperament. *Journal of Pediatrics, 77,* 188–194.

Carnegie Council on Adolescent Development. (1995). *Great transitions: Preparing adolescents for a new century.* New York: Carnegie Corporation.

Carpo, R. H. (1995). Factors in the cross-cultural patterning of male homosexuality: A reappraisal of the literature. *Cross-Cultural Research, 29,* 178–202.

Carraher, T. N., Schliemann, A. D., & Carraher, D. W. (1988). Mathematical concepts in everyday life. In G. B. Saxe & M. Gearhart (Eds.), *Children's mathematics: New directions in child development* (pp. 71–87). San Francisco: Jossey-Bass.

Casey, M. B. (1996). Understanding individual differences in spatial ability within females: A nature/nurture interactionist framework. *Developmental Review, 16,* 241–260.

Cassidy, C. M. (1991). The good body: When big is better. *Medical Anthropology, 13,* 181–213.

Catell, R. B. (1963). Theory of fluid and crystallized intelligence: A critical experiment. *Journal of Educational Psychology, 54,* 1–22.

Caudill, W., & Weinstein, H. (1969). Maternal care and infant behavior in Japan and America. *Psychiatry, 32,* 12–43.

Centers for Disease Control. (1992). Selected behaviors that increase the risk for HIV infection among high school students—U.S. 1990. *Morbidity and Mortality Weekly, 41,* 231–240.

Chagnon, N. A. (1983). *Yanomamo: The fierce people* (3rd ed.). New York: CBS College Publishing.

Chamberlain, P., & Patterson, G. R. (1995). Discipline and child compliance in parenting. In M. Bornstein (Ed.), *Handbook of parenting* (Vol. 4, pp. 205–225). Hillsdale, NJ: Erlbaum.

Chao, R. K. (1994). Beyond parental control and authoritarian parenting style: Understanding Chinese parenting through the cultural notion of training. *Child Development, 65,* 1111–1119.

Chao, R. K. (1996). Chinese and European American mothers' beliefs about the role of parenting in children's school success. *Journal of Cross-Cultural Psychology, 27*(4), 403–423.

Charles, M., & Hopflinger, F. (1992). Gender, culture and the division of household labor: A replication of U.S. studies for the case of Switzerland. *Journal of Comparative Family Studies, 23,* 375–387.

Cheek, J. M. (1989). *Conquering shyness.* New York: Putnam.

Chen, C., & Uttal, D. H. (1988). Cultural values, parents' beliefs, and children's achievement in the United States and China. *Human Development, 31,* 351–358.

Cherlin, A. J., & Furstenberg, F. F., Jr. (1986). *The new American grandparent: A place in the family, a life apart.* New York: Basic Books.

Chodorow, N. (1978). *The reproduction of mothering.* Berkeley: University of California Press.

Clark, K. B., & Clark, M. P. (1947). *Racial identification and preference in Negro children.* New York: Holt.

Cogan, J. C., Bhalla, S. K., Sefa-Dedeh, A., & Rothblum, E. D. (1996). A comparison study of United States and African students on perceptions of obesity and thinness. *Journal of Cross-Cultural Psychology, 27*(1), 98–113.

Cole, M. (1990). Cognitive development and formal schooling: The evidence from cross-cultural research. In L. C. Moll (Ed.), *Vygotsky and education* (pp. 89–110). Cambridge, England: Cambridge University Press.

Cole, M. (1992a). Culture and cognitive development: From cross-cultural comparisons to model systems of cultural mediation. In A. F. Healy, S. M. Kosslyn, & R. M. Shiffrin (Eds.), *Essays in honor of William K. Estes* (pp. 279–305). Hillsdale, NJ: Erlbaum.

Cole, M. (1992b). Culture in development. In M. H. Bornstein & M. E. Lamb (Eds.), *Developmental psychology: An advanced textbook* (3rd ed., pp. 731–789). Hillsdale, NJ: Erlbaum.

Cole, M. (1995). Culture and cognitive development: From cross-cultural research to creating systems of cultural mediation. *Culture and psychology, 1,* 25–52.

Cole, M., & Cole, S. R. (1989). *The development of children.* New York: Freeman.

Cole, M., & Cole, S. R. (1993). *The development of children* (2nd ed.). New York: Freeman.

Cole, M., & Cole, S. R. (1996). *The development of children* (3rd ed.). New York: Freeman.

Collins, W. A. (1990). Parent-child relationships in the transition to adolescence: Continuity and change in interaction, affect, and cognition. In R. Montemayor, G. Adams, & T. Gullotta (Eds.), *Advances in adolescent development: From childhood to adolescence: A transitional period?* (Vol. 2, pp. 85–106). Beverly Hills, CA: Sage.

Collins, W. A., & Russell, G. (1991). Mother-child and father-child relationships in middle childhood and adolescence: A developmental analysis. *Developmental Review, 11,* 91–136.

Coltrane, S. (1996). *Family man: Fatherhood, housework, and gender equity.* New York: Oxford University Press.

Condon, J. C. (1984). *With respect to the Japanese.* Yarmouth, ME: Intercultural Press.

Connolly, M. (1990). Adrift in the city: A comparative study of street children in Bogota, Colombia and Guatemala City. In N. Boxhill (Ed.), *Homeless children: The watchers and the waiters* (pp. 129–149). New York: Haworth Press.

Cook, P. (1994). Chronic illness beliefs and the role of social networks among Chinese, Indian, and Angloceltic Canadians. *Journal of Cross-Cultural Psychology, 25,* 452–465.

Cooley, C. H. (1902). *Human nature and the social order.* New York: Scribner's.

Coren, S. (1992). *The left-hander syndrome.* New York: Free Press.

Coren, S., & Halpern, D. F. (1991). Left-handedness: A marker for decreased survival fitness. *Psychological Bulletin, 109,* 90–106.

Corman, H. H., & Escalona, S. K. (1969). Stages in sensori-motor development: A replication study. *Merrill-Palmer Quarterly, 15*(4), 351–361.

Corsaro, W. A. (1988). Routines in the peer culture of American and Italian nursery school children. *Social Education, 61,* 1–14.

Corsaro, W. A., & Eder, D. (1990). Children's peer cultures. *Annual Review in Sociology, 16,* 197–220.

Cosgrove, J. (1990). Towards a working definition of street children. *International Social Work, 33,* 185–192.

Cosminsky, S. A., Mhlovi, M., & Ewbank, D. (1993). Child feeding practices in a rural area of Zimbabwe. *Social Science and Medicine, 36,* 937–947.

Cotran, R. S., Kumar, V., & Robbins, S. L. (1994). *Robbins' pathologic basis of disease* (5th ed.). Philadelphia: Saunders.

Cousins, S. D. (1989). Culture and self-perception in Japan and the United States. *Journal of Personality and Social Psychology, 56,* 124–131.

Coverman, S. (1985). Explaining husband's participation in domestic labor. *Sociological Quarterly, 26,* 81–97.

Covey, S. R. (1990). *The 7 habits of highly effective people.* New York: Simon & Schuster.

Coward, R. T., Horne, C., & Dwyer, J. W. (1992). Demographic perspectives on gender and family caregiving. In J. W. Dwyer & R. T. Coward (Eds.), *Gender, families and elder care.* Newbury Park, CA: Sage.

Cox, C. (1993). Hispanic culture and family care of Alzheimer's patients. *Health and Social Work, 18*(2), 92–101.

Crittenden, K. S. (1991). Asian self-effacement or feminine modesty? Attributional patterns of women university students in Taiwan. *Gender and Society, 5*, 98–117.

Cross, S. E. (1990). *The role of the self-concept in cross-cultural adaptation.* Unpublished doctoral dissertation, Department of Psychology, University of Michigan, Ann Arbor.

Cross, S. E. (1995). Self-construals, coping, and stress in cross-cultural adaptation. *Journal of Cross-Cultural Psychology, 26*(6), 673–697.

Cross, W. (1978). The Thomas and Cross models of psychological nigrescence: A literature review. *Journal of Black Psychology, 4*, 13–31.

Csikszentmihalyi, M., & Beattie, O. V. (1979). Life themes: A theoretical and empirical exploration of their origins and effects. *Journal of Humanistic Psychology, 19*, 45–63.

Cummings, L. L. (1994). Fighting by the rules: Women street-fighting in Chihuahua, Mexico. *Sex Roles, 30*, 189–198.

Cushner, K. (1990). Cross-cultural psychology and the formal classroom. In R. W. Brislin (Ed.), *Applied cross-cultural psychology* (pp. 98–120). Newbury Park, CA: Sage.

Damon, W. (1973). Early conceptions of positive justice as related to the development of logical operations. *Child Development, 46*, 301–312.

D'Andrade, R. (1990). Some propositions about the relations between culture and human cognition. In J. W. Stigler, R. A. Shweder, & G. Herdt (Eds.), *Cultural psychology* (pp. 65–129). New York: Cambridge University Press.

D'Andrade, R. G., & Strauss, C. (Eds.). (1992). Human motives and cultural models. New York: Cambridge University Press.

Dasen, P. R. (1972a). Cross-cultural Piagetian research: A summary. *Journal of Cross-Cultural Psychology, 7*, 75–85.

Dasen, P. R. (1972b). The development of conservation in Aboriginal children. A replication study. *International Journal of Psychology, 7*, 75–85.

Dasen, P. R. (1975). Concrete operational development in three cultures. *Journal of Cross-Cultural Psychology, 6*, 156–172.

Dasen, P. R. (1984). The cross-cultural study of intelligence: Piaget and Baoule. *International Journal of Psychology, 19*, 407–424.

Dasen, P. R. (1988). Les activities quotidiennes d'enfants africains dans leur contexte naturel: La methode des observations pontuelles. *Enfance, 41*, 3–24.

Dasen, P. R. (1994). Culture and cognitive development from a Piagetian perspective. In W. J. Lonner & R. Malpass (Eds.), *Psychology and culture.* Boston: Allyn & Bacon.

Dasen, P. R. (Ed.). (1977). *Piagetian psychology: Cross-cultural contributions.* New York: Gardner Press.

Dasen, P. R., & Heron, A. (1981). Cross-cultural tests of Piaget's theory. In H. C. Triandis & A. Heron (Eds.), *Handbook of cross-cultural psychology* (Vol. 4). Boston: Allyn & Bacon.

Dasen, P. R., Inhelder, B., Lavellee, M., & Retschitzki, J. (1978). *Naissance de l'intelligence chez l'enfant Baoule de Côte d'Ivoire.* Berne: Hans Huber.

Datan, N., Antonovsky, A., & Moaz, B. (1984). Love, war, and the life cycle of the family. In K. A. McCluskey & H. W. Reese (Eds.), *Life-span developmental psychology: Historical and generational effects* (pp. 143–159). New York: Academic Press.

Davenport, D. S., & Yurich, J. M. (1991). Multicultural gender issues. *Journal of Counseling and Development, 70,* 64–71.

Davidson, A. R. (1994). Problems of rapid population growth. In W. J. Lonner & R. Malpass (Eds.), *Psychology and culture.* Boston: Allyn & Bacon.

Dawes, A. (1990). The effects of political violence on children. A consideration of South African and other studies. *International Journal of Psychology, 25,* 13–31.

Day, R., Nielsen, J., Korten, A., Ernberg, M., et al. (1987). Stressful life events preceding the onset of schizophrenia: A cross-cultural study from the World Health Organization. *Culture, Medicine, and Psychiatry, 11,* 123–205.

Declercq, E. R. (1993). Where babies are born and who attends their births: Findings from the revised 1989 United States standard certificate of live births. *Obstetrics and Gynecology, 81,* 997–1004.

Delaney, C. H. (1995). Rites of passage in adolescence. *Adolescence, 30,* 891–897.

Dennis, W., & Dennis, M. G. (1940). The effect of cradling practices upon the onset of walking in Hopi children. *Journal of Genetic Psychology, 56,* 77–86.

Dentan, R. K. (1968). *The Semai: A nonviolent people of Malaya.* New York: Holt, Rinehart & Winston.

DeRosier, M. E., & Kupersmidt, J. B. (1991). Costa Rican children's perceptions of their social networks. *Developmental Psychology, 27,* 656–662.

Desmond, M., Price, J. H., Gray, N., & O'Connell, J. K. (1986). The etiology of adolescents' perceptions of their weight. *Journal of Youth and Adolescence, 15,* 461–474.

Dettwyler, K. A. (1989). Style of infant feeding: Parental/caretaker control of food consumption in young children. *American Anthropologist, 91,* 696–703.

DeVries, M. W. (1994). Kids in context: Temperament in cross-cultural perspective. In W. B. Carey & S. C. Devitt (Eds.), *Prevention and early intervention: Individual differences as risk factors for the mental health of children.* New York: Brunner/Mazel.

DeVries, M. W., & Sameroff, A. J. (1984). Culture and temperament: Influences on temperament in three East African societies. *American Journal of Orthopsychiatry, 54,* 83–96.

Dexter, C. R. (1985). Women and the exercise of power in organizations: From ascribed to achieved status. *Women and Work, 1,* 239–258.

Dhawan, N., & Roseman, I. J. (1988). *Self-concept across two cultures: India and the United States.* Paper presented at the ninth conference of the International Association for Cross-Cultural Psychology, Newcastle, Australia.

Dion, K. L., & Dion, K. K. (1993). Gender and ethnocultural comparisons in styles of love. *Psychology of Women Quarterly, 17,* 463–473.

Dohrenwend, B. P., & Dohrenwend, B. S. (1969). *Social status and psychological disorder.* New York: Wiley.

Domino, G. (1992). Cooperation and competition in Chinese and American children. *Journal of Cross-Cultural Psychology, 23*(4), 456–467.

Dornbusch, S. M., Ritter, P. L., Leiderman, P. H., Roberts, D. F., & Fraleigh, M. J. (1987). The relation of parenting style to adolescent school performance. *Child Development, 58,* 1244–1257.

Douki, S., & Tabbane, K. (1996). Culture and depression. *World Health Magazine, 49*(2), 22–26.

Draguns, J. (1990a). Applications of cross-cultural psychology in the field of mental health. In R. Brislin (Ed.), *Applied cross-cultural psychology* (pp. 302–324). Newbury Park, CA: Sage.

Draguns, J. G. (1990b). Normal and abnormal behavior in cross-cultural perspective: Toward specifying the nature of their relationship. In J. J. Berman (Ed.), *Nebraska symposium on motivation 1989* (pp. 236–277). Lincoln: University of Nebraska Press.

Draguns, J. G. (1994). Pathological and clinical aspects. In L. L. Adler & U. P. Gielen (Eds.), *Cross-cultural topics in psychology.* Westport, CT: Praeger.

Draper, P., & Cashdan, E. (1988). Technological change and child behavior among the !Kung. *Ethnology, 27,* 348.

Duda, J. L., & Allison, M. T. (1990). Cross-cultural analysis in exercise and sport psychology: A void in the field. *Journal of Sport and Exercise Psychology, 12,* 14–131.

Durbin, D. L., Darling, N., Steinberg, L., & Brown, B. B. (1993). Parenting style and peer group membership among European-American adolescents. *Journal of Research on Adolescence, 3,* 87–100.

Dybdahl, R. (1996, August). The child in context: Exploring childhood in Somalia. Paper presented at the Twenty-sixth International Congress of Psychology, Montreal.

Eckensberger, L. H. (1994). Moral development and its measurement across cultures. In W. J. Lonner and R. S. Malpass (Eds.), *Psychology and culture* (pp. 71–78). Boston, MA: Allyn & Bacon.

Edwards, C. P. (1989). The transition from infancy to early childhood: A difficult transition, and a difficult theory. In V. R. Bricker & G. H. Gossen (Eds.), *Ethnographic encounters in Southern Mesoamerica: Essays in honor of Evon Z. Vogt, Jr.* (pp. 167–175). Austin: University of Texas.

Edwards, C. P. (1996). Parenting toddlers. In M. H. Bornstein (Ed.), *Handbook of parenting* (Vol. 1, pp. 41–63). Hillsdale, NJ: Erlbaum.

Edwards, M. (1994). Pollution in the former U.S.S.R.: Lethal legacy. *National Geographic Magazine, 186*(2), 70–99.

Eisenberg, N., Boehnke, K., Schuhler, P., & Silbereisen, R. K. (1985). The development of prosocial behavior and cognition in German children. *Journal of Cross-Cultural Psychology, 16,* 69–82.

Ekvall, S. W. (1993). Nutritional assessment and early intervention. In S. W. Ekvall (Ed.), *Pediatric nutrition in chronic diseases and developmental disorders: Prevention, assessment, and treatment.* New York: Oxford University Press.

Elder, G. H., Modell, J., & Parke, R. D. (Eds.). (1993). *Children in time and place.* New York: Cambridge University Press.

Elkin, F., & Handel, G. (1989). *The child and society: The process of socialization* (5th ed.). New York: Random House.

Elkind, D. (1984). *All grown up and no place to go.* Reading, MA: Addison-Wesley.

Elkind, D. (1988). *The Hurried Child: Growing up too fast too soon.* Reading, MA: Addison-Wesley.

Ellis, A. (1962). *Reason and emotion in psychotherapy.* New York: Carol Publishing Group.

Ember, C. R., & Ember, M. (1993). *Cultural anthropology* (7th ed.). Englewood Cliffs, NJ: Prentice Hall.

Ember, C. R., & Levinson, D. (1991). The substantive contributions of worldwide cross-cultural studies using secondary data. *Behavior Science Research, 25,* 79–140.

Engels, J. (1993). *Pocket guide to pediatric assessment* (2nd ed.). St. Louis: Mosby.

Engle, P. L., Zeitlin, M., Medrano, Y., & Garcia, L. M. (1996). Growth consequences of low-income Nicaraguan mothers' theories about feeding 1-year-olds. In S. Harkness & C. M. Super (Eds.), *Parents' cultural belief systems* (pp. 428–446). New York: Guilford Press.

Enright, R. D., Bjerstedt, A., Enright, W. F., Levy, V. M., Buss, R. R., Harwell, M., & Zindler, M. (1984). Distributive justice development: Cross-cultural, contextual, and longitudinal evaluations. *Child Development, 55,* 1737–1751.

Enright, R. D., Franklin, C. C., & Manheim, L. A. (1980). Children's distributive justice reasoning: A standardized and objective scale. *Developmental Psychology, 16,* 193–202.

Epstein, L. H. (1985). Family-based treatment for pre-adolescent obesity. In M. Wolraich & D. K. Routh (Eds.), *Advances in developmental and behavioral pediatrics* (Vol. 6). Greenwich, CT: JAI Press.

Epstein, L. H. (1992). Exercise and obesity in children. *Journal of Applied Sport Psychology, 4,* 120–133.

Erikson, E. H. (1963). *Childhood and society* (2nd ed.). New York: Norton.

Erikson, E. H. (1969). *Gandhi's truth.* New York: Norton.

Erikson, E. H. (1982). *The life cycle completed.* New York: Norton.

Erikson, E. H., Erikson, J. M., & Kivnick, H. G. (1986). *Vital involvement in old age.* New York: Norton.

Espinosa, M. P., Sigman, M. D., Newmann, C. G., Bwibo, N. O., & McDonald, M. A. (1992). Playground behaviors of school-age children in relation to nutrition, schooling, and family characteristics. *Developmental Psychology, 28,* 1188–1195.

Essau, C. A., & Trommsdorff, G. (1996). Coping with university-related problems: A cross-cultural comparison. *Journal of Cross-Cultural Psychology, 27*(3), 315–328.

Fagot, B. I., & Leinbach, M. D. (1989). The young child's gender schema: Environmental input, internal organization. *Child Development, 60,* 663–672.

Falbo, T. (1991). The impact of grandparents on children's outcomes in China. *Marriage & Family Review, 16*(3–4), 369–376.

Farver, J. A. M., & Howes, C. (1988). Cross-cultural differences in social interaction: A comparison of American and Indonesian children. *Journal of Cross-Cultural Psychology, 19,* 203–215.

Farver, J. A. M., & Wimbarti, S. (1995). Indonesian children's play with their mothers and older siblings. *Child Development, 66,* 1493–1503.

Farver, J. M. (1993). Cultural differences in scaffolding pretend play: A comparison of American and Mexican mother-child and sibling-child pairs. In K. MacDonald (Ed.), *Parent-child play* (pp. 349–366). Albany: State University of New York Press.

Fay, W. B. (1993). Families in the 1990s. *Marketing Research, 5*(1), 47.

Feldman, S. S., & Elliott, G. R. (Eds.). (1990). *At the threshold: The developing adolescent.* Cambridge, MA: Harvard University Press.

Ferrante, J. (1992). *Sociology: A global perspective.* Belmont, CA: Wadsworth.

Field, T. (1992). *Massaging high-risk infants.* Paper presented at the International Conference on Infant Studies, Miami Beach, FL.

Figler, S. K., & Whitaker, G. (1995). Sport and play in American life. Dubuque, IA: Brown & Benchmark.

Fischer, K. (1987). Relations between brain and cognitive development. *Child Development, 58,* 623–632.

Fishbein, H. D. (1984). *The psychology of infancy and childhood: Evolutionary and cross-cultural perspectives.* Hillsdale, NJ: Erlbaum.

Fisher, C. B., & Brone, R. J. (1991). Eating disorders in adolescence. In R. M. Lerner, A. C. Petersen, & J. Brooks-Gunn (Eds.), *Encyclopedia of adolescence.* New York: Garland.

Fishman, J. A. (1971). *Advances in the sociology of language* (Vol. 1). The Hague: Mouton.

Fitzgerald, M. H. (1990). The interplay of culture and symptoms: Menstrual symptoms among Samoans. *Medical Anthropology, 12,* 145–167.

Fleming, J., Watson, C., McDonald, D., & Alexander, K. (1991). Drug use patterns in Northern Territory Aboriginal communities, 1986–1987. *Drug and Alcohol Review, 10,* 367–380.

Floderus-Myrhed, B., Pedersen, N., & Rasmuson, I. (1980). Assessment of heritability for personality, based on a short form of the Eysenck Personality Inventory: A study of 12,898 twin pairs. *Behavior Genetics, 10,* 153–162.

Ford, D. L., & Lerner, R. M. (1992). *Developmental systems theory: An integrative approach.* Newbury Park, CA: Sage.

Forman, G. E., & Sigel, I. E. (1979). *Cognitive development: A life-span view.* Monterey, CA: Brooks/Cole.

Forman, S. G. (1993). *Coping skills interventions for children and adolescents.* San Francisco: Jossey-Bass.

Freedman, D. G. (1974). *Human infancy: An evolutionary perspective.* Hillsdale, NJ: Erlbaum.

Freeman, D. (1983). *Margaret Mead and Samoa*. Cambridge, MA: Harvard University Press.

Freund, C. S. (1990). Maternal regulation of children's problem-solving behavior and its impact on children's performance. *Child Development, 61,* 113–126.

Friedman, A., Todd, J., & Kariuki, P. W. (1995). Cooperative and competitive behavior of urban and rural children in Kenya. *Journal of Cross-Cultural Psychology, 26*(4), 374–383.

Fukada, N. (1991). Women in Japan. In L. L. Adler (Ed.), *Women in cross-cultural perspective* (pp. 204–219). New York: Praeger.

Fuller, M. L. (1992). Today's demographics don't leave it to Beaver. *Education Digest, 58*(6), 54–57.

Furnham, A., & Alibhai, N. (1983). Cross-cultural differences in the perception of female body shapes. *Psychological Medicine, 13,* 829–837.

Gallimore, R., Goldenberg, C. N., & Weisner, T. S. (1993). The social construction and subjective reality of activity settings: Implications for community psychology. *American Journal of Community Psychology, 21,* 537–559.

Gallimore, R., Weisner, T. S., Kaufman, S. Z., & Bernheimer, L. P. (1989). The social construction of ecocultural niches: Family accommodation of developmentally delayed children. *American Journal on Mental Retardation, 94,* 216–230.

Gander, M. J., & Gardiner, H. W. (1981). *Child and adolescent development*. Boston: Little, Brown.

Gangestad, S. W., Thornhill, R., & Yeo, R. A. (1994). Facial attractiveness: Implications for mating dynamics. *Human Nature, 4,* 205–236.

Garbarino, J. (1985). *Adolescent development: An ecological perspective*. Columbus, OH: Merrill.

Gardiner, A. J., Gardiner, H. W., & Gardiner, O. S. (1994). Support groups in higher education: The Asian-American experience. In A. White-Parks, D. D. Buffton, U. Chiu, C. M. Currier, C. G. Manrique, & M. M. Piehl (Eds.), *A gathering of voices on the Asian-American Experience* (pp. 145–150). Fort Atkinson, WI: Highsmith Press.

Gardiner, H. W. (1994). Child Development. In L. L. Adler & U. P. Gielen (Eds.), *Cross-cultural topics in psychology* (pp. 61–72). New York: Praeger.

Gardiner, H. W. (1995, March/April). The life of a Buddhist monk. *Calliope.*

Gardiner, H. W. (1996). *Cross-cultural content in contemporary developmental textbooks*. Paper presented at the thirteenth congress of the International Association for Cross-Cultural Psychology, Montreal, Canada.

Gardiner, H. W., & Gardiner, O. S. (1991). *Women in Thailand*. In L. L. Adler (Ed.), *Women in cross-cultural perspective* (pp. 174–187). New York: Praeger.

Gardiner, H., & Mutter, J. D. (1992a). *Developing multicultural awareness: A model for integrating learning and culture*. Paper presented at the eleventh international congress of the International Association for Cross-Cultural Psychology and the Association for Intercultural Research, Liege, Belgium.

Gardiner, H. W., & Mutter, J. D. (1992b). *Positive attitudes and cross-cultural experiences.* Paper presented at the twenty-first annual meeting of the Society for Cross-Cultural Research, Santa Fe, NM.

Gardiner, H. W., & Mutter, J. D. (1993). *An approach to integrating teaching and formal learning in a multicultural context.* Paper presented at the twenty-second annual meeting of the Society for Cross-Cultural Research, Santa Fe, NM.

Gardiner, H. W., & Mutter, J. D. (1994). *Measuring multicultural awareness and identity: A model.* Paper presented at the twenty-third annual meeting of the Society for Cross-Cultural Research, Santa Fe, NM.

Gardiner, H. W., Mutter, J. D., & Kosmitzki, C. (1997). *A model for understanding cultural identity.* Unpublished manuscript.

Gardner, H. (1983). *Frames of mind: The theory of multiple intelligences.* New York: Basic Books.

Garvey, C. (1990). *Play.* Cambridge, MA: Harvard University Press.

Geertz, C. (1973). *The interpretation of cultures.* New York: Basic Books.

Gergen, K. J. (1994). *Realities and relationships: Soundings in social construction.* Cambridge, MA: Harvard University Press.

Gergen, K. J., Gulerce, A., Lock, A., & Misra, G. (1996). Psychological science in cultural context. *American Psychologist, 51,* 496–503.

Gibbons, J. L., Stiles, D. A., & Shkodriani, G. M. (1991). Adolescents' attitudes toward family and gender roles: An international comparison. *Sex Roles, 25,* 625–643.

Gibson, J. T., Westwood, M. J., Ishiyama, F. I., Borgen, W. A., et al. (1991). Youth and culture: A seventeen nation study of perceived problems and coping strategies. *International Journal for the Advancement of Counselling, 14,* 203–216.

Gielen, U. P. (1994). American mainstream psychology and its relationship to international and cross-cultural psychology. In A. L. Comunian & U. P. Gielen (Eds.), *Advancing psychology and its applications: International perspectives* (pp. 26–40). Milan, Italy: FrancoAngeli.

Gilligan, C. (1982). *In a different voice: Psychological theory and women's development.* Cambridge, MA: Harvard University Press.

Gladwin, T., & Sarason, S. B. (1953). *Truk: Man in paradise.* (Viking Fund Publications in Anthropology No. 20). New York: Wenner-Gren Foundation for Anthropological Research.

Goldberg, D. P. (1972). *The detection of psychiatric illness by questionnaire.* Windsor: NFER.

Goldberg, S. (1972). Infant care and growth in urban Zambia. *Human Development, 15,* 77–89.

Gonzales, G. F., & Villena, A. (1996). Body mass index and age at menarche in Peruvian children living at high altitudes and at sea level. *Human Biology, 68*(2), 265–276.

Goode, E. E. (1993). The cultures of illness: Health care professionals learn to appreciate immigrants' beliefs. *U.S. News and World Report, 114*(6), 74–77.

Goodnow, J. J. (1962). A test of milieu effects with some of Piaget's tasks. *Psychological Monographs, 76*(36, Whole Issue No. 555).

Goodnow, J. J. (1988). Parents' ideas, actions, and feelings: Models and methods from developmental and social psychology. *Child Development, 59,* 289–320.

Goodnow, J. J. (1990). The socialization of cognition. In J. W. Stigler, R. A. Shweder, & G. Herdt (Eds.), *Cultural psychology: Essays on comparative human development.* Cambridge, England: Cambridge University Press.

Goodnow, J. J., & Bethon, G. (1966). Piaget's tasks: The effects of schooling on intelligence. *Child Development, 37,* 573–582.

Goodnow, J. J., & Collins, W. A. (1990). *Development according to parents: The nature, sources, and consequences of parents' ideas.* Hillsdale, NJ: Erlbaum.

Gopal-McNicol, S. (1995). A cross-cultural examination of racial identity and racial preference of preschool children in the West Indies. *Journal of Cross-Cultural Psychology, 26,* 141–152.

Gormly, A. V., & Brodzinsky, D. M. (1993). *Lifespan Human Development* (5th ed.). Orlando, FL: Harcourt Brace Jovanovich.

Gotowiec, A., & Beiser, M. (1993). Aboriginal children's mental health: Unique challenges. *Canada's Mental Health, 41,* 7–11.

Grant, J. P. (1994). *The state of the world's children.* New York: UNICEF and Oxford University Press.

Greenfield, P. M., Brazelton, T. B., & Childs, C. P. (1989). From birth to maturity in Zinacantan: Ontogenesis in cultural context. In V. R. Bricker & G. H. Gossen (Eds.), *Ethnographic encounters in Southern Mesoamerica: Essays in honor of Evon Z. Vogt, Jr.* (pp. 177–216). Austin: University of Texas.

Greenfield, P. M., & Cocking, R. R. (1994). *Cross-cultural roots of minority child development.* Hillsdale, NJ: Erlbaum.

Grossman, B., Wirt, R., & Davids, A. (1985). Self-esteem, ethnic identity, and behavioral adjustment among Anglo and Chicano adolescents in West Texas. *Journal of Adolescence, 8,* 57–68.

Grossmann, K., Grossmann, K. E., Huber, F., & Wartner, U. (1981). German children's behavior towards their mothers at 12 months and their fathers at 18 months in Ainsworth's strange situation. *International Journal of Behavioral Development, 7,* 157–181.

Grotevant, H., & Cooper, C. (1985). Patterns of interaction in family relationships and the development of identity exploration in adolescence. *Developmental Psychology, 56,* 415–428.

Grusec, J. E., & Goodnow, J. J. (1994). Impact of parental discipline methods on the child's internalization of values: A reconceptualization of current points of view. *Developmental Psychology, 30,* 4–19.

Gustafson, G. E., Green, J. A., & Kalinowski, L. L. (1993). *The development of communicative skills: Infants' cries and vocalizations in social context.* Paper presented at the biennial meeting of the Society for Research in Child Development, New Orleans, LA.

Gustafson, G. E., & Harris, K. L. (1990). Women's responses to young infants' cries. *Developmental Psychology, 26,* 144–152.

Haan, N., Aerts, E., & Cooper, B. B. (1985). *On moral grounds: The search for a practical morality.* New York: New York University Press.

Haley, A. (1974). *Roots.* New York: Dell.

Hall, G. S. (1904). *Adolescence.* New York: Appleton-Century-Crofts.

Hall, G. S. (1922). *Senescence: The last half of life.* New York: Appleton-Century-Crofts.

Halpern, D. F. (1996). Sex, brain, hands, and spatial cognition. *Developmental Review, 16,* 261–270.

Halverson, C. F., Kohnstamm, G. A., & Martin, R. P. (Eds.). (1994). *Development of the structure of temperament and personality from infancy to adulthood.* Hillsdale, NJ: Erlbaum.

Hardy, J. A., & Higgins, G. A. (1992). Alzheimer's disease: The amyloid cascade hypothesis. *Science, 256,* 184–185.

Harkness, S. (1992). Cross-cultural research in child development: A sample of the state of the art. *Developmental Psychology, 28,* 622–625.

Harkness, S., & Super, C. M. (1985). The cultural context of gender segregation in children's peer groups. *Child Development, 56,* 219–224.

Harkness, S., & Super, C. M. (1992a). The cultural foundations of fathers' roles: Evidence from Kenya and the U.S. In B. S. Hewlett (Ed.), *The father-child relationship: Anthropological perspectives* (pp. 191–212). New York: Aldine.

Harkness, S., & Super, C. M. (1992b). The developmental niche: A theoretical framework for analyzing the household production of health. *Social Science and Medicine, 38,* 217–226.

Harkness, S., & Super, C. M. (1995). Culture and parenting. In M. Bornstein (Ed.), *Handbook of parenting* (Vol. 2, pp. 211–234). Hillsdale, NJ: Erlbaum.

Harkness, S., & Super, C. M. (Eds.). (1996). *Parents' cultural belief systems: Their origins, expressions, and consequences.* New York: Guilford Press.

Harlow, H. F., & Harlow, M. K. (1962). Social deprivation in monkeys. *Scientific American, 207,* 136–146.

Harlow, H. F., & Zimmermann, R. R. (1959). Affectional responses in the infant monkey. *Science, 130,* 421–432.

Harris, M. G. (1994). *Cholas,* Mexican-American girls, and gangs. *Sex Roles, 30,* 289–301.

Harrison, A. O., Stewart, R. B., Myambo, K., & Teveraishe, C. (1995). Perceptions of social networks among adolescents from Zimbabwe and the United States. *Journal of Black Psychology, 21,* 382–407.

Harter, S. (1982). The perceived competence scale for children. *Child Development, 53,* 87–97.

Hatfield, E., & Rapson, R. L. (1996). *Love & sex: Cross-cultural perspectives.* Boston: Allyn & Bacon.

Hatfield, E., & Sprecher, S. (1995). Men's and women's mate preferences in marital partners in the United States, Russia, and Japan. *Journal of Cross-Cultural Psychology, 26,* 728–750.

Hauser, S. T., & Kasendorf, E. (1983). *Black and white identity formation* (2nd ed.). Malabar, FL: Krieger.

Heinicke, C. M. (1995). Determinants of the transition to parenting. In M. H. Bornstein (Ed.), *Handbook of parenting* (Vol, 3, pp. 277–303). Mahwah, NJ: Erlbaum.

Helson, R., Mitchell, V., & Moane, G. (1984). Personality patterns of adherence and nonadherence to the social clock. *Journal of Personality and Social Psychology, 46,* 1079–1096.

Hendrick, J. B. (1990). Early childhood. In R. M. Thomas (Ed.), *The encyclopedia of human development and education: Theory, research, and studies.* Oxford: Pergamon.

Hendry, J. (1986). *Becoming Japanese.* Honolulu: University of Hawaii Press.

Hendry, J. (1993). Becoming Japanese: The arenas and agents of socialization. In R. H. Wozniak (Ed.), *Worlds of childhood reader.* New York: HarperCollins.

Herdt, G. (1986). Aspects of socialization for aggression in Sambia ritual and warfare. *Anthropology Quarterly, 59,* 160–164.

Heron, A., & Kroeger, E. (1981). Introduction to developmental psychology. In H. C. Triandis, & A. Heron (Eds.), *Handbook of cross-cultural psychology,* (1st ed., Vol. 4). Boston: Allyn & Bacon.

Herskovits, M. J. (1948). *Man and his works: The science of cultural anthropology.* New York: Knopf.

Hewlett, B. (Ed.). (1992). *Father-child relations: Cultural and biosocial contexts.* Hawthorne, NY: Aldine De Gruyter.

Hindley, C. B., Filliozat, A. M., Klackenberg, G., Nicolet-Neister, D., & Sand, E. A. (1966). Differences in age of walking for five European longitudinal samples. *Human Biology, 38,* 364–379.

Hitchcock, D. I. (1994). *Asian values and the United States: How much conflict?* Washington, DC: Center for Strategic and International Studies.

Hoffman, H. J., & Hillman, L. S. (1992). Epidemiology of the sudden infant death syndrome: Maternal, neonatal, and postneonatal risk factors. *Clinics in Perinatology, 19*(4), 717–737.

Hofstede, G. (1980). *Culture's consequences: International differences in work-related values.* Beverly Hills, CA: Sage.

Holland, D. C., & Valsiner, J. (1988). Cognition, symbols, and Vygotsky's developmental psychology. *Ethos, 16,* 247–272.

Hollos, M., & Leis, P. E. (1989). *Becoming Nigerian in Ibo society.* New Brunswick, NJ: Rutgers University Press.

Hollos, M., & Richards, F. A. (1993). Gender-associated development of formal operations in Nigerian adolescents. *Ethos, 21,* 24–52.

Holmbeck, G. N., Paikoff, R. L., & Brooks-Gunn, J. (1995). Parenting adolescents. In M. H. Bornstein (Ed.), *Handbook of parenting* (Vol. 1, pp. 91–118). Mahwah, NJ: Erlbaum.

Hong, L. K. (1987). Potential effect of the one-child policy on gender equality in the People's Republic of China. *Gender and Society, 1,* 317–326.

Hopkins, B. (1991). Facilitating early motor development: An intracultural study of West Indian mothers and their infants living in Britain. In J. K. Nugent, B. M. Lester, & T. B. Brazelton (Eds.), *The cultural context of infancy* (Vol. 2). Norwood, NJ: Ablex.

Hopkins, B., & Westra, T. (1988). Maternal handling and motor development: An intracultural study. *Genetic, Social and General Psychology Monographs, 14,* 377–420.

Hopkins, B., & Westra, T. (1990). Motor development, maternal expectations and the role of handling. *Infant Behavior and Development, 13,* 117–122.

Horn, J. L., & Cattell, R. B. (1967). Age differences in fluid and crystalized intelligence. *Acta Psychologica, 26,* 107–129.

Horn, J. L., & Donaldson, G. (1980). Cognitive development: II. Adulthood development of human abilities. In O. G. Brim & J. Kagan (Eds.), *Constancy and change in human development.* Cambridge, MA: Harvard University Press.

Horn, J. L., & Hofer, S. M. (1992). Major abilities and development in the adult period. In R. J. Sternberg and C. A. Berg (Eds.), *Intellectual development.* Cambridge, England: Cambridge University Press.

Houston, L. (1984). Black consciousness and self-esteem. *Journal of Black Psychology, 11,* 1–7.

Hsu, F. L. K. (1985). The self in cross-cultural perspective. In A. J. Marsella, G. DeVos, & F. L. K. Hsu (Eds.), *Culture and self: Asian and Western perspectives* (pp. 24–55). New York: Tavistock.

Hsu, F. L. K., Watrous, B. G., & Lord, E. M. (1961). Culture pattern and adolescent behaviour. *International Journal of Social Psychiatry, 7,* 33–53.

Hsu, L. K. G. (1986). The treatment of anorexia nervosa. *American Journal of Psychiatry, 143,* 573–581.

Hudgins, J. E., & Williams-Snyder, V. (1995). *African wedding guide.* Netscape: New Perspectives Technologies Company. (http://www.melanet.com/wedding/wed.html)

Huebner, A. M., & Garrod, A. C. (1993). Moral reasoning among Tibetan monks. A study of Buddhist adolescents and young adults in Nepal. *Journal of Cross-Cultural Psychology, 24,* 167–185.

Hutchinson, J. (1991, Spring). What crack does to babies. *American Educator: The Quarterly Journal of the American Federation of Teachers,* 31–32.

Ikels, C. (1989). Becoming a human being in theory and practice: Chinese views of human development. In D. I. Kertzer & K. W. Schaie (Eds.), *Age structuring in comparative perspective* (pp. 109–141). Hillsdale, NJ: Erlbaum.

Indran, S. K. (1995). Brief report: Eating attitudes among adolescent girls in Malaysian secondary school using the EAT questionnaire. *International Journal of Social Psychiatry, 41*(4), 299–303.

Ingram, D. D., Makuc, D., & Kleinman, J. C. (1986). National and state trends in use of prenatal care, 1970–1983. *American Journal of Public Health, 76*(4), 415–423.

Inhelder, B., & Piaget, J. (1958). *The growth of logical thinking from childhood to adolescence.* New York: Basic Books.

Inhelder, B., & Piaget, J. (1959). *The early growth of logic in the child: Classification and seriation.* New York: Harper & Row.

Isralowitz, R. E., & Hong, O. T. (1990). Singapore youth: The impact of social status on perceptions of adolescent problems. *Adolescence, 98,* 357–362.

Iwawaiki, S., & Kerner, R. M. (1974). Cross-cultural analysis of body build stereotypes of Japanese and American males and females. *Psychologia, 17,* 75–81.

Jablensky, A., Sartorius, N., Ernberg, G., Anker, M., Korten, A., Cooper, J. E., Day, R., & Bertelsen, A. (1992). Schizophrenia: Manifestations, incidence and course in different cultures: A World Health Organization ten-country study. *Psychological Medicine (Monograph Suppl. No. 20).*

Jackson, L. A. (1992). *Physical appearance and gender: Sociobiological and sociocultural perspectives.* Albany, NY: SUNY Press.

Jackson, S. (1987). Great Britain. In M. E. Lamb (Ed.), *The father's role: Cross-cultural perspectives* (pp. 29–57). Hillsdale, NJ: Erlbaum.

Jacobson, J. L., Jacobson, S. W., & Humphrey, H. E. B. (1992). Effects of in utero exposure to polychlorinated biphenyls and related contaminants on cognitive functioning in young children. *Journal of Pediatrics, 116,* 36–45.

Jacobson, S., Fein, G., Jacobson, J., Schwartz, P., & Dowler, J. (1984). Neonatal correlates of prenatal exposure to smoking, caffeine, and alcohol. *Infant Behavior and Development, 7,* 253–265.

Jahoda, G. (1986). A cross-cultural perspective on developmental psychology. *International Journal of Behavioral Development, 9,* 417–437.

James, K. E. (1991). Migration and remittances: A Tongan perspective. *Pacific Viewpoint, 32,* 1–23.

Jeffreys, M. D. W. (1952). Samsonic suicide or suicide of revenge among African Americans. *African Studies, 11,* 118–122.

Jegede, R., & Bamgboye, E. (1981). Self-concept in young Nigerian adolescents. *Psychological Reports, 49,* 451–454.

Jemmott, J. B., III, & Jemmott, L. S. (1993). Alcohol and drug use during sexual activity. Predicting the HIV-risk-related behavior of inner-city black male adolescents. *Journal of Adolescent Research, 8,* 41–57.

Johnson, C. L. (1988). Relationships among family members and friends in later life. In R. M. Milardo (Ed.), *Families and social networks* (pp. 168–189). Newbury Park, CA: Sage.

Johnson, M. M. (1988). *Strong mothers, weak wives.* Berkeley: University of California Press.

Johnston, L. D., O'Malley, P. M., & Bachman, J. G. (1992). *Smoking, drinking, and illicit drug use among American secondary school students, college students and young adults, 1975–1991.* Rockville, MD: National Institute on Drug Abuse.

Jones, D., & Hill, K. (1993). Criteria of facial attractiveness in five populations. *Human Nature, 4,* 271–296.

Jones, R. L., & Kurz Jones, S. (1976). *The Himalaja woman.* Palto Alto, CA: Mayfield.

Jordan, B. (1978). *Birth in four cultures: A crosscultural investigation of childbirth in Yucatan, Holland, Sweden and the United States.* St. Albans, VT: Eden Women's Publications.

Jordan, B. (1993). *Birth in four cultures: A crosscultural investigation of childbirth in Yucatan, Holland, Sweden and the United States* (4th ed.). Prospect Heights, IL: Waveland Press.

Jourard, S., & Secord, P. (1955). Body cathexis and personality. *British Journal of Psychology, 46,* 130–138.

Kaffman, M. (1993). Kibbutz youth: Recent past and present. *Journal of Youth and Adolescence, 22,* 573–604.

Kagan, J. (1994). Yesterday's premises, tomorrow's promises. In R. D. Parke, P. A. Ornstein, J. J. Rieser, & C. Zahn-Waxler (Eds.), *A century of developmental psychology.* Washington, DC: American Psychological Association.

Kagan, J., Kearsley, R. B., & Zealazo, P. (1978). *Infancy: Its place in human development.* Cambridge, MA: Harvard University Press.

Kagan, J., & Klein, R. E. (1973). Cross-cultural perspectives on early development. *American Psychologist, 28,* 947–961.

Kagan, J., Snidman, N., & Arcus, D. (1993). On the temperamental categories of inhibited and uninhibited children. In K. H. Rubin & J. B. Asendorpf (Eds.), *Social withdrawal, inhibition, and shyness in childhood.* Hillsdale, NJ: Erlbaum.

Kagitcibasi, C. (1990). *A critical appraisal of individualism and collectivism: Towards a new formulation.* Paper presented at the International Conference on Individualism and Collectivism: Psychological Perspectives from East and West, Seoul, Korea.

Kagitcibasi, C. (1995). Is psychology relevant to global developmental issues? Experience from Turkey. *American Psychologist, 50,* 293–300.

Kagitcibasi, C. (1996). *Family and human development across cultures.* Mahwah, NJ: Erlbaum.

Kalu, W., & Kalu, O. (1993). Nigeria. In L. L. Adler (Ed.), *International handbook on gender roles* (Chap. 17). Westport, CT: Greenwood Press.

Kamara, A. I. (1971). *Cognitive development among school-age Themne children of Sierra Leone.* Unpublished doctoral dissertation, University of Illinois.

Kamara, A. I., & Easley, J. A., Jr. (1977). Is the rate of cognitive development uniform across cultures? A methodological critique with new evidence from Themne children. In P. R. Dasen (Ed.), *Piagetian psychology: Cross-cultural contributions* (pp. 26–63). New York: Gardner/Wiley.

Katz, D., & Braly, K. W. (1933). Racial stereotypes of 100 college students. *Journal of Abnormal and Social Psychology, 28,* 280–290.

Kaufman, S. R. (1986). *The ageless self: Sources of meaning in late life.* New York: Meridian.

Kelly, M. (1977). Papua New Guinea and Piaget—An eight-year study. In P. R. Dasen (Ed.), *Piagetian psychology: Cross-cultural contributions* (pp. 169–202). New York: Gardner Press.

Kelso, B. J. (1994, September/October). Movement to combat female mutilation. *African Report,* 60–61.

Kenkel, W. F. (1985). *The family in perspective* (5th ed.). Houston, TX: Cap and Gown Press.

Kerig, P. K., Alyoshina, Y. Y., & Volovich, A. (1993). Gender-role socialization in contemporary Russia: Implications for cross-cultural research. *Psychology of Women Quarterly, 17,* 389–408.

Kett, J. (1977). Rites of passage: *Adolescence in America, 1790 to the present.* New York: Basic Books.

Khan, A., & Cataio, J. (1984). *Men and women in biological perspective.* New York: Praeger.

Kim, U., Triandis, H. C., Kagitcibasi, C., Choi, S., & Yoon, G. (1994). *Individualism and collectivism: Theory, method, and applications.* Thousand Oaks, CA: Sage.

Kinzie, J. D., Tran, K. A., Breckenridge, A., & Bloom, J. D. (1980). An Indochinese refugee psychiatric clinic: Culturally accepted treatment approaches. *American Journal of Psychiatry, 139*(10), 1276–1281.

Kleinman, A. (1982). Neurasthenia and depression: A study of somatization and culture in China. *Culture, Medicine, and Psychiatry, 6,* 117–190.

Koff, E., Rierdan, J., & Stubbs, M. L. (1990). Gender, body image, and self-concept in early adolescence. *Journal of Early Adolescence, 10,* 56–68.

Koffka, K. (1935). *Principles of gestalt psychology.* New York: Harcourt Brace.

Kohlberg, L. (1981). *Essays on moral development* (Vol. 1). New York: Harper & Row.

Kohlberg, L., & Gilligan, C. (1971). The adolescent as philosopher: The discovery of self in a post-conventional world. *Daedalus, 100,* 1051–1086.

Kohler, K. (1938). *The place of value in a world of facts.* New York: Liveright.

Konner, M. J. (1976). Maternal care, infant behavior and development among the !Kung. In R. B. Lee & I. DeVore (Eds.), *Kalahari hunter-gatherers: Studies of the !Kung San and their neighbors.* Cambridge, MA: Harvard University Press.

Kopp, C. B., & Kaslow, J. B. (1982). *The Child.* Reading, MA: Addison-Wesley.

Korn, S., & Gannon, S. (1983). Temperament, culture variation, and behavior disorders in preschool children. *Child Psychiatry and Human Development, 13,* 203–212.

Kornhaber, A. (1996). *Contemporary grandparenting.* Thousand Oaks, CA: Sage.

Kosberg, J. I. (Ed.). (1992). *Family care for the elderly: Social and cultural changes.* Thousand Oaks, CA: Sage.

Kosik, K. S. (1992). Alzheimer's disease: A cell biological perspective. *Science, 256,* 780–783.

Kosmitzki, C. (1996). The reaffirmation of cultural identity in the context of cross-cultural encounters. *Personality and Social Psychology Bulletin, 22,* 239–249.

Kosmitzki, C. (1997). *Contextual views of culture and development: A discussion of selected studies.* Paper presented at the twenty-sixth annual meeting of the Society for Cross-Cultural Psychology, San Antonio, TX.

Kostelny, K., & Garbarino, J. (1994). Coping with the consequences of living in danger: The case of Palestinian children and youth. *International Journal of Behavioral Development, 17,* 595–611.

Kozulin, A. (1990). *Vygotsky's psychology: A biography of ideas.* New York: Harvester Wheatsheaf.

Kroeber, A. L., and Kluckhohn, C. (1952). *Culture, Part III.* Papers of the Peabody Museum of Harvard University.

Kuhn, M. H., & McPartland, R. (1954). An empirical investigation of self-attitudes. *American Sociological Review, 19,* 68–76.

Kulin, H. E. (1991a). Hypothalamic-pituitary changes of puberty. In R. M. Lerner, A. C. Petersen, & J. Brooks-Gunn (Eds.), *Encyclopedia of adolescence.* New York: Garland.

Kulin, H. E. (1991b). Spermarche. In R. M. Lerner, A. C. Petersen, & J. Brooks-Gunn (Eds.), *Encyclopedia of adolescence.* New York: Garland.

Kumari, R. (1988). *Female sexuality in Hinduism.* Delhi: Joint Women's Programme by ISPCK.

Labouvie-Vief, G. (1986). *Mind and self in life-span development.* Symposium on developmental dimensions of adult adaptation: Perspectives in mind, self, and emotion. Presented at the 1986 meeting of the Gerontological Association of America, Chicago, IL.

Lamb, D. R. (1984). *Physiology of exercise: Response and adaption* (2nd ed.). New York: Macmillan.

Lamb, M. E. (Ed.). (1987). *The role of the father: Cross-cultural perspectives.* Hillsdale, NJ: Erlbaum.

Lamb, M. E., Frodi, A. M., Hwang, C. P., Frodi, M., & Steinberg, J. (1982). Effects of gender and caretaking role on parent-infant interaction. In R. M. Emde & R. J. Harmon (Eds.), *Attachment and affiliative systems.* New York: Plenum.

Lamb, M. E., Hwang, C. P., Frodi, M., & Frodi, M. (1982). Security of mother- and father-infant attachment and its relation to sociability with strangers in traditional and non-traditional Swedish families. *Infant Behavior and Development, 5,* 355–367.

Lamb, M. E., Pleck, J., Charnov, E. L., & Levine, J. A. (1987). A biosocial perspective on paternal behavior and involvement. In J. B. Lancaster, J. Altmann, A. Rossi, & L. R. Sherrod (Eds.), *Parenting across the life span: Biosocial perspectives* (pp. 111–142). Chicago, IL: Aldine.

Lamb, M. E., Sternberg, K. L., Hwang, C.-P., & Broberg, A. C. (Eds.). (1992). *Child care in context: Cross-cultural perspectives.* Hillsdale, NJ: Erlbaum.

Lancy, D. (1980). Work and play: The Kpelle children during rapid cultural change. In D. F. Lancy & B. A. Tindall (Eds.), *The anthropological study of play: Problems and prospects.* West Point, NY: Leisure Press.

Langlois, J. H., & Roggman, L. A. (1990). Attractive faces are only average. *Psychological Science, 1,* 115–121.

Larson, R. (1991). Egocentrism theory and the "new look" at the imaginary audience and personal fable in adolescence. In R. M. Lerner, A. C. Petersen, & J. Brooks-Gunn (Eds.), *Encyclopedia of adolescence.* New York: Garland.

Laurendeau-Bendavid, M. (1977). Culture, schooling, and cognitive development: A comparative study of children in French Canada and Rwanda. In P. R. Dasen (Ed.), *Piagetian psychology: Cross-cultural contributions* (pp. 123–168). New York: Gardner Press.

Lave, J. (1977). Tailor-made experiments and evaluating the intellectual consequences of apprenticeship training. *Quarterly Newsletter of the Institute for Comparative Human Development, 1,* 1–3.

Lave, J. (1988). *Cognition in Practice: Mind, mathematics and culture in everyday life.* Cambridge, England: Cambridge University Press.

Lave, J., & Wenger, E. (1991). *Situated learning: Legitimate peripheral participation.* Cambridge, England: Cambridge University Press.

Leadbeater, B. (1986). The resolution of relativism in adult thinking: Subjective, objective, or conceptual. *Human Development, 29,* 291–300.

Lecours, A. R. (1982). Correlates of developmental behavior in brain maturation. In T. Bever (Ed.), *Regressions in mental development.* Hillsdale, NJ: Erlbaum.

Lee, R., & Daly, R. (1987). Man's domination and woman's oppression: The question of origins. In M. Kaufman (Ed.), *Beyond patriarchy: Essays by men on pleasure, power, and change* (pp. 30–44). New York: Oxford University Press.

Lee, R. B., & Devore, I. (1976). *Kalahari hunter-gatherers.* Cambridge, MA: Harvard University Press.

Lefrancois, G. R. (1996). *The lifespan* (5th ed.). Belmont, CA: Wadsworth.

Legault, F., & Strayer, F. F. (1990). The emergence of sex-segregation in preschool peer groups. In F. F. Strayer (Ed.), *Social interaction and behavioral development during early childhood.* Montreal: La Maison D'Ethologie de Montreal.

Lerner, R. M. (1990). Plasticity, person-context relations, and cognitive training in the aged years: A developmental contextual perspective. *Developmental Psychology, 26,* 911–915.

Lerner, R. M. (1991). Changing organism-context relations as the basic process of development: A developmental contextual perspective. *Developmental Psychology, 27,* 27–32.

Lerner, R. M., Castellino, D. R., Terry, P. A., Villarruel, F. A., & McKinney, M. H. (1995). Developmental contextual perspective on parenting. In M. Bornstein (Ed.), *Handbook of parenting* (Vol. 2, pp. 285–309). Hillsdale, NJ: Erlbaum.

Lester, B. M. (1984). A biosocial model of infant crying. In L. P. Lipsitt (Ed.), *Advances in infancy research.* New York: Academic Press.

Lester, B. M., Boukydis, C. F. Z., Garcia-Coll, C. T., Hole, W., & Peucker, M. (1992). Infantile colic: Acoustic cry characteristics, maternal perception of cry, and temperament. *Infant Behavior and Development, 15,* 15–26.

Levine, N. E. (1980a). Asian and African systems of polyandry. *Journal of Comparative Family Studies, 11,* 385–410.

Levine, N. E. (1980b). Nyinba polyandry and the allocation of paternity. *Journal of Comparative Family Studies, 11,* 283–298.

LeVine, R. A. (1988). Human parental care: Universal goals, cultural strategies, individual behavior. In R. A. LeVine, P. M. Miller, & M. M. West (Eds.), *Parental behavior in diverse societies. New directions for child development* (No. 40). San Francisco: Jossey-Bass.

LeVine, R. A., & Miller, P. (1990). Commentary. *Human Development, 33,* 73–80.

LeVine, R. A., Miller, P., & West, M. (Eds.). (1988). *Parental behavior in diverse societies. New Directions for Child Development* (No. 40). San Francisco: Jossey-Bass.

Levy, B. S., Wilkinson, F. S., & Marine, W. M. (1971). Reducing neonatal mortality rate with nurse midwives. *American Journal of Obstetrics and Gynecology, 109,* 50–58.

Lewin, K. (1935). *A dynamic theory of personality.* New York: McGraw-Hill.

Liddell, C., Kvalsvig, J., Qotyana, P., & Shabalala, A. (1994). Community violence and young South African children's involvement in aggression. *International Journal of Behavioral Development, 17,* 613–628.

Liebkind, K. (1996). Acculturation and stress: Vietnamese refugees in Finland. *Journal of Cross-Cultural Psychology, 27*(2), 161–180.

Lin, K. M, & Kleinman, A. M. (1988). Psychopathology and clinical course of schizophrenia: A cross-cultural perspective. *Schizophrenia Bulletin, 14,* 555–567.

Lock, M. (1991). Contested meanings of the menopause. *Lancet, 337,* 1270–1272.

Lockery, S. (1991). Caregiving among racial and ethnic minority elders. *Generations, 15*(4), 58–62.

Logan, D. D. (1980). The menarche experience in twenty-three foreign countries. *Adolescence, 58,* 247–256.

Long, G. M., & Crambert, R. F. (1990). The nature and basis of age-related change in dynamic visual acuity. *Psychology and Aging, 5,* 138–143.

Lonner, W. J., & Ibrahim, F. A. (1989). Assessment in cross-cultural counseling. In P. Pedersen, J. Draguns, W. Lonner, & J. Trimble (Eds.), *Counseling across cultures* (3rd ed., pp. 229–334). Honolulu: University of Hawaii Press.

Lonner, W. J., & Malpass, R. (Eds.). (1994). *Psychology and culture.* Boston: Allyn & Bacon.

Loscocco, K., & Kalleberg, A. (1988). Age and the meaning of work in the United States and Japan. *Social Forces, 67,* 337–357.

Low, B. S. (1989). Cross-cultural patterns in the training of children: An evolutionary perspective. *Journal of Comparative Psychology, 103,* 311–319.

Lozoff, B. (1989). Nutrition and behavior. *American Psychologist, 44,* 231–236.

Lubben, J. E., & Becerra, R. M. (1987). Social support among black, Mexican and Chinese elderly. In D. E. Gelfand & C. M. Barresi (Eds.), *Ethnic dimensions of aging* (pp. 130–144). New York: Springer.

Luria, A. R. (1981). *Language and cognition* (J. V. Wertsch, Ed.). New York: Wiley Intersciences.

Lusk, M. (1992). Street children of Rio de Janeiro. *International Social Work, 35,* 293–305.

Luster, T., & Okagaki, L. (Eds.). (1993). *Parenting: An ecological perspective.* Hillsdale, NJ: Erlbaum.

Ma, H. K. (1989). Moral orientation and moral judgment in adolescents in Hong Kong, Mainland China, and England. *Journal of Cross-Cultural Psychology, 20,* 152–177.

Maccoby, E. E. (1980). *Social development: Psychological growth and the parent-child relationship.* New York: Harcourt Brace Jovanovich.

Maccoby, E. E. (1990). Gender and relationships. A developmental account. *American Psychologist, 45,* 513–520.

Maccoby, E. E. (1992). The role of parents in the socialization of children: An historical overview. *Developmental Psychology, 28,* 1006–1017.

Mackey, W. C. (1985). *Fathering behaviors: The dynamics of the man-child bond.* New York: Plenum Press.

MacKinnon, C. A. (1987). *Feminism unmodified: Discourses in life and law.* Cambridge, MA: Harvard University Press.

MacLeod, R. B. (1947). The phenomenological approach to social psychology. *Psychological Review, 54,* 193–210.

Madsen, M. C. (1971). Developmental and cross-cultural differences in the cooperative and competitive behavior of young children. *Journal of Cross-Cultural Psychology, 2,* 365–371.

Mahler, M., & Pine, F. (1975). *The psychological birth of the infant.* New York: Basic Books.

Marcia, J. E. (1980). Identity in adolescence. In J. Adelson (Ed.), *Handbook of adolescent psychology* (pp. 150–187). New York: Wiley.

Markus, H., & Kitayama, S. (1991). Culture and the self: Implications for cognition, emotion, and motivation. *Psychological Bulletin, 98,* 224–253.

Markus, H. & Wurf, E. (1987). The dynamic self-concept. A social psychological perspective. *Annual Review of Psychology, 38,* 199–337.

Marshall, L. (1976). *The !Kung of Nyae Nyae.* Cambridge, MA: Harvard University Press.

Marton, F., Dall'Alba, G., & Tse, L. K. (1993). *The paradox of the Chinese learner.* Paper presented at the European Association for Research on Learning and Instruction, Aix-en-Provence, France.

Matthews, K. A. (1992). Myths and realities of menopause. *Psychosomatic Medicine, 54,* 1–9.

Maxwell, E., & Maxwell, R. (1980). Contempt for the elderly: A cross-cultural analysis. *Current Anthropology, 21,* 569–570.

McCrae, R. R., & Costa, P. C., Jr. (1984). *Emerging lives, enduring dispositions.* Boston, MA: Little, Brown.

McNabb, S. L. (1990). Self-reports in cross-cultural contexts. *Human Organization, 49,* 291–299.

Mead, G. H. (1934). *Mind, self, and society.* Chicago: University of Chicago Press.

Mead, M. (1973). *Coming of age in Samoa: A psychological study of primitive youth.* New York: American Museum of Natural History. (Original work published 1928.)

Medicus, G. (1992). The inapplicability of the biogenetic rule to behavioral development. *Human Development, 35,* 1–7.

Meijer, L., Super, C. M., & Harkness, S. (1997). *Culture, temperament, and parents' perceptions of children's "difficult" behavior in the Netherlands and the U.S.* Paper presented at the twenty-sixth annual meeting of the Society for Cross-Cultural Research, San Antonio, TX.

Meldrum, B. (1984). Traditional child-rearing practices of the Oje market women of Ibadan. In H. Curran (Ed.), *Nigerian children: Developmental perspectives* (pp. 174–196). London: Routledge & Kegan Paul.

Meng, J. M. (1991). The pattern of family and quality of life. *Journal of Gerontology, 3,* 135–140.

Meredith, H. V. (1978). Research between 1960 and 1970 on the standing height of young children in different parts of the world. In H. W. Reece & L. P. Lipsitt (Eds.), *Advances in Child Development and Behavior* (Vol. 12). New York: Academic Press.

Meredith, H. V. (1987). Variations in body stockiness among and within ethnic groups at ages from birth to adulthood. In H. W. Reese (Ed.), *Advances in child development and behavior* (Vol. 20). New York: Academic Press.

Merrill, T. (Ed.). (1994). *Nicaragua: A country study.* Library of Congress (3rd ed.). Washington, DC: U.S. Government Printing Office.

Meyers, S. A. (1993). Adapting parent education programs to meet the needs of fathers: An ecological perspective. *Family Relations, 42*(4), 447–453.

Michel, G. F. (1981). Right-handedness. *Science, 212,* 685–687.

Milardo, R. M. (Ed.). (1988). *Families and social networks.* Newbury Park, CA: Sage.

Miller, C. A. (1987). Infant mortality in the U.S. *Scientific American, 253,* 31–37.

Miller, E. (1975). Self-evaluation among Jamaican high school girls. *Social and Economic Studies, 22,* 407–426.

Miller, J., & Bersoff, D. M. (1994). Cultural influences on the moral status of reciprocity and the discounting of endogenous motivation. *Personality and Social Psychology Bulletin, 20,* 592–602.

Miller, J. G. (1984). Culture and the development of everyday social explanation. *Journal of Personality and Social Psychology, 46,* 961–978.

Miller, P. H. (1993). *Theories of developmental psychology* (3rd ed.). New York: Freeman.

Minkler, M., & Roe, K. (1991). *Preliminary findings from the grandmother caregiver study of Oakland, California.* Berkeley: University of California Press.

Mishra, R. C., Sinha, D., & Berry, J. W. (1996). *Ecology, acculturation and psychological adaptation.* Thousand Oaks, CA: Sage.

Miyake, K., Chen, S. J., & Campos, J. J. (1985). Infant temperament, mother's mode of interaction, and attachment in Japan: An interim report. In I. Bretherton & E. Waters (Eds.), Growing points of attachment theory and research. *Monographs of the Society for Research in Child Development, 50,* 276–297.

Modgil, S., & Modgil, C. (1976). The growth of logical concrete and formal operations. In *Piagetian Research* (Vol. 3.). Atlantic Highlands, NY: Humanities Press.

Moghaddam, F. M., Taylor, D., & Wright, S. C. (1993). *Social psychology in cross-cultural perspective.* New York: Freeman.

Mokuau, N., & Browne, C. (1994). Life themes of native Hawaiian female elders: Resources for cultural preservation. *Social Work, 39,* 43–50.

Molitor, A. E., & Eckerman, C. O. (1992). *Behavioral cues of distress/avoidance in preterm infants.* Paper presented at the International Conference on Infant Studies, Miami, FL.

Mollica, R. F., Wyshak, G., deMarneffe, D., Khuon, F., & Lavelle, J. (1987). Indochinese versions of the Hopkins Symptoms Checklist-25: A screening instrument for the psychiatric care of refugees. *American Journal of Psychiatry, 144*(40), 497–500.

Morelli, G. A., Rogoff, B., Oppenheim, D., & Goldsmith, D. (1992). Cultural variation in infants' sleeping arrangements: Questions of independence. *Developmental Psychology, 28,* 604–613.

Morinaga, Y., Frieze, I. H., & Ferligoj, A. (1993). Career plans and gender-role attitudes of college students in the United States, Japan, and Slovenia. *Sex Roles, 29,* 317–334.

Mukai, T., & McCloskey, A. A. (1996). Eating attitudes among Japanese and American elementary schoolgirls. *Journal of Cross-Cultural Psychology, 27*(4), 424–435.

Mumford, D. B., Whitehouse, A. M., & Choudry, I. Y. (1992). Survey of eating disorders in English-medium schools in Lahore, Pakistan. *International Journal of Eating Disorders, 11,* 173–184.

Mundy-Castle, A. C. (1974). Social and technological intelligence in Western and non-Western cultures. *Universita* (University of Ghana), *4,* 46–52.

Mundy-Castle, A. C. (1976). *Psychology and the search for meaning.* Unpublished manuscript, University of Lagos.

Mundy-Castle, A. C., & Okonji, M. D. (1976). *Mother-infant interaction in Nigeria.* Unpublished manuscript, University of Lagos.

Murdock, G. P. (1967). *Ethnographic Atlas.* Pittsburgh, PA: Pittsburgh University Press.

Muuss, R. E. (1988). *Theories of adolescence* (5th ed.). New York: Random House.

Muuss, R. E. (1996). *Theories of adolescence* (6th ed.). New York: McGraw-Hill.

Mwamwenda, T. S. (1992). Cognitive development in African children. *Genetic, Social, and General Psychology Monographs, 118*(1), 7–72.

Naisbitt, J. (1996). *Megatrends Asia.* New York: Simon & Schuster.

Nakajima, H., & Mayor, F. (1996). Culture and health. *World Health, 49*(2), 13–15.

Nasser, M. (1986). Comparative study of the prevalence of abnormal eating attitudes among Arab female students of both London and Cairo Universities. *Psychological Medicine, 16,* 621–625.

National Center for Health Statistics. (1994). *Births, marriages, divorces, and deaths for 1993* (Monthly Vital Statistics Rep. Vol. 42, No. 12). Hyattsville, MD: Public Health Service.

National Institute on Drug Abuse. (1994). *Monitoring the future of drug abuse survey.* Washington, DC: U.S. Government Printing Office.

Natsopoulos, D., Kiosseoglou, G., & Xeromeritou, A. (1992). Handedness and spatial ability in children: Further support for Geschwind's hypothesis of "pathology of superiority" and for Annett's theory of intelligence. *Genetic, Social, and General Psychology Monographs, 118*(1) 103–126.

Nelson, M. B. (1994). *The stronger women get, the more men love football: Sexism and the American culture of sport.* New York: Harcourt Brace.

Neugarten, B. L. (1979). Time, age, and the life cycle. *American Journal of Psychiatry, 136,* 887–894.

Nichter, M., & Nichter, M. (1991). Hype and weight. *Medical Anthropology, 13,* 249–284.

Nicolopoulou, A. (1993). Play, cognitive development, and the social world: Piaget, Vygotsky, and beyond. *Human Development, 36,1–23.*

Niedbala, B., and Tsang, R. (1993). The small for gestational age infant. In S. W. Ekvall (Ed.), *Prediatric nutrition in chronic diseases and developmental disorders: Prevention, assessment and treatment.* New York: Oxford University Press.

Niethammer, C. (1977). *Daughters of the earth: The lives and legends of American Indian women.* New York: Macmillan.

Nsamenang, A. B. (1992). *Human development in cultural context: A third world perspective.* Newbury Park, CA: Sage.

Nunes, T., Schliemann, A. D., & Carraher, D. W. (1993). *Street mathematics and school mathematics.* Cambridge, England: Cambridge University Press.

Nurmi, J. E. (1991). How do adolescents see their future? A review of development of future orientation and planning. *Developmental Review, 11,* 1–59.

Nyiti, R. M. (1982). The validity of "cultural differences explanations" for cross-cultural variation in the rate of Piagetian cognitive development. In D. A. Wagner & H. W. Stevenson (Eds.), *Cultural perspectives on child development.* San Francisco: Freeman.

O'Boyle, M. W., & Benbow, C. P. (1990). Handedness and its relationship to ability and talent. In S. Coren (Ed.), *Left-handedness: Behavior implications and anomalies.* Amsterdam: North-Holland.

Ochse, R., & Plug, C. (1986). Cross-cultural investigation of the validity of Erikson's theory of personality development. *Journal of Personality and Social Psychology, 50*(6), 1240–1252.

Oetting, E. R., & Beauvais, F. (1986). Peer cluster theory: Drugs and the adolescent. *Journal of Counseling and Development, 65*(1), 17–22.

Oetting, E. R., & Beauvais, F. (1987a). Common elements in youth drug abuse: Peer clusters and other psychosocial factors. *Journal of Drug Issues, 17*(1–2), 133–151.

Oetting, E. R., & Beauvais, F. (1987b). Peer cluster theory, socialization characteristics and adolescent drug use: A path analysis. *Journal of Counseling Psychology, 34*(2), 205–213.

Offer, D., Ostrov, E., Howard, K. I., & Atkinson, R. (1988). *The teenage world: Adolescents' self-image in ten countries.* New York: Plenum.

Ojanuga, D. (1990). Kaduma beggar children: A study of child abuse and neglect in northern Nigeria. *Child Welfare, 69,* 371–380.

Okafor, N. A. O. (1991). Some traditional aspects of Nigerian women. In L. L. Adler (Ed.), *Women in cross-cultural perspective* (pp. 134–141). Westport, CT: Praeger.

Olowu, A. A. (1983). A cross-cultural study of adolescent self-concept. *Journal of Adolescence, 6,* 263–274.

Olowu, A. A. (1990). The self-concept in cross-cultural perspective. In A. A. Olowu (Ed.), *Contemporary issues in self-concept studies.* Ibadan, Kenya: Shaneson C.I. Ltd.

Olson, L. K. (Ed.). (1994). *The graying of the world: Who will care for the frail elderly?* Binghamton, NY: Haworth Press.

Omoluabi, P. F. (1990). Assessment of self-concept. In A. A. Olowu (Ed.), *Contemporary issues in self-concept studies.* Ibadan, Kenya: Shaneson C.I. Ltd.

Ortiz, S., & Poertner, J. (1992). Latin American street children: Problem, programmes and critique. *International Social Work, 35,* 413–415.

Page, R. C., & Berkow, D. N. (1991). Concepts of the self: Western and Eastern perspectives. *Journal of Multicultural Counseling and Development, 19,* 83–93.

Paikoff, R. L., & Brooks-Gunn, J. (1991). Do parent-child relationships change during puberty? *Psychological Bulletin, 110,* 47–66.

Pareek, U. (1990). Culture-relevant and culture-modifying action research for development. *Journal of Social Issues, 46*(3), 119–131.

Paris, S. G., & Cross, D. R. (1988). The zone of proximal development: Virtues and pitfalls of a metaphorical representation of children's learning. *Genetic Epistemologist, 26,* 27–37.

Parke, R. D. (1995). Fathers and families. In M. H. Bornstein (Ed.), *Handbook of parenting* (Vol. 3, pp. 27–63). Mahwah, NJ: Erlbaum.

Parke, R. D., Ornstein, P. A., Rieser, J. J., & Zahn-Waxler, C. (Eds.). (1994). *A Century of Developmental Psychology.* Washington, DC: American Psychological Association.

Parke, R. D., & Stearns, P. N. (1993). Fathers and child rearing. In G. H. Elder, J. Modell, & R. D. Parke (Eds.), *Children in time and space* (pp. 147–170). New York: Cambridge University Press.

Paul, M., & Fisher, J. (1980). Correlates of self-concept among black early adolescents. *Journal of Youth and Adolescence, 9,* 163–173.

Paxton, S. J., Wertheim, E. H., Gibbons, K., Szmukler, G. I., Hillier, L., & Petrovich, J. L. (1991). Body image satisfaction, dieting beliefs, and weight loss behaviors in adolescent girls and boys. *Journal of Youth and Adolescence, 20,* 361–377.

Peabody, D. (1985). *National characteristics.* New York: Wiley.

Perlman, D. (1988). Loneliness: A life-span, family perspective. In R. M. Milardo (Ed.), *Families and social networks* (pp. 190–220). Newbury Park, CA: Sage.

Peterson, E. T. (1989). Grandparenting. In S. J. Bahr & E. T. Peterson (Eds.), *Aging and the family.* Lexington, MA: Lexington Books.

Philip, H., & Kelly, M. (1974). Product and process in cognitive development: Some comparative data on the performance of school age children in different cultures. *British Journal of Educational Psychology, 44,* 248–265.

Phillips, A. S. (1973). *Adolescence in Jamaica.* Kingston: Jamaica Publishing House.

Phinney, J. S. (1990). Ethnic identity in adolescents and adults: Review of research. *Psychological Bulletin, 108,* 499–514.

Phinney, J. S., Lochner, B., & Murphy, R. (1990). Ethnic identity development and psychological adjustment in adolescents. In A. Stiffman & L. Davis (Eds.), *Ethnic issues in adolescent mental health.* Newbury Park, CA: Sage.

Piaget, J. (1954). *The construction of reality in the child.* New York: Basic Books.

Piaget, J. (1972). Intellectual evolution from adolescence to adulthood. *Human Development, 15,* 1–12.

Pipher, M. (1995). *Reviving Ophelia: Saving the selves of adolescent girls.* New York: Ballantine Books.

Pitskhelauri, G. Z. (1982). *The long-living of Soviet Georgia* (Trans. Gari Lesnoff-Caravaglia). New York: Human Science Press.

Plomin, R., DeFries, J. C., & McClearn, G. E. (1980). *Behavioral genetics: A primer.* San Francisco: Freeman.

Pollitt, E., Gorman, K. S., Engle, P., Martorell, R., & Rivera, J. (1993). Early supplemental feeding and cognition: Effects over two decades. *Monographs of the Society for Research in Child Development, 235*(58), No. 7.

Poortinga, Y. (1997). Towards convergence? In J. W. Berry, Y. H. Poortinga, & J. Pandey (Eds.), *Handbook of cross-cultural psychology* (2nd ed., Vol. 1, pp. 347–387). Boston: Allyn & Bacon.

Pratt, M. W., Hunsberger, B., Pancer, S. M., Roth, D., & Santolupo, L. (1993). Thinking about parenting: Reasoning about developmental issues across the life-span. *Developmental Psychology, 29,* 585–595.

Pratt, M. W., Kerig, P., Cowan, P. A., & Cowan, C. P. (1988). Mothers and fathers teaching 3-year-olds: Authoritative parenting and adult scaffolding of young children's learning. *Developmental Psychology, 24*(6), 832–839.

Price-Williams, D. R., Gordon, W., & Ramirez, M., III. (1969). Skills and conservation: A study of pottery-making children. *Developmental Psychology, 1,* 769.

Purdie, N., Douglas, G., & Hattie, J. (1996). Student conceptions of learning and their use of self-regulated learning strategies: A cross-cultural comparison. *Journal of Educational Psychology, 88*(1), 87–100.

Quadrel, M. J., Fishoff, B., & Davis, W. (1993). Adolescent (in)vulnerability. *American Psychologist, 48,* 102–116.

Queen, S. A., Habenstein, R. W., & Quadagno, J. S. (1985). *The family in various cultures* (5th ed.). New York: Harper & Row.

Radin, N. (1993). Primary caregiving fathers in intact families. In A. Gottfried & A. Gottfried (Eds.), *Redefining families* (pp. 11–54). New York: Plenum.

Rahula, W. (1959). *What the Buddha taught.* New York: Grove Press.

Raich, R. M., Rosen, J. C., Deus, J., Perez, O., Requene, A., & Gross, J. (1992). Eating disorders symptoms among adolescents in the United States and Spain: A comparative study. *International Journal of Eating Disorders, 11,* 63–72.

Rakowski, W., & Mor, V. (1992). The association of physical activity with mortality among older adults in the Longitudinal Study of Aging. *Journal of Gerontology, 47*(4), 122–129.

Raphael, D., & Davis, F. (1985). *Only mothers know: Patterns of infant feeding in traditional cultures.* Westport, CT: Greenwood Press.

Recio Adrados, J. L. (1995). The influence of family, school, and peers on adolescent drug misuse. *International Journal of the Addictions, 30,* 1407–1423.

Reid, I. R., Ames, R. W., Evans, M. G., Gamble, G. D., & Sharpe, S. J. (1993). Effect of calcium supplementation on bone loss in postmenopausal women. *New England Journal of Medicine, 328*(7), 460–464.

Reilly, R. (1988, August). Here no one is spared. *Sports Illustrated,* 70–77.

Reisberg, B. F., Steven, D. L., Mony, J., & Crook, T. (1985). Age-associated cognitive decline and Alzheimer's disease: Implications for assessment and treatment. In M. Bergener, M. Ermini, & H. B. Stahelin (Eds.), *Thresholds in aging.* London: Academic Press.

Repetti, R. L. (1993). Short-term and long-term processes linking job stressors to father-child interaction. *Social Development, 3,* 1–15.

Reskin, B. F. (1988). Bringing the men back in: Sex differentiation in the devaluation of women's work. *Gender and Society, 2,* 58–81.

Retschitzki, J. (1989). Evidence of formal thinking in Baule airele players. In D. M. Keats, D. Munro, & L. Mann (Eds.), *Heterogeneity in cross-cultural psychology.* Amsterdam: Swets & Zeitlinger.

Reynolds, P. (1989). *Children in cross-roads.* Grand Rapids, MI: Eerdmans.

Rhode, D. L. (Ed.). (1990). *Theoretical perspectives on sex differences.* New Haven, CT: Yale University Press.

Rice, F. P. (1992). *Intimate relationships, marriages, and families.* Mountain View, CA: Mayfield.

Richman, A. L., LeVine, R. A., New, R. S., Howrigan, G. A., Welles-Nystrom, B., & LeVine, S. (1988). Maternal behavior to infants in five cultures. In R. A. LeVine, P. M. Miller, & M. M. West (Eds.), *Parental behavior in diverse societies: New directions for child development* (No. 40). San Francisco: Jossey-Bass.

Riegel, K. F. (1975). Toward a dialectical theory of development. *Human Development, 18,* 50–64.

Roberts, G. W. (1994). Brother to brother. African-American modes of relating among men. *Journal of Black Studies, 24,* 379–390.

Rogoff, B. (1981). Schooling and the development of cognitive skills. In H. C. Triandis & A. Heron (Eds.), *Handbook of cross-cultural psychology* (Vol. 4, pp. 233–294). Boston: Allyn & Bacon.

Rogoff, B. (1990). *Apprenticeship in thinking: Cognitive development in social context.* New York: Oxford University Press.

Rogoff, B., & Chavajah, P. (1995). What's become of research on the cultural basis of cognitive development? *American Psychologist, 50,* 859–873.

Rogoff, B., and Morelli, G. (1989). Perspectives on children's development from cultural psychology. *American Psychologist, 44,* 343–348.

Rohner, R. P. (1986). *The warmth dimension: Foundations of parental acceptance-rejection theory.* Newbury Park, CA: Sage. (Reprinted by UConn Coop, U-19, Storrs, CT, 1991.)

Rohner, R. P. (1994). Patterns of parenting: The warmth dimension in worldwide perspective. In W. J. Lonner & R. Malpass (Eds.), *Psychology and culture* (pp. 113–120). Boston: Allyn & Bacon.

Roopnarine, J. L., & Carter, D. B. (1992a). The cultural context of socialization: A much ignored issue! In J. L. Roopnarine & D. B. Carter (Eds.), *Parent-child socialization in diverse cultures*. Norwood, NJ: Ablex.

Roopnarine, J. L., & Carter, D. B. (Eds.). (1992b). *Parent-child socialization in diverse cultures*. Norwood, NJ: Ablex.

Rosenblith, J. F. (1992). *In the beginning* (2nd ed.). Newbury Park, CA: Sage.

Rosenthal, D. A., Moore, S. M., & Taylor, M. J. (1983). A study of the self-image of Anglo-, Greek, and Italian-Austrian working class adolescents. *Journal of Youth and Adolescence, 12*(2), 117–135.

Rosenthall, E. (1992). Innovation for premature babies: Snuggling with loving parents. *New York Times,* B7.

Roth, M. W., Claude, M., Evans, N., & Mountjoy, C. (1985). Convergence and cohesion of recent neurobiological findings in relation to Alzheimer's disease and their bearing on its etiological basis. In M. Bergener, M. Ermini, & H. B. Stahelin (Eds.), *Thresholds in aging*. London: Academic Press.

Rozee, P. D. (1993). Forbidden or forgiven? Rape in cross-cultural perspective. *Psychology of Women Quarterly, 17,* 499–514.

Ruan, F. F. (1991). *Sex in China: Studies in sexology in Chinese culture*. New York: Plenum Press.

Rubin, K. H., Fein, G. G., & Vandenberg, B. (1983). Play. In Paul H. Mussen (Ed.), *Handbook of child psychology: Vol. 4. Socialization, personality and social development*. New York: Wiley.

Rushton, J. P., Fulker, D. W., Neale, M. C., Nias, D. K., & Eysenck, H. J. (1986). Altruism and aggression: The heritability of individual differences. *Journal of Personality and Social Psychology, 50,* 1192–1198.

Russell, G., & Russell, A. (1987). Mother-child and father-child relationships in middle childhood. *Child Development, 58,* 1573–1585.

Ryan, A. S., Rush, D., Krieger, F. W., & Lewandowski, G. E. (1991). Recent declines in breast-feeding in the United States, 1984 through 1989. *Pediatrics, 88,* 719–727.

Sagi, A., Lamb, M. E., Lewkowicz, K. S., Shoham, R., Dvir, R., & Estes, D. (1985). Security of infant-mother, -father, and -metaplot attachments among kibbutz-related Israeli children. In I. Bretherton & E. Waters (Eds.), *Growing points of attachment theory and research. Monographs of the Society for Research in Child Development, 50,* 257–275.

Sahin, N., & Sahin, N. H. (1995). Dimensions of concerns: The case of Turkish adolescents. *Journal of Adolescence, 18,* 49–69.

Salamone, F. A. (1983). Children's games as mechanisms for easing ethnic interaction in ethnically heterogeneous communities: A Nigerian case. In J. C. Harris and R. J. Park (Eds.), *Play, games, and sports in cultural contexts* (pp. 461–472). Champaign, IL: Human Kinetics.

Salthouse, T. A. (1987). The role of experience in cognitive aging. In K. W. Schaie & K. Eisdorfer (Eds.), *Annual Review of Gerontology and Geriatrics* (Vol. 7). New York: Springer.

Salthouse, T. A., & Coon, V. E. (1993). Influence of task-specific processing speed on age differences in memory. *Journal of Gerontology, 48,* 245–255.

Sanchez, L. (1993). Women's power and the gendered division of labor in the third world. *Gender and Society, 7,* 434–459.

Sangree, W. H. (1992). Grandparenthood and modernization: The changing status of male and female elders in Tiriki, Kenya, and Irigwe, Nigeria. *Journal of Cross-Cultural Gerontology, 7,* 331–361.

Sapir, E. (1951). The status of linguistics as a science. In D. Mendelbaum (Ed.), *Selected writings* (No. 5, pp. 207–214). Berkeley: University of California Press. (Original work published 1929.)

Sartorius, N. R. (1993). A WHO method for the assessment of health-related quality of life (WHOQOL). In S. R. Walker & R. M. Rosser (Eds.), *Quality of life assessment: Key issues in the 1990s* (pp. 201–207). London: Kluwer Academic Publishers.

Sartorius, N. R. (1994). Description of WHO's Mental Health Programme. In W. J. Lonner & R. Malpass (Eds.), *Psychology and culture.* Boston: Allyn & Bacon.

Sartorius, N. R., Jablensky, A., Korten, A., Ernberg, G., Anker, M., Cooper, J. E., & Day, R. (1986). Early manifestations and first contact incidence of schizophrenia in different cultures: A preliminary report on the initial evaluation phase of the WHO Collaborative Study on Determinants of Outcome of Severe Mental Disorders. *Psychological Medicine, 16,* 909–928.

Scarr, S. (1993). Biological and cultural diversity: The legacy of Darwin for development. *Child Development, 64,* 1333–1353.

Schaie, K. W. (1977–1978). Toward a stage theory of adult cognitive development. *Journal of Aging and Human Development, 8,* 129–138.

Schaie, K. W. (1984). The Seattle Longitudinal Study: A 21-year exploration of psychometric intelligence in adulthood. In K. W. Schaie (Ed.), *Longitudinal studies of adult psychological development.* New York: Guilford.

Schaie, K. W. (1989). Individual differences in rate of cognitive change in adulthood. In V. L. Bengston & K. W. Schaie (Eds.), *The course of later life.* New York: Springer.

Schaie, K. W., & Willis, S. L. (1993). Age differences in patterns of psychometric intelligence in adulthood: Generalizability within and across ability domains. *Psychology and Aging, 8,* 44–55.

Scheper-Hughes, N. (1990). Mother love and child death in northeast Brazil. In J. W. Stigler, R. A. Shweder, & G. Herdt (Eds.), *Cultural psychology: Essays on comparative human development* (pp. 542–565). Cambridge, England: Cambridge University Press.

Schlegal, A., & Barry, H. (1991). *Adolescence: An anthropological inquiry.* New York: Free Press.

Schliemann, A., Carraher, D., & Ceci, S. J. (1997). Everyday cognition. In J. W. Berry, P. R. Dasen, & T. S. Saraswathi (Eds.), *Handbook of cross-cultural psychology* (Vol. 2, 2nd ed., pp. 177–216). Boston: Allyn & Bacon.

Schwartz, T. (1981). The acquisition of culture. *Ethos, 9,* 4–17.

Schwartzman, H. B. (1983). Socializing play: Functional analysis. In J. C. Harris & R. J. Park (Eds.), *Play, games, and sports in cultural contexts.* Champaign IL: Human Kinetics.

Scott, J. P. (1992). Aggression: Functions and control in social systems. *Aggressive Behavior, 18,* 1–20.

Searleman, A., Porac, C., & Coran, S. (1989). Relationship between birth order, birth stress, and lateral preferences: A critical review. *Psychological Bulletin, 105,* 397–408.

Searle-White, J. (1996). Personal boundaries among Russians and Americans: A Vygotskian approach. *Cross-Cultural Research, 30*(2), 184–208.

Segall, M. H. (1979). *Cross-Cultural Psychology.* Belmont, CA: Wadsworth.

Segall, M. H., Dasen, P. R., Berry, J. W., & Poortinga, Y. H. (1990). *Human behavior in global perspective.* New York: Pergamon Press.

Seligman, M. E. P. (1989). Research in clinical psychology: Why is there so much depression today? In I. Cohen (Ed.), *The G. Stanley Hall Lecture Series* (Vol. 9). Washington, DC: American Psychological Association.

Seligman, M. E. P. (1990). *Learned optimism.* New York: Pocket Books.

Serpell, R. (1993). *The significance of schooling: Life-journeys in an African society.* New York: Cambridge University Press.

Sharabany, R., & Wiseman, H. (1993). Close relationships in adolescence: The case of the kibbutz. *Journal of Youth and Adolescence, 22,* 671–695.

Shavelson, R. J., & Bolus, R. (1982). Self-concept: The interplay of theory and method. *Journal of Educational Psychology, 74,* 1–17.

Shea, J. D. (1985). Studies of cognitive development in Papua New Guinea. *International Journal of Psychology, 20,* 33–61.

Sheriff, M., & Cantril, H. (1947). *The psychology of ego involvement.* New York: Wiley.

Shields, D. L. L., & Bredemeier, B. J. L. (1995). *Character development and physical activity.* Champaign, IL: Human Kinetics.

Shostak, M. (1981). *Nissa: The life and words of a !Kung woman.* Cambridge, MA: Harvard University Press.

Shucard, J. L., & Shucard, D. W. (1990). Auditory evoked potentials and hand preference in 6-month-old infants: Possible gender-related differences in cerebral organization. *Developmental Psychology, 26,* 923–930.

Shwalb, B. J., Shwalb, D. W., & Shoji, J. (1994). Structure and dimensions of maternal perceptions of Japanese infant temperament. *Developmental Psychology, 30,* 131–141.

Shweder, R., Mahapatra, M., & Miller, J. G. (1987). Culture and moral development. In J. Kagan & S. Lamb (Eds.), *The emergence of morality in young children* (pp. 1–82). Chicago: University of Chicago Press.

Siegert, R. J., & Chung, R. C. (1995). Dimensions of distress: A cross-cultural factor replication. *Journal of Cross-Cultural Psychology, 26*(2), 169–175.

Sigel, I. E. (Ed.). (1985). *Parental belief systems: The psychological consequences for children.* Hillsdale, NJ: Erlbaum.

Sigel, I. E., McGillicuddy-DeLisi, A. V., & Goodnow, J. J. (Eds.). (1992). *Parental belief systems: The psychological consequences for children* (2nd ed.). Hillsdale, NJ: Erlbaum.

Sigelman, C. K., & Shaffer, D. R. (1995). *Life-Span Human Development.* Pacific Grove, CA: Brooks/Cole.

Sigman, M., McDonald, M. A., Newmann, C., & Bwibo, N. O. (1991). Prediction of cognitive competence in Kenyan children from toddler nutrition, family characteristics and abilities. *Journal of Child Psychology and Psychiatry, 32,* 307–320.

Sigman, M., & Sena, R. (1993). Pretend play in high-risk and developmentally delayed children. In M. H. Bornstein & A. W. O'Reilly (Eds.), *The role of play in the development of thought: New directions for human development* (No. 59). San Francisco: Jossey-Bass.

Singh, S., Forrest, J. D., & Torres, A. (1989). *Prenatal care in the United States: A state and county inventory.* New York: Alan Guttmacher Institute.

Sinha, J. B. P. (1984). Toward partnership for relevant research to the third world. *Indian Journal of Psychology, 19,* 169–178.

Sinha, J. B. P. (1993). The bulk and the front of psychology in India. *Psychology and Developing Societies, 5,* 135–150.

Skoog, L., Nilsson, L., Palmertz, B., Andreasson, L., & Svanborg, A. (1993). A population-based study for dementia in 85-year-olds. *New England Journal of Medicine, 328,* 153–158.

Slaby, A. E., & Dwenger, R. (1993). History of anorexia nervosa. In A. J. Giannini and A. E. Slaby (Eds.), *The eating disorders.* New York: Springer-Verlag.

Slonim, M. B. (1991). *Children, culture, and ethnicity.* New York: Garland.

Smith, D. E., & Blinn Pike, L. (1994). Relationship between Jamaican adolescents' drinking patterns and self-image: A cross-cultural perspective. *Adolescence, 29,* 429–437.

Smith, D. E., & Cogswell, C. (1994). A cross-cultural perspective on adolescent girls' body perception. *Perceptual and Motor Skills, 78,* 744–746.

Smith, D. E., & Reynolds, T. E. (1992). Adolescents' self-image: A cross-cultural perspective. *Child Study Journal, 22,* 303–315.

Smith, J., & Baltes, P. B. (1990). Wisdom-related knowledge: Age/cohort differences in response to life-planning problems. *Developmental Psychology, 26*(3), 494–505.

Smith, J. S. (1992). Women in charge: Politeness and directiveness in the speech of Japanese women. *Language in Society, 21,* 59–82.

Smith, M. G. (1965). The Hausa of northern Nigeria. In J. L. Gibbs, Jr. (Ed.), *Peoples of Africa* (pp. 119–155). New York: Holt, Rinehart & Winston.

Smith, P. K. (1991). Introduction: The study of grandparenthood. In P. K. Smith (Ed.), *The psychology of grandparenthood: An international perspective* (pp. 1–16). London: Routledge & Kegan Paul.

Smith, P. K. (1995). Grandparenthood. In M. H. Bornstein (Ed.), *Handbook of parenting* (Vol. 3, pp. 89–112). Mahwah, NJ: Erlbaum.

Snarey, J. R. (1985). Cross-cultural universality of socio-moral development. A critical review of Kohlbergian research. *Psychological Bulletin, 97,* 202–232.

Solomon, G. B. (1996). *Fair play in the gymnasium: Promoting socio-moral development among children at risk.* Unpublished manuscript, Texas Christian University, Fort Worth.

Sommers, I., Fagan, J., & Basin, D. (1993). Sociocultural influences on the explanation of delinquency for Puerto Rican youths. *Hispanic Journal of Behavioral Sciences, 15,* 36–62.

Song, M., Smetana, J. G., & Kim, S. Y. (1987). Korean children's conceptions of moral and conventional transgressions. *Developmental Psychology, 23,* 577–582.

Sonko, S. (1994). Fertility and culture in sub-Saharan Africa. *International Social Science Journal, 46,* 397–411.

Sparkes, K. K. (1991). Cooperative and competitive behavior in dyadic game-playing: A comparison of Anglo-American and Chinese children. *Early Child Development and Care, 68,* 37–47.

Spence, A. P. (1989). *Biology of human aging.* Englewood Cliffs, NJ: Prentice-Hall.

Spirduso, W. W., & MacRae, P. G. (1990). Motor performance and aging. In J. E. Birren & K. W. Schaie (Eds.), *Handbook of the psychology of aging* (3rd ed., pp. 184–200). San Diego, CA: Academic Press.

Spiro, M. E. (1993). Is the Western conception of the self "peculiar" within the contexts of world cultures? *Ethos, 21,* 107–153.

Spock, B., & Rothenberg, M. B. (1992). *Dr. Spock's baby and child care.* New York: Pocket Books.

Stack, C. B. (1974). *All our kin: Strategies for survival in a black community.* New York: Harper & Row.

Staples, R. (1952). Appreciations and dislikes regarding grandmothers as expressed by granddaughters. *Journal of Home Economics, 44,* 340–343.

Stein, R. C. (1986). *South Africa.* Chicago: Childrens Press.

Steinberg, L. (1990). Interdependence in the family: Autonomy, conflict, and harmony in the parent-adolescent relationship. In S. S. Feldman & G. L. Elliott (Eds.), *At the threshold: The developing adolescent* (pp. 255–276). Cambridge, MA: Harvard University Press.

Steinberg, L., & Brown, B. B. (1989). *Beyond the classroom: Parent and peer influences on high school achievement.* Invited paper presented to the Families as Educators Special Interest Group at the annual meetings of the American Educational Research Association, San Francisco.

Sternberg, R. J. (1985). *Beyond IQ: A triarchic theory of human intelligence.* Cambridge, England: Cambridge University Press.

Sternberg, R. J., & McGrane, P. A. (1993). *Intellectual development across the life span.* Unpublished manuscript, Yale University, New Haven, CT.

Stevenson, H. W., Chen, C., & Lee, S. (1991). Chinese families. In J. L. Roopnarine & D. B. Carter (Eds.), *Parent-child socialization in diverse cultures* (pp. 17–33). Norwood, NJ: Ablex.

Steward, E. P. (1994). *Beginning writers in the zone of proximal development.* Hillsdale, NJ: Erlbaum.

Stiles, D., De Silva, S. S., Gibbons, J. (1996). Girls' relational self in Sri Lanka and the United States. *Journal of Genetic Psychology, 157,* 191–203.

Stiles, D., Gibbons, J., & de la Garza-Schnellman, J. (1990). Opposite sex ideal in the U.S.A. and Mexico as perceived by young adolescents. *Journal of Cross-Cultural Psychology, 21,* 180–199.

Stiles, D. A., & Gibbons, J. L. (1995). *Gender role expectations of Norwegian adolescents.* Paper presented at the twenty-fourth annual meeting of the Society for Cross-Cultural Research, Savannah, GA.

Storz, N., & Greene, W. H. (1983). Body weight, body image, and perception of fad diets in adolescent girls. *Journal of Nutrition Education, 15,* 15–18.

Stratton, P. (1988). Parents' conceptualization of children as the organizer of culturally structured environments. In J. Valsiner (Ed.), *Child development within culturally structured environments: Vol. 1. Parental cognition and adult-child interaction* (pp. 5–29). Norwood, NJ: Ablex.

Strom, R. D., Strom, S., Collinsworth, P., Sato, S., Makino, K., Sasaki, Y., Sasaki, H., & Nishio, N. (1995). Grandparents in Japan: A three-generational study. *International Journal of Aging and Human Development, 40*(3), 209–227.

Strom, R. D., & Strom, S. K. (1993). Grandparents raising grandchildren: Goals and support groups. *Educational Gerontology, 19,* 705–715.

Super, C. M. (1976). Environmental effects on motor development: The case of "African infant precocity." *Developmental Medicine and Child Neurology, 18,* 561–567.

Super, C. M. (1979). *A cultural perspective on theories of cognitive development.* Paper presented at the meeting of the Society for Research in Child Development, San Francisco.

Super, C. M. (1981). Cross-cultural research on infancy. In H. C. Triandis and A. Heron (Eds.), *Handbook of cross-cultural psychology: Vol. 4. Developmental Psychology.* Boston: Allyn & Bacon.

Super, C. M., & Harkness, S. (1982). The infants' niche in rural Kenya and metropolitan America. In L. L. Adler (Ed.), *Cross-cultural research at issue* (pp. 47–55). New York: Academic Press.

Super, C. M., & Harkness, S. (1986). The developmental niche: A conceptualization of the interface of child and culture. *International Journal of Behavioral Development, 9,* 545–570.

Super, C. M., & Harkness, S. (1994a). The developmental niche. In W. J. Lonner & R. Malpass (Eds.), *Psychology and culture* (pp. 95–99). Needham Heights, MA: Allyn & Bacon.

Super, C. M., & Harkness, S. (1994b). Temperament and the developmental niche. In W. B. Carey & S. C. Devitt (Eds.), *Prevention and early intervention: Individual differences as risk factors for the mental health of children.* New York: Brunner/Mazel.

Super, C. M., & Harkness, S. (1997). The cultural structuring of child development. In J. W. Berry, P. R. Dasen, & T. S. Saraswathi (Eds.), *Handbook of cross-cultural psychology* (Vol. 2, 2nd ed., pp. 1–39). Boston: Allyn & Bacon.

Super, C. M., Harkness, S., & Blom, M. (1997). *Cultural differences in Dutch and American infants' sleep patterns: How do they get that way?* Paper presented at the twenty-sixth annual meeting of the Society for Cross-Cultural Research, San Antonio, TX.

Super, C. M., Herrena, M. G., & Mora, J. O. (1990). Long-term effects of food supplementation and psychosocial intervention on the physical growth of Colombian infants at risk of malnutrition. *Child Development, 61,* 29–49.

Susman, E. J., & Dorn, L. D. (1991). Hormones and behavior in adolescence. In R. M. Lerner, A. C. Petersen, & J. Brooks-Gunn (Eds.), *Encyclopedia of adolescence.* New York: Garland.

Swaim, R. C., Oetting, E. R., Thurman, P. J., Beauvais, F., & Edwards, R. W. (1993). American Indian adolescent drug use and socialization characteristics: A cross-cultural comparison. *Journal of Cross-Cultural Psychology, 24*(1), 53–70.

Swart, J. (1988). *An anthropological study of street children in Hillsbrow, Johannesburg, with special reference to their moral values.* Unpublished master's thesis, University of South Africa, Pretoria.

Tajfel, H. (1981). *Human groups and social categories.* Cambridge, England: Cambridge University Press.

Takada, K. (1993). Aging workers in Japan: From reverence to redundance. *Aging International, 20,* 17–20.

Takahashi, K. (1990). Are the key assumptions of the "strange situation" procedure universal? A view from Japanese research. *Human Development, 33,* 23–30.

Tamis-LeMonda, C. S., Bornstein, M. H., Cyphers, L., Toda, S., & Ogino, M. (1992). Language and play at one year: A comparison of toddlers and mothers in the United States and Japan. *International Journal of Behavioral Development, 15,* 19–42.

Tanner, J. M. (1989). *Fetus into man: Physical growth from conception to maturity.* Cambridge, MA: Harvard University Press.

Tape, G. (1987). *Milieu africain et developpement cognitif: Une etude du raisonnement experimental chez l'adolescent ivoirien.* [The African environment and cognitive development: A study of experimental reasoning in adolescents from Cote d'Ivoire.] Unpublished doctoral dissertation, Universite de Caen, France.

Thoman, E. B. (1993). Obligation and option in the premature nursery. *Developmental Review, 13,* 1–30.

Thomas, A., & Chess, S. (1977). *Temperament and development.* New York: Brunner/Mazel.

Thomas, W. I., & Znaniecki, F. (1927). *The Polish peasant in Europe and America.* New York: Knopf.

Thompson, R. A., & Lamb, M. E. (1983). Security of attachment and stranger sociability in infancy. *Developmental Psychology, 19,* 184–191.

Tien, H. Y., & Lee, C. F. (1988). New demographics and old designs: The Chinese family and induced population transition. *Social Science Quarterly, 69,* 605–628.

Tiggemann, M., & Rothblum, E. D. (1988). Gender differences in social consequences of perceived overweight in the United States and Australia. *Sex Roles, 18,* 75–86.

Ting-Toomey, S. (1991). Intimacy expressions in three cultures: France, Japan, and the United States. *International Journal of Intercultural Relations, 15,* 29–46.

Tinsley, B. J., & Parke, R. D. (1984). Grandparents as support and socialization agents. In M. Lewis (Ed.), *Beyond the dyad* (pp. 161–194). New York: Plenum.

Tremblay, Helene. (1988). *Families of the world.* New York: Farrar, Straus & Giroux.

Triandis, H. C. (1989). The self and social behavior in differing cultural contexts. *Psychological Bulletin, 96,* 506–520.

Triandis, H. C., Brislin, R., & Hui, C. H. (1988). Cross-cultural training across the individualism-collectivism divide. *International Journal of Intercultural Relations, 12,* 269–289.

Triandis, H. C., McCusker, C., & Hui, C. H. (1990). Multimethod probes of individualism and collectivism. *Journal of Personality and Social Psychology, 59,* 1006–1020.

Tronick, E. Z., Morelli, G. A., & Ivey, P. K. (1992). The Efe forager infant and toddler's pattern of social relationships: Multiple and simultaneous. *Developmental Psychology, 28,* 568–577.

Tse, S., & Bailey, D. M. (1992). Tai chi and postural control in the well elderly. *American Journal of Occupational Therapy, 46*(4), 295–300.

Tseng, W., & Hsu, J. (1980). Minor psychological disturbances of everyday life. In H. C. Triandis & J. Draguns (Eds.), *Handbook of cross-cultural psychology* (Vol. 6, pp. 61–97). Boston: Allyn & Bacon.

Tu, W. (1978). The Confucian Perception of Adulthood. In E. Erikson (Ed.), *Adulthood* (pp. 113–127). New York: Norton.

Tu, W. (1985). *Confucian thought: Selfhood as creative transformation.* Albany: State University of New York Press.

Tylor, E. B. (1871). *Primitive culture* (2 vols.). London: Murray.

Tzuriel, D. (1992). The development of ego identity at adolescence among Israeli Jews and Arabs. *Journal of Youth and Adolescence, 21,* 551–571.

UNICEF. (1993). *Child malnutrition: Progress toward the world summit for children goal.* New York: Statistics and Monitoring Section, United Nations International Children's Emergency Fund.

United Nations. (1990). *Human Development Report, 1990.* New York: United Nations Development Program.

U.S. Bureau of the Census. (1992). *Statistical abstract of the United States: 1992* (112th ed.). Washington, DC: U.S. Government Printing Office.

U.S. Bureau of the Census. (1993). *Statistical abstract of the United States: 1993* (113th ed.). Washington, DC: U.S. Government Printing Office.

U.S. Department of Health and Human Services (USDHHS). (1992). *Health United States 1991, and Prevention Profile.* (DHHS Pub. No. PHS 92–1232). Washington, DC: U.S. Government Printing Office.

Uzgiris, I. C., & Raeff, C. (1995). Play in parent-child interactions. In M. H. Bornstein, *Handbook of parenting* (Vol. 4). Mahwah, NJ: Erlbaum.

Valsiner, J. (1987). *Culture and the development of children's action.* Chichester: Wiley.

Valsiner, J. (1988). Organization of children's social development in polygamic families. In J. Valsiner (Ed.), *Child development in cultural context* (pp. 67–86). Toronto: Hogrefe & Huber.

Valsiner, J. (1989a). *Child development in cultural context.* Toronto: Hogrefe & Huber.

Valsiner, J. (1989b). *Human development and culture.* Lexington, MA: Heath.

Valsiner, J., & Benigni, L. (1986). Naturalistic research and ecological thinking in the study of child development. *Developmental Review, 6,* 203–223.

Valsiner, J., & Lawrence, J. (1997). Human development in culture across the life span. In J. W. Berry, P. R. Dasen, & T. S. Saraswathi (Eds.), *Handbook of cross-cultural psychology* (Vol. 2, 2nd ed., pp. 69–106). Boston: Allyn & Bacon.

Van den Heuvel, H., Tellegen, G., & Koomen, W. (1992). Cultural differences in the use of psychological and social characteristics in children's self-understanding. *European Journal of Social Psychology, 22,* 353–362.

Van Esterik, P. (1989). *Beyond the breast-bottle controversy.* New Brunswick, NJ: Rutgers University Press.

Van Ijzendoorn, M. H., & Kroonenberg, P. M. (1988). Cross-cultural patterns of attachment: A meta-analysis of the strange situation. *Child Development, 59,* 147–156.

Van Reek, J., Adriaanze, H., & Knibbe, R. (1994). Alcohol consumption and correlates among children in the European Community. *International Journal of the Addictions, 29,* 15–21.

Veale, A. (1992). Towards a conceptualization of street children: The case from Sudan and Ireland. *Troaire Developmental Review* (Dublin), 107–128.

Visano, L. (1990). The socialization of street children: The development and transformation of identities. *Sociological Studies of Child Development, 3,* 139–161.

Voda, A. M., Dinnerstein, M., & O'Donnell, S. (1982). *Changing perspectives on menopause.* Austin: University of Texas Press.

Vondra, J., & Belsky, J. (1993). Developmental origins of parenting: Personality and relationship factors. In T. Luster & L. Okagaki (Eds.), *Parenting: An ecological perspective* (pp. 1–33). Hillsdale, NJ: Erlbaum.

Vygotsky, L. S. (1978). *Mind in society: The development of higher psychological processes.* Cambridge, MA: Harvard University Press.

Vygotsky, L. S. (1986). *Thought and language* (Trans./rev. by A. Kozulin). Cambridge, MA: MIT Press. (Original work published 1934.)

Wachs, T. D. (1987). *Comparative salience of physical and social environmental differences.* Paper presented at the biennial meeting of the Society for Research in Child Development, Baltimore, MD.

Wallace, A. F. C. (1961). Mental illness, biology, and culture. In F. Hsu (Ed.), *Psychological anthropology.* Cambridge, MA: Schenkman.

Wallen, K. (1989). Mate selection: Economics and affection. *Behavioral and Brain Sciences, 12,* 37–38.

Wardlaw, G. M., & Insel, P. M. (1993). *Perspectives in nutrition* (2nd ed.). St. Louis: Mosby.

Watanabe, Y. (1986). Distributive justice development. *Japanese Journal of Educational Psychology, 34,* 84–90.

Waterson, E. J., & Murray-Lyon, I. M. (1990). Preventing alcohol related birth damage: A review. *Social Science and Medicine, 30,* 349–364.

Watkins, D., & Dhawan, N. (1989). Do we need to distinguish the constructs of self-concept and self-esteem? *Journal of Social Behavior and Personality, 4,* 555–562.

Weill, J., & Le Bourhis, B. (1994). Factors predictive of alcohol consumption in a representative sample of French male teenagers: A five-year prospective study. *Drug & Alcohol Dependence, 35,* 45–50.

Weisfeld, C., Weisfeld, G. & Callaghan, J. (1982). Female inhibition in mixed-sex competition among young adolescents. *Ethology and Sociobiology, 3,* 29–42.

Weisfeld, G. (1997). Puberty rites as clues to the nature of human adolescence. *Cross-Cultural Research, 31*(1), 27–54.

Weisner, T. S. (in press). The 5-to-7 transition as an ecocultural project. In A. J. Sameroff & M. M. Haith (Eds.), *Reason and responsibility: The passage through childhood.* Chicago: University of Chicago Press.

Weisner, T. S., Matheson, C. C., & Bernheimer, L. P. (1996). American cultural models of early influence and parent recognition of developmental delays: Is earlier always better than later? In S. Harkness & C. M. Super (Eds.), *Parents' cultural belief systems: Their origins, expressions, and consequences* (pp. 496–531). New York: Guilford.

Wellman, H. M., & Gelman, S. A. (1992). Cognitive development: Foundational theories of core domains. *Annual Review of Psychology, 43,* 337–375.

Werner, E. E. (1979). *Cross-cultural child development.* Belmont, CA: Wadsworth.

Werner, E. E. (1989). Children of the garden island. *Scientific American, 260,* 101–111.

Wertsch, J. V., & Tulviste, P. (1994). Lev Semyonovich Vygotsky and contemporary developmental psychology. In R. D. Parke, P. A. Ornstein, J. J. Rieser, & C. Zahn-Waxler (Eds.), *A Century of Developmental Psychology.* Washington, DC: American Psychological Association.

Wertz, R. W., & Wertz, D. C. (1979). *Lying-in: A history of childbirth in America.* New York: Schocken.

West, C., & Zimmerman, D. H. (1987). Doing gender. *Gender and Society, 1,* 125–151.

Westermeyer, J., & Peake, E. (1983). A ten-year follow up of alcoholic Native Americans in Minnesota. *American Journal of Psychiatry, 140,* 189–194.

Whitall, J. (1991). The developmental effect of concurrent cognitive and locomotor skills: Time-sharing from a dynamical perspective. *Journal of Experimental Child Psychology, 51,* 245–266.

White, C., & Burke, P. (1987). Ethnic role identity among black and white college students: An interactionist approach. *Sociological Perspectives, 30,* 310–331.

White, M. (1987). *The Japanese educational challenge: A commitment to children.* New York: Free Press.

White, M. (1993). *The material child: Coming of age in Japan and America.* New York: Free Press.

Whiting, B. B. (1963). *Six cultures: Studies of child rearing.* Cambridge, MA: Harvard University Press.

Whiting, B. B., & Edwards, C. P. (1988). *Children of different worlds: The formation of social behavior.* Cambridge, MA: Harvard University Press.

Whiting, B. B., & Whiting, J. W. M. (1975). *Children of six cultures: A psycho-cultural analysis.* Cambridge, MA: Harvard University Press.

Whiting, J. W. M., Burbank, V. K., & Ratner, M. S. (1986). The duration of maidenhood. In J. B. Lancaster & B. A. Hamburg (Eds.), *School age pregnancy and parenthood.* Hawthorne, NY: Aldine de Gruyter.

Williams, J., & Best, D. (1990). *Sex and psyche: Gender and self viewed cross-culturally.* Newbury Park, CA: Sage.

Wilson, J. O., & Herrnstein, R. J. (1985). *Crime and human nature.* New York: Simon & Schuster.

Wilson-Oyelaran, E. B. (1988). Toward contextual sensitivity in developmental psychology: A Nigerian perspective. In J. Valsiner (Ed.), *Child development in cultural context* (pp. 51–66). Toronto: Hogrefe & Huber.

Winegar, L. T., & Valsiner, J. (Eds.). (1992a). *Children's development within social context: Vol 1. Parental cognition and adult-child interaction.* Hillsdale, NJ: Erlbaum.

Winegar, L. T., & Valsiner, J. (Eds.). (1992b). *Children's development within social context: Vol 2. Research and methodology.* Hillsdale, NJ: Erlbaum.

Wiseman, H., & Lieblich, A. (1992). Individuation in a collective community. *Adolescent Psychiatry, 18,* 156–179.

Wolf, A. M., Gortmaker, S. L., Cheung, L., & Gray, H. M. (1993). Activity, inactivity, and obesity: Racial, ethnic, and age differences among schoolgirls. *American Journal of Public Health, 83,* 1625–1627.

Wolf, A. P. (1964). *Marriage and adoption in a Hokkien village.* Unpublished doctoral dissertation, Department of Anthropology, Cornell University.

Wolf, A. P. (1978). *Studies in Chinese society.* Stanford, CA: Stanford University Press.

Wolf, A. W., Lozoff, B., Latz, S., & Pauladetto, R. (1996). Parental theories in the management of sleep routines in Japan, Italy and the United States. In S. Harkness & C. M. Super (Eds.), *Parents' cultural belief systems*. New York: Guilford Press.

Wolf, M. (1972). *Women and the family in rural Taiwan*. Stanford, CA: Stanford University Press.

Wolffers, I. (1997). Culture, media, and HIV/AIDS in Asia. *Lancet, 349* (9044), 52–59.

Wood, D. J. (1989). Social interaction as tutoring. In M. H. Bornstein, & J. S. Bruner (Eds.), *Interaction in human development*. Hillsdale, NJ: Erlbaum.

Wood, D. J., & Middleton, D. (1975). A study of assisted problem solving. *British Journal of Psychology, 66*, 181–191.

World Health Organization. (1979). *Schizophrenia: An international follow-up study*. New York: Wiley.

Worthman, C. M. (1994). Developmental microniche: A concept for modeling relationships of biology, behavior, and culture in development. *American Journal of Physical Anthropology Supplement, 18*, 210.

Worthman, C. M. (1995). Biocultural bases of human variation. *ISSBD Newsletter, 27*(1), 10–13.

Worthman, C. M., Stallings, J. F., & Jenkins, C. L. (1993). Developmental effects of sex-differentiated parental care among Hagahai foragers. *American Journal of Physical Anthropology Supplement, 16*, 212.

Wylie, L. (1974). *Village in the Vaucluse* (3rd ed.). Cambridge, MA: Harvard University Press.

Yi, S. H. (1993). Transformation of child socialization in Korean culture. *Early Childhood Development, 85*, 17–24.

Ying, Y., & Liese, L. (1990). Initial adaptation of Taiwan foreign students to the U.S.: The impact of pre-arrival variables. *American Journal of Community Psychology, 18*(6), 825–845.

Ying, Y., & Liese, L. H. (1994). Initial adjustment of Taiwanese students to the United States: The impact of post-arrival variables. *Journal of Cross-Cultural Psychology, 25*(4), 466–477.

Yu, L. C. (1993). Intergenerational transfer of resources within policy and cultural contexts. In S. H. Zarit, L. I. Pearlin, & K. W. Schaie (Eds.), *Caregiving systems*. Hillsdale, NJ: Erlbaum

Zammuner, V. L., & Fischer, A. H. (1995). The social regulation of emotions in jealousy situations: A comparison between Italy and the Netherlands. *Journal of Cross-Cultural Psychology, 26*(2), 189–208.

Zarit, S. H., & Eggebeen, D. J. (1995). Parent-child relationships in adulthood and old age. In M. H. Bornstein (Ed.), *Handbook of parenting* (Vol. 1, pp. 119–140). Hillsdale, NJ: Erlbaum.

Zeskind, P. S. (1983). Cross-cultural differences in maternal perceptions of cries of low- and high-risk infants. *Child Development, 54*, 1119–1128.

Zeskind, P. S., Klein, L., & Marshall, T. (1992). Adults' perceptions of experiential modifications of durations of pauses and expiratory sounds in infant crying. *Developmental Psychology, 28*, 1153–1162.

Zeskind, P. S., Sale, J., Maio, M. C., Huntington, L., & Weiseman, J. R. (1985). Adult perceptions of pain and hunger cries: A synchrony of arousal. *Child Development, 56,* 549–554.

Zhang, Y., Proenca, R., Maffel, M., Barone, M., et al. (1994). Positional cloning of the mouse obese gene and its human homologue. *Nature, 372,* 425–442.

Zimmerman, B. J. (1990). Self-regulated learning and academic achievement: An overview. *Educational Psychologist, 25,* 3–17.

AUTHOR INDEX

SUBJECT INDEX